Highgate

The London Rich

*

*   *   *

The London Rich
The Creation of a Great City, from 1666 to the Present

Peter Thorold

*

St. Martin's Press  New York

ISBN 0-312-26616-2

First published in the United Kingdom by Penguin Books Ltd.
First U.S. Edition: October 2000
1 3 5 7 9 10 8 6 4 2

942.1
T516

For Anne

Contents

List of Colour Illustrations

Acknowledgements

I would like gratefully to acknowledge the help I have received from Valerie Barker of the Moravian Union, Eleanor Boyle, Michael Constantinidi, my daughter-in-law Madeleine Lim, the Portman Estate Office, Nicholas Roskill, Ian Scott, Sir James Spooner, David Tucker, and from Barry Till, an encyclopaedia of knowledge on the Thames Valley.

I wish also to thank Trevor Abramsohn of Glentree Estates, Yolanda Barnes of FPD Savills and Richard Crosthwaite of Knight Frank for sparing the time to discuss the current market for expensive property in London. My thanks also to David Spittles.

I owe much to the resources of the Guildhall Library and to the assistance of its staff, and to the London Library. I am also obliged to the Governors of the North London Collegiate School at Canons Park and to the Shakespeare Birthplace Trust Records Office at Stratford-upon-Avon.

Note on Value of Money

The conversion of prices and monetary values in general into current terms is based on *A Perspective of Wages and Prices* (1981) by Sir Henry Phelps Brown and Sheila Hopkins, and on figures published by the *Economist*. While historically money could change value sharply from year to year, over long periods there was little or no overall inflation. For the sake of simplicity, and bearing in mind the inevitable imprecision involved in the translation of old money into new, a multiple of 115:1 has been generally adopted for the period to 1770, and 58:1 for that from 1820 to 1914. For the intervening inflationary years, an appropriate modification has been made.

Picture Acknowledgements

The author and publishers are grateful to the following for permission to reproduce illustrations: National Gallery, London, 181; National Portrait Gallery, London 34, 104, 192; Hulton Getty Images, 269, 305, 313, 324, 327; Steve Stephens, 177; Fishmongers' Company, London, 143; Museum of London, 23, 217, 247, 256, 308; London Metropolitan Archives, 185, 290, 309; British Museum, 155, 173; Courtauld Institute of Art, 150; The Marquess of Tavistock and the Trustees of the Bedford Estates, 13, 192; London Borough of Wandsworth, 225; Royal Collection Enterprises, 114; Highgate Literary and Scientific Institution, 158; Royal Borough of Kensington and Chelsea Libraries and Arts Service, 74, 287, 299, 317 (top), 344; Guildhall Library, 81, 92, 115, 148–9, 154, 167, 212, 260; London Borough of Lambeth Archives Department, 231, 234, 236; Mary Evans Picture Library, 342; Royal Commission on the Historical Monuments of England, 64, 67, 259, 271, 288, 306, 317 (bottom), 321; Fritz von der Schulenburg, 345; Trustees of Sir John Soane's Museum, 141; *Country Life* Picture Library, 320.

I

Before the Fire

*

In a matter of a few days during the first week of September 1666, the Great Fire of London obliterated the ancient city so completely that popular memory retains hardly more than a snapshot of flimsy timber buildings, their roofs brushing each other over tortuous and narrow little alleys. To a quiz-show sort of question on the lines of 'Who is the most famous Londoner?' most people would probably nominate Dick Whittington along with, perhaps, Dr Johnson. But eighteenth-century Johnson brings with him a host of associations, while Whittington, living at the turn of the fourteenth and fifteenth centuries, comes almost alone. His affinities are those of a nursery rhyme – Bow Bells, his cat (mythical or not, certainly London's most famous animal) and the fact that he was several times Lord Mayor. Few people apart from scholars would be able to name any other of the great London merchants of the Middle Ages; indeed, with the exception possibly of Sir Thomas Gresham, they would do no better with the Renaissance.

This book will add little to the store of knowledge about the old city. Its subject is the new London that grew up outside its walls and the people who created it. It is about the transformation of the embryo city of Westminster, in 1666 not much more than a collection of monumental buildings with a slum attached, and the voracious expansion through which it swallowed up the villages and countryside around. The rebuilt City of London, destined to emerge as the financial capital of the world, was to supply much of the money for the new town as well as some of its wealthiest inhabitants.

Nevertheless, the ancient walled city left legacies to the composite town which replaced it. Some, like the Tower and sections of the wall, are physical, others are more abstract, characteristics and patterns of life which carried – carry – on over generations. It was not a giant among cities – Paris and others were larger – and the tribute that it was 'the flower of cities all' seems overblown. Medieval and Renaissance London was though a great trading centre. It was extremely cosmopolitan, with the Steelyard for instance, on the Thames near our Cannon Street station, a three-acre self-governing precinct allotted to the Hansa merchants for their Baltic trade. It was, in summer at least, a commuters' town; at the time of the Fire many of the better-off Londoners were still at their country homes.

While there were exceptions such as the banking families of the Hoares and Childs, business dynasties in the London of the later

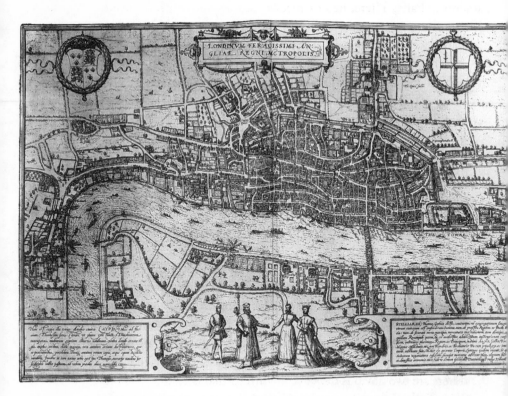

London in the time of Queen Elizabeth I, from Braun and Hogenberg, *Civitates Orbis Terrarum*, 1572

seventeenth century, and of the eighteenth century as well, were transient. Partly that was a result of the hazards of trade: as the proverb went, 'the winds and waves are not more uncertain than the circumstances of the merchants & tradesmen of the City of London'. Sons and heirs might be well advised to take the money and run. And anyway the seductions of a dignified country life as a local pillar of society were very strong in England. They always had been, it appears: William Caxton observes how short-lasting were London families when compared to their counterparts in the Low Countries. It is one of the reasons we have so few names to put alongside Dick Whittington.

At the end of the seventeenth century a doctor, Martin Lister, who had been attached to the English embassy in France, compared London to Paris. There, he observed,

> the palaces & convents have abolished the dwellings of the people, and crowded them excessively together, occupying far the greatest part of the ground; whereas in London the contrary may be observed, viz. that the people have destroyed the palaces, and seated themselves upon the foundations . . .

The massive expansion of London which was underway by Lister's time can be described as the rich striking out to settle new ground, or, equally, as the rich fleeing the irresistible onrush of the poor. Either interpretation meant old town houses abandoned to demolition or conversion. Such houses were to be a familiar part of the landscape in the years immediately preceding the Fire, as the patrician rich migrated westwards or to the chic suburb of Aldersgate, a district just outside the walls where the Museum of London now stands. Even in earlier times the shifting of population within the city had the same effect. Where, as often happened, the people did not, to follow Lister's words, 'destroy the palaces', but turned them to other uses, the process of decline could be long drawn-out.

There are two obvious City examples. The first is unique: it is the survivor of the Fire and countless later indignities and threats, and now, thanks to the energy and resolution of a successful businessman, is in course of restoration on the Chelsea Embankment. This is the magnificent Crosby Hall, with painted hammerbeam roof and three oriel windows, the centrepiece of a mansion built by the merchant Sir John Crosby in the fifteenth century. Over its lifetime it has housed an amazing variety of people and institutions. In its heyday, it was the lodging of Richard III when Duke of Gloucester; later it was the headquarters of the East India Company. It escaped a fire which destroyed the rest of the complex, one part to become a Presbyterian chapel, the other to be taken by the General Post Office. Some of the ornamental stonework was removed to decorate a dairy near Henley; a firm of packers moved in. During the early nineteenth century – and this was unusual – a subscription was raised to save the buildings. Crosby Hall stayed up, a wine merchant took over, and it ended its City days as a restaurant, to be reinstated in Chelsea in 1910. The other example dates from the beginning of the seventeenth century. In *Bishopsgate Street*, a striking engraving of 1872, Gustave Doré depicts a seedy pub called the Sir Paul Pindar Stout House. It was the remains of a mansion built for Sir Paul Pindar, an immensely rich businessman. It was very grand and ornate, five storeys high, with a chapel, stables, park and garden, and what seems to have been a separate banqueting house. A section of the timber façade can still be seen, attached to the wall of the gift shop in the Victoria and Albert Museum.

With a thriving economy and a growing population, London obviously could not be constrained indefinitely within its walls, within its 'square mile'. As it happened, the overflow into the country around was delayed by two factors. One was the Black Death which ravaged the population, the other was the release on to the market from the 1530s of land confiscated by the Crown at the Reformation from the Church and religious orders, land which from an urban point of view had been 'underused'. Some of this newly available property was leased out and much of it was privatized on favourable terms to the purchaser. The quantity – and the value – of the real estate belonging to the twenty-three religious houses in London and Westminster was colossal. Outside the City, they, with the Church itself, owned Soho, lands which were to be Piccadilly, Covent Garden, the great houses along the river, and much else. Inside the City, they were

The remains of Sir Paul Pindar's superb Bishopsgate
mansion, built at the beginning of the seventeenth
century. By 1872, the date of this engraving by
Gustave Doré, what survived had degenerated into a
down-at-heel pub.

substantial landlords who themselves occupied a number of the choicest sites. The fortunes of the Priory of the Salutation, known to later generations as the Charterhouse and one of three religious houses in Clerkenwell, provide an example of what happened. The prior and the twelve monks refused to recognize Henry VIII as head of the Church, and were removed for execution. Their treasure was taken for the King's personal use and the priory was converted into a private mansion, the residence first of the North family and then of the Duke of Norfolk. The new owners of ecclesiastical property lost no time: mansions, tenements, warehouses and other business premises were erected on gardens and fields, and sometimes on churchyards. In fact, not only on the churchyards, for eight churches were converted to secular uses. In Austin Friars, off Throgmorton Street, Sir William Paulet stored corn and coal in the steeple and choir of his local church, while his son, the first Marquess of Winchester, sold the church monuments and turned part of the building into stables.

An invaluable and melancholy witness was John Stow, the son of a City tailor and author of *A Survey of London* first published at the end of the sixteenth century. By taste, Stow was profoundly conservative. He regretted the archery grounds now converted into gunnery ranges for cannon; he deplored the ever-increasing traffic that jammed the City's alleys and the pollution and blocking of watercourses such as the Walbrook. He lamented that rich men were no longer building alms houses. Against Thomas Cromwell, successor to Cardinal Wolsey and the minister responsible for the dissolution of the religious orders, Stow took special umbrage. He had good reason, for Cromwell built himself a large house in Austin Friars on the site of old tenements, and arbitrarily enclosed land round about. One of those who suffered was Stow's father.

My father had a garden there, and a house standing close to his south pale; this house they loosed from the ground, ere my father heard thereof; no warning was given him, nor other answer, when he spake to the surveyors of that work . . .

'The sudden rising of some men causeth them to forget themselves,' commented John Stow acidly. It was a complaint which in one form or another was to reverberate again and again throughout London's later history.

By the last half of the sixteenth century, however, the pressure of population was becoming insupportable. In 1550, the inhabitants of London were estimated to number some 70,000, of whom three quarters lived within the City limits. But the population was starting to multiply at the sort of breakneck pace we now associate with Cairo or Mexico City. By 1600 it is reckoned to have reached around 200,000; by the time of the Fire, 400,000. 'People fill the cellars,' wrote the French ambassador in the 1660s. By then the proportions had reversed, with only a quarter of the population living inside the City limits. Rich and poor both moved out; broadly speaking, they went in opposite directions. To the east, workshops and cheap housing uprooted the hedges and overlaid the fields of Spitalfields and Whitechapel and Houndsditch. To the west and the north-west migrated the more well-to-do.

The people concerned in the movement westwards tended natur-ally to be those who did not work in the City. The wealthy ones were mainly patrician rich. Even at the time of the Fire a few noble families lingered in the City, although by then they were concentrated mainly in Aldersgate. Christian, the dowager Countess of Devonshire, was one, however, who had no intention of changing her style – or place – of living. Her residence continued to be Devonshire House in Bishopsgate, a large and beautiful mansion with a fine garden which had been built by a goldsmith, Jasper Fisher, in the sixteenth century. Every afternoon, amid all the commercial bustle of the City, she took a drive in her gilded coach, escorted by her chaplain, her doctor, her chief steward and footmen. When she left and when she returned to Devonshire House, twelve waiting women stood to receive her on each side of the steps.

Lady Devonshire was an anachronism. In his *Londinopolis*, pub-lished in 1657, James Howell laments the fate of old private mansions in the City, taking as an example Northumberland House, close to the present Fenchurch Street station and remembered in the name Northumberland Alley. It had been abandoned by the earls of North-umberland when they took possession of a new palace at Charing Cross. Howell writes that the house

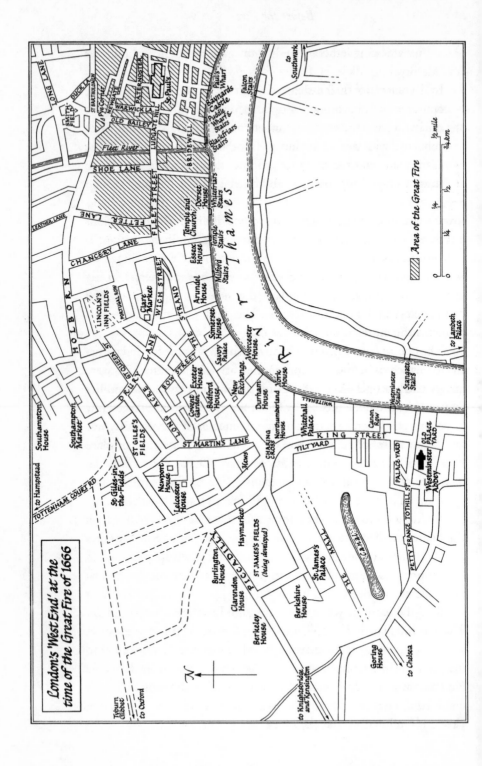

London's 'West End' at the time of the Great Fire of 1666

... of late being left by the Earls, the gardens thereof were made into Bowling Alleys, and other parts into Dicing Houses, common to all comers, for their money, there to bowl & recreate themselves. But now of late, so many Bowling Alleys, and other houses for unlawful gaming, have been raised in other parts of the City & suburbs, that this ... [place] ... is left and forsaken of the Gamesters, and therefore turned into a number of great Rents, small cottages, for strangers and others.

It was a common enough fate, though some of the mansions, Thomas Cromwell's among them, enjoyed a short extended life as livery halls until consumed in the Fire.

The patrician rich did not of course move out alone. They went in the company of a multitude of servants and dependents. Nevertheless, their migration marked the beginnings of a shift towards an increasing segregation of social classes which in later times would be a significant – and baleful – characteristic of London. In the old city, crowded as it was, social isolation was more complicated, for traditionally people lived next to each other not so much because they were of the same income group as because they shared the same trade and were members of the same guild. For instance, scriveners were likely to live in Paternoster Row, and drapers in Lombard Street. Even in old London, however, by the time of the Great Fire the tendency was towards a more defined separation between rich and poor. It can be seen in the notorious Pudding Lane.

Pudding Lane has always suffered from a bad press. W. G. Bell, the main authority on the Fire, described it as 'A line of tottering houses [which] ran unevenly down the steep hill to the Thames'. A contemporary writer called it 'a pitiful lane'. It was not the sort of place a City grandee would choose to find himself at any time, least of all in the early hours of the morning. That was the fate of Sir Thomas Bludworth, Lord Mayor of London and MP for Southwark, who was called from his bed on the night of 1 September 1666 to inspect a fire at Farriner's the bakers, which had got out of hand. In memorable words he expressed his opinion: 'Pish! a woman might piss it out.' Two days later Bludworth's own home, Camden House, near the Guildhall at the other end of the City, went up in smoke

9

along with most of the rest of London. Yet the character of Pudding Lane as revealed by a census of 1638 is rather different from that associated with it a generation later. This narrow little street was mostly populated by small craftsmen and tradesmen – coopers, tailors, fishmongers, joiners, tallow chandlers and clothworkers. It is possible that the houses were packed with lodgers, but even so, it is surprising that their average rental value is assessed at a shade over £10 as against a City average which falls into a band of £6–£10. (The census was held for purposes of tithe, and the assessment understates actual rents by a quarter.) There were some very poor residents, including Widow Thomas with a house – or more probably a hovel – 'in the backyard' assessed at £2. At the same time, though, also in Pudding Lane in 1638, were Mr Beard 'next below the Church way, a great house' assessed at £30 and Mr Ward 'in a great house that Mr How lived in' at £26. What is more, Mr Beard had just taken over an additional dwelling valued at £6. These were substantial rents for what must have been substantial properties and, as a comparison, one can note that Anthony van Dyck and Izaak Walton, living elsewhere in the City, were assessed at £20 and £25 respectively. Yet just short of thirty years later, in 1666, on the eve of the Fire, the hearth tax returns bring the street closer to Bell's 'line of tottering houses'. There is no sign of any substantial buildings. The inference is that those belonging to Mr Beard and Mr Ward had been pulled down or broken up into rooming houses.

There were Pudding Lanes outside the walls as well. In Westminster itself, less than two miles away and the focus of the emerging new town, jostling the houses and apartments of the courtiers were little alleys with equally picturesque names and of an equally sordid type – Pensioners' Alley, Poulterers' Yard, Clinkers Court. To someone looking out towards Westminster from London proper, perhaps from the tower of old St Paul's, the view would have been imposing. On the way, beyond the commotion of Fleet Street, stood two lines of palaces spaced out along the Strand. So grand, so large, so numerous were they that it would be easy to see them as symbolic, as an affirmation of the structure of seventeenth-century society, formal, hierarchical, ostentatious. That it was these things we shall see in a moment. More difficult would have been to find symbols to represent that other more relaxed social current, apparent in diaries and memoirs, which paradoxically runs through the life of the time. An example is a vignette of Mrs Backwell, wife of the leading banker of his time, leaning from her window in Fleet Street to greet Samuel Pepys as he walks by. Pepys in fact often appears to move with surprising ease between social classes. Another example is the less familiar Sir Humphrey Mildmay in the 1630s.

Humphrey Mildmay was of a much more established background and of infinitely less push and ability than Pepys. He was easygoing to the point of indolence, a good fellow, a decent landlord, with an interest in public affairs which hardly extended further than an interest in who was to be hanged at Tyburn. Here is an extract from his diary in 1640, just as the crisis breaks which leads to the Civil War:

> ... to dinner at Graces [the house of some Essex cousins] – there I laughed heartily at the Puritans and came home to my other affairs, and so continued until night where came to supper Parson Vincent drunk, Alex not much better, Parson Webb to laugh at them and so I laughed away the time.

Mildmay was a substantial Essex landlord and like his father he served his term as high sheriff of the county. His income was roughly £1,000 a year, say £115,000 in our money, and his house at Danbury consisted of forty-three rooms. He was then at least well-off, even if not remotely in the category of his contemporaries, the magnificent grandees painted by van Dyck with their £10,000 or more.

Mildmay's friends were mostly of similar temperament, a heavy-drinking lot of country neighbours and London merchants, although it is unexpected to find among them Isaac Dorislaus, a Dutchman and Oxford don who was to be judge-advocate of the parliamentary army, organizer of the arrangements for the King's trial, and who was ultimately to be assassinated by Royalists. (It is something of a surprise too to learn from Mildmay, who was to be firmly on the side of the King, that Dorislaus's nickname for the parliamentary leader, Mr Pym, was Mr Pimp.) The diary shows a blurring of distinctions among his friends and acquaintance, between private and public or professional life, and also between social classes. Will Hothersall,

Mildmay's estate manager at Danbury, and Will Perry, the manager for his Somerset estate, were employees, tenants and friends. They and Mildmay not only eat together and go drinking at the inn together, but when one of them comes up to London he is likely to accompany his employer on his usual social rounds.

Humphrey Mildmay spent several months a year in London, renting a house outside the city in Clerkenwell. He was in London partly for business, and passed a great deal of his time at the law courts consulting what strikes one as an Inn-full of lawyers. It was not only a matter of actual litigation, but of coping with the general paraphernalia attached to land tenure at the time. While his wife occasionally makes an appearance, she tends to stay down in the country in Essex. Mildmay, though, is in London mainly for fun and, while not particularly extravagant, goes in for bursts of spending, as when he indulges in what he calls a debauch – a drinking session – with a garrulous friend up from Essex, his fellow justice of the peace and school governor, Sir John Tyrrell. Money also goes in presents to 'she-friends'.

Mildmay's is an easygoing life, far removed from the rituals which characterized society at a more elevated social level. Mildmay dismisses the Lord Mayor's Show as 'foolery', but its parade and ceremony were intrinsic to the nature of seventeenth-century society. The great lords were, to start with, nothing if not magnificent – in death as in life. Take their style of travelling. When the fourth Earl of Bedford died in 1641, in the midst of the most serious political crisis in English history, his body was accompanied by over three hundred coaches on its journey from Bedford House in the Strand to burial in the family mausoleum in Buckinghamshire. The Duke of Newcastle travelled 'like a prince' in three coaches with forty attendants; the Marquess of Winchester outdid him with four coaches and a hundred attendants. It almost goes without saying that they were heavy spenders. The Duke of Buckingham was rumoured to have paid £30,000 for his bejewelled coronation apparel in 1661. That represents well over three million pounds now. Probably the rumour grossly exaggerated the reality; the point though is that such a seemingly incredible figure could have been deemed possible.

Then there is the ceremony. To start with, it is just not possible

The fourth Earl of Bedford, who developed Covent
Garden, by Sir Anthony van Dyck, *c. 1636*.

to imagine, say, the Countess of Northumberland hailing acquaintances in the street from her windows at Charing Cross. Polite
behaviour is ponderous. Soon after the restoration of Charles II, the
Lord Chancellor, the Earl of Clarendon, with his wife and son, paid
a visit to his friend John Evelyn and his wife. It seems to have been
considered an informal sort of occasion; at any rate, they were all
'very merry'. Informal or not, though, the Lord Chancellor arrived
with his 'purse and mace borne before him'. A highly significant
influence on dress and protocol was Louis XIV's Versailles. The rules

in London were less rigid; for one thing Charles II's temperament was unlike that of his French cousin. The English did not go so far as the French; a Londoner, for instance, did not constantly refer to himself as 'a man of my quality' or 'a person of my rank'. Nevertheless, the rituals were precise and extreme, and manifested themselves in such matters as who walked where in the street, how gloves were to be worn, how you should knock on the door and enter a room, and, of great importance, what you should do with your hat. Here are two excerpts on hat-ceremony as set out in de Courtin's *Rules of Civility*, a book on etiquette published in England in the 1670s. The standard rule was that hats were worn indoors as a matter of course but taken off in the presence of superiors.

> The person of quality having oblig'd you to be covered in a place where you ought not to have done it but by particular command, you must pull off your hat as often as in the discourse his Lordship's name be mentioned, the name of any of his relations, or of any person of quality that is intimate with him . . .

Should too much name-dropping mean things got out of hand, the 'person of quality' might relax the rules. Still it was necessary to remain on your guard:

> If his lordship chances to sneeze, you are not to bawl out 'God *bless* you, Sir', but pulling off your hat, bow to him handsomely, and make that observation to yourself.

No wonder that there was apparently a Turkish curse which ran: 'I wish you as little rest as a Christian's hat.'

If the setting here is distinctly urban, the atmosphere that of a Court, the countryside in seventeenth-century England was never far away, physically or metaphorically. A difficulty in selecting names of famous Londoners is that the term itself is ambiguous. Whittington and Johnson and Dickens undoubtedly qualify, but the description fits only partially in the case, for instance, of many of the owners of the great London palaces. That would continue to be true in the eighteenth and nineteenth centuries. The Earl of Bedford, the Duke of Newcastle, the Marquess of Winchester, those examples of magnificent lordliness taken above, were country potentates, whom it would be misleading to represent only in a London setting. The Earl of Northumberland, with his vast estates in the north of England, could perhaps best be visualized as a feudal prince. The same was true of Lady Anne Clifford with her London house of Baynard's Castle, which stood at the western end of the City walls, a counterpart to the Tower of London in the east, and like the Tower, more fortress than palace. Baynard's Castle burned all through one night and was still ablaze the next morning, providing one of the most spectacular sights of the whole Fire. But Lady Anne was not in residence; she had left London in 1649 and never returned, spending the remaining twenty-seven years of her life on progresses between her castles in Westmorland.

To return to the earls of Bedford, important London landowners and very rich indeed. The fifth earl and his wife normally spent only three months a year in London, travelling in state between Bedford House in the Strand and Woburn, their country house in Bedfordshire, accompanied by numerous staff and a great quantity of furniture, plate, bedding and provisions. For the rest of the year, the household at Bedford House consisted of no more than a housekeeper, a watchman and a gardener, assisted when necessary by casual help. Indeed, Lord Bedford was a man of quiet, rural tastes. Lord Ailesbury, his political rival for the lord lieutenancy of the combined counties of Bedfordshire, Huntingdonshire and Cambridgeshire, thought of him as a 'graceful old nobleman', who kept to himself, with his guests in summer either his own relations or those who shared his love for bowling and cards.

This ambiguity applied also to Bedford House itself, to Northumberland House and the other palaces which stood along the Strand. A number of them were very old, spoils taken from the Church and the bishops at the Reformation, and visible on Agas's map of London and Westminster of 1560. Bedford House stood on the north side of the road and to its east were Lord Burghley's magnificent Exeter House and the smaller Wimbledon House. On the opposite side of the Strand, next to the Temple, were, among others, Essex House (the Duchess of Somerset), Arundel House (the Duke of Norfolk), the Savoy (dilapidated and used mainly as a hospital), Durham House (the Earl of Pembroke), York House (the Duke of Buckingham), and at the end of the row, Northumberland House. Some fronted directly on to the street, some were wholly or partially hidden by other buildings, while often their grounds swept down to the river and a private landing stage.

These great houses were really only 'London' in the sense that by the 1660s they were surrounded by the town. As buildings they might have been lifted from the countryside – or in some cases, given their quadrangles, from Oxford or Cambridge – to be dropped down next to each other complete with their appurtenances of stables, gardens and outbuildings. To add to the rural illusion, set every so often along the roadway, were little thatched cottages. The great mansions of the Strand escaped the Fire – it would be halted just in time – but, nonetheless, like the timber houses of the City, they were, as a few years would show, already an anachronism.

If Lord Bedford and other proprietors of the great houses in 1666 were at heart countrymen, their hearts bespoke by their rolling country acres, it would be wrong to consider them as necessarily provincial. Monsieur Sorbière, a scientist, remarked on the arrogance but also the erudition of the English nobility; during their withdrawal from public life during the Interregnum, many had turned to study. Henry Howard, the future Duke of Norfolk, in 1667 provided Arundel House as a meeting place for the Royal Society. This serious side of patrician London could occasionally collide with the frivolous. Sorbière described a comic if rather embarrassing moment when he and colleagues, adjusting their telescopes in St James's Park, encounter some courtiers, who had never dreamed of looking at the stars and 'would believe themselves dishonoured if they concerned themselves with anything but inventing new forms of dress'. These courtiers, after all, belonged to the Court of Charles II – the most sophisticated and probably the most frivolous in British history. They at least rate as wholehearted Londoners.

One might take two examples from among the most prominent members of the Court. The Duke of Buckingham of York House was a man who 'commonly turned day into night and night into day, and knew no order of life or time but after the calls of his appetite;

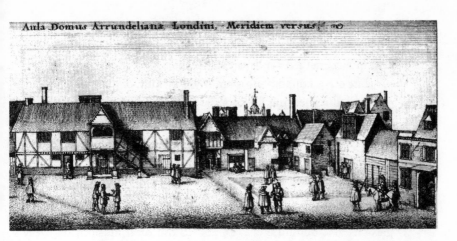

Aula Domus Arrundeliana Londini. Meridiem versus

The courtyard of Arundel House, Strand, 1646. Etching by Wenceslaus Hollar.

and those were either lewd or profane'. He never bothered to repair his houses in Rutland which Cromwell's soldiers had pillaged, and the country house he acquired was Cliveden in Buckinghamshire, situated as it was conveniently near to the metropolis. Then there is that most spectacular of rakes, Lord Rochester. For a neat metropolitan quip it would be hard to better his double-charged retort to a dog which had bitten him, 'I wish you were married and living in the country.' Or, for nerve, to improve on his foray into the City while in temporary disgrace at Court. Living there incognito 'he soon deeply insinuated himself into the esteem of the substantial wealthy aldermen, and into the affections of their more delicate, magnificent, and tender ladies'. He had a high old time and was such a success that he was bombarded by invitations. However, soon bored, Rochester moved to another part of the City, changing his identity into that of a supposedly famous German doctor and astrologer, whose remedies 'principally consisted in giving present relief to unfortunate young women in all manner of diseases, and all kinds of accidents incident to the fair sex, either from unbounded charity to their neighbors, or from too great indulgence to themselves'. It was for such-minded Londoners that the Restoration comedies were written. You men, says Hippolita in Wycherley's *The Gentleman Dancing-Master*, when you have girls in your clutches, 'you carry 'em into Yorkshire, Wales, or Cornwall, which is as bad as to Barbadoes'. And then, '[Are not] streets full of fine coaches better than a yard full of dung carts?' demands a character in Shadwell's *The Squire of Alsatia*.

The stage country bumpkin could be juxtaposed with City aldermen called something like Fondlewife or Gripe, or with Rochester-type rakes. However, in the example below from the Epilogue to *The Gentleman Dancing-Master*, Wycherley changes direction, hoping to lure the businessmen to the theatre as the patricians leave for the war. The appeal itself is – here – incidental; what is significant is the way it expresses the difference between the two groups, West End and City, as manifested in their clothes and general appearance.

> You we had rather see between our scenes,
> Than spend-thrift fops with better clothes and miens;
> Instead of laced coats, belt, and pantaloons,
> Your velvet jumps,* gold chains, and grave fur gowns,
> Instead of periwigs and broad cock'd hats
> Your satin caps, small cuffs, and vast cravats.

The migration of the patricians naturally emphasized the difference between them and the businessmen. For the latter, the reconstructed City was a natural habitat. It provided the access they required to docks and warehouses, and their culture was embedded in its structure and constitution, its wards and parishes. The more wealthy could find at least temporary relief from the hubbub and pollution by resort to a secondary home in the nearby countryside. So, the businessmen rebuilt their homes and offices after the Fire and stayed where they were. Only 4 per cent of those listed in a directory of nearly 2,000 bankers and merchants published in 1677 lived in the West End, and most of those were located in already declining areas close to the City boundary. Certainly some, such as the Houblon family – Huguenot by origin – who in the 1690s provided the first Governor of the Bank of England, lived grandly. John Evelyn, dining in 1679 with James Houblon, could describe his house in Great Winchester Street, just off London Wall, as being furnished '*en*

---

* A 'jump' was a short coat.

Prince'. More typical was the house of Alderman Backwell, incidentally the owner of considerable City property. In the basement were strongrooms, on the ground floor the 'shop' premises, and on the first floor a dining room, a small parlour and kitchen. Above, on the second floor, were two bedrooms, and then on the upper floor and in the attic a further five bedrooms, mainly for servants. The building was identified by the sign of a unicorn outside. If, as time went on, rich businessmen would increasingly move westwards – often when they had made their money and desired to become gentlemen – the custom of 'living over the shop' in the City persisted into the nineteenth century; even the great and immensely wealthy Nathan Mayer Rothschild did so.

A recent writer has taken a dramatic example of the disconnection between the City and Westminster at mid-century. The Great Fire had started soon after midnight and by morning was clearly out of control. The Lord Mayor was in a state of collapse and there was pandemonium in the streets. Samuel Pepys rushed to Whitehall to find the King and his brother, the Duke of York, apparently quite unaware of what was happening less than two miles away. The City came to see the West End as profligate, while to the patricians the City was boorish and materialistic. In the later eighteenth century, a foreign visitor was to write: 'Two towns a hundred leagues distant from each other, cannot have less resemblance than there is between the City and the other parts of London: the form of government; the regulations; the privileges; the taste and arrangement of the houses; the manner of living; everything in one word, renders this difference remarkable.'

How much then – apart from money – did the patrician rich and the business rich have in common? Financial relationships, sometimes grandchildren, and power. (Actually, the grandchildren can be subsumed under business, for marriage between the two classes of London rich was almost always a transaction to merge status with money.) As to power, between them, the rich of the City and those of the West End – a small proportion of the population – determined the prosperity of all London through their spending and through the employment they provided. Generations later, in 1861, the national census showed that one in every three women living in London aged between fifteen and twenty-four was a domestic servant. For the seventeenth century no such hard evidence exists. What is clear, however, is not only that domestic servants were very numerous, but alongside them was a very large number of others who depended directly on the wealthy for their livelihood: for instance, craftsmen of the type found in Pudding Lane, and washerwomen, road sweepers, prostitutes and innumerable retailers. As a result, the prolonged absence in the country during the year of so many of the rich caused serious seasonal unemployment.

It would be wrong to give the impression that by the time Pepys sped with news of disaster to Whitehall London had already settled into its future demographic shape. It only did so gradually in the face of stubborn opposition from existing interests. The rulers of the City, the Corporation of the City of London, were as apprehensive about the emerging new town as were their successors of many years later about the establishment of Canary Wharf. In 1609, Lord Salisbury, the Lord Treasurer, had opened the New Exchange on his own land at the Charing Cross end of the Strand. It was a hypermarket and trading exchange combined and presented direct competition to the Royal Exchange in the City. The Lord Mayor had written in protest to Salisbury:

> For a pawn [the New Exchange] being there erected and put into a prime course of trade, will take all resort from this place . . . [it] will draw Mercers, Goldsmiths and all other chief traders to settle themselves out of the City . . . to the great decay of the trade within the City.

The City authorities were also anxious to maintain their control over conditions of employment, fearing what they regarded as unfair competition from cheap or untrained labour. More threatening to would-be developers, however, was the hostility of the national government at Westminster. Some of the government's anxieties are familiar enough in our day to town planners and politicians in many parts of the world. How is it possible to maintain order in a megalopolis; how can it be made certain that resources are not chronically overstretched? For one thing, sewers and adequate water supplies cannot be established overnight. Even in Covent Garden, an early development and a model of planning, there were doubts. When in 1634 Sir Edmund Verney bought a lease there on two newly built houses with coach houses and stables, there was as yet no sewer. So he insisted on a clause which provided that, if living in Covent Garden proved so uncomfortable that he could not do it 'without any inconvenience', he could cancel his lease at six months' notice.

By 1666 London was not only far bigger – at least twenty times bigger – than any other town in England, in all Europe it was second in size only to Paris. But France accounted for a much larger population than England, so there the problem was, so to speak, diluted. The expert Sir William Petty calculated that half the King's revenue derived from London. Very worrying was the effect of London's growth on the outside, non-metropolitan world, as it sucked in labour to man its booming economy. The phenomenal increase in population was not the result of herculean efforts at procreation on the part of its inhabitants, but of sustained immigration. The Yorkshire landowner Sir John Reresby put the problem plainly in the House of Commons in 1685 when he declared that London drained all England of its people, 'especially the North, our tenants all coming hither, finding by experience that they could live here better in a cellar or a garret than they could . . . in the country on a farm of £30 rent.' The argument in adapted form applied to the rich as well, for the problem was worsened if important members of the community, people like Reresby himself, or Humphrey Mildmay, turned into more or less permanent Londoners. For one thing it was held that they might spend too much money on luxuries and upset the balance of payments by wasteful expenditure on imports. For another thing, and a much more fundamental one, there was the possible effect on the country-side. Take Mildmay. He was expected to act as leader of his local community: he was a justice of the peace, an unpaid civil servant appointed by the central government, whose job it was to deal summarily with petty criminals, to order the whipping of trespassers and to send vagabonds to gaol. For serious crimes, he and his fellow magistrates were responsible for the preliminary investigation. The hall of his house, Danbury Place, was no ordinary drawing room intended for private parties. It was furnished with long oak tables and benches and, in addition, sixteen chairs. It was there that taxes were assessed and reports received from the surveyor of highways and the overseer of poor relief. Mildmay and his colleagues were charged with the management of a highly regulated economy. As magistrates, they licensed ale-house keepers, supervised prices and bound apprentices; they even laid down an incomes policy and set terms of employment and a maximum wage. England was not like France, with its provincial civil servants and its grandees congregated at Versailles. The nobility and the country gentry were needed on the spot in their counties to make sure that the local economy worked. And for London above all the result would be catastrophic if the harvest failed and its teeming population were deprived of their supply of food.

Thus, the nobility and gentry, apart from those directly involved in running the country from Court, were not intended to be real Londoners. The Privy Council, buttressed by acts of parliament, issued proclamation after proclamation, and people were fined for staying too long. In 1632 the Star Chamber prosecuted some 250 peers, baronets, knights and gentlemen for remaining in London in defiance of an order directing them home. Proclamations also prohibited building on new foundations. Licences to build were often refused, as in the case of Lord Southampton in 1636 when he applied to develop land behind his old mansion in Holborn. Illicit buildings were demolished, others escaped undetected. But the government's attitude was in practice ambiguous. A list was drawn up in 1638 of new buildings erected without permission since 1603, buildings which had not been pulled down but where a fine had been levied instead. There were 1,361 of them – 618 to the west of the City, mainly in Holborn; 404 to the north, in Clerkenwell, Bishopsgate outside the walls, and Cripplegate; 282 in the area of Wapping. The modest balance had been built south of London Bridge. The problem with strict enforcement of the rules was that the government, with its chaotic finances, was always tempted to tax transgressors rather than to take steps to ensure that they never transgressed again. Still, the fines added to building costs and so inevitably acted as a discouragement to developers. Certainly landlords inside the permitted bounds were piling more and more people into existing buildings and squeezing shoddy housing into every alley or court they could annex. The health risk was of course frightful, as the Plague of 1665 – estimated to have killed between 70,000 and 80,000 people – bore witness. Moreover, building of this sort produced ready tinder for the Great Fire.

If, in September 1666, the tower of old St Paul's would have been the best place from which to observe the Strand palaces, equally it would have served for an inspection of the new West End. Monsieur Sorbière said that young French visitors, travelling by water as they did between west and east, thought of London as a place without hinterland. As Sorbière made plain, that was not the case. Holborn was already built up, and beyond was the development of Lincoln's Inn. Further to the west, around the area of our St Martin's Lane, was the residential estate built by Lord Salisbury early in the century, while behind the Strand lay the fashionable precinct of Covent Garden carved from the gardens of Bedford House.

It was through bargaining with the government that Covent Garden, the best-known of these early West End developments, came about. The fourth Earl of Bedford paid £2,000 (say £230,000 in our money) in 1631 for a licence to develop his ground on the north

Covent Garden, the first of the West End squares, laid out in the 1630s, showing Inigo Jones's St Paul's Church. Etching by Wenceslaus Hollar, 1646.

side of the garden wall of Bedford House. In return, he undertook to maintain the road at Long Acre, a district from which he was already collecting rent from tenants. He also agreed to accept the services of the Royal Surveyor, Inigo Jones. Covent Garden, with its elegant and italianate houses set in arcaded terraces, was an outstanding success, and the residential development was followed up under the fifth earl by a fruit and vegetable market. This coupling of residential and commercial was not unique. Lord Clare, the heir of a City family, did the same at Clare Market, now a dingy little alley half a mile or so away attached to the uncharismatic bulk of the London School of Economics and Political Science. In fact, by the end of the Civil War, the second Lord Clare's income from London property was running at about £2,800, considerably more than the fifth Lord Bedford was drawing from his. What was original about the Bedford project was the inclusion of a church, St Paul's, built on the western side of the square. It was the first new church to be built in London since the Reformation and the predecessor of all the other churches which the West End landowners would find it necessary to provide – usually simply by presenting the land – for their wealthy leaseholders.

Clare Market lies off Kingsway near the boundary with the City, and it was natural that much of the early development should be established in its vicinity. On the other side of Kingsway, the western side, is Great Queen Street, named after James I's queen, with some of its buildings still revealing their venerable origins. Round the corner from Clare Market is the large space of Lincoln's Inn Fields, which, with its imposing houses, was to be one of the most fashionable addresses in London and the first garden square. It consisted originally of three fields, Cup Field, Purse Field and, mainly outside the eventual square, Fickets Field. In the sixteenth century they were the place of execution of the conspirator Babington, and in the seventeenth – after development – of the Exclusionist Lord Russell. The first attempt to build was made by the Kentish and City family of Cornwallis, who, in the eighteenth century, were to produce one of the most eminent public figures of his time, the Marquess Cornwallis, a man who in his reserve and dignity was almost a caricature of the English *Milord*. His antecedents, however, were less exalted. James Howell in *Londinopolis* reported that a Mrs Cornwallis had so delighted Henry VIII with the quality of her puddings that he awarded her a fine house in Aldgate. Her grandson Sir Charles, rising in the world, bought what was later to become Devonshire House in Bishopsgate. In 1613, he turned his attention to Lincoln's Inn Fields, took a lease on Purse Field from the Crown and applied for a licence to build himself a house.

While the fields were Crown property, they lay on the edge of legal London, a district standing back from the Strand around Chancery Lane which was occupied for most of the year by lawyers. It is another example of the old residential grouping by trade or profession, an analogy (which the lawyers might not have appreciated) with the scriveners gathered together in Paternoster Row. The Society of Lincoln's Inn protested vigorously at the threat of development, arguing in a petition to the Crown that the fields should be preserved as a public park on the lines of Moorfields in the City. Their petition was sympathetically received, and commissioners led by Inigo Jones appeared on site to make a survey, the object of which was to lay out the fields for walks and to pull down illegally erected tenements. Had Lincoln's Inn then applied for a lease and carried out improvements, probably the Fields would have been saved from development. But they did not, and shortly before the Civil War, the widowed Lady Cornwallis sold her interest to William Newton from Bedfordshire who had already acquired the lease of Cup Field. He applied for a licence, this time to build thirty-two houses, reminding the Crown how wretchedly small a rent it was paid under existing arrangements. The Society once more objected, arguing annoyance and smells, and the 'disquieting of their studies', but by now, the Crown, in desperate straits for money, found the prospect of extra rents too alluring to forego.

By 1664, twenty-one peers and forty-two gentlemen were listed as living around the Fields. Lindsey House, Nos 59–60, built in 1640, though modified architecturally in the eighteenth century, survives as an example of the handsome buildings in which they lived. The Duke of York's [theatre] Company moved to the Fields from the Strand and Samuel Pepys frequently attended their plays. But Pepys also came to see his patron Lord Sandwich, and to dine at the

'Blue Balls' tavern, or with Sandwich's father-in-law Lord Crew. Sometimes he went there just for the walking. Pepys's colleague Thomas Povey was another resident, with a remarkable house which contained that rarity, a bathroom. John Evelyn records dining in Lincoln's Inn Fields with Sir John Banks, 'a merchant, of small beginnings, but by usury etc. amassed an estate of 100,000 pounds', and who was now in the process of turning himself into a gentleman.

Before the century was out, the area was thick with buildings, and to its inhabitants the new London was becoming formidably large and confusing. Here are directions on how to find a house in Chancery Lane in the days before street-numbering:

> A great house in Chancery Lane, over against Lincoln's Inn, near the Three Cranes, next door to the Hole in the Wall, within two doors of Mr Farmer's and one door of Judge Ackings.

The visitor was also advised to keep an eye open for the pump which was nearby.

As landowner and landlord in west London, the Crown was predominant. Nevertheless there existed a multitude of smaller proprietors, particularly in the City. There, livery companies, charities, widows and the City Corporation itself were significant property investors. Many noblemen drew rent from land in London. Lord Bridgwater had accumulated property around his house in the Barbican, and the Earl of Dorset, owner of Dorset House in Fleet Street – one of the largest buildings in London – invested in leases, mostly of pubs, in the area round the Savoy. Lord Cleveland owned all the manors in Stepney and Hackney, including the land on which the East India dock stood. But Bedford, Clare and the descendants of the first Lord Salisbury were the most prominent. Before moving on to the whirlwind development of London in the last decades of the seventeenth century, however, there must be added to this exclusive list the more proletarian, not to say juvenile, figure of Miss Mary Davies, in September 1666 aged nineteen months.

The Davies inheritance, known to later generations as the Grosvenor Estate, had reached Mary Davies through her father Alexander Davies, who was carried off by the Plague in the summer of 1665. He had himself inherited from his great uncle, a largely self-made lawyer and scrivener named Hugh Audley who made his fortune principally through lending money and through a place on the Court of Wards, an institution for raising a complex form of inheritance tax. Audley died, rich and famous for his business acumen, in extreme old age in 1662. So famous indeed was he that in the same year there was published his biography, *THE WAY TO BE RICH According to the practice of the Great Audley.* 'Some good things worth my minding', was Samuel Pepys's comment as he bought a copy. The book, a pamphlet really, is actually rather disappointing as an attempt to explain the methods of a man who must qualify as one of the most successful investors of all time; one would expect a great deal more from somebody distilling for us now the wisdom of George Soros or Warren Buffett. Essentially, except for its emphasis on hard work, the moral of the biography is negative – the need for extreme, Scrooge-like thrift and inordinate scepticism. 'Fie, fie, why are you so idle?', so Audley would lecture young men, '. . . there is not an hour in the day, but you might gain sixpence in, and sure two pence.' He was a sanctimonious man who built up an undeserved reputation for piety by taking care always 'to accompany himself with some grave and reverend divine'.

Since Hugh Audley in old age, almost maddened by the attentions of avaricious friends and relations, was forever redrawing his will, Alexander Davies could count himself lucky (though much good it did him personally) to have been picked at the right moment. Still, he could hardly guess how lucky. Audley's bequest to Davies was the manor of Ebury, which he had bought years before in 1626 for £9,400 (over a million pounds today) from the politician and businessman Lionel Cranfield, Earl of Middlesex, who had fallen on hard times. This manor, comprising only part of Audley's real-estate holdings – he was also a considerable buyer of country property – formed slightly under half of the greater manor of Eia, 1,090 acres of arable and pasture lying along the whole west side of London. The north-western section, a segment of Hyde Park, belonged to the Crown, and two other portions – for simplicity's sake modern designations are used – southern Mayfair, and part of Pimlico, were also outside the manor of Ebury. What is remarkable about the whole area is that a map of

1614, sufficiently in date fifty years later to be used by Alexander Davies, shows an almost total absence of buildings. There are three farm buildings near the site of Buckingham Palace, and a slaughter-house close by. There is Ebury Farm, south-west of Victoria Station, and Neyte House on the southern end of Ebury Bridge and known by the 1660s as the Neat Houses, when it had evolved into a collection of market gardeners' cottages and taverns. The Davies estate was divided into two parts. The northern section was bordered by Park Lane on the west, Oxford Street on the north, a line just west of Bond Street on the east, and another line parallel to the top of Berkeley Square to the south. The southern section consisted of Belgravia and most of Pimlico. It was real estate which eventually would be of almost incalculable value.

2

London Breaks Its Bounds

*

Nothing now remains of the great palaces of the Strand but an ornate seventeenth-century watergate standing behind the cluster of streets – Buckingham Street, York Buildings, George Court, Villiers Street – which recall the site of York House. The construction of the Embankment in the nineteenth century has left it beached well back from the now narrowed Thames, but in its day it provided a suitably impressive place of disembarkation for visitors to the house. York House was sold for demolition in 1672 by its owner, the Duke of Buckingham. One by one the others followed – Essex House next door, Exeter House, Worcester House, Little Salisbury House, Salisbury House itself – their sites and grounds to be replaced by the houses and tenements (and in one case a shopping centre) for which there was so much demand after the Great Fire. John Evelyn, uncharacteristically mistaking the trend, had tried in 1671 to persuade his friend Henry Howard, the future Duke of Norfolk, one of the few owners with money in hand, actually to rebuild his dilapidated palace of Arundel House; he failed, and it too came down in the 1680s after Howard's death. By the end of the century only a handful of the great buildings were still there.

Up to 1666 the withdrawal of the nobility and gentry from the City and its immediate neighbourhood had been steady rather than precipitate. Now it was made urgent by the crowds of homeless flooding westwards, fleeing 'the ruinous heap, or that *Chaos* which we now call London'. The Fire, with its destruction of so much of London's housing, acted as detonator for a demographic explosion, a massive migration which was anyway inevitable. It was a flight by the rich, but hardly a reluctant one, for they were happy to go, to take their money and abandon to speculators and builders the massive, often obsolete buildings descended to them from other, different times. Many of the Strand mansions were no longer even occupied by their owners but hired out as embassies or split up into lodgings. And then there was the pollution. Sir Dudley North inhabited a large mansion in the City behind Goldsmiths' Hall. He caulked up windows and chimneys but, even so, clouds of dust penetrated the house to the extent that some of the rooms had to be stripped of their furniture. John Evelyn's fondness for the Strand certainly did not imply an indifference to the filth and pollution of Thames-side London. In his book *Fumifugium** published in 1661, he writes that smoke from breweries near Northumberland House at Charing Cross filled the galleries of the Court at Whitehall. Elsewhere he noted that 'I have been in a spacious church where I could not discern the minister for the smoke; nor hear him for the peoples barking.' For that dense fog which was to haunt London for another three centuries, the best description is perhaps that of the early nineteenth-century visitor Louis Simond:

> The air . . . is loaded with small flakes of smoke, in sublimation, – a sort of flower of soot, so light as to float without falling. This black snow sticks to your clothes and linen, or lights on your face. You just feel something on your nose, or your cheek, – the finger is applied mechanically, and fixes it into a black patch!

In times when people anywhere, town or country, were so often afflicted by chronic ill-health, the desire to escape at least the worst of the pollution was an important factor in the decision on where to live in London and in the 'colonization' of the countryside.

The traditional residential pattern continued to break up. As the rich moved west, they were followed by the trades which depended on them, and on which of course they in their turn depended. But the tradesmen and the poor were now to be more neatly tucked away; the days of mixed residential areas when rich and poor lived cheek

---

* Its full title was *Fumifugium: or the inconvenience of the aer and smoak of London dissipated.*

by jowl were passing. In the 1660s and long afterwards, a vivid memory
lingered of what had approached class warfare. The Civil War, the
execution of the King, the major-generals, the humiliation of the
country's traditional leaders were not to be forgotten. Lord Clarendon
recalled that 'a more inferior sort of common people' took over, 'who
. . . exercised so great an insolence over those who were in quality
above them, that was very grievous . . . all distinction of quality being
renounced.' Sir John Reresby returned from abroad in 1658 to find
that the citizens and ordinary people of London could barely stand
the sight of a gentleman. Walking one day in the street with his valet
who sported a feather in his hat, the two of them were set upon by
workmen and escaped only with difficulty. During the Republic
there had also occurred an unprecedented upheaval in manners. A
description is given by Evelyn in his *Character of England*:

> Do but imagine how it would become our ladies to call *Monsieur*
> N. *Jack* N. What more frequent than this? *Tom* P. was here today,
> I went yesterday to the Course with *Will* R. and *Harry* M. treated
> me at such a tavern.

This is to be compared with standard patrician protocol, as when
Rachel, Lady Russell, a woman of the highest social standing, writes
to her thirteen-year-old niece Elizabeth Ogle – already married –
she addresses her as 'Lady Ogle' and refers to 'your ladyship's letter'.

The country immigrants were not confined to artisans and
would-be apprentices. The prosperous families with established
London roots, now on the move, were joined by country gentry who,
remembering the austerities of the Republic, wanted fun, and found
the money to obtain it. They flocked to town, letting, so it was said,
'even to the very door of their mansion house', land which once they
had farmed themselves. Here, in Etherege's *She Would if She Could*,
is Sir Oliver Cockwood back in London:

> Indeed I have been an age absent . . . Well, faith, a man had
> better be a vagabond in this town than a justice of the peace in
> the country. I was e'en grown a sot for want of gentlemanlike
> recreations.

It was not just a question of pleasure and excitement. More business was done in London now, it was there you went for mortgages and for the regular sittings of the House of Commons. Sir Oliver is returning to old haunts, but many of the country gentry who arrived were from families who in earlier times would seldom have left their local parishes or foregone their local pursuits. They constituted new demand on London, for houses or lodgings, and for services. Lord Clarendon's father, a reasonably substantial Wiltshire squire, never visited London at all during the last thirty years of his life. One country gentleman, talking to Pepys and some companions, recalled his father telling him that in his time it was so rare for a country gentleman to come to London that, when he did, he would make his will before setting out.

With the atrocious, narrow and often waterlogged country roads and the unstable and uncomfortable wagons which served as coaches, alarm over the dangers of the road was not wholly fanciful. Sometimes it was necessary to travel by litter rather than on horseback or by coach. Lady Anne Clifford travelled that way on one occasion from London to Knole in Kent. In 1619 a sick James I started a journey by litter but ended carried by his guards because of the intolerable jolting. The introduction of the new travelling coach around the middle of the century greatly improved communications, and indeed the transition has been compared by one expert to that in the nineteenth century from coach to railway. To travel from Bath to London, a distance of 109 miles, took three days by the old stagecoach. But there was now in summer what was called a 'flying coach' which accomplished the fifty-nine mile journey between Oxford and London in a single day, taking thirteen hours. By the 1680s London was linked by stagecoach to eighty-eight towns.

Edmund Bohun was one of the countrymen who tried his luck in London. He was a Suffolk squire and magistrate, possessed, as he put it, of 'a competent though limited patrimony'. Ambition was one motive, for he had two highly placed contacts through whom he hoped to secure a profitable job. The desire for new friends was another, since Bohun, an intellectual by temperament, found himself perpetually at odds with his fox-hunting neighbours. So when by chance in the mid-1680s most of his seven servants for one reason or another gave notice, he and his wife took the plunge and let their country estate. Bohun reckoned that the move would bring a further advantage, for whereas to give up the manor house and most of the servants and continue to live in Suffolk would occasion serious loss of face, in London they could make do with lodgings without a qualm. They decided to settle in Clerkenwell, still respectable but less fashionable than it had been fifty years before in Humphrey Mildmay's time. But their lodgings proved to be too shabby and Mrs Bohun insisted on moving. However, even in the new lodgings, Bohun admitted to embarrassment at welcoming friends. In the end, the experiment failed, partly because Bohun was a most tactless and inept person socially who would find it difficult to fit in anywhere. He had been too unrealistic; he had arrived, he admitted to himself, believing – shades of Etherege's Oliver Cockwood – that a beggar in London was happier than a gentleman in the country. Bohun was devout and deplored the moral atmosphere of the city: 'As the air and streets of London do foul the body and dirty the clothes and linen above all other, so there is the greatest corruption of the soul too, if great care be not taken.' It was difficult to educate the children and, above all, to obtain the rents from his country estate. Finally, one of his possible patrons died and he quarrelled with the other. The only job that was offered proved unsatisfactory and the experiment lapsed. (There is, though, a sort of happy ending, for years later, after his diary finishes, Bohun turns up as Chief Justice of South Carolina.)

Bohun's Clerkenwell was a long way from Whitehall, the seat of government and fashion, a district which, if far from unpolluted, by virtue of its importance inevitably attracted many of the wealthiest patricians. The difficulty was the lack of suitable housing. It was at this point that there intervened the man with the best claim to be regarded as the founder of the West End – Henry Jermyn, Earl of St Albans, three times ambassador to France, a man of huge physique and one of whom it was said that his 'entire person . . . must be a moving trophy, and monument of the favours and freedoms of the fair sex'. Happily – in the context of real-estate development – one of the trophy holders was Henrietta Maria, the Queen Mother, to whom indeed St Albans was rumoured to be secretly married. Happily too, for the same reason, St Albans was more than a sexual prodigy, he was also extremely shrewd. John Evelyn wrote of him that 'it is incredible how easy a life this Gent. has lived, & in what plenty even abroad, whilst his Majesty was a sufferer'.

St Albans pointed out to Charles II that 'the beauty of this great Town and the convenience of your Court are defective in point of houses fit for the dwellings of noble men and other persons of quality'. A solution was found in the Crown land of St James's Fields in the neighbourhood of St James's Palace – within striking distance of Whitehall – which formed part of the jointure settled for her lifetime on the Queen Mother. The King appointed the fields under lease to St Albans. Such grants of land, either in the form of a gift or at a price below market value, were a standard method of rewarding loyal

Henry Jermyn, Earl of St Albans, the developer of St James's Square and the man with the best claim to be regarded as the founder of the West End. An etching by R. Godfrey, 1793, taken from a portrait by Lely.

service, and, in any event, the King had borrowed money from St Albans during his exile. The fields, as it happened, were not exactly untouched by man, for in 1661, the year of the appointment, they were already occupied by more than 220 houses and sheds. Still – even ignoring the sheds – the buildings were quite unsuitable for what was required. The transfer to St Albans was effected in stages. In 1661 he held the lease as the Queen Mother's trustee; the next year Henrietta Maria resigned her interest and Charles II granted the lease to St Albans personally, also extending it for a charge of £6,000. St Albans now had a sixty-year lease, but five years had already expired and none of the houses was yet built. Except in the case of a house for himself, he did not intend to pay for the building; the question was whether people would be prepared to pay for very grand and thus expensive houses when their ownership (or their family's ownership) would last for so limited a time. Here was a fundamental and enduring question which would confront every substantial landowner and landlord in London. St Albans convinced the King that unless would-be buyers obtained the freehold and so were able to pass on these mansions to their heirs, they were not interested. So, in 1665, the King granted St Albans the freehold on approximately half the estate so that he in turn could sell it on. There followed the development of Pall Mall, and, despite protests from the City that it infringed their rights, a new covered market.

So important was the Court as the focus of the new London that it was natural for the traveller Celia Fiennes to write at the turn of the seventeenth and eighteenth centuries, 'London is the City properly for trade, Westminster for the Court'. Whitehall, a Tudor palace appropriated from Cardinal Wolsey, was enormous, stretching half a mile down the Thames, a jumble of buildings containing something like 2,000 rooms, with, however, the notable addition of Inigo Jones's Banqueting House, externally much the same as it is today. Down the middle, straddled by two covered bridges, ran King Street, to the west but parallel to our Parliament Street. At its southern end stood Westminster Abbey, and, slightly off to the side in Old Palace Yard, the medieval palace of Westminster which accommodated the chambers of the Lords and Commons, and the lawcourts. All around crowded in hovels and tenements, and unsalubrious little alleys.

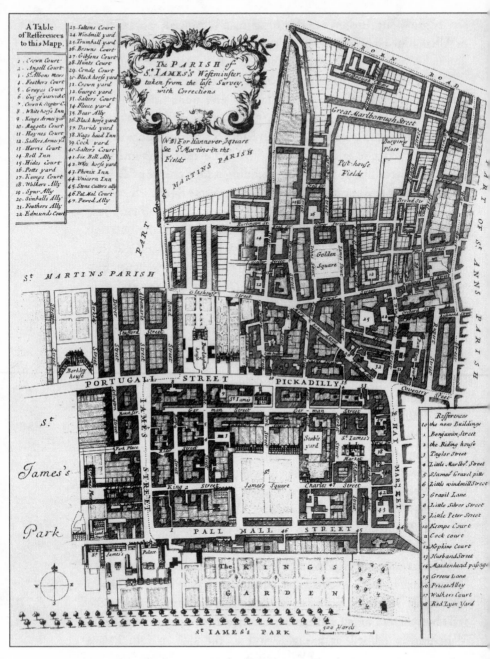

St James's and the West End, detail from a map by
Ogilby and Morgan, *London etc. Actually Survey'd*,
1681–2.

Edward Waterhouse described the function of the Court in his *Gentleman's Monitor* of 1665:

> To [the Court], as the centre of greatness and pomp, fashion and civility, honour and advancement, do all persons of ambition, lustre, or any remarkable conspicuity, come, in hope to make their interest in, and their advance by it: Hither comes the proper man, who is fit to stand before the King . . . and the delicate woman to advance herself by an honourable match, and the eloquent divine to get preferment by courtly tongue and apposite discourse . . .

It is a wide definition. To Swift and to Boswell, the Court was an excellent coffee-house, useful for meeting people and keeping up with the news. To many, like the courtiers met by Sorbière in St James's Park, it was the centre of social life, the abode of fashion, a view which lent itself to numberless satires like that of Samuel Butler depicting the epicene courtier who 'flutters up and down like a butterfly in a garden, and while he is pruning of his peruke takes occasion to contemplate his legs and the symmetry of his breeches.' In Charles II's time, the Court provided a wealth of sexual opportunity. At other times it was seen as a bastion of respectability. One thinks of Queen Victoria or of a censorious and betoqued Queen Mary. Dorothy Osborne wrote of the pre-Civil War Court in a letter to her future husband William Temple that, though 'it was no perfect school of virtue, yet Vice there wore her mask, and appeared so unlike herself that she gave no scandal.' But Temple himself, after a lifetime's experience of government and diplomacy, had no truck with anything incidental. The Court was simply a place of business, he noted:

> A Court [is] properly a fair, the end of it trade and gain: for none would come to be jostled in a crowd, that is easy at home, nor go to service, that thinks he has enough to live well of himself. Those that come to either for entertainment, are the dupes of the traders, or, at least, the raillery.

Participants could find it extremely demanding. As Lord Chesterfield was to put it, 'Favour at courts depends upon so many, such trifling, such unexpected, and unforeseen events, that a good courtier must attend to every circumstance, however little.' Sir John Reresby would have agreed. A 'Moorish' slave belonging to him died during an operation. Reresby was accused of responsibility for the death and, as a result, his estate was in danger of forfeiture to the Crown, and thus, in accordance with normal practice, available to be passed on as reward to some deserving public figure. The conspiracy to deprive Reresby – for that is what it was – seems to have involved the Lord Treasurer, the Duke of Norfolk and perhaps even the Lord Chief Justice. It was only through his connection as a Yorkshireman with Danby, who took him to see the King, that Reresby frustrated the plotters. Reresby's ambition was official employment in his home county, but self-protection as well as self-advancement compelled his constant presence in London. Sir John Bramston – like Reresby, of impeccable Royalist credentials, a deputy lieutenant of Essex and, as knight of the shire, one of the two representatives of the county in the House of Commons – was under the necessity of continual attendance at Court in order to recover three and a half years of pension owed to his late brother. At Court, he declared, it was a question of out of sight, out of mind; to obtain what you needed (or simply were owed) you had to be 'often in view'.

But if you were 'in view', 'in mind', a loyal supporter of the government or particularly influential, the rewards could be immense. They came in the form of jobs, of sinecures, of pensions, and, like titles – another important form of patronage – they could be hereditary. The Post Office pensioners' list gives an idea of some leading beneficiaries; none of the people concerned had any other connection with the Post Office. In the financial year to March 1704, the list includes Queen Anne's husband, Prince George of Denmark; the commander-in-chief of the army, the Duke of Marlborough; the Duke of Schomberg; the Duchess of Cleveland, ex-Castlemaine, once mistress to Charles II; and Reresby's patron, the Earl of Danby, now Duke of Leeds. Among the handful of minor beneficiaries was Titus Oates, rewarded with £300 a year as the key 'witness' in the Popish Plot and as compensation for the painful revenge he had afterwards suffered at the hands of the Stuarts. It was useful money, with the Duchess of Castlemaine drawing an income of £4,700, equivalent to over half a million pounds now. Sometimes the system of what came to be called Old Corruption seems weird: in the early nineteenth century, for instance, there was a baroness paid £340 a year, nearly £20,000 in our money, as hereditary sweeper of the Mall in St James's Park.

Yet, to be rewarded in this way, it was usually essential to be resident in London over long periods, and not just when parliament was sitting. And resident nearby: Lord Ailesbury wrote that his father, a privy councillor from an important family, was at a great disadvantage because he persisted in living in Clerkenwell. When William III moved the Court to Kensington, courtiers and politicians went along too.

Robert Baker, the founder of Piccadilly, only moved in such circles by way of commerce. He was a member of one of the trades – luxury goods, clothing and catering, building and decorative – which followed the rich westwards. His father was a Somerset corn merchant who died young, leaving Robert to a hard childhood and a cheating uncle, and to apparently no schooling whatever. In 1600 he arrived in London, an insignificant country tailor who three years later opened what was described by a neighbour as a 'poor little shop' in the Strand backing on to the gardens of York House, where he and his family worked and lived. However, the choice of site was excellent; the Strand was booming commercially and Baker's shop found itself placed next door to Lord Salisbury's New Exchange which opened a few years afterwards. Baker supplied expensive haberdashery to the rich noblemen and to the Court, his wife was skilful with linens, and soon he was employing sixty men at a time when few employers aspired to more than half a dozen. The Strand premises became overcrowded and Baker moved his household ten minutes' walk away, into the open country of Windmill Fields on the western edge of Soho, where for £50 he bought 1⅜ acres of freehold. Here he built his house, with cow barn attached, quickly nicknamed by such neighbours as there were Pickadilly Hall after the pickadillies – borders to ruffs and collars – which were apparently a speciality of his business. (In the same way Shaver's Hall, a gaming house with gardens covering 3½ acres on land that Baker later acquired, was named after its proprietor, a barber.) Then he turned his attention to wider development, continuing to purchase land and erect houses, having in one instance to buy common grazing rights which applied to some of the ground. By the time he died in 1623, Baker had accumulated considerable property and built houses around our Piccadilly Circus, in the Haymarket, Whitcomb Street and Golden Square. He was a rich man, no longer a tailor but a gentleman who married his daughter and heir into one of the leading families of Kent.

Problems followed Robert Baker's death. Mary Baker, his young widow and second wife, ran headlong into one of them. She had erected buildings without licence which polluted the water supply to Whitehall and Somerset House, and, in February 1638, the Star Chamber ordered that all the houses in Piccadilly dating from 1616 be demolished. Mary Baker was obliged to undertake extensive drainage schemes and to pay a £1,000 fine before the order was rescinded. There was pressure too from more recent developers, most notably the rakish Cavalier, Colonel Thomas Panton, like St Albans at first sight an unlikely devotee of real-estate development. It was said of him that 'he cared not what expenses he was at to carry on an intrigue of love'. He was an inveterate gambler; but then one night at Court he won enough money to buy an estate in Herefordshire worth £1,500 a year (£170,000 in our money), and immediately gave up gambling. Panton turned into a very serious businessman who saw advantage to be gained by mixing in the lengthy lawsuits which racked the Baker family and in the end destroyed most of Robert Baker's legacy.

Mary Baker was long-lived and still living at Pickadilly Hall in 1668, nearly half a century after the death of her husband. By then Piccadilly was transformed. Three great palaces with their gardens, stables and outbuildings occupied the north side of the road down to what is now Green Park and what was then the edge of London. First, from the east, was the sumptuous Burlington House, fragments of which survive in the Burlington House that today accommodates the Royal Academy. Next to it came the mammoth Clarendon House built for the chief minister, Lord Clarendon, by 1668 disgraced and in exile, which with 101 hearths was one of the largest buildings in the country and stood in eight acres granted to Clarendon by the King. Last was Berkeley House.

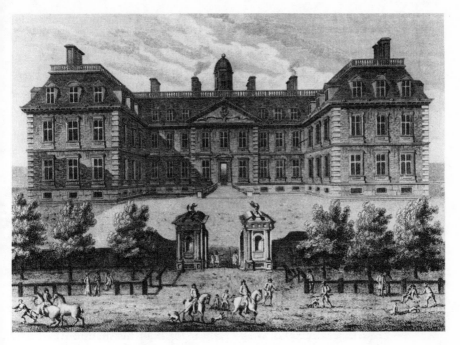

Clarendon House, Piccadilly, built 1664–7, described
by John Evelyn as being 'without hyperbole', the most
magnificent house in England. Etching by J. Dunstall.

The building of these three Piccadilly mansions in the 1660s gave
a powerful impetus to West End building. It was not so much that
they encouraged other grandees to build on a comparable scale but that
they set the scene for further development. There was a trickle-down
effect. Just as the palace of the sovereign drew to it the mansions of
the high nobility, so in turn did these mansions attract others. In
Covent Garden and in Bloomsbury, for instance, a great house acted
as the nucleus to a new community. The economist Richard Cantillon
explains the process in his *Essai sur la nature du commerce en général*
published in 1755.

If a Prince or Nobleman . . . fixes his residence in some pleasant
spot, and several other Noblemen come to live there to be within
reach of seeing each other frequently and enjoying agreeable
society, this place will become a City. Great houses will be built

there for the Noblemen in question, and an infinity of others for the Merchants, Artisans, and people of all sorts of professions whom the residence of these Noblemen will attract thither. For the service of these Noblemen, Bakers, Butchers, Brewers, Wine Merchants, Manufacturers of all kinds, will be needed. These will build houses in the locality or will rent houses built by others . . . all the little houses in a City such as we have described depend upon and subsist at the expense of the great houses . . .

It is a quotation which goes to the heart of this book, for it describes not only the classical way in which a city such as London developed, but it emphasizes too the fundamental importance of decisions made by rich individuals.

Leicester Fields, containing the later Leicester Square, were other Crown lands which had been granted outright, in their case to James I's minister Lionel Cranfield, who had included them in his sale of land to Hugh Audley. The latter had sold them on to the second Lord Leicester, who in the early 1630s built his mansion Leicester House at the northern end of the fields. Dealings before the Civil War between Leicester and St Albans, then Henry Jermyn, illustrate some of the differences in character between the two developers. Leicester was ambassador in Paris and anxious to obtain the lord lieutenancy of Ireland. The key to the appointment was seen to be Queen Henrietta Maria, and the key to her, even in those days, was Jermyn. Only money made Jermyn 'quick and stirring', reported Leicester's agent at Court, for he was a man who had never been known to do anything for free. Matters dragged on until the Civil War – Jermyn had to make a quick escape to France – with Leicester never quite able to screw himself up to meeting Jermyn's price. Cultivated, but vacillating, and by reputation impractical, he nevertheless managed to build up a significant London estate.

The government's licence to build Leicester House with its stables and coach houses was made dependent on the planting of the rest of the fields with trees and on laying out walks for common use. Lord Leicester was even obliged to retain the area set aside for clothes drying. Steadily, however, following the example of countless country landlords, Leicester encroached on this common land. Between 1663 and 1665 he was granting leases wholesale on the east side of the fields, and in 1670 he obtained official retrospective sanction for what he had done, and was awarded a licence for further building. The system of controls was crumbling. As the rate of building gathered pace, in St James's, Leicester Fields, then in Soho and Mayfair, the restraints imposed through building licences jarred increasingly with the King's need to reward his supporters and to fulfil old obligations, and with the general pressure on land.

What is more, members of the House of Commons holding a direct interest – or through their patrons an indirect one – in property development wanted not to halt the growth of London but rather to prevent the swamping of the new fashionable areas by the proletariat. Sir Christopher Wren submitted a petition to the King expressing anxiety about new housing in Soho designed for workmen and small tradesmen who were fleeing the irksome regulations of the City of London. In January 1671 matters came to a head with a debate in the House. 'This enlarging of London makes it filled with lacqueys and pages,' declared one member. Another asserted that he would have 'the tradesmen enjoined to return again into the City who are planted in this part of the town'. These were hardly very practical suggestions for, apart from anything else, the rich needed their 'lacqueys and pages', and indeed could hardly be served effectively by tradesmen whose premises were several miles away. Sir William Coventry intervened with a compromise suggestion: restrict the type of building, limit height, so that it will suit the nobility and ambassadors but be unsuitable for tradesmen, who of course combined shops and living quarters under one roof.

The momentum behind further action at the time was lost, but in 1678 the issue was again sufficiently alive to oblige Richard Frith to give a bond indemnifying the purchaser of a house he was selling in St James's Square against any tax which might be imposed. One reason for hesitation in the 1670s was, it seems, that the House of Commons, increasingly at odds with the Crown, was reluctant to allow taxes which, by augmenting the King's revenue, would make him less amenable to pressure. But by the 1680s the Stuarts were back in control. James II's attitude was that people did not *have* to build any more than they were obliged to make themselves drunk '. . . if they will drink, let them pay for it'. Lord Ailesbury approached the question rather more drily. The alternative to raising taxes on new buildings (and he included houses built since 1660 on ground granted by the King) was to increase import duties. Ailesbury considered a buildings tax as a lesser evil, and was later convinced that failure to take his advice had damaged trade with the American colonies. His advocacy of a buildings tax deeply affronted many in the House of Commons: 'It is naturally to be believed that the beginning of my disgrace was on the account of my proposing a tax on new foundations.'

The sense of outrage was palpable: Sir Thomas Clarges, whose fortune was based on royal grants of land in the West End, violently attacked the proposal and, according to Ailesbury, 'went out of the House foaming at [the] mouth'. Clarges, his name given to Clarges Street and Clarges Mews near Shepherd Market, collaborated with St Albans in St James's Square. But unlike St Albans or Sir Thomas Bond, another prominent developer who has left his name on one of London's best-known streets, he was not a member of Henrietta Maria's entourage. He was the son of a farrier in the Savoy, but he was also brother-in-law to George Monck, Duke of Albemarle, whose call on the King's goodwill as the restorer of the monarchy was almost limitless. In his Roundhead background and his modest social roots, Clarges was closer to Nicholas Barbon, with the possible exception of Wren, the most famous and most important London developer of the time.

Dr Barbon – a medical doctor, although he did not practice – was an extraordinary man. He was the son of 'Praise God Barebones', the Puritan zealot who gave his name to one of Cromwell's parliaments, and indeed was himself usually called 'Barebone' by his contemporaries. He was, though, no political revolutionary, but equally he was no Court sycophant. The episode of Essex House gives an idea of his character. In 1674 the Strand palace of Essex House was put up for sale. Arthur Capel, the then Earl of Essex (of a different family from that which had given its name to the house) came on the scene as a prospective purchaser, with the King – who wished to reward him for services in Ireland – as his backer. Barbon, however, was already in negotiation and, without waiting for the formal contract, had uprooted the garden and laid out the plans for a street.

Great pressure was brought to bear on him to withdraw, and he was twice summoned before the Privy Council. He nevertheless refused to give in.

Barbon was very tough and very shrewd. His method of financing his land purchases and developments is illustrative. A conventional loan was chargeable at 10 per cent interest. Barbon's approach was to obtain credit from a scrivener or goldsmith and by delays, subterfuge and injunctions hold off payment, until finally, when he was forced to disburse, he could do so at 5 per cent interest on arrears. He was a classic entrepreneur. In 1667, the year after the Great Fire, he founded, and managed, the first fire insurance office in England. He was also a theoretician, who experimented with banking and wrote extensively on finance and economics. In *An Apology for the Builder* of 1685 he set out a spirited defence of London's expansion and thus of the role of the developer. 'The cause of the increase of Building is from *the natural increase of Mankind*,' he insisted. Every year a new town is added to London, and people blame the builders. But new buildings should be welcomed for they raise the rents of the old ones; the bigger a town is, the more valuable are the houses within it. Building, Barbon reminded his readers in another book, creates employment on a large scale.

Nicholas Barbon was involved as a developer all over London. In the Strand he carried through the redevelopment of the Duke of Buckingham's York House and its grounds as well as that of Essex House; he worked with St Albans in St James's Square; he was to be found in the City in Mincing Lane, and participated in a syndicate which redeveloped the site of Devonshire House after the death of the old Lady Devonshire in 1675. In Holborn he drove through his plans for Red Lion Fields in the face of determined opposition from the members of Gray's Inn who descended on the field and assaulted the workmen. When asked by an acquaintance why he always undertook such ambitious schemes, he replied loftily that small ones were fit only for bricklayers. At the end he overstretched himself and went bankrupt, characteristically leaving instructions in his will that his debts should not be paid.

Soho, with Barbon one of the principal contractors, was an old hunting ground, its name deriving from So-Ho, a hunting call. Even in the 1660s it was sparsely inhabited. To us in our day it is planted firmly north of Shaftesbury Avenue, separated distinctly from the area of Leicester Square. In the seventeenth century, there was no dividing line, and on a map the two districts appear to flow naturally into one another. Obviously Soho was unlikely to remain long in its pristine state. Nor did it, for by 1670 with Leicester Square largely completed, landowners and landlords, contractors and builders, turned their attention northwards. During the 1670s and 1680s a sustained burst of building swept over the district and for a brief period made Soho Square one of the most fashionable addresses in London. Sir Roger de Coverly for instance was placed there by his creator when he was in town. Soho was again part of the now deceased Queen Mother's jointure and even though the land had reverted to the King, the indefatigable St Albans obtained a lease (but not a freehold) on 22 acres. In fact, this time he took little part in development, subleasing almost all of it to Richard Frith, whose name has become attached to one of the district's best-known streets. The Pulteney family, who were squeezed out of their Crown tenancy of Sandpit Fields to allow for Green Park – as well as from other land north of Piccadilly – were compensated by a lease on a long strip of ground in western Soho.

Yet Soho, large as it was, did not turn into quite the gold mine that had been anticipated. It could claim no great mansions unless one counts Leicester House, which anyway had already established its own enclave. There was Newport House, but that was quickly demolished by Nicholas Barbon to make room for houses, tenements and a market. In 1681–2 the magnificent Monmouth House was built for the ill-fated duke of that name in Soho Square, but placed as it was at one end of the district, its stimulative effect was restricted. Barbon and Frith both ran into trouble with their speculations, and Lord Macclesfield as head lessee tried to organize countermeasures which would force Barbon to pay up the rent he owed. In parts of Soho the standard of building was low and the street planning poor. A survey of 1693 reported that houses dating from the 1670s on the Pulteney land of Windmill Fields were of such inferior quality that it was doubtful whether they would even survive to the end of their thirty-year leases. Cheap housing naturally did not attract the rich, and

Soho Square in 1731. Engraving by Sutton Nicholls.
The hills of Hampstead and Highgate can be seen in
the distance.

Soho quickly became the focus of massive immigration by persecuted
French Huguenots, whose skills and industry, though of great advantage to the London economy, were not calculated to appeal to rich
rentiers.

From Lincoln's Inn Fields on the east to Soho on the west,
residential London outside the City had, on its northern side, reached
a natural boundary. While there existed no visible barrier, no actual
wall such as that which defined the limits of Paris and which was to
serve a very practical purpose as late as 1870/71, the high road that
ran north of this developed area – followed now by High Holborn,
New Oxford Street and Oxford Street – in effect attained formal
recognition as a boundary during the Civil War, when it became the
northern section of the defensive line of forts and ramparts constructed
as protection against Royalist attack. It was a sort of *périphérique*,
carrying a stream of goods traffic around the built-up area. At the

47

eastern end, on the edge of the City of London, Henry VIII's Lord Chancellor, Thomas Wriothesley, created Earl of Southampton, had been granted the manor of Bloomsbury and a parcel of land at Holborn Bars. The property empire built up by his descendants was initially a commercial one based on a toll gate at Holborn Bars and the demand for housing and shops along the busy main road. Development was gradual and interrupted by political complications, but by the 1620s and 1630s Southampton House on the south side of Holborn was surrounded by building. More and more of the grounds were built over; the tennis court went, and the chapel, and finally in 1638, the house itself. Lord Southampton bought more land along Holborn and took the step of moving his household across the way into the countryside of Bloomsbury. Here, in the late 1650s, in what was to be Bloomsbury Square, he built a new Southampton House on the site of one of the Civil War forts.

So far in this book two women have appeared in prominent roles – the Queen Mother Henrietta Maria, whose jointure lands formed the core of much of the original West End, and Mary Davies, the progenitor, so to speak, of the Grosvenor Estate. But though prominent, they were largely passive. Rachel Wriothesley, daughter of the Earl of Southampton and heiress to Bloomsbury, falls into a different category. Under her direction, while Holborn continued to produce a useful commercial revenue, the essential nature of the estate shifted to smart residential. The appeal of Bloomsbury depended to a great extent on its healthy situation. In 1665 an eminent doctor wrote of it:

> I cannot but take notice of Bloomsbury . . . for the best part about London, both for health and pleasure exceeding other places. It is the best air and finest prospect, being the highest ground, and overlooking other parts of the city. The fields bordering upon this place are very pleasant and dry grounds for walking and improving of health.

To Rachel Wriothesley, however, there fell far more than mere superintendence of a change in policy. In 1669, two years after her father's death, she married – for love – William Russell, who on the death of his elder brother succeeded as heir to his father, the Earl of Bedford. The marriage thus led to the linking of two great London estates, Bloomsbury and Covent Garden. Then followed disaster: Russell, a leading politician fiercely opposed to the Court, was found guilty of treason, of conspiring to assassinate the King in the Rye House Plot of 1683. He was beheaded. The heartbroken Rachel set herself two tasks. One was to rehabilitate her husband's reputation, and the other, first to preserve and then to extend the family's wealth and standing. So successful was she – with her friends – in the first that William Russell was established in history as the great Whig martyr who had sacrificed his life in the cause of liberty. On the second she was much more on her own, for the Earl of Bedford was now an old man. Part of William Russell's property was safely in trust, out of harm's way, but the rest was liable to confiscation by the Crown. Rachel's pleading at an interview with Charles II averted the immediate peril, but the danger remained. She cut herself off from social life, determined, she said, 'to converse with none but lawyers and accountants'. With the accession of William and Mary, the Russell family was restored to high favour and the old earl advanced to a dukedom. Rachel Russell was able to spend the rest of her long widowhood in promoting her children's welfare and consolidating the family's property holdings.

'Westminster is in a fair way to shake hands with Chelsea as St Giles is with Marylebone,' wrote Daniel Defoe. Contemporaries had only to look around them to see the extraordinary growth of London. Lord Berkeley of Stratton was another member of Henrietta Maria's entourage, and he owed much of his rise to fortune to his cousin Lord St Albans, whose sole redeeming quality has been described as being 'that he was never at a loss to discern merit in his relatives'. But Berkeley was an able man in his own right, a prominent Royalist general during the war, viceroy of Ireland, ambassador to France, a successful businessman who came close to bringing off a spectacular merger of his own lands north of Piccadilly with Audley's manor of Ebury, which adjoined them to the west. In 1672, he signed on behalf of his young son a contract for marriage with the seven-year-old Mary Davies, though the marriage itself never took place as in the end Berkeley could not raise the money required of him. In 1675 Lord Berkeley suffered a stroke and John Evelyn, as a close friend, found himself taking responsibility for the family's affairs: 'what will not friendship & love make one do!' he wrote in his diary. After Berkeley's death, Evelyn advised his widow, herself the daughter of a leading City businessman, on how to develop the Berkeley lands. Already the splendid Piccadilly houses, built only twenty years before, were turning over their grounds for development. Clarendon House was demolished. Of that immense building Evelyn was left with a poignant memory. The last time he had seen Lord Clarendon he was sitting in the garden there in a wheelchair, overcome by depression. Dismissed and in disgrace, Clarendon was accused by his enemies of every sort of villainy. One charge was that he had pocketed the money received from the sale of Dunkirk to the French. It was also alleged that to build his great house he had diverted for his own use the stone meant for the repair of St Paul's and timber intended for the navy. The night following Evelyn's visit he fled to France.

It is unlikely, however, that Evelyn would have shared that memory with Lady Berkeley, for her late husband, once a close friend of Clarendon's, had taken a vigorous part in his dismissal from power. His mood, though, was sombre. The entry in his diary after a visit to Lady Berkeley is a lament for the houses and their parks and gardens and for London itself:

> . . . I could not but deplore that sweet place (by far the most pleasant & noble Gardens Courts and Accommodations, [stately] porticos etc. anywhere about the Town) should so much of it (be) streitned & turned into Tenements; but that magnificent pile and Gardens contiguous to it (built by the late L. Chancellor Hyde [Clarendon] with so vast a cost) being all demolished, & designed for *piazzas* & buildings, was some excuse for my Lady Berkley's resolution of letting out her ground also, for so excessive a price as was offered, advancing her revenue near 1000 pounds per Ann: in mere ground rents; to such a mad intemperance the age was come of building about a City, by far too disproportionate already to the Nation, I having in my time seen it almost as large more than it was within my memory.

The man who had made Lady Berkeley this irresistible offer was John Hinde, of a City family and himself a goldsmith banker who lived in Cornhill and owned Lauderdale House, which is now incorporated in the mansion at Waterlow Park on Highgate Hill. He was an experienced developer and also a partner with Barbon in fire insurance projects. However, the building of Mayfair failed to proceed with the speed and success which had become almost customary. Houses no longer seem to spring almost automatically from the ground, to be filled within a few years by dukes. As Evelyn suspected, Hinde had paid too much for the Berkeley land; the piazzas and buildings intended to cover it and the Clarendon House grounds and the neighbouring Conduit Mead estate were to be long delayed. The speculative boom was disintegrating. There were problems with drainage and water supply, and with interest due from the syndicate which he led. By 1684, Hinde and his partners were forced to mortgage the unsold parts of the estate and to sell off freeholds. He was imprisoned for debt and made bankrupt, dying in prison. Richard Frith, his partner, suffered the same fate. Tenements came first in much of Mayfair, not houses for the wealthy nor elegant squares, and it was not until the end of the War of the Spanish Succession in 1713 that recovery took place. After that appeared Hanover Square, then Grosvenor Square and Berkeley Square.

It is time to distinguish more clearly between the person who owned the ground and the one who actually developed it. They were seldom the same. The developer was a speculator who took the risk, accepting financial liability without the certainty of a buyer. By background he might be a doctor such as Barbon, a goldsmith such as Hinde, or, like the men who eventually succeeded in building the Conduit Mead estate, a scrivener who invested his clients' money. Thomas Neale was Master of the Mint, and also held the right to license and suppress gaming houses, and to conduct the national lottery. Hinde's downfall was precipitated by his problems as a Tax farmer. Sir Thomas Bond was a protégé of St Albans and controller of Henrietta Maria's household. Sometimes developers were members of the trade, builders or craftsmen, hiring themselves, so to speak, for part of the project.

The system worked through the sale by the landowner (soon to be landlord) of a 'building lease' to the developer, charging him probably only a nominal rent during the period of the building works. The developer in his turn would sell on the lease to whoever wanted the completed house, often before the works were finished and when only the carcase of the building existed. Nicholas Barbon in fact often preferred to sell to builders as soon as he had cleared the site and laid out the plots on which to build. As a landowner, Lord St Albans was unusual in that he parted with his freeholds; most landowners retained theirs. Nevertheless, they all faced the St Albans problem: if people were to pay for the cost of the buildings – for obviously the price charged by the contractor reflected his costs – how long a lease would they demand? Lord Southampton started by selling building leases of forty-two years, but, as time went on, landowners were compelled to grant longer and longer terms, until in the nineteenth century the normal period was ninety-nine years. At the end of the term, the house reverted to the landowner, who would probably grant the lessee or whoever else might be interested a repairing lease of, say, twenty-one years. If he decided to redevelop, then the whole process would start again. Their investment in London property was to make London landowners among the very richest of the London rich. However, while the system allowed them to transfer the cost of building to someone else, it meant that for generations their only direct interest was in the rent received. In 1664, Lord Lisle, Lord Leicester's eldest son, was opposed to long leases, 'by which leases I should have given away my right, and my son's, for . . . many years.' The landowner nevertheless did have a strong indirect interest during the years of waiting since the last thing he wanted, when the time for repossession arrived, was a pile of ruins or a slum. Thus he laid down conditions in his leases intended to preserve the standards of the estate and to encourage its general coherence. These are set down by Lord Leicester for the building of Leicester Square:

> That all builders fronting to the field called Leicester field shall plant so many and such trees before their several grounds and houses as the Earl of Leicester or his assigns shall appoint, and maintain the same during the term granted.

That they shall pave and rail before their own house the whole proportion of their ground.

That they shall to every house build a balcony.

The property was not to become a slum, or, for that matter, an industrial estate or shopping centre. That proved an insurmountable difficulty with the area immediately to the east of our Regent Street, what we would think of as the western edge of Soho. The rich – the patrician rich and professional people – had quit the eastern side of London mainly to be free of that type of environment. They had no intention of settling among the breweries in Colman Hedge Close or Brewer Street, or in the area of Broadwick Street and Marshall Street where a pest house had been established at the time of the Plague of 1665, and where indeed building was thought unsafe on medical grounds until the 1730s. In Grosvenor Square, when it was built early in the eighteenth century, ground rents were weighted should the premises be used for certain specified trades such as a distillery or butcher's shop; the clause was intended as a deterrent rather than as a means to make money.

Whatever the differences in detail, later building, such as Grosvenor Square, Berkeley Square and the other Mayfair streets and squares, in general design followed their seventeenth-century predecessors. Legislation too encouraged a degree of uniformity. Moreover, a tried and tested plan had clear attractions. Another clause in Lord Leicester's contract with builders laid down 'that everyone shall build in such manner and form and with such proportions and scantlings [dimensions] as those houses are built in the Pal Mal in St James's field fronting to the south, and to be obliged to such articles as those builders were obliged to.' In any event, developers in one district were employing builders and workmen who came from another; those who constructed the Grosvenor Estate were at the same time, almost all of them, busy in the adjoining Conduit Mead.

Nicholas Barbon and Christopher Wren leave very different legacies. Of Barbon, Roger North, who knew him, wrote, 'His talent lay more in economising ground for advantage and the little contrivances of a family than the more noble aims of architecture, and all his aim was at profit.' His importance was that he devised the basic

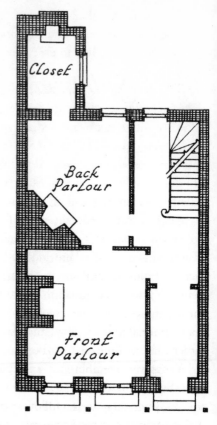

Elevation and plan of the type of house built by
Nicholas Barbon between 1670 and the end of the
seventeenth century. It was to serve as a model for the
standard West End house of the future.

model for the 'terrace house'. He was, said North, 'the inventor of
the new method of building, by casting of ground with streets and
small houses, and to augment their number with as little front as
possible'. All over London you found – and still find – variations of
his method. In the version intended for the rich the house characteristically is three storeys high with a basement, and with the 'area'
being set against a built-up roadway. The site, in Sir John Summerson's words, was a long strip of ground running back from the street.
The house covered the front part of the strip, the middle was a garden
or courtyard, and at the back was a coach house and stable served
from a subsidiary road.

54

3

Suburban Splendour

*

In 1546, an old and sick Henry VIII, nearing the end of his life, travelled back in slow stages to London from his palace of Oatlands near Weybridge. His first stop was at the mansion he had appropriated from Cardinal Wolsey on the River Mole near Esher, the next his palace of Nonsuch at Ewell, a mile from Epsom, and after that his manor house at Wimbledon. By the time of the restoration to the throne of his great-great-great-nephew not much more than a century later, while all four of these houses were still extant, only Wimbledon, by now in private hands, and probably the Esher house, could claim to be properly habitable. Oatlands was soon demolished and Nonsuch went before the end of the century. Windsor and Hampton Court survived, but there were still other royal palaces which disappeared. The most important was Sheen at Richmond, dating from the Middle Ages and rebuilt from time to time, and which had been particularly favoured by Queen Elizabeth. In 1660 it was restored to Henrietta Maria but in so dilapidated a condition that she had no wish to live there. Its demise followed a familiar pattern: it was not demolished outright but broken up and parcelled into tenements. Further east, at Greenwich, still south of the Thames, were Eltham, which was described by Froissart in the fourteenth century as 'a very magnificent palace', but by John Evelyn in 1656 as 'miserable ruins', and Greenwich House, which Charles II was anxious to save. Little, though, was done and eventually Wren's Greenwich Hospital was built on its site. Only Eltham, by the present Blackheath golf course, still exists, still 'ruinous', but with its Great Hall partially restored by a private benefactor in the 1930s.

The country houses of wealthy individuals which surrounded

London lasted no longer. The difference was that they were replaced: their owners required something more modern and fashionable, and probably more comfortable. That was true elsewhere in England. But in much of the country around London, the manor houses which dotted the landscape were not, as they were likely to be in other parts, the habitations of ancient families of country squires, but rather those of *nouveaux riches* Londoners. It was a land of secondary homes, subject to frequent changes of ownership. So universal among prosperous London families was the desire for a secondary house, in the country but close to London, a refuge at weekends and in summer, that it is rare to find a London-based diary or memoir of the time where the writer, or his or her family, does not possess a suburban house. Pepys is an exception, for after some thought he and his wife decided to spend their money on a coach instead, but even Pepys lived out his last years in Clapham. His friend John Evelyn (with a house at Deptford), a busy, well-connected committee man, was always making trips into the surrounding country. He visits the physicist Robert Boyle at Chelsea and then hurries on to Kensington; he goes to Camberwell to see a friend or an archaeological dig; to Fulham to the Bishop of London; to Hammersmith for a look at some gardens. He dines at Twickenham.

Within the built-up area of modern London there remain several houses dating from the seventeenth century or earlier which were originally the nuclei of agricultural estates. Valence House in East London, in Dagenham, is one, with part of its moat still in place. It was for centuries owned by the Dean and Chapter of Windsor and let out until its sale to the London County Council in 1921. Forty Hall in Enfield, north London, less than two miles inside the M25 motorway and standing close to the site of Theobalds, yet another lost royal palace, was built by a one-time Lord Mayor of London, Sir Nicholas Rainton, between 1629 and 1636. It remained in private hands, passing through various families, until the death of its last private owner, Sir Henry Carrington Bowles MP, in 1943. Forty, like Valence, is now a museum. Architecturally, the most spectacular is Charlton Park, built at the beginning of the seventeenth century by Adam Newton, secretary and tutor to Henry, Prince of Wales, the elder son of James I, and placed conveniently near to the royal palaces of Greenwich and Eltham. John Evelyn, who lived nearby, knew Charlton well and wrote in his diary – a sweeping statement indeed – that the view from Charlton '(after Constantinople) is doubtless for city, river, ships, meadows, hill, woods, & all other distinguishable amenities, the most noble the whole world has to show'. His only complaint seems to have been that, when he dined there in 1669, the servants of the house made his coachmen so drunk that they both fell off the coach on the way home. During the eighteenth century Charlton was leased out – often an ominous portent for a mansion – but to tenants who were irreproachable financially and socially. In fact, Charlton was always backed by ample money and passed into the hands of the Maryon-Wilson family, who, in the nineteenth century, were also to be one of the most important, as well as the most controversial, landowners in Hampstead. The sale of the house and its park in 1925 to the Greenwich Borough Council was the first time Charlton had come on the market since 1680.

Forty and Charlton were preserved because they were owned by wealthy families prepared to ignore the inconveniences brought about

Charlton House at the end of the eighteenth century.

by the encroachment of metropolitan London and the temptation either to sell to developers or to carry out development themselves. Eventually these families lost the means or the will to continue, but at least they had persevered long enough for public money or private benefaction to have become available as a possible source of rescue. The owners of Valence could afford to take a similar view. There are, however, two surviving one-time country houses within London which fall into a different category. Bruce Castle, once the manor house of Tottenham in north London, dates from the sixteenth century although significant alterations were made later. In 1827 it was bought by the Hill family of Birmingham who established there a famous school with Rowland Hill, later the originator of the penny post, as headmaster. For a private house to be converted into a school, however, was another bad sign. As the century progressed, the Bruce Castle school became less famous and its situation more precarious. Finally, the house and its grounds were acquired by Tottenham Council in the 1890s.

The last erstwhile country house, Eastbury House (or Eastbury Manor House or Eastbury Hall as it has variously been known), is a curiosity. Internally, because while stripped of most of its panelling and virtually everything else many years ago, it still displays in its main reception room some fine sixteenth-century wall paintings. From the outside it is striking, a red-brick, time-battered Elizabethan country mansion, its park long gone, standing on a green in Barking in the middle of a large housing estate completed soon after the First World War. The house was built by a rich merchant from East Ham whose heirs in 1650 sold it along with its farmland to Thomas Vyner, a member of an important City banking family. From 1690, with the male Vyners dying out, ownership became divided between several heirs for whom it was simplest to let the house and its land to tenant farmers. In the 1720s Defoe described Eastbury as 'a great house, ancient, and now almost fallen down'. A hundred years later, it was still standing – just. In 1834 there was published an illustrated account of its architecture and history. Across the ploughed fields, it was said, the house still gave out a grand appearance. But its state seemed almost hopeless, it was likely 'to be sold piecemeal, and levelled into ground'. Only two rooms plus the kitchen were occupied, each of them by employees of the farmers who held the lease, brothers apparently who lived in Dagenham. The forebodings were all but justified: in the 1840s the owner, who died mad, severely damaged the interior and was on the point of pulling the house down. A local enthusiast came to the rescue but by the First World War Eastbury was again in danger, this time as a result of the inexorable spread of London and the plans for a housing estate. However, immediately after the war the National Trust bought the house and began restoration. It seemed that at last Eastbury was safe. No doubt had it been located in west London it would have been, but, as things were, it was marooned in one of the least alluring parts of the country. Part of the building was converted into an ex-servicemen's club, but tribulations continued. In the thirties it was damaged by vandals; in 1935 it was leased to the Barking Borough Council for a museum. That closed with the Second World War, and the house was damaged by bombing. Nevertheless, Eastbury has survived, to be one of the most evocative memorials to the old rich in London.

Valence, Forty, Charlton, Bruce Castle, Eastbury were houses of the wealthy rather than of the very rich, large certainly but not 'palaces', defined in Johnson's dictionary as houses which are 'eminently splendid'. They were not on the scale of the biggest country houses of their time near London such as Theobalds and Hatfield, nor could they compare with two giants built within a few miles of the capital in the later stages of the great, if fluctuating, boom which started in 1660 and, gathering pace after 1680, came to an end with the South Sea disaster of 1720. One was Wanstead. The original Wanstead manor house had been bought in 1667 by the immensely rich Sir Josiah Child, for years the chairman and driving force of the East India Company. The house and its estate lay on the edge of Epping Forest on the road to Essex, the park at its eastern edge abutting what is now the North Circular Road. Past owners of the estate included a son-in-law of Sir Thomas More, Queen Elizabeth's Robert Dudley, Earl of Leicester, and James I's Duke of Buckingham. After the Civil War it had passed to the regicide Henry Mildmay, a brother of Sir Humphrey, and at the Restoration to the King's brother, James, Duke of York, from whom it was bought by Child. Josiah Child spent lavishly on the grounds but it was left to his son to launch out on a new house, one intended in its magnificence to be to east London what Hampton Court was to the west. The other house was Canons, five miles away from Wanstead, just north of Edgware on the old Roman road of Watling Street. James Brydges, soon to be created Duke of Chandos, bought it from the family of his first wife and took possession in 1713. Chandos (as it is simplest to call him from the start) was even richer than Child, and he almost immediately started on building a new house, a palace which during its short life became a legend.

The links between Wanstead and Canons were close. Chandos watched carefully as the architect Colen Campbell's plans for Wanstead took shape. He was well placed to do so, for his aunt was Josiah Child's first wife and the younger Child her son. Furthermore, his wife – his second wife Cassandra Willoughby – was also his first cousin, Lady Child's daughter by her first husband. It is to Duchess Cassandra's letters that we owe much of what we know about Canons and something more therefore of life in the richest circles of society in the early eighteenth century. No one could have been better equipped than she to take on a large part of the management of a great establishment. She was well educated: her father was an eminent naturalist and a founding fellow of the Royal Society, and she herself wrote an interesting history of her family. She had grown up at Wanstead, helping her mother to handle the innumerable requests for favours addressed to Josiah Child, an experience which more directly she was to repeat when married to Chandos. From her youth she was used to managing large houses. At the age of sixteen she had left Wanstead to run her eighteen-year-old brother's huge Wollaton Hall in Nottinghamshire, one of the more extravagant of Elizabethan show houses, acting as his hostess and helping to repair the war-damaged mansion, to restock it with furniture and to re-create its splendid garden. From that she must have gained useful financial knowledge; and if she had wanted more, she had only to listen to her brothers' discussions on how to counter their stepfather's incursions on their fortunes. ('Most sordidly avaricious', was Evelyn's assessment of Child.) Like her contemporary Celia Fiennes, Cassandra was an indefatigable traveller; indeed, it has been estimated that between 1695 and her marriage in 1713 she spent a third of her time travelling around England. In her journal she makes some pithy comments. Longleat was admirable but apart from two or three very handsome apartments the rest of the rooms 'lie but ill'. A grotto at Wilton could have been constructed more cheaply. Of a Yorkshire house reckoned as particularly fine, she observed 'within it, all I found wonderful, was, that any man should have laid out so much money upon a house, & not make one good apartment in it, nay not one very handsome entertaining room'. She loved gardens (and those later at Canons were to be outstanding) with a particular fondness for fountains and ornamental water. In character, Cassandra Chandos was shrewd and good-natured, poised with that slightly intimidating coolness characteristic of her time, competent and conscientious.

Legend attached itself not just to Canons but also to its creator. The Duke of Chandos, wrote Arthur Onslow, for thirty years Speaker of the House of Commons,

> . . . was the most surprising instance of a change of fortune raised by a man himself, that has happened, I believe, in any age. When he came first into the office of paymaster of the army, he had little or no estate of his own, and never inherited more than a few hundred pounds a year; but by the means of this office, and the improvements of money, in little more than ten years, living expensively too in the mean while, he had accumulated a fortune of not less than six or seven hundred thousand pounds; I have heard more . . .

On money Chandos spoke with the utmost authority, and the news in February 1720 that he was investing heavily in South Sea stock gave an extra impetus to share prices as they started their rapid climb to disaster. It was not, however, quite a case of rags to riches, for Chandos was no parvenu. He was the eldest surviving son of a large family of the eighth Baron Chandos, an impoverished peer who lived in a ruined castle on the Wye in Herefordshire. Lord Chandos, poor as he was, nevertheless possessed through his wife's family quite excellent business connections. In consequence, as a boy the future Duke spent five years far removed from the ruined castle, in Constantinople where his father represented the Turkey Company. Chandos is virtually unique among the London rich, not just for the reason given by Onslow, but as a man of the bluest blood who was also dedicated to business. He relished his dukedom but he remained, in spirit as well as in fact, a thorough-going businessman. What the Duke hates is idleness, wrote Cassandra in a letter of reproof to an unsatisfactory stepson. In comparing him with those arrogant grandees, the great nobles of his time, his co-biographers described him as 'affably bourgeois'. He was unscrupulous, for he lived in a markedly unscrupulous age, and his eyes were fastened immovably on the main chance. But he was not callous or egocentric; rather the opposite, for he was a generous and affectionate man.

Advised by an assortment of architects, Chandos set about building on the site of the old Elizabethan manor house. The busy main road to London was diverted to allow a 400-acre park through which ran a drive of nearly a mile long, and broad enough to accommodate three carriages at the same time. On New Year's Day 1722 the household numbered ninety-three at a time when fifty would have been a normal maximum for the very wealthiest aristocrats. It included the family, the indoor staff, the Duke's private orchestra, farm workers, and the Chelsea Pensioners who lived in the lodges which guarded the park gates. Seating for meals in the hall at Canons was graded according to rank and occupation. The house was smaller than the very largest country houses such as Vanbrugh's Castle Howard or Blenheim, and its reception rooms were less spacious than, for instance, those at Buckingham House in St James's Park. Its fame owed something to its closeness to London, but mainly it rested on the opulence, the superb gardens, the collections of paintings and books, the quality of the fittings and furniture. The colonnaded marble staircase was a sensation; in later years it was installed in Chesterfield House, Mayfair, ending its life in the foyer of the Odeon Cinema, Southend, wrecked by a bomb during the Second World War. There were a bathroom, hot water pipes and washrooms and water closets. The superlatives run high. From Daniel Defoe: '. . . no nobleman in England, and very few in Europe, lives in greater splendor, or maintains a grandeur and magnificence, equal to the Duke of Chandos.' *Tales of Our Great Families*, published in 1880, declared that Chandos lived at Canons in a splendour 'to which probably no other subject of the English Crown had ever aspired since the days of Cardinal Wolsey'. There was poetry: here, for example, is Charles Gildon:

> Thus chosen Canons, with its groves and bowers,
> Its verdant launds, its dales and gentle hills,
> Its standing lakes and all its murmuring rills
> Its sunny banks and every shady glade,
> By consecrating hymns is sacred made.

Amicably bourgeois as the Duke may have been personally, he kept a princely state. When he attended services at the parish church he was attended by a squad of his Chelsea Pensioners, who served as a guard of honour. It was not unnatural then that there should be discordant voices. Here is the loudest, that of Alexander Pope in his poem *Timon's Villa*:

> But hark! the chiming clocks to dinner call;
> A hundred footsteps scrape the marble hall:
> . . . Is this a dinner? this a genial room?
> No, 'tis a temple, and a hecatomb.
> A solemn sacrifice, perform'd in state,
> You drink by measure, and to minutes eat.

Pope denied later that he intended a satire on Canons, but his disclaimer was judged implausible.

What are described here as suburban mansions were all close to London, at the most fifteen miles away, often no more than a mile or two. Distance, however, is relative in terms of accessibility: how, after all, can one without a smile compare the present Duke of Northumberland driving into London from Syon with his early eighteenth-century predecessor making the same trip? Close as Canons and Wanstead and the other houses were to London, they did not necessarily do away with the need for a base within the city. It could be a question of the cold in winter. It was very much a question of communications, for roads were still frequently very bad, and there were the obvious limitations of the transport available. As

The staircase from the first Duke of Chandos's early eighteenth-century palace of Canons, near Edgware, by Gibbs, *c.* 1715, as installed at Chesterfield House, Mayfair, in 1894.

a younger man the Duke of Chandos had frequently visited the old Canons, belonging at the time to his first wife's family, and also the neighbouring village of Stanmore. Sometimes he took the stagecoach, but that was a matter of four hours each way over the ten-mile distance. He could drive his own barouche, but on occasion that broke down on the road. In later times – and roads were improving – Cassandra and he would go up to London just for the day, although bad weather could oblige them to remain overnight. Highwaymen and footpads were a danger. On at least two occasions, the Duke's servants were set upon and robbed while on the London road. Once the Duke himself had a brush with highwaymen. It seems that as he was returning to London from Canons, his coach was hailed by a boy, who warned him of two highwaymen waiting in ambush up ahead. Accompanied by his armed servants, he chased them as far as the village of Paddington before finally securing their capture.

In his time, Chandos owned or leased a number of houses in London. He had lived north of Lincoln's Inn Fields in Red Lion Square, and in Golden Square, Soho, and in 1710 he acquired a house in Albemarle Street, north of Piccadilly. Most spectacular was Lord St Albans's old house in St James's Square, which Chandos bought from the Duke of Ormonde. It was enormous, the largest house in the square with some fifty rooms, where at one time the Ormondes had employed forty-five indoor servants, with stables accommodating twenty horses and five coaches, along with innumerable dogs. Country houses and London houses were closely linked. Bedford House in the Strand, for example, had supplied Woburn, the Russells' house in Bedfordshire, with a wide range of commodities – luxuries such as tea, coffee, champagne and other wines; clothes and furniture; and with plants, shrubs and fruit grown either in the garden at Bedford House or bought next door in the Covent Garden market. Some of the coal used at Woburn was shipped by sea to London and collected at Durham Yard which lay on the river a short distance from Bedford House. The farm at Canons sent up wagons with hay for sale to London stables which returned carrying loads of dung. It supplied Chandos House, St James's, with meat, fruit and vegetables. Laundry for the London house was washed at Canons, and a boy mounted on a Welsh pony rode up daily from the country to fetch letters.

There is a Canons Park still – now a school – just as there is a Wanstead Park and many other parks dotted over the map of outer London to mark the location of vanished country mansions and their grounds. Canons Park, though, can only be a passing reminder of Chandos and his great house, both of them now almost entirely forgotten. Two splendid memorials, however, remain. One is the parish church of St Lawrence's in Whitchurch Lane, near Canons Park underground station, with its finely restored eighteenth-century wall paintings and box pews. It was built by the Duke and contains an elaborate baroque monument to him, and to Cassandra and his first wife. The second is music. Among the rich of the time, only Chandos and the Duke of Bedford could boast private orchestras. But only Chandos could offer Handel as director of music. It was in St Lawrence's and at Canons that Handel enjoyed one of his most brilliant periods of creativity with *Acis and Galatea* and *Esther*, which in its original form was composed for the ceremonial opening of the chapel at Canons. It was at this time too that Handel composed the beautiful *Chandos Anthems*.

In 1724, Daniel Defoe published his *A Tour thro' the Whole Island of Great Britain*, an ebullient work, expansive on the subject of the growth of London and its suburbs. On all sides of London, he writes, the villages have increased in size amazingly within the last twenty or thirty years. Blackheath he admires, and Greenwich, which owes its beauty to 'the lustre of its inhabitants, where there is a kind of collection of gentlemen, rather than citizens, and of people of quality and fashion'. From the hills about Clapham you can look down on the pleasant villages of Peckham and Camberwell with some of the finest dwellings about London. He instances Lord Powis's house at Peckham and the Duchess of Bedford's at Streatham. For the Thames to the west of London, Defoe's enthusiasm is boundless. Richmond, nine miles from central London, everyone admired, its view was almost a wonder of the world. One foreign visitor, the Abbé Le Blanc, who disliked London, described Richmond and its surroundings as an immense garden, which 'offers to the eye a kind of image of earthly paradise'. For Defoe,

From Richmond to London, the river sides are full of villages, and those villages so full of beautiful buildings, charming gardens,

The Chandos Monument, St Lawrence's, Whitchurch
Lane, Little Stanmore. The monument was designed in
1717 by Grinling Gibbons and shows the Duke with his
first two wives, Mary Lake and Cassandra Willoughby,
kneeling on either side.

and rich habitations of gentlemen of quality, that nothing in the world can imitate it.

The Thames was not only beautiful, it was convenient and familiar. It was the great thoroughfare within London itself. In 1664 Samuel Sorbière recorded that when his neighbours in Covent Garden wanted, as they put it, to go to London, that is to the City, they sometimes found it much quicker to do so by boat than on foot; walking, he said, might take two hours, the trip by water a quarter of an hour. It is significant that Pepys's urgent dash to Whitehall with news of the Fire was made by boat. As late as 1710, to the visitor Zacharias von Uffenbach, London was still a town for the most part built along the river. What was more, the river boats, which reminded another visitor of the Venetian gondolas, were more comfortable than the hackney carriages with their incessant jolting. The one drawback, according to von Uffenbach, was that the wind blew men's wigs about so much. The Thames was also the main thoroughfare out of London to the west, providing easy and safe access to the riverside villages and mansions. Like many wealthy people, William Russell's grandfather, the fourth Earl of Bedford, kept a private barge – moored just across the way from Bedford House – to travel to Old Corney House, his riverside mansion at Chiswick. The Thames too was a delight for those attracted by the idea of an excursion. Samuel Pepys noted in his diary for 12 May 1662 that the weather was so hot he and his wife could not sleep. So, they rose at four in the morning, and together with a friend who brought along his son and daughter, they set off upstream from their house on Tower Hill in the Navy Board barge. They disembarked at Mortlake, walking on to Richmond, where they rejoined the barge. Pepys and his friend continued their walk and met the women at Hampton Court. They were shown around the palace, dined and were back home at 8 p.m. But the roads were improving and in 1712 the antiquary and topographer Ralph Thoresby found the journey to Hampton Court equally agreeable by road. He admired Syon on the way, then passed through 'Twistleworth and Twitnam' (Isleworth and Twickenham). On the return journey he and his party left their coach and walked to Lord Dysart's house at Ham. 'We met the Duke of Argyle with the Lady Dysart, and other nobles of both sexes, in the shady groves; we walked thence to Petersham.' Ham, a Jacobean house which belonged to the Dysarts, is still there.

However, it could not always be quite as blissful. The author of *A Voyage up the Thames*, sailing with a friend on the river in 1738, confirmed Defoe's account of the new houses along the banks but took a more analytical view. He observed old houses to which were attached stables and coaches, which he said, were fit to stand 'behind the most august palace', but also nearby houses and gardens 'render'd modern in every respect, by the consumption of ancient Estate'. He also remarked on new buildings intended to last for generations which were sold before the foundations were well settled. And even Defoe's effervescence evaporated at one moment as he wrote of 'the overthrow, and catastrophe of innumerable wealthy City families, who after they have thought their houses established, and have built their magnificent country seats, as well as others, have sunk under the misfortunes of business, and the disasters of trade.' Four years before there had occurred the collapse of the South Sea Company, and with it the long-lasting bull market. The affadavits of the South Sea directors give a clear idea of how widely the leading men of the City had been buying property.

In the uproar which followed the bursting of the Bubble, politicians and public turned furiously on those held responsible. The government fell, the Chancellor of the Exchequer was sent to the Tower, and the directors of the South Sea Company, often with prison thrown in, were subjected to penal fines. The thirty-three directors and senior officials were required to submit a detailed list of their assets to the House of Commons, which turned itself into a court of law. Seven possessed little or no real property. Two, Sir Harcourt Master and Sir Robert Chaplin, were from old-established county families and almost as a matter of course owned extensive estates in Kent and Lincolnshire respectively. Many of the others had been buying country estates, often in the last few months of the boom. In an orgy of buying, the deputy cashier Robert Surman had acquired, or contracted to acquire, property in Gloucestershire, Lincolnshire, Warwickshire, Dorset, Yorkshire, Suffolk, and Essex. Some of this buying was intended simply as an investment and as a way of spreading risk; that was particularly true of purchases in London itself. However, most probably a good deal of it was driven by the perennial desire of City businessmen to translate themselves, or at least their families, into country gentry. It was not just a question of snobbery. The fear of ruin and perhaps the debtors' prison hung heavy. (The turbulence in the 1990s at Lloyd's, in structure an ancient 'regulated company', is a sharp reminder of life under unlimited liability.) Moreover, the appeal of a life divorced from trade was strengthened by gentlemanly education and culture. As Sir Robert Clayton, thinking of a nephew who had been sent on the Grand Tour, remarked sardonically, 'Few of the travelled Monsieurs' wished to become bankers. Clayton's heir, another nephew, chose to enjoy life as a country baronet. The Houblons withdrew to the tranquillity of the countryside. The Clitherows, a wealthy business family owning considerable City real estate, settled at the Jacobean Boston Manor, Brentford, which survives still in the shadow of the M4 motorway.

While many of the South Sea directors invested in west London property, only three, the untypical Chaplin, Sir Theodore Janssen and another, actually lived in the West End proper; in London the rest were to be found in or near the City. Where their country estates were close to London, they again were often towards the eastern end of the city. However, there were a number of exceptions, with Sir William Chapman at Hampstead and two other directors at Carshalton in Surrey, also now part of Greater London, and described by Defoe as 'a whole town of fine houses'. Edward Gibbon, grandfather of the historian, owned a house at Putney, and Peter Delaporte houses at Wandsworth and Esher. Living in undoubted suburban splendour was Sir Theodore Janssen of Wimbledon and Hanover Square, one of the two richest directors, whose holding of South Sea stock in June 1720, before the crash, was worth a million pounds (£115 million in our money). Janssen was a Huguenot who had emigrated to England in 1683, become an MP and a baronet, and was for many years a director of the Bank of England. One of the most respected men in the City, by 1720 he had acquired all twenty-four houses in Queen Anne's Gate (then Queen Square), as well as a Wimbledon manor house – the one-time royal palace taken by Charles I for Henrietta Maria – which he bought from the second Duke of Leeds, son of Lord Danby, chief minister under Charles II and in effect under William III. Faced with a fine which allowed him to keep only £50,000 out of assets of £243,000, he was obliged to sell up, with the Wimbledon property passing to Sarah, Duchess of Marlborough. Janssen was at least more fortunate than the other richest director, the sub-governor of the South Sea Company, Sir John Fellowes, who was permitted only £10,000 out of what was virtually the same amount of assets.

Another director of the company was Stephen Child of the banking branch of the family, who was himself not particularly rich. He owned a number of houses in Richmond and another at Isleworth as well as the lease of a house in Lombard Street which, he stated in his affadavit, 'I deem an incumbrance, and not of any value, the rents of houses being considerably fallen.' He was, though, closely associated with conspicuous wealth, since his brother was the owner of Osterley Park, Isleworth, on the edge of present-day west London. As already mentioned, the Childs, like the Hoares – who purchased the manor of Barnes – were one of the important seventeenth-century families who did continue in business. Osterley stood on the site of a farmhouse and was built by Sir Thomas Gresham as a complement to his mansion in Bishopsgate. A hundred years after Gresham's death, the estate was bought by the ubiquitous Nicholas Barbon, and eventually passed to Francis Child as one of Barbon's mortgagees. Osterley's neighbour Syon, a mile or two away on the Thames, had an unimpeachably aristocratic background, at least since the original abbey buildings had been commandeered and allocated to the Duke of Somerset, going by marriage at the end of the sixteenth century to the earls of Northumberland. In the early eighteenth century both Osterley and Syon counted as great mansions, although it was mid-century before they were reconstructed by Robert Adam to that full glory which makes them today, along with Kenwood in Hampstead, the most splendid examples of suburban palaces once belonging to private individuals which have survived.

In 1678 the Marquess of Worcester, very grand and very rich, owned two great houses. One was Badminton in Gloucestershire, described by Cassandra Chandos, who visited it on her travels, as 'a very noble one ... very large and very convenient'. The other,

Worcester House in the Strand, was large but not at all convenient. Extensive repairs were necessary. To modernize it was impractical, since the steepness of the carriageway would then make it difficult for entertaining and for coaches. And besides, with the old neighbours going or gone, the Strand was not what it had been. Still the location was central and close to Whitehall Palace. So, Lord and Lady Worcester came to the conclusion that they should give over Worcester House for redevelopment, retaining on the site for themselves a smaller house with a view of the river. They started to look for a suitable replacement in the suburbs. One possibility was Sir Nicholas Crispe's house at Hammersmith, built in Charles I's reign for, it was said, £23,000 (£2.6 million or so in our money) and which Burke's *Extinct Peerage* of 1844 describes as a 'most magnificent mansion at the waterside'. Lady Worcester, however, ruled it out as 'the worst situated, and the worst house she ever saw'. She was not much more enthusiastic about Lord Paget's house at West Drayton (north of Heathrow airport); at fifteen miles from London it was too far away. Nevertheless, her husband started negotiating for a lease, withdrawing when he found Lord Paget too demanding in his terms. So they settled for renting Lord Berkeley's house at Cranford, in the same direction but rather closer in. Renting, however, was a temporary expedient and in December 1681 Lady Worcester wrote approving the purchase of the old manor house of Chelsea for £5,000.

John Evelyn knew the house of old and three years before had admired the extent of the grounds and its healthy situation. In September 1683 he was back to see the considerable alterations which had been carried out by Worcester, now Duke of Beaufort; with all that money spent, Evelyn thought, it could have been better done. Still, as a drawing by Leonard Knyff in the 1690s, engraved by Kip some years later, shows, Beaufort House and its surroundings were magnificent. The house had been built by Sir Thomas More in 1520 and it was there that More and his family lived and entertained Henry VIII. It stood back from our Embankment, at the southern end of the old Moravian graveyard just west of Beaufort Street and Battersea Bridge. Its owners since More's attainder had included Lord Burghley and his son Lord Salisbury, the creator of the New Exchange and developer of the Strand, who had greatly enlarged the house. There had followed Lionel Cranfield, the man who sold so much of his property to Hugh Audley, and the first and second Villiers, dukes of Buckingham. Next door was More's farmhouse, which in reconstructed form and named Lindsey House is now 95–100 Cheyne Walk, and nearby were the new manor house built by Henry VIII after More's execution and Lord Wharton's old Danvers House with its remarkable garden. Chelsea was celebrated for its gardens . . . and for its inhabitants. In a directory of peers and bishops for 1708–9, only three districts outside metropolitan London are mentioned. Fulham and Kensington, which rate a bishop each, and Chelsea, with two bishops and three peers, Beaufort, Shaftesbury and Carbury. Later other grandees arrived, including Sir Robert Walpole. Chelsea was known as the 'village of palaces'.

An attraction of the Chelsea house to the Duke of Beaufort was that though outside the town it was nevertheless easily accessible. He wrote to his wife before they moved that it usually meant no more than a quarter of an hour's walk to reach their new home from Arlington House, on the site of Buckingham Palace. Jonathan Swift, working closely with government ministers and a resident of Chelsea in 1711, was even more concerned about the walking: it would be exactly what his health needed, and he would walk to Westminster and back daily, taking rather less than an hour each way. In a series of letters to Esther Johnson ('Stella') in Ireland, Swift gives a vivid impression of communications between London and Chelsea. The lime trees in St James's Park were out in leaves, he wrote on 20 April 1711, and wise people were going to the country. A week later he followed, hiring lodgings in Church Lane which ran parallel to Lawrence Street, just beyond Chelsea Old Church.

For the first day or two all went well, and Swift declared with satisfaction that he 'was now a country gentleman'. There followed some days of unrelenting rain. All three stagecoaches to London were full; he hired a chaise, which was expensive, and spent the night in town. On 3 May he just stayed in his lodgings all day. Chelsea buns were another disappointment. Then the weather cleared. But walking home one night with his manservant Patrick, he came upon a drunken parson fighting with a seaman. Swift and Patrick managed to part the two men, who nevertheless carried on brawling all the way to

Chelsea. 'A pretty scene for one that just came from sitting with the Prime Ministers,' commented Swift; still 'I had no money in my pocket, and so could not be robbed.' However, 'nothing but Mr Harley [the "prime" prime minister] shall make me take such a journey again.' But by 19 May summer had arrived and hay-making was in full swing; '[the hay] smells so sweet as we walk through the flowery meads,' he wrote, not without adding a characteristic bite: 'the hay-making nymphs are perfect drabs, nothing so clean and pretty as farther in the country.' Summer brought the prospect of bathing in the Thames, but the stones proved too sharp for comfort and there were too many boats in the way. Still the boats came in useful as transport in hot weather and Swift took to travelling to town in the morning by boat and walking back. In the end, Secretary of State St John required him closer at hand, and so on 5 July he gave up his Chelsea lodgings and resolved he would get his walking in St James's Park and about London.

Swift's account is also a reminder of what to later generations is the peculiar nature of London's suburbs in the early eighteenth century and before. Swift walked out of St James's Park, past Buckingham House (the predecessor of Buckingham Palace) into open country, following the line of what is now Buckingham Palace Road, Pimlico Road and Royal Hospital Road. Had he walked along the river, he would have passed a terrace of houses at Millbank with the London mansion of the Grosvenors at the far end, and then nothing but the occasional farm building and the group of gardeners' cottages known as the Neat Houses until he reached Lord Ranelagh's house – next door to the Chelsea Hospital – which marked the start of the riverside high street of Chelsea. It was the same anywhere in western London, and even the smartest residential squares, Hanover Square and Grosvenor Square, led directly into the countryside. The suburbs on this side of London were not attached to the town, they were separate entities, separate villages, not in the least resembling the suburbs which were to be almost a trade mark of nineteenth-century London. The three private mansions generally regarded as the finest in London at this time were pitched on the very edge of the town. The Duke of Buckingham (a new creation, the Sheffield family) could talk contentedly of looking down from his drawing room at

Buckingham House on to 'the pleasantest park in the world'. True, the park was sometimes so crowded that you could not avoid literally rubbing shoulders with your neighbour, but on the other side of the house everything was peaceful and rural. The other two great houses were Bedford House and Montagu House, side by side in Bloomsbury. A painting of the 1740s shows them from the north across the corn fields.

London obviously had to stop somewhere, there had to come at least a breathing space after the frenetic expansion which lasted into the 1720s. It is less obvious why the West End was now tilting away from the river. The western 'frontier' at Westminster was much the same as it had been in 1660, not only in Swift's 1711 but in 1760 as well. The Grosvenors were slow to begin development of their estate, and when they did start, it was with Mayfair, not with what came to be known as Pimlico. One problem was the restraints imposed by feudal tenures. The fundamental difficulty along the Thames, however, was the intractable nature of the terrain. The road past Millbank

Approaching London from the country. Many of the grandest London houses stood on the very edge of the city. Here a carriage arrives from the country, crossing the cornfields of what is now Russell Square, Bloomsbury, heading towards Southampton House (Bedford House) and, to the right, Montagu House on the site of today's British Museum. Detail from a painting attributed to Samuel Scott, 1745.

was constructed over a marsh, and even with the ditching, it could turn quickly into a quagmire. It was wonderful soil on which to grow vegetables but impossible, in the circumstances, for building on.

Further north, the West End had indeed spread westwards halting at the natural barrier of the Crown-owned Hyde Park. On the other side of the park, a mile and a half away, was the village of Kensington. On its edge, facing east towards London, was another grand house, once Nottingham House, then Kensington House and later Kensington Palace, and in 1711 occupied for part of the year by Queen Anne. It had been bought in 1689 by William III, who found that the polluted air of the riverside Whitehall Palace exacerbated his asthma. Kensington can be seen in a sense as a replacement for the vanished Richmond and Nonsuch and the others, and was more convenient, especially in winter, than Windsor and Hampton Court. The approach road ran from Hyde Park Corner down Rotten Row, the name of which is supposed to be a corruption of *Route du Roi*. César de Saussure described it:

> Nothing is more beautiful than the road from London to Kensington, crossing Hyde Park. It is perfectly straight and so wide that three or four coaches can drive abreast. [There are] posts put up at even distances, on the tops of which lanterns are hung and lamps are placed in them, which are lighted every evening when the Court is at Kensington.

Hyde Park had been privatized briefly during the Republic. The Crown had repossessed it but there was no guarantee of preservation. However solid the walls which surrounded the park might appear, it was a moot point whether in practice they represented a bulwark capable of resistance to the pressure for more living space. The issue came to a head over a replacement for Whitehall Palace, which had burned down in 1698.

Among the papers of Robert Harley, Earl of Oxford, the Lord Treasurer, is a memorandum dated 1712, unsigned but apparently in the handwriting of John James, a distinguished architect and planner, which sets out cogently a proposal for establishing a new royal palace in Hyde Park, where the Queen would normally live while keeping an apartment 'in town', possibly at St James's Palace. (It is noteworthy that neither St James's nor Kensington House, adapted though it had been by Christopher Wren, was regarded as suitable.) The argument was that it would be prohibitively expensive to rebuild on the Whitehall site and to buy the land and houses around about. The proposal was far from philistine. To rebuild at Whitehall would entail pulling down Inigo Jones's Banqueting House ('and it were a pity so fine a building be lost') and spoiling St James's Park. On that park the memorandum stated, 'The town must either be deprived of the use of the park, which would make living in town intolerable, or else the Palace would have no private gardens, which sure even to a Court is necessary as public gardens.' The memorandum went on to urge that the new palace would help solve another problem, the provision of suitable living space for the rich. It stated:

> A late years [*sic*] the town is so increased and tenement buildings so much run on, that most of the great houses which belonged to people of quality are thrown down, and turned into tenements, and there is hardly to be got ground about the town fit for people of quality to build houses in.

The Queen might sell or give land for building right along the north side of Piccadilly down to Hyde Park Corner, and if that were insufficient, she could make over the eastern perimeter of Hyde Park (following our Park Lane) up to Marble Arch, or as it was then, Tyburn. In future, of course, executions would have to take place somewhere else.

So fundamental a shift in the balance of London would have drawn in Knightsbridge and Kensington a century earlier than in fact happened. But the plan contained further, extremely ambitious recommendations. Kensington House was to be either used to accommodate courtiers or pulled down to allow better views. A great deal of emphasis was placed on the outlook, on the views that befitted a great palace. To the north an avenue would be planted the length of Hampstead Heath, and to the south there would be another avenue, possibly with a canal, to open out the country towards Wimbledon. And as part of the Wimbledon plan, a bridge would be built across the Thames. This was quite revolutionary, for London at this time possessed one bridge only, the venerable London Bridge.

Nothing came of the proposal, and, as will be seen in the next chapter, the demand for new land on the part of the rich was to be nothing like so pressing as the writer of the memorandum assumed. Instead, Kensington House was remodelled and turned into a palace. But it was a declining palace, less and less used by the sovereign. Not only did Kensington and Knightsbridge remain separate, but Wimbledon, attractive place to live as it was and is, has never been sucked into the orbit of central London. An attempt in the nineteenth century to draw the south bank of the Thames into the West End was to prove a failure.

If Chelsea was the 'village of palaces', Kensington was 'the court suburb', where patricians bought or rented houses, or took lodgings, living there during the months of the year that the monarch was in residence. What had been a sleepy village was transformed into a thriving community. Kensington had first taken shape, so to speak, at the beginning of the seventeenth century, when Sir Walter Cope, courtier, businessman and incidentally patron of Robert Baker of Piccadilly, attempted to invest his fortune as Hugh Audley invested his, by buying up a block of country to the west of the capital. In Cope's case the financial strain was too much and he was obliged in the end to divest himself of much of what he had acquired. Cope bought the four manors and sub-manors that comprised Kensington – Earlscourt, the most southerly; Abbots Kensington and West Town, westwards of Kensington Palace; and Nutting Barns, beyond Notting Hill. In all, it was an estate of nearly 500 acres, which to the south extended almost to the Fulham Road. Cope sold 36 acres on the eastern boundary to another courtier, Sir George Coppin, who built on them what later became Kensington Palace, and other land to the mercer Baptist Hicks, Lord Campden, who then built another large mansion, Campden House. These two houses and another, Cope's own residence Holland House, can be seen in the distance in the drawing by Knyff of Beaufort House. When the Court was established at Kensington House, other large houses were built. The wealthy Colby brothers, Thomas, a director of the East India Company, and Philip, who made a fortune through the supply of cloth to the army, built a pair of mansions near the palace, while army commanders, companions to King William, favoured Kensington Square. Later on, the future Queen Anne hired Campden House, and other grandees established themselves in the locality.

After Sir Walter Cope's death in 1614, his daughter and heiress married Henry Rich, shortly to be made Earl of Holland, the grandson of Richard Rich, the traducer of Thomas More, and who as Chancellor of Henry VIII's Court of Augmentations implemented the sale of the monastic lands and thus probably had more influence than Audley, Bedford, St Albans or any developer on the eventual demography of the rich in London. Of the estate of which Henry Rich took possession – Holland House and its lands – there remain now only the ruins of the house, and the park, perhaps the prettiest in London. What is left of the façade to the house serves in our day as a backdrop in summer for plays and concerts, standing like the set for an opera to provide a perfect memorial to a dramatic and colourful past. In the nineteenth century, George Augustus Sala was to write, '. . . as for Holland House . . . It came in naturally with the Conqueror and the first Lord Holland.' It is a way of putting it. Built by Cope, its antiquity among London's major private houses was rivalled only by Northumberland House, which predeceased it by seventy years. The particular attention given to Holland House in this book is based partly on that, but more on its importance as an example of the great house as a political and social centre. There were other influential political houses, such as Cecil House, Lansdowne House and Londonderry House, and other 'social' houses; yet on both counts Holland House remains supreme.

About the early stories there is a touch of legend. In the front, on what are now playing fields, Oliver Cromwell and his son-in-law General Ireton discuss matters of state and revolution away from the ears of the world, and there is John Aubrey's ghost story of Lady Diana Rich, Lord Holland's daughter, out walking one morning in the grounds behind the house who encounters her *Doppelgängerin*, her own apparition, with 'Habit, and everything as in a Looking-Glass', and is dead within a month.

Lord Holland was charming, exceptionally good-looking, the archetypal courtier of his time . . . and in the end, tragic. In Claren-

Holland House, Kensington, engraved from a drawing
of 1817 by J. C. Smith.

don's words, he was 'a very well-bred man, and a fine gentleman in
good times; but too much desired to enjoy ease and plenty when the
King could have neither; and did think poverty the most insupportable
evil that could befall any man in this world.' He was not a country
landowner; he lived on his earnings from politics, and so had nothing
to fall back on when the Civil War confronted him with ruin. Holland
did not know which way to turn, that is he could not tell which side
was going to win. He succeeded in antagonizing both and ended up
on the scaffold. After a few years, the confiscated Holland House
was returned to the family, and the widow of the third Earl of
Holland, who had inherited the additional title of Warwick, married
Joseph Addison, an outstanding figure in English literature who also
became a Secretary of State. Even then, in the early eighteenth
century, Addison could describe Holland House as 'classic ground'.
But by his time the old houses were out of fashion – all around
London they were being replaced or remodelled. Kensington too was
losing its allure and after the death of Queen Caroline in 1737, the

Court was seldom there. The fact that the village was so near to London was of some help, but though turnpikes were constructed for parts of the way, the roads were by no means safe. Lady Cowper, wife of the Lord Chancellor, made this entry in her diary in October 1715, a time when troops were being mobilized to resist the Jacobite uprising: 'I was now at Kensington, where I intended to stay as long as the Camp was in Hyde Park, the roads being so secure by it, that one might come from London any time of the night without danger . . .'

Both Holland House and Campden House were affected by the change in taste. Campden House was turned into a girls' school and Holland House was split into rented apartments. In 1721, Holland House and its estate passed through a Rich daughter to the Edwardes family, who thus became one of the major Kensington landowners. Salvation occurred in 1746 in the form of Henry Fox, who took a ninety-nine-year lease, paying a rent which was barely more than that he was paying for his far smaller house in Conduit Street, Mayfair. Immediately Fox and his wife set about restoration of their new property, lavishing on it money and care. Later Fox bought the freehold.

Henry Fox was the son of Stephen Fox, who started as a page-boy and ended up an extremely successful businessman equally at home in the City and in Whitehall, a person much respected and much liked. One of Henry Fox's own sons was Charles James Fox, a man who was positively adored. Henry Fox himself was one of the most important politicians of the eighteenth century and was almost universally loathed. Lord Chancellor Hardwicke described him in parliament as 'a dark and insidious genius, the engine of personality and faction.' In a petition to the King in 1769, the City of London accused him of being 'the public defaulter of unaccounted millions'. Although he was incomparably more able than the Earl of Holland, his seventeenth-century predecessor at Holland House, the two men had much in common. They were both younger sons and so without the capital resources available to most of the owners of large houses. Henry Fox was as dependent as his predecessor on Court favour and perquisites, and, like him, was an acknowledged expert in obtaining them. There is a cheeky little story of Fox complaining about one of his colleagues at an interview with George II. He got nowhere with his complaint, but 'Before he quitted the royal presence, Fox, utilising the opportunity with an effrontery which was all his own, had contrived to extract from His Majesty the promise of a small sinecure.'

In 1762, George III, moving against the old political leaders such as the Duke of Newcastle, reluctantly accepted Fox as leader of the House of Commons in order to secure ratification of the treaty which ended the Seven Years War. Fox pushed the treaty through the Commons all right but did so amid charges of unprecedented bribery, horrifying politicians by the savagery of his attack on his principal opponents and erstwhile friends and his purge of a whole multitude of their appointees. 'Those phantoms they talk of so much', was Fox's contemptuous description of the Whig patriciate. Fox was an original. He was not like the grandees. He married one in Caroline, eldest daughter of the Duke of Richmond, a great hostess who received only the very best society. But an elopement had been necessary, since the Richmonds, regarding the Foxes as parvenus, refused their consent. Henry Fox's attitude to the young was most unusual: his maxim was that they were always in the right and their elders in the wrong. The Whig oligarchs of the eighteenth century took their pleasure (as well as much of their income) from spacious landed estates, but Henry Fox, like his father Stephen, was no countryman. While he supplemented Holland House with Sunderland House, on the site of the present Albany in Piccadilly, which he bought from the Duke of Bedford, his only truly country house – leaving out a Wiltshire hunting box purchased for his eldest son – was Kingsgate, a small place built on the edge of the cliffs on the wind-blown north-east coast of Kent, where, now Lord Holland, he amused himself in his old age by bathing and putting up romantic ruins which included a Roman villa.

The unorthodoxy, but not the ferocity, was inherited by Fox's descendants. The word could be used too about Holland House itself. Though the great American historian John Lothrop Motley, in London as United States Minister in the 1860s, could say that 'Certainly, if ever a house deserved to be haunted, it is Holland House', the reason was less complex. Holland House was the enduring suburban mansion, old-style, and long after the fields and cottages around about had been swallowed by the metropolis, a sense of the country lingered. Right up to October 1940, when it was destroyed by bombing, a commonplace description of Holland House was that it was 'just like a country house in London'.

Above: an interior, possibly that of Durham House, Strand, with Charles I, Henrietta Maria, the third and fourth earls of Pembroke and the King's dwarf Jeffrey Hudson. British School, seventeenth century.

Below: Charles II and courtiers on Horseguards Parade about 1680, with the Palace of Whitehall in the background. From a painting by an unknown artist.

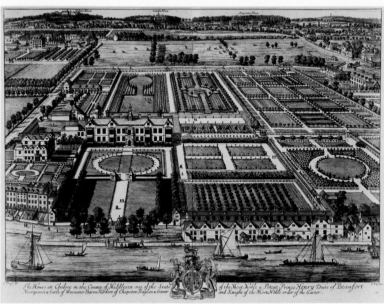

Above: Chiswick from the River painted by Jacob Knyff, *c.*1675–80, showing Old Corney House, the riverside house of the fourth Earl of Bedford.

Below: Beaufort House, Chelsea in the mid-1690s. Holland House, Campden House and Kensington House can be seen on the hills in the distance. The engraving by Kip is from a drawing by Knyff.

A series of spectacular masquerades were organized at the Haymarket Theatre in the early eighteenth century by the Swiss impresario John James Heidegger. The picture here was painted by Giuseppi Grisoni in 1724.

Above: Covent Garden, the piazza and market by John Collet, 1770s.

Below: North-Country Mails at the Peacock Inn, Islington, where they took on board passengers from the West End. Aquatint by James Pollard of 1823.

4

Casualties

*

Building has always been a notoriously cyclical business and almost as a matter of course the end of every boom leaves developers stranded, hobbled by the unfinished, unpaid for and unsellable buildings left on their hands. In the late seventeenth and early eighteenth centuries, the dangers of speculative building were magnified by usury laws that capped the rates of interest at which developers could borrow – at 6 per cent until 1714, and then at 5 per cent. As soon as the yield on government loans or other longer-term debt approached these levels, lenders naturally enough switched their money away, leaving developers high and dry. Evelyn had called the boom 'a mad intemperance' and, as we have seen, a downturn in the market had ruined Barbon, Hinde and Frith, as well as others. To build the new West End required steady nerves; speculative building demanded a speculator's temperament and it is no coincidence that so many of the promoters and developers were natural gamblers. It was as true of Panton and St Albans, a man reputed to live for play, as it was of those who came to grief.

Disaster hit less obvious targets as well. Mary Davies, the great heiress whose lands became the Grosvenor estate, never developed anything. Real estate nevertheless was her undoing: she did not go bankrupt, she went mad. Her mother married again while she was a young child, putting Mary in the care of an aunt. The mother may have neglected her emotionally, but she never for an instant neglected her value as an heiress. In Simon Jenkins's words, Mary was guarded like 'a porcelain doll crammed with gold'. With Lord Berkeley failing to produce the money contracted for, the twelve-year-old Mary was married to Sir Thomas Grosvenor. When he died, Mary Davies –

or more properly now Mary Grosvenor – already showing signs of mental instability, was entrapped by a plot aimed at capturing her fortune through remarriage. She could not cope, and it took years of litigation before a court declared her the victim of conspiracy. By the time of her death in 1730, she had been mad for twenty-five years. There is also the case of John Barkstead. Any list of early West End landowners who met disaster can hardly ignore him even though the property he owned had no influence, or at least no direct influence, on his undoing. He is a figure who flickers in and out of history books, sometimes called Barkstead, sometimes Berkstead, sometimes Berksted. Pepys, who wasted days searching for treasure this elusive person was supposed to have buried in the Tower of London, once refers to him as Baxter. In a 1657 act of parliament (his name incidentally spelt in two different ways within the act itself) Barkstead is established with Lord Bedford and Lord Clare as a founding father of the nascent West End. He was a member of Cromwell's Upper House and one of his major-generals, and a temporary beneficiary of the transfer to the victors of royal and Church lands after the Civil War. Other beneficiaries of this sort were General Lambert, who acquired the great manor of Wimbledon, and General Harrison, who took possession of the manor of Marylebone. Barkstead's investments, funded by money owed by the state, were in Thames-side property at Deptford, and notably in a reversion to Church lands in Shoe Lane, a road thrusting up from Fleet Street near the foot of Ludgate Hill. His career as a developer – and anything else – came to an abrupt end at the Restoration. Barkstead was a regicide, he fled to the Continent, was tricked by Sir George Downing, and brought back to England for execution.

To reintroduce here the Duke of Chandos appears incongruous. Having served his turn as a model of triumphant wealth, how should he be placed in the company of Barbon and Hinde and suchlike exemplars of disaster? The fact is that the last half of Chandos's career, from the South Sea collapse of 1720 to his death in 1744, proved almost as ruinous as the first half had been successful. Duchess Cassandra's letters tell of increasing money worries. In 1733 she writes to her sister apologizing that she can no longer continue with gifts of money on the old scale; 'indeed at present it has been hard for me to raise £20'. In March 1735 she writes to her sister-in-law refusing money: '. . . make yourself easy if you can, for I now know but too well how to pity your case, my Lord having now pd. debts for other people so long, that we both know the pain of not being able to pay our own.' In the same year Chandos, to save expense, allowed the gardens at Canons to fall into such neglect that they were shut to the public. If he was far from losing everything, his decline was sufficiently marked for Speaker Onslow, who had described his rise in such ringing terms, to write also that finally '. . . he fell (for so indeed it should be called) pitied and lamented by all who knew him.'

In August 1720 the Duke's holding in the South Sea Company was worth the colossal sum of £855,000 (close on a hundred million pounds today); less than two months later he owed around £70,000. He was not, however, the man to retire burned from the disaster; he remained an undiscourageable speculator, an incorrigible South Sea spirit. The losses piled up as time went on: £35,000 went on Law's Mississippi Scheme and later £125,000 in the Royal Africa Company and the slave trade. He plunged into everything, into government office, soap and glass-making, into coal, into insurance and the East India Company, into oyster fisheries. And in real estate there were investments in Georgia and Nova Scotia and New York and, at home, in country estates, and in property in Bath and Bridgewater in Somerset, and above all in London.

The Treaty of Utrecht had given new life to the London property market. Interest rates fell, and it has been calculated that over the three years 1716–18 the number of new buildings erected in London amounted to a fifth of the total in existence twenty years before. Between 1717 and 1719, Hanover Square, the first of the Mayfair squares, was laid out and was shortly to draw fashionable London away from Soho. The promoter was the first Earl of Scarbrough, who bought and leased the land, and among those who joined him was a fellow general, Lord Cadogan, whose family were later on to become one of the best known of London landlords. Hanover Square was an example of a grouping of rich with common sympathies, in this case – as the name shows – Hanoverian, Whig and military. In 1717, running slightly behind, a group of prominent Tories, among them Chandos, then still Lord Carnarvon, launched an ambitious scheme which centred on land owned by Lord Harley, the son of Swift's chief, the ex-Prime Minister, who was now Earl of Oxford. The Harleys had emerged as important London landowners through Lord Harley's marriage to Henrietta Cavendish, the heiress daughter of the Duke of Newcastle, who was also the fourth Earl of Clare. The scheme entailed pushing directly north of Hanover Square, over the barrier of Oxford Street, into the almost untouched parish of St Marylebone. A ground plan for the new Cavendish Square was drawn up. The development was to be on the grandest scale, its houses the largest of any London square, and with a church and market. Advance publicity stressed the convenience of the location, that it was relatively close to Westminster – and indeed it was nearer than, for instance, Bloomsbury. James Gibbs was supervising architect, and, in the usual way, there was to be overall control of much of the architectural detail. For the Harleys the signs were encouraging, with interest shown by some of the wealthiest and most influential people in the country. Lord Harcourt, ex-Lord Chancellor, agreed to take a 75-foot frontage and to start building at once; the Duke of Norfolk chose the west side of the square; Lord Carleton committed himself to another substantial plot. Lord Bathurst and Sir William Wyndham applied. Above all, there was the Duke of Chandos, leasing land on the north side of the square. An architect's plan prepared for him in 1720 shows that he had in mind a house of much the same size as Canons itself.

The Cavendish Square scheme, however, was a failure, not least because a number of the would-be leaseholders were heavy losers in the South Sea crash. The Duke of Norfolk backed out. Some buildings did indeed go ahead, with Lord Bingley, ex-Chancellor of the Exchequer, and Lord Harcourt staying the course. But progress overall was very slow. Unlike Hanover Square, which formed the centre of a new district, the Harley development by 1730 lay isolated, without hinterland, jutting into the countryside. Certainly what there was looked imposing, but nevertheless it was to be fifty years after the formulation of the original plans before Cavendish Square was finally completed. Defoe's declaration that St Giles was in a fair way to shake hands with Marylebone was as premature as his assertion that

Westminster was to join with Chelsea. At Cavendish Square, wrote the rather sanctimonious author of *A New Critical Review of the Public Buildings . . . in and about London and Westminster*, published in 1736, we 'see the folly of attempting great things, before we are sure we can accomplish little ones. Here 'tis, the modern plague of building was first stayed, and I think the rude, unfinish'd figure of this project should deter others from a like infatuation.' The fact was, the rich no longer wanted big London houses: fashion had changed. Horace Walpole, writing to Sir Horace Mann in 1743, looked back. I suppose, he said,

> . . . in a term we shall revert to York Houses, Clarendon Houses etc. But from that grandeur, all the nobility had contracted themselves to live in coops of a dining-room, a dark back room . . . and a closet. Think what London would be, if the chief houses were in it, as in the cities in other countries, and not dispersed like great rarity plums in a vast pudding of country!

The attitude to country and London property was indeed different. The nobility and gentry stuck tenaciously to their country houses, and if they found them too small, or too inconvenient, or too old-fashioned, they probably rebuilt on the same site. In all likelihood, after all, the country house was an integral part of an agricultural estate which provided its owner with much of his income and much of his importance in his county. In fact, status in London too probably depended on that local importance. As to London property, country grandees might well own none at all, neither freehold nor on long lease. Even Leicester House, one of the grandest of London mansions, was almost permanently let, with tenants who, before the Civil War, included Charles I's Earl of Strafford, and afterwards, the Queen of Bohemia and Thomas Verbecq, a wealthy merchant. In the eighteenth century, the Imperial ambassador, the future George II, and his son Frederick, Prince of Wales, who died there in 1751, were tenants. Tenancies might in fact be very short. Two surveys on place of residence in the capital of the families of peers and bishops – one of them referred to in the last chapter – show that only about a quarter of them were living in the same house or street in 1708 as they had

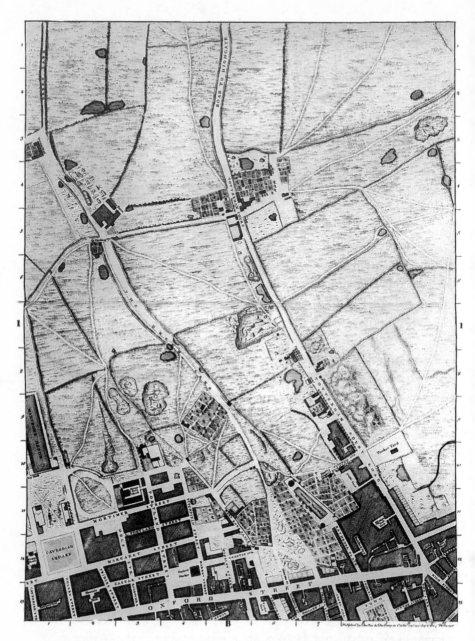

The frustrated development of Cavendish Square and its neighbourhood. On the far left is Chandos's Marylebone reservoir, 'the terror of many a mother'. Detail from a map by John Rocque, 1746.

been ten years before. There was obviously an overwhelming reliance on short tenancies.

Some bought or leased houses, or kept those they had inherited, simply for investment. Charles Bennet, second Baron Ossulston, with an income of £8,500 (nearly a million pounds in our money) was richer than most peers and proprietor of extensive country estates. Ossulston, incidently the great-nephew by marriage of Sir Humphrey Mildmay, inherited what are now Nos. 1 and 2 St James's Square. He also owned seven houses in adjacent Charles II Street, four tenements in St James's Market just east of the square, and another tenement near Piccadilly. Outside the West End he owned twenty houses in Spitalfields, in the City, some land and tenements over the edge of London, in Marylebone, and what were termed two mansion houses in Charterhouse Yard. From time to time he did occupy his fine St James's Square house, but he split it in two, letting out one part on a twenty-one-year lease. To travel about London and to reach his main country property in Middlesex, he kept a hackney carriage and horses, and a barge at Brentford. The later period of his life in London Ossulston spent almost entirely in lodgings or rented houses scattered all over the newly built West End. In 1698 he was in Golden Square; later he moved to Soho Square; then near Leicester Fields; then on the west side of St James's Street, and on to Poland Street off Tyburn Road (Oxford Street). In 1715, Ossulston was back in Soho Square. He moved to Dover Street, and finally to Conduit Street, where he died.

By the 1720s, the Duke of Chandos, Ossulston's neighbour in St James's Square, was in full retreat. By 1723 he appears to have dropped the idea of a single great mansion in Cavendish Square, and at the end of the following year he was in fact the owner of two houses in the square, each half-built. That to the west was to be for him and Cassandra, while the other was to be let as an investment. Chandos set about finding a buyer for his house in St James's Square, but none was forthcoming: it was too large for the times and his asking price slipped year by year. Finally it was bought by the builder Benjamin Timbrell who pulled it down, providing a replacement in the form of six houses of more manageable size, three of them fronting on to St James's Square and three on to Duke of York Street. The

The West End in the mid eighteenth century, taken from George Foster, *A new and exact Plan of London and Westminster.*

air in Cavendish Square was good, wrote Cassandra, but used as she was to palaces – though she did not put in quite that way – she found the new house too small.

Chandos owned other London property, for instance leases on houses in Scotland Yard, as well as a wharf and part of a dock. It was not, though, the building of houses or the buying and selling of property which was so damaging to Chandos in his London investments. It was his involvement with the London water supply. No business could appear more promising, for the expansion of the capital depended on an adequate supply of water. Back in the 1660s the Lord Mayor had pointed out to Samuel Pepys how the building of St James's Square would raise the price of water. For Chandos, there was the added attraction that he could supply elm wood for water mains from Canons and from an estate he owned in Berkshire. By the 1720s, a number of water companies were in existence and in fierce competition. There were the Shadwell and London Bridge companies, and the Chelsea Waterworks, founded in 1724, which constructed a large reservoir south of the Chelsea Road, near Buckingham House, and further reservoirs in Green Park and Hyde Park. There was also the New River Company which drew its supplies from springs in Hertfordshire rather than from the Thames. Chandos's choice for investment and for a partner was characteristically the most erratic and speculative of them all, the York Buildings Company (of which he had at one stage been governor), with its works on the site of the old Strand palace of York House.

St James's Square presented Chandos with a special opportunity. Westminster, though technically a 'City', was actually run by parish vestries working in conjunction with local magistrates. While they might be appropriate to country villages, they possessed quite inadequate resources and powers to administer a great town. The result was that parliament, through what were called Local Acts, was obliged to create supplementary authorities, the initiative for which rested with local inhabitants. These acts regulated every sort of amenity from roads and drains to poor relief. In 1726, a local act for St James's Square empowered residents, through trustees elected from among themselves, to clean, repair and beautify the square, and to levy rates. In Westminster, Golden Square, Berkeley Square and Grosvenor

Square were to benefit from similar acts of parliament. (The payment of extra tax for amenities survives now in the levies made on residents for the use of private square and communal gardens.) In St James's Square, the trustees wasted no time in clearing the rubbish dumped in the square, the central part of which they decided to cover in gravel and surround by posts and railings. For the very middle they determined on an ornamental basin which would also serve as a reservoir. Three water companies tendered and, after some canvassing by Chandos, York Buildings emerged as winner. The Duke was in the market for other reservoirs as well and while he failed to persuade the trustees of the fourth Duke of Bedford (a minor at the time) to allow a York Buildings basin in Bloomsbury Square, he was successful on his own land just to the north of Cavendish Square, roughly where Queen Anne Street now stands. The St James's project worked satisfactorily for a time, but with the failure of the Harley estate to grow, the Cavendish Square venture was a disaster; the reservoir – 'the terror of many a mother' who worried about her children falling in – lay useless until demolition in the 1760s, twenty years after the Duke's death.

The Duke of Chandos died in 1744 – Cassandra having predeceased him – with his once legendary wealth much reduced. His successor, his son by his first marriage, was extravagant and incapable, and in 1747 Canons was pulled down, a white elephant impossibly expensive to maintain, with its marvellous contents put up for auction. It had lasted hardly more than twenty-five years. Still, that was longer than Clarendon House in Piccadilly, which with its 101 hearths was one of the largest houses in England and which survived less than twenty years. Clarendon House provided an object lesson in the dangers of building. Its cost of around £50,000 (£5.75 million today) was three times what Lord Clarendon had anticipated. There were all sorts of reasons for this. The architect reminded him that changes had been made while work was under way, that there had been weather damage during the winter to put right, that timber prices had risen because of the Dutch war, that the price of bricks and of labour had gone up as a result of the Plague. Whatever the details, Clarendon House stood as a monument to *folie de grandeur*. Lord Clarendon himself, in exile after his fall from power, admitted

St James's Square with the Duke of Chandos's
reservoir at its centre. Engraving by Sutton Nicholls in
the early 1720s.

as much in his autobiography. He could not, he wrote, think of
anything of which he was so much ashamed, 'as he was of the vast
expense he had made in the building of his house; which had more
contributed to that gust of envy that had so violently shaken him . . .
and which had infinitely discomposed his whole affairs, and broken
his estate'.

Even then Clarendon could not bring himself to follow the advice
of his family and friends that he should sell the house. Perhaps after
all, one day, he would be recalled to office. And he was reluctant to
sell at what would inevitably be a substantial loss. In fact, the price
realized by his son after his death in a sale to the second Duke of
Albemarle was £26,000. The giant houses indeed proved precarious

investments. The Duke of Beaufort had considered it a bargain when in 1682 he paid £5,000 for Beaufort House, Chelsea, with its magnificent grounds and setting. Yet his great-grandson could obtain only half that amount when in 1737 he sold it to the eminent doctor and philanthropist Sir Hans Sloane, and that despite the substantial sums spent by the old duke on renovation. Part of the trouble was that the old duke had been too grasping: he had assumed ownership of the water conduit, threatening to deprive the lord of the manor, Lord Newhaven, of its use. There was a prolonged lawsuit, renewed by Hans Sloane when he bought the manor of Chelsea, which was settled only when the house had been left empty for twenty years.

There is a vivid account of Beaufort House in its last days left by its caretaker Edmund Howard in an autobiographical sketch. Howard was a Quaker, a bachelor, and a gardener who learned some of his craft from a cousin who worked at Canons. He had been for some years an apprentice in Chelsea before meeting Sloane, who told him that he was in the process of buying Beaufort House and needed a caretaker who could also do some gardening. Sloane himself was living in the 'new' manor house built by Henry VIII, on the site of 19–26 Cheyne Walk, and did not require Beaufort House to live in. Anyway, after the years of unoccupancy the place was in a ruinous condition and, it seems, without furniture. Howard was provided with a table, a stool, a candlestick and a bed, and left to get on with the job. His description of life in Beaufort House would easily fit into a nineteenth-century Gothic tale. Sloane, Howard wrote,

> sent me (only) into this old and Desolate place to live & lodge alone in such a frightfull place surounded with high Trees and overgrown with Briars of thorns and high Brick walls where had I been ever so much distressed and called aloud no chance of being heard for the house was situate about half way between the Thames & the Kings Road.

The house, he added, 'was more fit for the harbour of owls and batts or the Habitation of an Hermit than for a man in the full vigour of youth'. Howard's morale was not improved by the story of a ghost, apparently that of a man murdered in the house in the old Duke of Beaufort's time. It was said that workmen on the place had discovered some human bones. It was no wonder that Howard was alarmed when disturbed during the night by noises overhead. They proved, however, to have been caused neither by a ghost nor – another thought – by thieves stealing lead from the roof, but by the collapse of part of a ceiling.

Nobody seems to have thought it practicable to keep Beaufort House standing. Even to board up the windows and carry out rudimentary weatherproofing would cost £500 (£57,000 today) according to the estimate given by Sloane's surveyor. Potential buyers did, however, materialize. One group considered building a distillery in the garden, and another consisted of people who were later to open the pleasure gardens of Ranelagh next door, and who thought the Beaufort site might do for their purposes. In the end, the mansion was sold, or apparently sold, to contractors whose interest lay in the materials they could glean from the buildings, the lead, stone, bricks, timber, iron, a marble pavement. Howard was moved out into a riverside cottage, freed from the ghost and the hazard of collapsing roofs. His carefree life, though, did not last, for one of the contractors went bankrupt and the sale was cancelled. Nevertheless workmen continued to appear on site, intent on making away with whatever they could. When Howard was not fighting off these marauders he was trying – reluctantly, on Sloane's orders – himself to supervise the demolition and to sell the salvage. Not unreasonably, he felt himself out of his depth, and nor was he, a gardener after all, entranced by involvement with the move from Bloomsbury to Chelsea of Sloane's 'collection of gimcracks', the objects which a few years later were to form the basis of the British Museum collection. He gave up his job, married, and went in for clock-making. Beaufort House came down, the land for years left unbuilt over.

As we have seen, Nicholas Barbon had argued that the growth of a town increased the value of existing buildings. He went further; the buildings in the centre would be more valuable than those on the periphery. Leaving the special case of the City out of account, that turned out *not* to be so in much of London, least of all in the Strand and along the riverside to Blackfriars. It was a district which by the end of the seventeenth century contained an unusually mixed community. There were the poor who had crowded in from the east; slums were entrenched and proliferating, and in particular there existed the notorious criminal community of Alsatia, ironically placed close by the lawyers of the Inner Temple, who themselves represented an important section of the local population. There was a vigorous commercial life embodied most obviously in the New Exchange; and then there were the fashionables, people of the highest social standing who had not yet brought themselves to leave for the West End.

The exodus by the rich from any district, be it Aldersgate in the City, or Clerkenwell or the Strand, was a lengthy process. There would always be people reluctant to leave an area with which they had strong family or other emotional ties. The Duke of Bedford, William Russell's father, was one, refusing to leave Bedford House, the demolition of which had to wait on his death in 1700. The Duke of Beaufort, it may be remembered, had arranged to keep a house for himself on the site of Worcester House as an adjunct to his Chelsea mansion. And if the dukes of Norfolk failed to stay on it was not for want of trying. John Evelyn's friend, the sixth duke, employed a surveyor to lay out a plan for the Arundel estate which was sanctioned by an act of parliament. The intention was that Arundel Street and adjacent streets would produce sufficient rents to support a rebuilt Arundel House. Indeed, in 1677, work on the new mansion started. The idea proved impracticable and the seventh duke moved off to St James's Square. The Earl of Dorset, whose assembly of properties at Blackfriars included Dorset House, Little Dorset House, a theatre and some forty smaller buildings, all completely destroyed by the Great Fire, also took a house in St James's Square, although in the 1680s, he actually returned to one of the new streets off the Strand.

Between November 1698 and May 1700, the journalist Ned Ward wrote and published a series of articles on London in his monthly journal the *London Spy*. The theme was a tour of the city made by Ward posing as an ingenuous narrator accompanied by a knowledgeable and worldly companion. Here they are in the Temple gardens among the lawyers:

... I observed abundance of masked ladies with rumpled hoods and scarves, their hands charged with papers, bandboxes and rolls of parchment, frisk in and out of their staircases, like coneys in a warren bolting from their burrows.

'Are all these women come hither about law business?' Ward enquires.

'No, no,' replied my companion, 'these are ladies that come to receive fees, instead of giving any ... they give credit during a law vacation, and now, in term time, they are industrious in picking up their debts.'

This sounds more like good fun than hard historical evidence about life around the lawcourts. However, when the articles come to the palaces and the New Exchange and the Dorset House estate, the impression they give is convincing, and it is an impression of decline. Ward looks at the immense and imposing Northumberland House at Charing Cross, one of the last survivors of its species, which with the earldom of Northumberland in what was to be a long abeyance, lay more or less abandoned. Ward's words must have summed up what many people felt: 'What a thousand pities ... is it that so noble a palace, which appears so magnificent and venerable, should not have the old hospitality continued within, answerable to its outward grandeur.' And here Ward and his companion arrive by river at Dorset Gardens and the adjoining Salisbury Court. Ward, gazing at a 'stately edifice (the front supported by lofty columns)' enquires who lives there, what 'magnificent Don Croesus'? The companion answers nobody, so far as he knows, apart from rats and mice and perhaps a superannuated caretaker. What they were looking at, in fact, was a theatre, a building attributed to Wren, which had opened in 1671 and was more or less abandoned ten years later. It reopened in 1706 mainly for acrobatic and wild animal shows, to close finally three years afterwards. The 'stately edifice' was demolished.

The redevelopment of the Dorset House estate was a good example of how the rich attempted to adapt their property to new circumstances. Lord Dorset, moreover, went further than most, for he also took a lease from the Crown on land near Somerset House by which he undertook to rebuild the tenements which stood on it. As an investor, however, he was not to be compared with the Cecil family, represented in the Strand by two branches, one headed by Lord Salisbury, the other by Lord Exeter. The Salisburys' New Exchange supplied the western end of London with a formidable rival to the City's Royal Exchange. It did particularly well in the decade after the Fire, when there was no Royal Exchange – and not much else for that matter – to provide competition. So well indeed, that the third Lord Salisbury, pulling down Little Salisbury House and converting Great Salisbury House into a more manageable property, used part of the site to build a further large hypermarket of sixty shops which he named the Middle Exchange. A year or two later, his cousin Lord Exeter followed suit with his Exeter Exchange. But the boom days were over, there was too much capacity, and within ten years of its opening, in 1694, the Middle Exchange, nicknamed the 'Whores' Nest', was closed down. In 1737 the New Exchange went the same way. Nevertheless, while there was severe residential decline, the Strand was in the longer term to maintain itself as an important shopping centre, and Exeter Exchange, in later times famous for its menagerie, survived until 1830, when it was demolished as part of a road-widening scheme.

Investment was directed at residential use as well as at commerce. Landowners, and contractors such as Barbon, generally intended attractive streets and well-built houses. There were, of course, exceptions, those who, through lack of capital or a need for immediate returns, allowed their property to deteriorate. A classic example is Henry Rich, the Earl of Holland of Holland House. He had inherited land in 1612 from his father on the site of St Bartholomew's hospital in Smithfield. He took a short-term view, developing a further section of the site, encroaching on the celebrated fairground and continuing with his father's policy of granting thirty-one-year leases. Such a term was not long enough to encourage solid building. The leaseholders subdivided again and again, turning houses intended for one family into tenement buildings, used often for commercial as well as residential purposes. It was the classic way by which a slum came into being. A fundamental problem was that houses in central London were

The Unlucky Glance, 1772, an engraving attributed to
Hubert-François Gravelot: the setting is a fashionable
London shop.

seldom built with the poor in mind: just as the poor got cast-off
clothing from the rich, so they got their cast-off buildings. Crosby
Hall and the Paul Pindar house are just early examples.

It was, however, not the imprudence of the landowners which
drove away the well-to-do of the Strand, but the steady decline of
the neighbourhood, the continued influx of the poor and, frequently,
the disreputable. When in 1695 the Duke of Beaufort's house in
Beaufort Buildings – on the site of the entrance way to the present
Savoy Hotel – was destroyed by fire, the Duke did not move back.
By 1721 Charles Howard, the Duke of Norfolk's brother, was the only

titled resident left on the decaying Arundel estate. A drawing in the British Museum's Crace Collection shows the estate in 1734 with the deterioration unmissable. By then, at the other end of the Strand, the residential development on the site of the old Duke of Buckingham's York House was dominated by the York Buildings Company's noisy steam engine for pumping water from the Thames – a 'Wild-Fire Engine' as it was called by the author of the 1738 *A Voyage up the Thames* as he passed it by.

Nowhere, though, was the change more dramatic than at Clare Market and at Covent Garden, the very birthplace of the West End. Clare Market by 1708 was composed mainly of taverns and tenements, with a clamorous population of markedly homosexual prostitutes. The once-fashionable St Clement's Lane was described in 1730 as 'a disgraceful Rookery, filthy and squalid and disreputable to the last degree'. Covent Garden illustrated how, just as the existence of a great house generated residential outgrowth, so did its absence work the other way. Bedford House came down in 1705. The market thrived, and it became more difficult to sustain the balance of commerce and private housing. There were also the two theatres, the Covent Garden Theatre and the Theatre Royal, Drury Lane, adding colour and indeed distinction to the district, but which attracted not only playgoers (themselves adding to the bustle of the neighbourhood) but also hordes of prostitutes. Then there were the gangs, including that odd phenomenon of the time, the aristocratic gangs known as 'Mohocks', with robberies galore and fighting in the streets at night. By then, the elegant private houses were being displaced by retail shops, hotels, coffee- and chocolate-houses, and taverns, and the elegant Inigo Jones piazza was cluttered with stalls and shacks. The rich continued to visit Covent Garden but they came most probably as visitors to its gaming houses or as customers of its brothels.

Obviously, for those short of money, there were advantages in the fall of rents which resulted from the decline. When the nearly penniless Samuel Johnson arrived in London with his former pupil David Garrick in 1737, he found himself cheap lodgings in Exeter Street opposite the present Savoy Hotel. Dr Johnson was to turn into a devoted Londoner, finding charm in the most unlikely parts of the capital, as, for instance, in Wapping, which Boswell visited on his recommendation only to be obliged to admit that it did not live up to expectations. And in Southwark as well, where in his later years Johnson was to have an apartment in the house of his friends Mr and Mrs Thrale. Southwark, 'the Borough' as it was called, stands across the river from the City, linked to it now by Blackfriars Bridge and London Bridge. It was ancient indeed, a Roman town, and before that an Iron Age settlement. In the Middle Ages it was London's twin, a flourishing town with its own jurisdiction, distinguished by its cathedral and other magnificent buildings. The palace of the Bishop of Winchester on Bankside was particularly grand, and there were also the town house of the abbots of Waverley and, from the early sixteenth century, a great mansion built for Charles Brandon, Duke of Suffolk, married to the King's sister, the dowager Queen of France. At the western end of the borough stood a house belonging to Sir John Fastolf, with its moat of a quarter mile in circumference. After the Reformation, palaces and fashion faded away, but Southwark remained vibrant, a centre of London's entertainment well known for its brothels, its bear and bull baiting, and, as the modern replica of Shakespeare's Globe reminds us, its theatres.

At the close of the twentieth century, Bankside in particular – the strip of land running along the Thames, with its river walk, the Globe Theatre and the new Tate Gallery – is an exciting and attractive part of London. It is so for the first time in centuries. For the brothels, the theatres and the rest followed the palaces into oblivion, leaving the Borough to degenerate into a filthy and down-at-heel industrial slum, 'London's scrap-heap, the refuge of its excluded occupations and its rejected residents.' To the visitor of the eighteenth century, Bankside and Southwark generally appeared as a conspicuous casualty of London's evolution. One arrival, no visitor but an involuntary resident, was the sociable, country-loving, snobbish Hester Thrale.

She was born Hester Salusbury, an only child, of a family of country gentry down on their luck. Her father was incapable of making money and quite improvident, and her mother in desperation had thrown her considerable jointure into the common bottomless pot. Hester was early put to work: it became her job so to enchant her childless uncles that they bequeath her their substantial fortunes, and in the meantime keep her family afloat. She tried hard, it looked as if she would succeed, but in the end what she salvaged was a £10,000 (over a million pounds today) portion and an introduction to a rich brewer, the handsome and debonair Henry Thrale. Hester did not much like him but her training had hardly favoured advanced thinking about marriage. So, aged twenty-two, she married him in compliance with family duty; as a cousin put it, she was 'sold for a barrel of porter'.

Henry Thrale was not quite what he seemed. While he possessed his own pack of fox hounds, temperamentally he was a dedicated Londoner. His wife said of him that he was 'like Millament in Congreve's comedy, he abhorred the country and everything in it'. He was also a very ambitious businessman, the inheritor of a large brewery on Bankside. His beer, 'Thrale's Intire' porter, was allegedly

Mrs Thrale, *c.* 1785, in Italy after her marriage to Signor Piozzi. The painter is unknown.

well known as delicious 'from the frozen regions of Russia to the burning sands of Bengal and Sumatra'. His passion was to make his brewery the biggest in the country; he was going to outbrew Whitbread. Hester of course knew about the brewery; what she had not fully appreciated was that she would be expected to spend her winters there. Her husband was understandably reticent on the subject since other women he had considered as wives had turned down flat the prospect of living in Southwark. What Hester had expected, and what indeed she got most of the time, was a fine house, Streatham Park, set in nearly ninety acres of Tooting Common on land bought by the Thrale family from the Duke of Bedford, the local lord of the manor. Streatham was one of the fashionable country suburbs, and it was there that the third and fourth dukes of Bedford were brought up. At Streatham, in good time, Hester Thrale was to establish a salon, to attract as dazzling a group of friends as anyone could well possess – Samuel Johnson, above all, and Edmund Burke, Joshua Reynolds, David Garrick (though she knew him less well), Oliver Goldsmith. When Fanny Burney was admitted, her beloved Samuel Crisp – a sort of honorary godfather to her – wrote: 'Where will you find such another set? Oh, Fanny, set this down as the happiest period of your life.'

Nothing had prepared the sophisticated and lively young Mrs Thrale for Southwark, or for the brewery situated in a 9-acre compound abutting the site of the old Globe Theatre. She arrived for the first time in January 1764, shortly after her marriage. She could put up with the house which stood, offices attached, at the entrance to the brewery yard, where were to be found the clerks' quarters, store houses, vaults and vats, dung pits and stabling for nearly 100 horses. It was plain, even bleak, but comfortable enough. It was the surroundings which appalled her. Upstream towards Blackfriars Bridge (opened in 1769, during the Thrales' time in Southwark), some decent riverside houses had been built, but virtually everywhere else in the Borough there existed nothing more appealing than a jumble of workshops and poor workmen's cottages. The very names of the streets were cheerless. The Thrales lived in Deadman's Place, which led into Dirty Lane on one side and Foul Lane on the other; just by was the more sportive but uncouth Cuckold's Court. Maid Lane, which joined

The Thrales' house at Streatham from Walford, *Old
and New London*, 1897, vol. vi.

Deadman's Place at the river end, according to Dodsley's *London and
Its Environs Described*, published three years before Mrs Thrale's
arrival, was 'a long straggling place with ditches on either side; the
passages to the houses being over little bridges'. The whole area was
subject to flooding. Over the road was Clink Street, handy for the
Clink Prison, described at the time as 'a very gloomy hole'. Virtually
on the brewery premises was a stone-cutter's yard, noisy and dusty
but presumably not too smelly. Behind lay an old burial ground, and
behind that an open sewer. Then there were the tanneries and Messrs
Potts's vinegar factory. Mixed in were odd patches of open space
used as tenter grounds for stretching cloth, but only a strong imagination could have compared them to the green fields so loved by the
country-bred Hester Thrale.

If there was nothing in Southwark to delight the eye, let alone
the nose, equally there was nothing to gratify Hester's enjoyment of
good society. Certainly, some upper-class people were buried in the

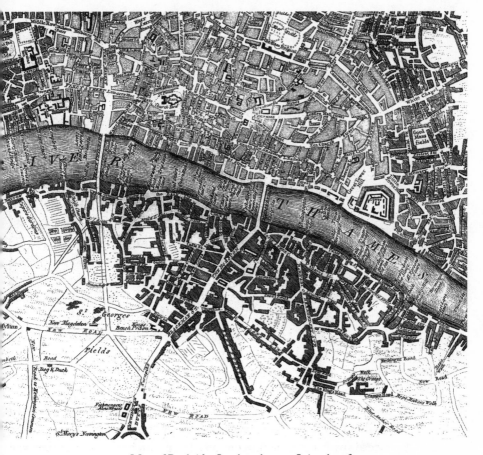

Map of Bankside, Southwark, 1770. It is taken from
London, Westminster and Southwark, 1770, in Henry
Chamberlain, *A New and Compleat History and Survey
of the Cities of London & Westminster*, 1770, vol. ii.

nearby graveyard; however, it seems that they had been brought
there, not from elegant houses within reach of the brewery but from
local prisons. For Southwark boasted not just the Clink, but the
Marshalsea, the King's Bench, the Counter and the White Lion as
well. (One prison, let alone an array of them, lowered the standing
of any residential district and, in fact, it seems to have been the
prospect of a prison nearby which precipitated the Grosvenors' final
desertion of their Millbank house for Mayfair.) For friends and
acquaintances elsewhere in London, the brewery was a difficult place

to visit. To start with, cabmen could not find the way and boatmen did not wish to. James Boswell one afternoon failed to persuade the boatmen at Hungerford Stairs – by Charing Cross – to go further than to ferry him over to the bank of the Thames immediately opposite, leaving him to walk the rest of the way. After all, there were few return fares to be picked up in Southwark. Later that night at 1 a.m., Boswell counted himself lucky to secure a hackney coach for the return journey. Society at the brewhouse then, Hester Thrale found very circumscribed, particularly in her early years there. It was some consolation that she had two carriages at her disposal, and she took to paying extended daily visits to her mother in Dean Street, Soho.

Then Samuel Johnson came on the scene. His delight in London, coupled with his taste for paradox, did lead him to assert that Pepper Alley, a nearby lane leading down to the Thames, was as healthy a spot as Salisbury Plain and a much happier one. At the same time his feet were never far off the ground. When the local clergyman preached on friendship, Johnson declared him a blockhead for choosing a subject so ill-fitted to such a busy place, where 'the men are thinking on their money, I suppose, and the women are thinking of their mops'. Johnson argued that Hester must come to terms with Southwark. To linger in the country, 'feeding the chickens till she starved her understanding', would do her no good and in particular it would sour her relations with her husband. In November 1779 he wrote to her: 'I do not see with so much indignation Mr Thrale's desire of being the first Brewer, as your despicable dread of living in the borough . . . it is the business of the one to brew in a manner most advantageous to his Family, and of the other to live where the general interest may best be superintended.' Four days later, he added: 'You must take physick, or be sick; you must live in the Borough, or live still worse.'

Fanny Burney, who knew both women well, went so far as to compare Hester Thrale with Madame de Stael. That seems extravagant, and indeed Fanny Burney qualified her words. Nevertheless, Mrs Thrale was much more than just a gifted hostess. Robust, energetic and quick, urged on by Johnson, she buckled to. Her life, she was to write years later, 'had been been one long canvass'. She meant it in a general sense, but the word applied too in its familiar political context, for Henry Thrale, like his father before him, was one of Southwark's two MPs. The constituency was no pocket borough; it numbered two thousand far from somnolent voters and general elections demanded unremitting work which, with her husband's health failing, fell more and more to her. Even more exacting was the brewery. For Thrale turned out to be a failure, a wretched businessman living in fantasy, gambling on everlasting good times, who came near to wrecking his business. Increasingly Hester was drawn into the firm. She laboured to understand how it worked, she canvassed for business. It was she, not her demoralized husband, who saved the brewery in the slump year of 1772, and who raised loans and restored confidence among the workforce.

The debts were paid off, the business again flourished, and then, in 1779, Thrale suffered a stroke and once more it was for her to take charge. In her journal-cum-commonplace book which she called *Thraliana*, Hester lamented the '*Borough Winter* which of all other things I most abhor', but determined that she must go to the Southwark house '& hack at the Trade myself. I hate it heartily, yea heartily! but if living in Newgate would be *right* I hope I should be content to live in Newgate.' In another entry, she added, 'my duty shall make it Pall Mall to me.'

Almost despite herself, she grafted on to her country background an abundant experience of business. She speaks with special authority when she draws a comparison between the life of the wife of a country gentleman and that of a wealthy businessman:

There is no doubt but that the wife of a trader who flatters himself that he has three or four thousand pounds o' year, lives in much more splendour than the wife of a gentleman who has three or four thousand pounds o' year estate: for the commercial man gains by his business a familiarity with money, tho' totally unmingled with *contempt* of it, which the aristocrat cannot possibly obtain – who sees his cash so seldom, & finds it so necessary to his happiness. Meantime my country baronet or squire *has* what he *thinks* he has, & his wife knows how much and how little that amounts to – as well as himself: but the merchant's *lady* never is informed of her husband's circumstances any more than his *whore* is; she cannot be let in to the mysteries of a large

& complicated business – probably she could not understand it if she was inform'd, more probably she would talk of it among her female companions, and *most* probably the acct. of it would interest her so little, she would drive away to the auction hoping wholly to forget it.

Thrale's condition did not improve, and he lost his seat in the general election of 1780. His wife decided that for health reasons it was urgent that he be distanced from the brewery. Increasingly erratic, Thrale talked of renting Lord Shelburne's house in Berkeley Square – best known as Lansdowne House – which Hester described as one of the finest in London. In the end they settled on 1 Grosvenor Square, which they took furnished from Sir Richard Heron, Chief Secretary for Ireland, at a rent of 11 guineas (£850 today) a week. On the face of it, nowhere could be more congenial than this, the most fashionable address in London, the antithesis of Bankside. In fact, Hester's joy was muted by worries about her husband and the future of the brewery. It was, however, much easier to see her friends. And the Square garden was more fun for her daughters to play in than 'Palmyra', the garden the Thrales had constructed out of rubble on the far side of Deadman's Place. Then Henry Thrale died. Neither of Hester's two sons had survived childhood, and it was not practicable to continue with the business. So she and Dr Johnson, as executors, sold out. Anyway, she did not want to carry on, not just because she disliked Southwark, but because of her inbred disdain for 'trade', its coarseness, as she saw it. 'Busy people,' she wrote in her journal, 'neither love nor hate, pin down the most delicate soul to a counting house desk, & in three years he will when his neighbour's family dwelling has caught fire, ask only, what money was lost?' Hester Thrale, born Salusbury, was restored to unalloyed gentility. 'It is the greatest event of my life,' she wrote. 'I have sold my brew-house to Barclay the rich Quaker for £135,000 ... I have by this bargain purchased peace & a stable fortune: restoration to my original rank in life, and a situation undisturbed by commercial jargon, unpolluted by commercial frauds; undisgraced by commercial connections.' And she finishes off: '... so adieu to brewhouse and Borough wintering, adieu to trade & tradesmen's frigid approbation.'

She married again, scandalizing Johnson and Fanny Burney and her other friends by choosing an Italian singer, Signor Piozzi, with whom she fell passionately in love. She neglected her daughters, she lost her touch with money. Sometimes she and her husband lived at the Streatham house, more often they rented it to tenants, later on it was sold. For some years she owned the lease of a house in Hanover Square. Hester Piozzi lived a long life, in her old age qualifying, as she put it, as one of the 'Antiquities of Bath'. Southwark crops up occasionally in her journal; it was being born there, she wrote, that made her daughters so 'purse-proud'. (One married a banker, Merrik Hoare, and another Admiral Lord Keith, who is said probably to have made more in prize-money than any other naval officer.) But looking at it from the outside one has a sense of anticlimax; and while it may be ironical, it is not quite a surprise, to find her writing to her friend Sir James Fellowes more than thirty years after she had parted from grim, run-down Southwark: 'The best years of *my* temporal existence – I don't mean the happiest; but the best for powers of improvement, observation etc. – were passed in what is now Park Street, Southwark, but then Deadman's Place.'

5

'Devouring Luxury'

*

The character of the West End of London was largely determined by its ownership, by the fact that a small number of rich families held fast to their land over a long period of time. They did so, first of all, because they believed it would prove a profitable investment. And mixed with this belief was their traditional conception of land as an assertion and symbol of the family's social and political status. Goodwill and a sense of responsibility, however, would not of themselves have been enough. They could be frustrated by confiscation for political reasons (as in the Civil War) or, more likely, because they were not qualities likely to be inherited in every generation. After all, what about a twenty-one-year old heir, newly come into possession, chancing on someone like Charles James Fox at the gaming table? And there was Lord Harcourt, who in 1825 lost the ninety-nine-year lease on his house in Cavendish Square at cards to the Duke of Portland. Hence, it was standard practice to safeguard the family assets by putting them into trust, into settlement. Such an arrangement most certainly helped to preserve London property holdings, but it also complicated their administration by constraining the family's freedom to move with the market. The remedy lay in private acts of parliament, known as estate acts. To take two eighteenth-century examples: in 1739, the Duke and Duchess of Portland, on behalf of themselves and their infant son, initiated a bill in parliament to enable them to grant building leases on their Soho property for a longer period than was authorized by their marriage settlement. In 1754, the executors of the late Duke of Somerset needed parliamentary authority to sell real estate in Lincoln's Inn and replace it with property elsewhere.

In the case of the Grosvenors, the protection given to wives by means of a life interest in assets – without which they would have lost all control of their money to their husbands – acted as a brake on the development of Mayfair. Until Mrs Tregonwell, Mary Davies's mother, died in 1717, the Grosvenors were powerless to grant worthwhile leases on her land. While Mary Davies might have agreed to some variation in the terms of her life interest, which notably included the site of the future Grosvenor Square, none was in any event possible until she came of age, nine years after her marriage. Even then she appears to have been in no hurry to agree to a new settlement, and matters were complicated by the death of her husband in 1700. It was only in 1711 that a private act of parliament opened the way for building. Even then, the Grosvenors were barred from granting leases of more than sixty years, although they managed to circumvent this rule in effect by arranging with contractors that an extension would be made as soon as circumstances allowed. Ninety-nine years then became the normal length of lease.

Next to Lincoln's Inn Fields, Grosvenor Square was the largest square in London and was mainly built between 1725 and 1731. Many of the thirty builders and building partnerships who leased or subleased its fifty-one sites were involved also in Hanover Square and Cavendish Square. One of them was Benjamin Timbrell, the man who bought Chandos House in St James's. Daniel Defoe described the scene in west London in 1725:

> I passed an amazing scene of new foundations, not of houses only, but as I might say of new Cities. New towns, new squares, and fine buildings, the like of which no city, no town, nay, no place in the world can shew; nor is it possible to judge where or when, they will make an end or stop of building . . . All the way through this new scene I saw the world full of bricklayers and labourers; who seem to have little else to do, but like gardeners, to dig a hole, put in a few bricks, and presently there goes up a house.

And he added '. . . as the people are run away into the country, the houses seem to be running away too.' It was an advantage of the leasehold system that by encouraging development on an extended

Frederick, Prince of Wales, walking in the Mall. From
a painting attributed to Samuel Wade, *c.* 1735.

scale, it tended to cheapen the price of houses and to speed their
construction.

From the start, Grosvenor Square formed the centre of the whole
Grosvenor development in Mayfair. The estate was planned so as to
look inwards, away from Hyde Park and from the Tyburn Road with
the noisy crowds who periodically passed along it on their way to an
execution at (our) Marble Arch. As a result, the view from Hyde
Park was on to the back of the houses along Park Lane, originally
called Tyburn Lane, although Sir Richard Grosvenor did recognize
the park's existence by providing a gate through its walls with a lodge
and lodge-keeper. He also took account of it by charging lower rents
for houses on the western side of Grosvenor Square. Where they
considered it worthwhile, the Grosvenors involved themselves closely
with the financing, allowing arrears of rents to accumulate, and
granting mortgages. Otherwise mortgages were drawn from wealthy

individuals with spare money to invest, from solicitors and barristers, and from widows, spinsters and clergymen. Hoare's Bank was one of the mortgagees.

The square was smart and remained smart. The houses were in terraces and not free-standing, but the scale was magnificent and design of the façades simulated that of palatial mansions. Its inhabitants were wealthy and grand. When Henry Thrale arrived in January 1781 he was something of an oddity. In the days before his stroke, only second-generation rich as he was, he carried himself, his hounds and his mistresses like an aristocrat. Nevertheless, he was – unless there were some temporary tenants of whom we are unaware – the sole businessman in Grosvenor Square. While the names of Delmé and Heathcote would to informed contemporaries have carried City resonances, the Grosvenor Square residents who bore them were well assimilated into the ruling class. Sir Peter Delmé, for instance, was married to the daughter of the Earl of Carlisle and best known for

A View of Grosvenor Square. Mezzotint after
Edward Dayes, 1789.

Westminster and Mayfair, by
John Rocque, 1746.

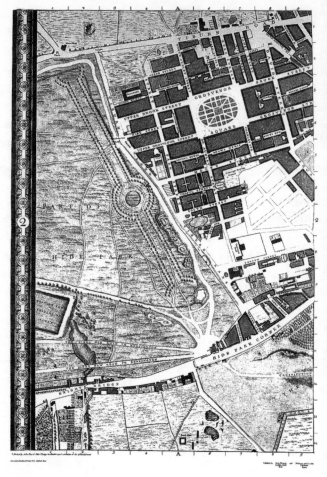

his love of racing. One resident, Lord North, was temporarily absent
in Downing Street, another was the Marquess of Rockingham, who
would replace him as Prime Minister the following year. There were
three bishops, among them a future Archbishop of Canterbury; a
field-marshal; four dukes, including the Duke of Beaufort, and also
the heir to a dukedom; and a long list of lesser peers, which included
the landlord, Mary Davies's grandson, Lord Grosvenor, and the Earl
of Thanet, who lived in one of the finest houses in the square. The
Thanets had moved on from Bloomsbury, to which they had migrated
from the City a century before. There was also a sprinkling of

well-born widows including the dowager Duchess of Chandos, widow of the second Duke. Of the commoners, a large number were members of parliament, and thus well placed to make money (as well as titles) even if they did not already possess it.

Grosvenor Square was not immune to the depression in the housing market which took place in the 1730s, 1740s and 1750s, when property prices in the West End stagnated and sometimes fell. Nos. 20 and 53 even had to be sold by means of a lottery. The depression reflected general economic pressures and an actual contraction in London's population. The West End was over-built. The Grosvenor estate, however, was much better able to withstand bad times than some of its neighbours. The Conduit Mead estate to its east, which had proved the downfall of John Hinde and others in the seventeenth century, was still a problem to its freeholders, the City of London. There was an incoherence about the building plan and about the road system which had been constructed within the estate. Leases were a jumble, and provided little incentive to tenants to look after their property. So, in the late 1740s, the City Corporation, badly needing money, resolved to grasp the nettle, and, as existing contracts allowed, establish standard leases with forty-year terms. Since the new leases were automatically renewable, the fact that they were shorter than those on the Grosvenor and most other private estates was not important. Where they were indeed original – and from the landlord's point of view highly injurious – was that they allowed perpetual renewal at the same rent and same renewal premium. The City simply ignored the risk of inflation. As it happened, prices in the 1750s, when the new provisions started coming into effect, were generally much the same as they had been a hundred years before; they fluctuated wildly in the very short term and in different areas, but there was no overall inflation. But, in the 1770s, prices took off in an inflation which was not to be seen again until the twentieth century. Marvellous for the leaseholders, a nightmare for the landlords. The same situation existed on the small Berners Estate on the north side of Oxford Street. The estate surveyor, writing in 1918, deplored the legacy of eighteenth-century leases with which he had to deal. In 1915, for example, the Berners Estate was forced to extend the lease of 21 Berners Street, already lengthened to 1993, for a further twenty-one years to 2014 at a rent of £14 a year (the eighteenth-century rent) with a fine (a premium) of £14. That was bad enough in 1915; it is of course grotesque now.

Like Grosvenor Square, St James's Square, a hundred years after its foundation, still ranked as a most desirable address. Both succeeded in keeping out trade, banishing it to the side streets. Soho Square, so fashionable at the start of the eighteenth century, and fashionable still when compared to the Soho district as a whole, was a different matter. In 1763, when Casanova arrived to visit his one-time lover Teresa Cornelys at Carlisle House on the eastern side of the square, he found, opposite him on the other side, the Venetian embassy where he was distinctly *non-grata*. Mrs Cornelys was 'trade' – though of a spectacular sort – but there did remain high-flying private residents like the Duke of Argyll, a local landowner; the (far from wealthy) Duchess of Wharton; and the immensely rich William Beckford. Monmouth House was still in place on the north side, although its ducal occupants had moved elsewhere. Other residents, however useful, were less prestigious. They included the portrait painter Allan Ramsay; the Soho workshops, upholsterers and manufacturers of the famous Soho tapestries; and the Soho Academy, one of the best schools in London, to which the sons of Edmund Burke and James Boswell were later sent. About to open around the corner in Carlisle Street was Domenico Angelo's finishing school for young gentlemen desirous of perfecting their horsemanship and swordplay.

London in the eighteenth century was a boom town for foreigners, at least as attractive as it had been in the past to Lombards, Flemings and Hansa merchants and the myriad others who followed them. Many of the immigrants, particularly the Dutch, took jobs in commerce and finance, but those most frequently to be seen in the West End were engaged in consumer services, a great envelope of a term which encloses both Handel and the most insignificant valet. Restaurants and hotels were often run by foreigners, and rich Londoners employed French cooks, a boon to visitors, since English food, without soups or sauces, was something of a trial. Somewhere between Handel and the valet can be placed a group of people, those like Teresa Cornelys, Domenico Angelo, and the Swiss impresario John James Heidegger (who organized a series of spectacular masquerades at the Haymarket Theatre in the earlier part of the century), not strictly speaking creative artists themselves, but people connected with the arts, who supplied Londoners with something of the glitter of Paris. Teresa Cornelys in the 1760s rates as the most successful of all. She was a one-time courtesan, theatrical producer and opera singer, who, at her house in Soho Square, organized a series of immensely successful assemblies, masquerades and concerts. Her brilliance as an entrepreneur was in recognizing that the London rich demanded a suitably lavish outlet for their spending. In February 1770 Horace Walpole wrote to Sir Horace Mann:

The ball was last night at Soho, and if possible, was more magnificent than the King of Denmark's ... The mob was beyond all belief; they held flambeaux to the windows of every coach, and demanded to have the masks pulled off and put on at their pleasure, but with extreme good humour and civility.

As Mrs Cornelys explained to Casanova, 'when it is a question of pleasure, the English do not care what they spend'. Casanova was himself very extravagant and very experienced in the great world. As he put it, grandly and with understatement, 'economy in pleasure is not to my taste'. But even his breath was taken away by the lavishness of his friend's entertaining – 600 people in an evening was not out of the way – and at the sumptuous apartments and furnishings. She employed, he noted, three secretaries; a female confidante; another, dumb attendant; and thirty-two ordinary servants.

From a social point of view, Casanova made the mistake of arriving near mid-summer. To sample the season at its best, it was necessary to be in London before the end of May, for by July the patricians had left for the country and the West End struck visitors as practically deserted. 'I hear there's nothing left in London but Lying-in-ladies, [and] those who are expecting every day to be in that situation,' wrote Lady Dalkeith one 6 July. Whatever the time of year, however, arrival in England was likely to be disagreeable. It was not just the sea crossing, which could prove lengthy and arduous, but the reception, with notoriously rude and venal customs officials and mobs of urchins yelling, 'French Dog! French Dog!' Madame du Bocage, arriving at an hotel in Deal, was importuned by a crowd of sailors and porters demanding money for drink. At least, that is what she thought they must be after. She, like most of the foreign visitors of the early and mid-eighteenth century, ambassadors included, spoke no English. In London, a well-dressed foreigner who strayed too far afield risked physical assault, although happily the patricians of the West End could normally speak French, and – the men – would normally have done the Grand Tour.

The travellers from the Continent who flocked to London during the last half of the eighteenth century have left numerous accounts of life in the West End. When they happen to mention the City, it is

Le Français à Londres by J. Collet, engraved by
C. White, mid-eighteenth century. A well-dressed
foreigner in eighteenth-century London who strayed
too far afield risked physical assault.

usually to dwell on its differences – in appearance, in manners, in
attitude – to the West End. There is what appears an almost total
separation socially. The Hanoverian, Count Frederick Kielmansegge,
at a ball near Gray's Inn one evening, was invited with his party by 'a very
pleasant and rich merchant's wife' to a dinner with a City subscription

ball to follow. When they went, they noticed that, apart from some other foreign guests, there was nobody present from the West End. Kielmansegge, in London in 1761 to attend George III's coronation, passed his time mainly in the very grand houses. He much approved of Northumberland House with, so he said, its more than 140 rooms. His criticism was that the gateway was too narrow and the courtyard too cramped for the number of carriages and sedan chairs which crowded in for parties. In that respect he much preferred the Duke of Bedford's mansion in Bloomsbury, where the Duchess held assemblies every Friday during the season. What Kielmansegge, like other visitors, much disliked about the conventions of high society was the ritual of tipping. After a magnificent dinner at the Duke of Newcastle's, he found it difficult to identify the servants. They were dressed, he complained, not in livery, but so stylishly that they were hard to distinguish from the guests. Moreover, the elegance of the servants increased the cost, since 'to a gold-laced coat you cannot offer a solitary shilling'.

Everyone remarks on the obsession with money. The scale of spending, the taste for 'devouring luxury', to use the words of the German J. W. von Archenholz, in no way implied an indifference towards money on the part of the men or, for that matter, the women. To the contrary. Saussure asserted that the first question a woman asked you if you mentioned the name of a man whom she did not know was, 'Is he rich?' Pricing was down to a fine art, everything was measured in terms of money, not least adultery. Casanova and others were told that it was known for husbands to set traps for their wives in order to obtain damages from their lovers. Even to Casanova, a man who lived off the rich, the materialism grated. One day he went to the City to change some money, and talking with his banker, enquired the name of a person nearby. 'He's worth a hundred thousand,' replied the banker. 'And who is that man over there?' 'He's not worth a ten-pound note.' Casanova protested that he had asked their names, not how much they were worth. But the banker could not help there, explaining that 'Names don't go for anything here. What we want to know about a man is *how much he has got.*'

The visitor could adapt to the fixation with money as he did to the extravagance and to the sound of the language. More difficult was getting to grips with the character of his hosts. The grand

Londoner possessed a veneer of French sophistication, but through-out society there existed a certain hardness, a roughness expressed most clearly perhaps in the passion for sports such as bull-baiting and cock-fighting. First impressions were often unfavourable, for the men seemed cold, lifeless and excessively reserved, following no doubt the precept of Lord Chesterfield that while one may be seen to smile, one should never, ever, laugh. The baffling English reserve applied to those who supplied pleasure as much as to those who purchased it. The landlord of the bagnio (one of the few public places open in London on a Sunday) to which Casanova was sent by his friend Lord Pembroke appeared to be a man of such gravity and respectability that Casanova hardly dared explain what he wanted. A later visitor had the same experience. He declared that a notary, or a confessor for that matter, could not have been more solemn had he asked, 'Sir, where would you be buried?' than the waiter who enquired of him and his friend what they wanted in the way of women.

The foreigner might attribute the cold manner to the weather: Voltaire was told that if you had a favour to ask at Court, the rule was to wait until the wind was in the south or west. The charitable, in describing the English, might use a word like 'phlegmatic' – a quality the Duchesse de Gontaut said they lost only at the races – while others, less kindly disposed, would accuse them of being morose. Their case appeared strengthened by the notoriously high rate of suicide. From time to time though, everyone agreed, the reserve gave way ... to a lecture on the superiority of all things British, and in particular on that liberty which was supposedly unique to the British nation. This last line of argument could actually be less irritating than one might imagine, since to see how British liberty worked was often one of the reasons the traveller had for being here in the first place. Few visitors seem to have lost patience, although Monsieur Grosley quotes a story told about Lord Tyrconnel who did, and cut his visit short. Educated in France, and bored to tears by the endless discussion of politics in London drawing rooms, he invited four courtesans to a bagnio, where, to his despair, they fell into an argument among themselves about a forthcoming parliamentary debate.

But persevere, urged those foreigners who understood the Eng-lish. The anglophile Archenholz warned readers of his book *A Picture of England* (first English translation 1789) not to judge them by their members of parliament, by their rapacious soldiers and privateers, or by their record in India. Underneath the difficult exterior, they were warm and generous and even passionate, though that last quality revealed itself mainly in the manic gambling. They were, he wrote, straightforward and sincere – which, after all, was more, some visitors thought, than could be said for the French. Nor – in the eighteenth century – were they considered hypocrites; in fact it was the reverse. Soon after Casanova's arrival he met Augustus Hervey, who had been second-in-command of the naval force which had taken Havana and had been largely responsible for the expedition's success. The prize money had been stupendous. In his typical fashion, Casanova opened the conversation on a high moral tone, with a question about personal honour. Hervey brought him down to earth. In England, he said, if you break the law and you pay for it, no more is owed to society. Dishonour comes about only if the criminal tries to escape punishment by base or cowardly actions. He concluded, 'I have taken Havana from Spain: this was robbery on a large scale.'

The candour of the English might be disconcerting, as indeed it was to Casanova in this instance, but it was refreshing, and while their friendship might be hard to win, once gained, it was the real thing. Intellectually, they were notable for a strong common sense and an aptitude for solid reasoning. Even the apparent arrogance should not be taken at face value: certainly they were arrogant about the alleged superiority of their country, but about themselves as individuals they were really quite modest. Above all, and this was generally seen as being on the credit side, they displayed an originality and independence of character. There are numerous examples quoted by visitors of generosity with money. To take one example. Madame de La Tour du Pin was living as a refugee from the French Revolution in a small house at Richmond. Her next-door neighbour was a rich City alderman with whom one day her young son fell into conversation. The alderman, having enquired about the family, thenceforward sent over regular presents of fruit from his garden – very welcome in the straitened circumstances of refugees – and allowed the son a free run of his house. But though the alderman and Mme. de La Tour du Pin saw each other frequently over the garden wall, so to speak, never did he make the slightest move to speak to her or to acknowledge her existence. She thought it odd, but, as it happened, she had had the same sort of experience already. Several years before, she, her husband and a friend, all three having narrowly escaped the guillotine, were farming in New York State on very limited funds. One day they were visited by Talleyrand, also a refugee, who was accompanied by a British 'nabob', a Mr Law. To the Frenchwoman, Law went rather far even by British standards, for he hardly spoke at all and was immersed in the deepest melancholy. Yet, after a couple of days, impressed by their fortitude and shocked by their poverty, he asked Talleyrand to persuade the La Tour du Pins to accept a loan so that they could set themselves up properly.

Like its inhabitants, London as a city evoked mixed feelings. No one could be enthusiastic about the great smog which hung over the city, implanting its grime everywhere and penetrating the lungs of native and visitor alike. It was also extremely expensive. 'I am frighted at the expense attending one's living here: Oh Joney, you have no idea of it,' wrote the businessman Joshua Johnson back home to America in 1771. On the whole, London was thought to lack a certain visual excitement. Inside, the houses were marvellously clean despite the smog; the mahogany gleamed, the comfort was appreciated by everyone. Outside, visitors – at least from the 1780s on – praised the street lighting and the pavements, and the bridges over the Thames, where the old London Bridge had been now reinforced by Blackfriars and Westminster. They admired too the parks and the West End squares, St Paul's and some of the other public buildings. However, they were often disappointed by the general architecture. To the Duc de Levis, London brought to mind a vision of iron railings stretching as far as the eye could see; to Louis Simond, at the beginning of the nineteenth century, the streets often enough were pervaded by a 'sort of uniform dinginess'; to the Abbé Le Blanc, a duke in London lived in a smaller house than many a Paris tradesman. It was also considered that there were too many beggars and prostitutes. The fascination of London lay in its vitality, its enormous size, the choice of things to do, the ease of living, the clamour, the sheer metropolitan sensation. When Carl Philip Moritz arrived from Germany in 1782, he and his companions disembarked downstream from Dartford, because, he said, the Thames was so congested that it could take several days for a ship to work its way through the last ten miles. G. C. Lichtenberg approached London by road from Harwich, reaching the city at 10.30 in the evening. It took him until midnight to attain the house where he was staying, and in the streets, he said, it was as noisy as in other cities at midday.

So large had London grown as the century came to an end that in 1791 Horace Walpole was writing to Miss Berry that sedan chairs were obsolete, for 'Hercules and Atlas could not carry anybody from one end of this enormous capital to the other'. At least the demise of sedan chairs, while it may have saddened older Londoners, served to clear the pavements for the crowds hastening to buy from shops filled with the luxuries of all the world. In 1786, a rather breathless visitor, the German writer Sophie von la Roche, described her encounter with 'lovely Oxford Street'.

'Just imagine,' she wrote home,

> . . . a street taking half an hour to cover from end to end, with double rows of brightly shining lamps, in the middle of which stands an equally long row of beautifully lacquered coaches, and on either side of these there is room for two coaches to pass one another; and the pavement, inlaid with flag-stones, can stand six people deep and allows one to gaze at the splendidly lit shop fronts in comfort. First one passes a watchmaker's, then a silk or fan store, now a silversmith's, a china or glass shop. The spirit booths are particularly tempting, for the English are in any case fond of strong drink. Here crystal flasks of every shape and form are exhibited: each one has a light behind it which makes all the different coloured spirits sparkle. Just as alluring are the confectioners and fruiterers, where, behind the handsome glass windows, pyramids of pineapples, figs, grapes, oranges and all manner of fruits are on show.

Madame von la Roche went on to Hatchetts, a master saddler employing several hundred workmen, where she admired the coaches on display and saw the drawing of one ordered for the Nawab of Arcot, which was priced at the staggering figure of 15,000 guineas

(£1.2 million today). Drawn back to Oxford Street, she is struck by a shop selling a great range of women's shoes. Inside a woman was buying shoes for herself, while her small daughter, 'was searching amongst the dolls' shoes for some to fit the doll she had with her'.

In 1774, the daughter of Governor Hutchinson of Massachusetts wrote home to her sister-in-law after a month in London: 'London my dear is a world in itself: you ask me how I like it? very well for a little while; it will do to see once in ones life, and to talk of ever after; but I would not wish to fix my abode here.' The last few words adjusted, the name of London replaced, and it might be a letter from a visitor writing home about twentieth-century New York.

By 1800, London was not only the largest, but much the largest city in Europe. Its population of 900,000 was a third more than that of Paris, double that of Madrid or Naples, and five times greater than that of its old commercial rival, Amsterdam. In the world as a whole, only Peking was bigger, but it was in rapid decline, and otherwise London was challenged only by Edo (Tokyo). London owned and built more ships than anywhere else, it was the centre of international trade, finance and insurance, and it remained an important manufacturing city. In the great consumer boom of the later eighteenth century, it seemed that its streets were indeed paved with gold; there was an extra urgency in the money-making, people were dazzled by the wealth all about them. And there was more to be had, for money was spinning down the social hierarchy. Dr Johnson regretted the breakdown of 'subordination', declaring that there were many causes but that the chief one was the 'great increase of money'. Dr Trusler, an interesting character who wrote a number of books on money and the effect of inflation, declared that the 'Great degree of luxury . . . within a few years, is not only astonishing but almost dreadful to think of.' In Samuel Foote's *The Cozeners*, first performed in 1774, Mrs Aircastle reproaches her husband:

What! have you no ambition? no soul? Could you be easy to stand stock-still, whilst your neighbours are advancing all round you? Cottagers are become farmers; farmers are made justices; and folks that travelled barefoot to London, roll down again in their coaches and chariots; but still we stick!

That Britain was rich was not in doubt. Whether the prosperity was solidly based was a more open question. Gouverneur Morris, the distinguished American diplomat and politician, in London in 1790 to negotiate a commercial treaty, wrote to President Washington that 'Perhaps there never was a moment in which this country felt herself greater.' But – in another letter – he said that 'The supposed prosperity of this country is a bubble', that 'Britain resembles a very fine but very complicated machine. It goes well and tells truly the year, day, hour and second but the least accident to a part will derange the whole.' To other Americans, luxury and extravagance had reached such a pitch as to have corrupted the nation. Of no one was that more true than the American loyalists who stood by the Crown during the War of Independence and who lived out a sad exile in London. To Peter Van Schaack, corruption pervaded every channel of power: 'The great officers [of state] are abandoned to luxury and dissipation . . . I find the British spirit extinct.'

The new riches, the sense of their brittleness, the recasting of attitudes to money and display, the indifference to traditional values, including that of social 'subordination', seemed to many embodied in two groups of people who erupted on to the London scene – the 'nabobs' from India and the 'West Indians' from the sugar islands of the Caribbean. Perhaps no words can better illustrate their importance than those of Disraeli in *Endymion*, writing of society in 1827. 'The great world then,' he says, 'consisted mainly of the great landed aristocracy, who had quite absorbed the nabobs of India, and had nearly appropriated the huge West Indian fortunes.' Such words could not have been written about the Josiah Childs and Stephen Foxes, the new rich of the Restoration. That these people, British, but so alien in attitude and behaviour, would be absorbed by no means appeared a foregone conclusion at the time. Would they in the end really want to accept the old conventions with which few of them had more than the most meagre acquaintance? Why, with their vast wealth, should they not buy up the House of Commons? Lord Chesterfield offered a broker £2,500 (£285,000 in today's money) in 1767 for a parliamentary seat for his son. The broker laughed; East and West Indians had pushed up prices, sometimes to two or three times that level. William Pitt the elder – incidentally grandson of the

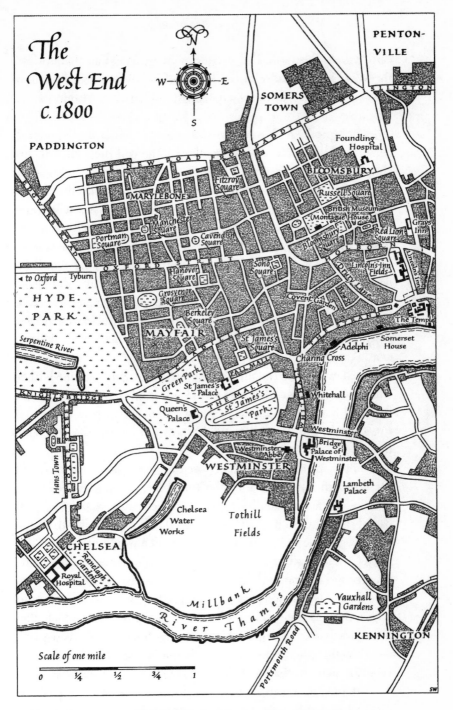

The West End, about 1800. From Christopher
Hibbert, *London: The Biography of a City*, 1969.

early nabob 'Diamond Pitt' – close as he was to William Beckford, the West Indian leader in the House of Commons, pondered how private hereditary fortunes could withstand 'such a torrent of corruption'.

The typical nabob was not in the mould of Mr Law, Talleyrand's generous friend. He was more like Matthew Mite, the principal character in Foote's play *The Nabob* of 1778. The haughty Lady Oldham rebukes her husband for asking help of his brother who is in trade. She concedes that younger brothers may have little choice in what they do, but in words which might come straight from the mouth of Mrs Thrale, pronounces that 'there is a nicety, a delicacy, an elevation of sentiment, in this case, which people who have narrowed their notions with commerce, and considered during the course of their lives their interest alone, will scarce comprehend.' When the family gets down to it, however, their differences shrivel away when confronted by a nabob, a man who, in Lady Oldham's words, 'came thundering among us . . . profusely scattering the spoils of ruined provinces.' A man too of the lowest origins, for Sir Matthew Mite was born Mat Mite, son of old John and Margery Mite at the Sow and Sausage in St Mary Axe, who stole tarts from the man at Pye-Corner, and was sent to the East for fear he would go from bad to worse.

As it happened, the threat posed by the nabobs was transient. Only superficially were they the forerunners of the Anglo-Indian families of the nineteenth and twentieth centuries, who – slightly to paraphrase Correlli Barnett – felt a moral responsibility for the future of India and the welfare of her peoples which would have astonished Lord Clive. They bought large houses and entertained lavishly in the country and in London, but they founded no dynasties. Partly it was that their interests were short term, partly that the opportunity for such wealth as theirs did not last long, and often too because their lives ended sadly and with their fortunes dissipated. Clive himself, who bought a house in Berkeley Square, ended as a suicide. Paul Benfield, who purchased the lease of 19 Grosvenor Square from Lord Thanet, built up a banking business, but ended bankrupt and in exile. General Richard Smith, on whom Foote is supposed to have based his nabob character Matthew Mite, was in continual trouble for bribing electors, and finished his life in obscurity, having lost £180,000 along the way to Charles James Fox at cards. Warren Hastings became the focus of moral outrage, to an extent the scapegoat for his fellows.

There was some overlap between East and West Indians, with a number of families holding interests in both the Caribbean trade and the East India Company. In London, they might live next door to each other, not least in the melting pot of Soho Square, which in the 1760s and 1770s housed the nabobs John Grant and Crisp Molyneux, and the West Indians William Beckford and Sir George Pigot. But the nabobs were not so much City families with overseas investments as adventurers intent on making a fortune on the spot which they could bring home with them. The West Indians were a different matter. The basis of their wealth was sugar plantations worked by slave labour which some families had owned since the seventeenth century. Eric Williams, in his *Capitalism and Slavery*, compared the place of sugar in the eighteenth-century economy to that held by steel in the nineteenth, and oil in the twentieth. The ramifications of this vital product ran wide and deep, involving bankers, merchants and rentiers as well as planters and shippers, and numerous ordinary middle-class families. West Indians and those with West Indian interests appear in Jane Austen, with the Northamptonshire baronet Sir Thomas Bertram in *Mansfield Park* who goes on a lengthy business trip to his plantation in Antigua, and the seventeen-year-old, 'half-mulatto' Miss Lambe in the unfinished *Sanditon*. Not all were rich: at the same time – October 1779 – as he is urging Hester Thrale to do her duty by Southwark, Dr Johnson wants her to persuade her husband to help 'some old gentlewomen at the next door [who] are in very great distress'. They lived on a small annuity from Jamaica which could no longer be relied on since the French appeared likely at any moment to capture the island. Many of the West Indians never went near their plantations. The Lascelles family were sugar factors and bankers. During the last part of the eighteenth century there were three Lascelles MPs in the House of Commons, none of whom, as far as it is known, ever visited the family's Barbados estates.

Richard Cumberland in his play *The West Indian* was noticeably kinder to his eponymous hero than Foote was to Matthew Mite. The West Indians were flamboyant and ostentatious, but because of the nature of their wealth were not so much violent as harsh. Nevertheless, just as the old rich sensed that too many of the vices of the Orient had rubbed off on the British who returned from India, so did they remark an alien streak in the West Indians with their singsong accents and sallow complexions. Most prominent of all were the Beckfords, who leave behind them two of the most tangible monuments to West Indian wealth and power. One is a house on the corner of Soho Square, now 1 Greek Street, built by Richard Beckford in 1750, which is still in place, open to the public, with magnificent plasterwork ceilings and walls. The other, very striking, is at the Guildhall, in the form of a giant statue of Richard's brother, William Beckford, one of a group which otherwise honours only the very greatest of British heroes – Churchill, Nelson, Wellington and the two Pitts. Beckford – always excluding Alexander Hamilton – was the dominating figure produced by the British Caribbean islands. He was twice Lord Mayor, richer than most of the peerage and owned more land than most dukes. He also embodied the contradictions in the position of the West Indians in British society. He is both commemorated in a pantheon of Britishness, and, though married to the grand-daughter of the sixth Earl of Abercorn, was also a figure quite at odds with traditional patrician society. In the House of Commons Beckford not only denounced the 'little paltry rotten boroughs', but demanded 'as to your nobility, about 1,200 men of quality, what are they to the body of the nation? Why, Sir, they are subalterns . . . they receive more from the public than they pay to it. If you were to cast up all their accounts and fairly state the balance, they would turn out debtors to the public for more than a third of their income.' It is easy to see why people were nervous. In the countryside Beckford stood out uncomfortably. At Fonthill, the estate he bought in Wiltshire, there were too many girls around; and he was judged excessively louche by his neighbours.

Yet to the West Indians, Britain was Home. That, the difficult climate of the tropics, and the need to educate their children, led them back, to the extent that in 1778 an anonymous West Indian was writing that few proprietors stayed on in the islands who could afford to move to Britain. It remained of course of overriding importance to protect the capital they had invested in the plantations or in trade with the Caribbean. It was vital to maintain their monopoly on the sale of sugar to Britain and to the American colonies – French sugar was much cheaper than British – and to be assured of the support of the government and the Royal Navy. To accomplish this they formed what was perhaps the most effective business lobby in the history of parliament. In the end, the West Indians showed no wish to supplant the old rich; they wanted to join them. Their money, through marriage, sustained many old patrician families whose fortunes were in need of replenishment. In more specifically London terms, their enduring contribution lay in the vital role they played in the building of what to contemporaries seemed a huge, new city – Marylebone.

Henry Fielding in 1752 encapsulated in a few, highly coloured words the movement out of central London:

> Within the memory of many now living the circle of the people of Fascination included the whole parish of Covent Garden and a great part of St Giles in the Fields [Lincoln's Inn Fields area]; but here the enemy broke in and the circle was presently contracted to Leicester Fields and Golden Square. Hence the People of Fashion again retreated before the foe to Hanover Square; whence they were once more driven to Grosvenor Square and even beyond it, and that with so much precipitation, that had they not been stopped by the walls of Hyde Park, it is more than probable they would by this time have arrived at Kensington.

By 1752, the 'people of fashion' had been in Grosvenor Square for a generation, the depression was coming to an end, the old impetus towards growth of the town was reviving, and with even greater intensity. The prosperity which followed the successful ending of the Seven Years War in 1763 was to necessitate more living space for the wealthy, not so much because of pressure exerted by the poor, but because they themselves were more numerous as well as richer than ever. Fashion had once more changed, with the nobility and gentry yet more eager for the pleasures of the capital. In 1777, James Boswell, visiting the Duke of Devonshire's Derbyshire palace of Chatsworth, noted the gradual change of living habits over three generations; whereas the Duke's grandfather had spent nine months a year in the country, and his father six months, he himself spent no more than three.

The infilling of Mayfair was more or less complete. Berkeley Square was finished at last. Piccadilly was built up. Horace Walpole wrote to a friend in 1759: 'When do you come? if it is not soon, you will find a new town. I stared today at Piccadilly like a country squire: there are twenty new stone houses; at first I concluded that all the grooms that used to live there, had got estates and built palaces.' A property boom ends with too many unsold houses on the market, a property depression ends with too few. Extra demand could be satisfied only by building on new land and, almost as inevitably, that land would be the fields and gardens of the parish of St Marylebone, the area which lay around Fielding's 'even beyond', the becalmed enclave of Cavendish Square. A map published by Dodsley in 1761 shows buildings occupying virtually the whole of the south side of Oxford Street (still called Tyburn Road), but the north side, on the ground above Grosvenor Square, remains largely open country. Opposite our Bond Street tube station, at what became Stratford Place, was land belonging to the Corporation of the City of London, on which, until 1736, had stood a modest building grandly named the Lord Mayor's Banqueting House, a relic of the days when the City was supplied with water from conduits in Marylebone. Here, once a year, the Lord Mayor arrived to inspect the conduit heads, and then to do some hunting and hold a banquet. Further on, beyond Marylebone Lane, was the old Harley estate, with Oxford Street – called after Edward Harley, Lord Oxford – built up on both sides, and with the Cavendish Square development to the north.

At the end of the seventeenth century, Marylebone was a village of less than 100 houses flung out along Marylebone Lane, with its manor house and parish church at the top end of our Marylebone High Street. It grew as time went on, but remained firmly 'country'. In October 1728, the *Daily Journal* referred to people arriving in London from their country houses in Marylebone. The manor house was originally a hunting box used as an occasional royal residence in the reigns of Mary and Elizabeth. In James I's time, the freehold of the manor and its park had been bought by Edward Forsett, whose grandson in 1708 sold it to the Duke of Newcastle for £17,500 (£2

The Lord Mayor's Banqueting House, on the site of
what is now Stratford Place on the north side of
Oxford Street, in 1750. Reproduced from Walford, *Old
and New London*, 1897, vol. iv.

million today). By then, the manor house had been converted into a
school. The headmaster, the Revd John Fountayne, made it one of
the best in London, much patronized by the West End rich. The
gardens had become the Marylebone pleasure gardens which, in one
form or another, had flourished since the middle of the seventeenth
century, and improved steadily afterwards to take advantage of the
increased accessibility of Marylebone, and of the presence of potential
customers from the Cavendish Square area. There was in fact a
connecting footpath which ran from the corner of Wigmore Street
and Harley Street. Marylebone Gardens were firmly established as a
well-known London resort. Henry Fielding's brother, the much
respected London magistrate Sir John Fielding, declared that Londoners should have no need of Mrs Cornelys's Soho entertainments
when they had Ranelagh with its music and fireworks, and

Marylebone with its music, wine and plum cakes. Still, Marylebone Gardens could not match Ranelagh in terms of high fashion and there was the disadvantage that the fields by Dagetts Farm, just west and beyond the gardens, and elsewhere, were notoriously dangerous. At one stage, the proprietor of the gardens was obliged to hire a guard of soldiers to protect his customers on their way to and from London.

Marylebone was in an odd situation. It was not, as were Kensington and Chelsea and Pimlico, shielded from the great town by natural barriers; to the contrary, it lay for decades, largely rural, staring London in the face across Oxford Street. And the fact of Oxford Street, and of Edgware Road on its western flank, involved it in intolerable expense, for Marylebone was required to pay half the upkeep of these busy metropolitan highways. 'Turnpiking' produced tolls, but even so the costs for roads were only lightened, not abolished. Then there were uncomfortable relations with the grandees of Cavendish Square, who had nothing in common with the tradesmen who composed the parish vestry. At least they left the tradesmen in place, since they regarded it as beneath their dignity to mix directly in local politics. While Cavendish Square must have added something to general prosperity, it also added to the vestry's costs for poor relief, since many of the labourers and craftsmen employed in its building had settled at the eastern end of Oxford Street. The existing churchyards could not cope with increased burials and it was necessary to find a new burial ground and to spend money on walling it in. More parish constables were needed, and there was the expense of the upkeep of a new courthouse, although the building itself was supplied free by Lord Oxford. In fact, until an act of parliament in 1756, Marylebone was 'having to cope with a town but basically coping as a village'.

The two principal landowners in Marylebone, or, to be more precise, in that part of the original great sprawling parish which today we think of as Marylebone, were the Duke of Portland, proprietor of the old Harley estate, and – to the west, towards Marble Arch – the Portman family. Portland was the legatee through the marriage in 1734 of the second duke with Margaret Cavendish Harley, daughter and heiress of the Lord Harley, later the second Earl of Oxford, from whom Chandos had bought his land, and of his heiress wife Henrietta, daughter of the Duke of Newcastle. The Portmans were an old established and wealthy Dorset family, closely associated with the Berkeleys, who originally obtained their land from the Crown in the sixteenth century when Sir William Portman was Lord Chief Justice. Alongside these two large landowners were several smaller ones, the City Corporation in the Stratford Place enclave, the Milners, the Hope Edwards and the Berners. It was the last of these who launched the second great wave of London's expansion. The Berners land at the eastern end of Oxford Street had been bought in 1654 by Josias Berners, the son of a Clerkenwell shopkeeper. The family lived in Hertfordshire, doing little with their London property until William Berners signed a contract with a gardener turned builder, Thomas Hubble, whereby he constructed the sewers and Hubble demolished what old buildings there were and erected new ones. Between 1750 and 1763 the existing streets, notably Berners Street, came into being and the site of the Middlesex Hospital was let on a 999-year lease.

It would be repetitive to describe in detail contemporaries' reactions to the construction of Marylebone. Defoe's words on west London in the 1720s – 'the world full of bricklayers and labourers; who . . . like gardeners . . . dig a hole, put in a few bricks, and presently there goes up a house' – would need no modification. People of the time, and historians later, have talked of Marylebone as one huge building site, and of 'houses [which] rose like exhalations'. What was new, however, was the scale. Later on, Macaulay, speaking on the Reform Bill, expressed it in this way, imagining himself showing London to a stranger:

> I would conduct him through that immense city which lies to the north of Great Russell Street and Oxford Street, a city superior in size and in population to the capitals of many mighty kingdoms; and probably superior in opulence, intelligence, and general respectability, to any city in the world.

At the start, the prosperous families who lived up at the top near the old manor house, as yet remote from the building works, still 'kept their coaches, and . . . considered themselves to be living in the country.' Marylebone, though, was not a suburb in the sense of

Kensington, where the local houses were often supplemented by winter accommodation in Mayfair. It was part of the district's attraction that it combined easy access to central London with space to allow for substantial town houses.

In 1772 Boswell arrived in London after a lengthy stay in his native Scotland. He went to look at Portman Square and at some of the new streets: 'The increase of London is prodigious. It is really become too large.' So he wrote in his journal. 'The consequence is that people live at such a distance from each other that it is very inconvenient for them to meet.' The old Chandos reservoir disappeared, and Marylebone Gardens – which gave room for Harley Street to take proper shape – as also did the executions at Tyburn with their boisterous crowds. Long streets were laid down, and the customary squares. As the Duke of Portland developed his land, so did Henry William Portman, who succeeded to his family's estates in 1761. In 1765, when the first Portman land agreements were signed, more land contracts were registered in Middlesex than in any year since 1725. Large houses appeared. One was the Duke of Manchester's Manchester House, which became the centre of the square which bears his name, and was the forerunner of Hertford House, now the museum for the Wallace Collection. Another was Stratford House, named for Edward Stratford, Earl of Aldborough, built on the City of London land at the bottom of Marylebone Lane. It is still there, standing back genteelly from Oxford Street, and now called Derby House after a later owner. However, the nucleus of the Portman estate was Portman Square, the equivalent of Cavendish Square to the Portlands and Grosvenor Square to the Grosvenors.

Portman Square and Portland Place were intended for the very rich. The contractor with the major share in their building, John Elwes, born Megot, was himself a very wealthy man who had inherited from his father, a Southwark brewer, some property around the Haymarket. He was also without question the most eccentric developer in London's history. Elwes possessed charming manners, was an enthusiastic fox hunter, an MP and a voracious gambler – so far then a characteristic wealthy gentleman of his time. Where gambling debts were owed to him, he could also be generous. However, he was also a miser, an extreme miser, who so fascinated his contemporaries that a book published about him soon after his death was reprinted again and again. The miserliness was congenital: his mother was left £100,000 by her husband but, we are told, starved herself to death; his uncle, immensely rich, presented 'the most perfect picture of human penury that ever existed'. Elwes, devoted to the uncle, inherited his fortune, changed his name to the uncle's, and steadily invested in Marylebone real estate. There are many stories told of him. That, for instance, he happily wore an old cast-off wig he picked up out of a country ditch; that he disapproved of education for his sons on the grounds that 'Putting things into people's heads was the sure way to take money out of their pockets.' He resented turnpike roads, and one day, returning from Newmarket and obliging his companion to follow him, he veered suddenly off the road up a precipitous bank. Never pay a toll if you can avoid it, he explained afterwards to his exhausted friend. At one stage during his development of Marylebone property, Elwes did without a permanent London house of his own, settling into whichever of his properties happened to be empty. Should a tenant present himself, he happily moved out at a minute's notice, taking with him a couple of beds, a pair of chairs, a table, and the old woman who looked after him. One summer in his old age he spent at a house belonging to him in Welbeck Street, visiting those of his properties round about where work was in progress. He got up at 4 a.m. and would sit down happily on the steps of one or other of these houses, patiently waiting for the workmen to arrive. To the neighbours he was known as the 'old carpenter'.

The early development of Marylebone coincides with a period of especial excellence in London building, perhaps for domestic architecture the greatest period of all. The eminent architectural historian Sir John Summerson in his *Georgian London* singles out four houses designed by Robert Adam in the 1770s as perhaps representing 'the highest point of imagination and artistry in the handling of the London house ... The rooms in an Adam house are ... a harmony of spaces – a harmony in which many contrasts reside.' They are, he goes on, devised for an elaborate social parade, built for public life, for continual entertaining. These houses are: 20 St James's Square, built for Sir Watkin Williams Wynn (which is partially preserved); Derby House in Grosvenor Square (demolished); and two in Marylebone – Chandos House, built close by Cavendish Square for the third Duke of Chandos, and Home House in Portman Square, although the exterior there was designed by James Wyatt. Both of these last two survive.

That such a sample should turn up so large a proportion of survivors is a surprise. Almost as a matter of course, houses, and buildings in general, were demolished or left to rot once they had served their original purpose. Many never even had time to become obsolete; they were burned down while in their full glory. Even if the disaster of 1666 is ignored, the victims of fire make a formidable list. One of the last of the aristocratic City mansions, Lord Bridgwater's house in the Barbican, burned down in 1687. In the West End there perished the highly admired Montagu House in Bloomsbury, and Arlington House, the predecessor of Buckingham House. The palace of Whitehall, seriously damaged by fire in 1691, was altogether destroyed seven years later. In the eighteenth century went Powis House in Great Ormond Street and Devonshire House (originally Berkeley House) in Piccadilly, and there was a very serious fire in Exchange Alley in the City in 1748. One of the most sensational fires destroyed the Pantheon assembly rooms on Oxford Street in 1792. The Pantheon had opened to a gathering of 1,500 guests twenty years before and had – with assistance from exasperated Soho neighbours – put Mrs Cornelys out of business. 'Imagine Balbec in all its glory,' wrote Horace Walpole of this amazing building with its main hall a rotunda based on Santa Sophia. But from now on, the list of fire casualties diminishes as the stringent provisions set for new buildings by the 1774 Building Act took effect. Marylebone was by and large to be a safer place than its predecessors.

Home House, one of the first houses to be built to the new standard, is placed at the northern end of Portman Square. Its flank, over Gloucester Place, faced Montagu House. Neither house was speculative – both were made to order and both were assessed at a rateable value (in 1784) of £600. They differed architecturally: Montagu House was designed not by Adam but by James (Athenian) Stuart, and Horace Walpole preferred it – disliking, as he said, 'all the harlequinades of Adam which never let the eye repose a moment'. Otherwise, they most obviously differed in that while, like most

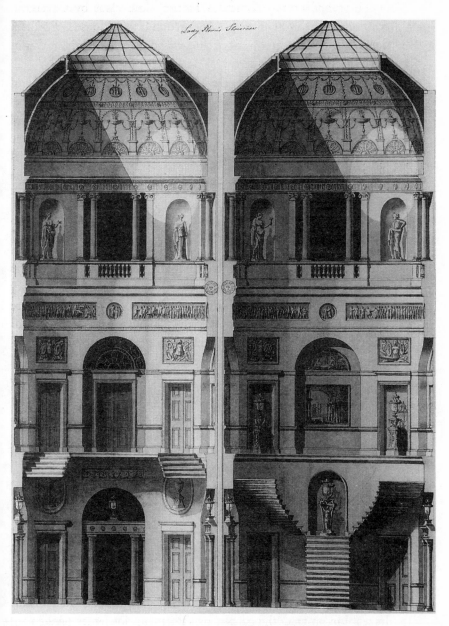

Lady Home's staircase at Home House, Portman
Square, designed by Robert Adam in the mid-1770s.

of the grandest town houses, Montagu House was free-standing, positioned within its own grounds, Home House formed part of a terrace. In this seemingly more modest category, however, it was in the excellent company of the Williams Wynn house and Norfolk House in St James's Square, Derby House in Grosvenor Square and the smaller but superb Clermont House by William Kent in Berkeley Square. The contrast between the two houses was reflected in the antipathy that existed between their owners. Montagu House was built for a Tyneside coal owner, the intellectual and society hostess Mrs Elizabeth Montagu, who moved there from Mayfair. Home House belonged to the Countess of Home who previously occupied a house on the south side of Portman Square.

Lady Home was a West Indian and, as such, correlates more closely with the nature of this new area of London. She was born Gibbons of Jamaica, and married first James Lawes, elder son of the island's governor, and, after his death, Lord Home, a husband who rapidly disappeared from the scene. Home House provided a natural centre for West Indians. There were excellent practical reasons for this convergence on the new district. The 1760s and 1770s were the time when the planters and their families thronged to London, awash with money, seemingly like the hero of Cumberland's play *The West Indian*, which opened in 1771, who 'has rum and sugar enough belonging to him, to make all the water in the Thames into punch'. Like the Jews and before them the Huguenots, like most minorities in fact, they formed a clique, in their case with a sense of community based not just on their situation in London, but on the clan-like family ties which had supported them in the islands. A number, such as the rich and influential Beeston Long, lived on their office premises in the City, in Long's case in some state at 17 Bishopsgate. But, correctly, in the public mind, Marylebone and the West Indians became closely identified. When, in *Mansfield Park*, Sir Thomas Bertram's elder daughter marries, she and her husband take a house in Wimpole Street which had recently belonged to 'Lady Lascelles'. In real life, in 1784, the gardener of Portman Square prepared a list of residents. It was far from comprehensive; possibly it comprised only those he knew personally. Nevertheless, the weighting is significant. Those on the list were: William Beckford (the son, the future 'caliph

The Custom House Quay, painted by Samuel Scott in
1757. Through London's docks passed the immense
imports of West Indian sugar that created some of the
largest of eighteenth-century fortunes.

of Fonthill'), Mrs William Beckford senior (the widow), Lady Home, Lord Maynard, Mr Erle Drax, Sir Peter Parker, Admiral Lord Rodney, the Earl of Tankerville, the Earl of Middleton, Lady Egmont, the Earl of Ducie and Samuel Whitbread. Of these twelve, the first seven owned West Indian plantations. It seems only fitting then that both of the principal Marylebone landlords acquired West Indian connections: Edward Berkeley Portman married Lady Emma Lascelles; and the Howard de Waldens, who inherited from the Portlands in the late nineteenth century, are descended from the Ellises and Palmers, both important Jamaican families.

The West Indian connection with Marylebone was to last for many years, as long perhaps as the description held anything other than an historical meaning. By the early nineteenth century, as a result of a fall in sugar prices, the effect of absentee landlordism, and then in the 1830s of slave emancipation, sugar wealth thinned to a shadow of what it once had been. The model to take of a West Indian

Marylebone from the site of present-day Wigmore Street, in 1750. Reproduced in Walford, *Old and New London*, 1897, vol. iv.

would less resemble the Beckfords than Edward Moulton-Barrett, father of Elizabeth Barrett Browning, a member of one of the most important slave-owning families in the Caribbean. Financial pressures drove him and his family from the country to London, to Marylebone. While Elizabeth, as a semi-invalid, was receiving Robert Browning (also descended from a West Indian family) at 50 Wimpole Street, Moulton-Barrett was at his office struggling to keep afloat what had once been a flourishing business. Increasingly one would have heard more of East Indians, and it has been computed that in the early nineteenth century 80 per cent of East India Company directors lived in Marylebone. If nabobs of the old school had run their course, the district shared with St John's Wood a continuing appeal for returned Anglo-Indians.

As time goes on, however, one senses a loss of vitality. Marylebone was the largest, and for many years the wealthiest, of London's parishes, but it was no longer exciting. London streamed on by.

6

Migration to the North

*

By the mid-eighteenth century, the boundaries of the West End were sharply defined on three of its four sides. To the east there was a shading off into commercial and financial London; on the south the Thames formed a natural barrier; to the west were the two parks, St James's and Hyde Park; and to the north the frontier of Oxford Street, pierced only by the suburbs of Cavendish Square and Blooms-bury. Yet even without foreknowledge of the imminent establishment of a new town at Marylebone, it was evident that the northern line could not hold, and that Oxford Street, increasingly hemmed in by houses and beset by traffic, could no longer fulfil its function as the city's northern bypass. Thus, in 1755, a group of gentlemen, farmers and tradesmen, representing the villages of Paddington, St Marylebone and Islington and other parishes which lay along the northern edge of London, combined to present a bill to parliament sanctioning the construction of a new and uncluttered highway half a mile or so to the north. The New Road, as it was to be called, would run from Paddington to Islington and would be built jointly by the Marylebone and Islington turnpike trusts. It would, so its sponsors claimed, improve communication between Essex and Middlesex, and would free London streets from congestion, not least from the herds of cattle driven through on their way to the market at Smithfield. It was also argued – and memories of Prince Charles Edward and the Forty-Five were very recent – that the road would provide a line of defence in the event of war, and allow easy movement of troops.

The New Road ran through farmland, with landowners along the way usually happy enough to be bought out; after all, they gained

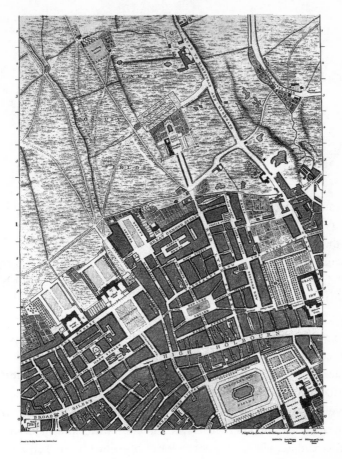

The northern limits of London in 1746. From the map
by John Rocque.

not only compensation but improved communications. The Duke of
Grafton was one, and Grafton Way and Grafton Mews, just south
of Euston Road, mark the position of his fields. The most prominent
objector was the Duke of Bedford on his estate in Bloomsbury, half
a mile to the south. John, fourth Duke of Bedford, grandson of
Rachel Russell, was immensely rich, very grand socially, and one of
the most important politicians of his day. Though not a man of
exceptional ability, by a shrewd employment of his wealth he put
together and sustained a powerful political faction; over many years

147

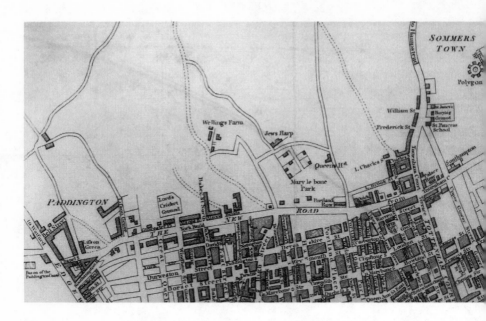

it was difficult to form a government without his support and partici-
pation. He was famously good with money. He rebuilt his great
palace at Woburn and between succeeding as duke on the death of
his elder brother in 1732 and his own death in 1771, he managed to
increase the annual gross rental of the Bloomsbury estate from £3,700
to around £8,000. Nevertheless, he showed no enthusiasm for increasing its size, which he was content to leave much as he had found it,
a strip running two hundred yards north of Holborn along Great
Russell Street with hardly more than the two great buildings of
Bedford House and Montagu House (bought by the government for
– along with the smaller Thanet House – the British Museum)
standing out into the countryside. Once the New Road was in place,
Bedford accepted the fact and cut a private drive – following the line
of today's Southampton Row and Woburn Place – out through his
fields to join it, so shortening his journey to Woburn. But he did not
at all welcome it. Even taking account of the fact that in the 1750s
demand for building land had yet to recover, his was an unusual
attitude for a London landowner. As a breed the landowners were
likely to greet with enthusiasm any circumstances which made it
profitable to convert their farmland into urban housing.

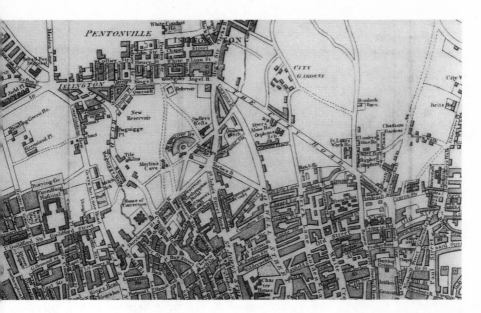

London's first bypass: the New Road from Paddington
← to Islington, 1755. A detail of a plan from B. Lambert,
History of London, 1806.

Nevertheless, the Duke's reaction is understandable; he did not
need the money and was comfortably settled. He resented the disturbance to his fields, to the arable land and to the pasture on which he
kept sheep and cattle brought up from Woburn and then sent on to
the Smithfield market. He was concerned about his tenants. With
good reason, for they had shown themselves extremely sensitive about
anything they regarded as intrusion on what they considered to be
an exclusive private estate. Some were ready complainers about traffic,
whether it passed along Holborn or took short cuts through Bloomsbury. Others objected over unruly behaviour in and around the local
market. The fields allegedly threatened by the New Road were the
occasion of many difficulties. It was not just a matter of keeping out
vagrants; there were complaints about 'a vile rabble of idle and
disorderly people' – sometimes insufficiently dressed – playing cricket
and suchlike games, and about boys flying kites and bathing in the
ponds. A Mrs Nash warned that if things did not improve, 'We must
all leave our homes, there is no bearing of it.' There was the vociferous

Miss Capper, the lessee of the bulk of the Duke's farmland, who declared that in view of the dust and dirt the New Road would cause, she was going to demand a reduction in her rent. She went further and wrote a submission on the subject to the House of Commons committee considering the New Road bill. (There is also a Capper Street almost next door to the Graftons.) And then what would happen to the view, for the road would certainly attract building? That was a question which affected the leaseholders in Bloomsbury Square and the Duke directly at Bedford House (even though Horace Walpole dismissed the Duke's personal objection on the grounds that he seldom came to London and anyway was half-blind). The road went ahead, made wider than planned as a result of the Duke's representations, and with a prohibition on buildings southwards towards Bloomsbury.

While happily the military possibilities of the road were never tested, the other advantages claimed for it were thoroughly justified.

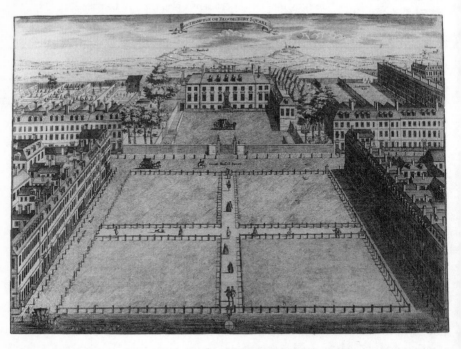

Bedford House and Bloomsbury Square. Engraving by Sutton Nicholls, 1754.

The New Road, while its name may be forgotten, remains even now one of the most important of London thoroughfares, its route traced by Marylebone Road and Euston Road – with its railway stations of Euston, King's Cross and St Pancras – and then by Pentonville Road leading on to the Angel at Islington. Finally, by an extension built virtually at the same time, there is a connection with the City of London by means of the City Road. The bonds between the metropolis and the outlying parishes were tightened and so were those that linked the parishes more closely together. In 1766, John Gwynn in his *London and Westminster Improved*, a book of great imagination and skill which put forward detailed proposals for a formal approach to the planning of London, saw the New Road as providing a natural boundary for restraining 'the rage of building'. That, however, it did not do.

For Islington, the effect of the New Road was dramatic. It stood now at a junction of the main roads leading west and south. And north as well, for the Great North Road ran up through the main street of Islington village. At the Peacock Inn, near the Angel, the northbound mail coaches collected passengers who arrived from the West End. By the 1790s, there were two local stagecoaches providing hourly return services to the City. Islington, being a mile from the City walls, had probably always attracted day-trippers from London. To Samuel Pepys it was the culmination of what he called his 'Grand Tour', as well as being the location of the King's Head, one of his favourite inns. Just outside the parish boundary in Clerkenwell, over the road from the Angel Inn, was the spa of Sadler's Wells, opened in 1683 by a Mr Sadler, and known variously in its time as Sadler's Music House, the Islington Spa, and the 'new Tunbridge Wells'. Nearby was another spa, Bagnigge Wells. Most of all, however, Islington's economy relied on milk production. It was 'London's Dairy', and a good proportion of its population seems to have been cows. It was a place for farmhouses rather than suburban palaces. Not even the ancient manor houses all survived into the eighteenth century: that of Barnsbury, for instance, early disappeared and seems not to have been occupied later than the fourteenth century. To its west, archaeologists have identified a moated site, but it is probable that it harboured nothing more exalted than a farm. A glance at an early nineteenth-century map may give a different impression, for it will show some individual houses of reasonable size set in the countryside. There is Copenhagen House, which was, though, just tea gardens; there is Cream Hall, but that, as its name suggests, was a farm, though later on turned into a villa; Upper Place was of no consequence. For the mansions, it was best to go over to Stoke Newington. The village of Islington – thunderous with traffic on its way to the docks – offered some fine buildings which originally housed people of means, but they were now mostly converted into inns and shops. There was, however, one outstanding exception, although by the eighteenth century it was much decayed: this was the fifteenth-century manor house of Canonbury, of which the tower, sixty foot high, still remains. In its best days, the house was very large and apparently occupied the whole of what is now Canonbury Place. At the beginning of the seventeenth century, the Canonbury and Clerkenwell manors with Crosby Hall in the City passed to the Comptons, earls of Northampton, through the marriage of Henry, Lord Compton, with Elizabeth, daughter of the immensely rich City merchant Sir John Spencer. There is a famous romantic tale attached to this union, which took place at a time when romantic marriages among the rich were in very short supply. The father, it goes, objected, and the couple eloped, with Compton disguised as a baker's boy and Elizabeth descending Canonbury tower in a baker's basket. Sadly, the story has been discredited. But romantic or not, the marriage established the Comptons, earls and later marquesses of North-ampton, as one of the major landowners, and subsequently landlords, of London until they sold their Islington property in 1954. They were, though, absentee like other proprietors of important London estates. After the Restoration, their London houses were to be found in other parts of town – in Northampton Square, Clerkenwell; in Lincoln's Inn Fields; in Bloomsbury Square; and, in the eighteenth century, in Marylebone – but not in Canonbury. In their absence, the manor house deteriorated, divided into separate apartments, with, so Daniel Lysons relates in his *The Environs of London* (1810–11 edition), 'the names of the lodgers being on the doors as in a College staircase or inn of court'. Among the later tenants were Speaker Onslow, the friend of the Duke of Chandos, and Oliver Goldsmith.

In 1770, there appeared on the scene an entrepreneurial stock-
broker named John Dawes, who acquired from the Lord Northampton of the day a sixty-one-year lease on a portion of the manor
buildings and some surrounding land. He demolished what was there
and put up modern buildings. Restless, he then sold out, and moved
up the hill to Highbury, where he acquired the manor, replacing the
manor house with a large new mansion, and selling building leases
on the lands around. By the 1790s (when Dawes was dead and his
property mainly disposed of to pay his debts), builders had completed
what is now Highbury Place and part of Highbury Terrace. This was
high and healthy land which, with the handsome new houses, soon
attracted wealthy residents, to whom their new district seemed definitely superior to Islington in general. In the 1820s, they installed
gates to create private roadways, and to block off Highbury from the
plebeian Holloway Road. In true West End fashion, they went a step
further and presented a bill to parliament, attempting to obtain a
local act which would give them responsibility for their own lighting
and security, and exemption from the general parish rate. Their bill,
however, was rejected.

Highbury and the acres of elegant squares and terraces which
followed it – Canonbury Square, Lonsdale Square, Myddelton
Square, some of Barnsbury, among the finest – constitute an impressive memorial to their builders and to the wealthy and well-to-do of
Islington. Many of them now stand on a par with the West End,
indeed they are usually better preserved, and it would be easy sometimes for a visitor to believe himself in Marylebone or Bayswater.
And the houses which front the stretch of the New River in Canonbury
Grove might be mistaken for those on the eastern side of Holland
Park. The New River Canal, and the statue of its founder, the early
seventeenth-century entrepreneur Sir Hugh Myddelton, which stands
a few hundred yards up from the Angel tube station at the divide of
Upper Street and Essex Road, are other monuments to Islington's
prosperity and, even more, to the prosperity of much of London
itself. The New River was a ten-foot-wide, forty-mile-long canal
carrying water down from a source near Ware in Hertfordshire, which
became the main water supplier to the City and north London. The
New River Company, which constructed it and owned it, ultimately

Rural Islington from C. and J. Greenwood, *Map of London . . .* of 1827.

Haymaking in the 1770s as the terraces make their
appearance on the Canonbury Estate, Islington, by
R. Dodd. Engraved by R. Pollard and J. Jukes, 1787.

became the largest water company in Europe as well as a shrewd
diversifier into real estate, and was to make large fortunes for its
shareholders, notably the Holford family, builders and owners of the
most spectacular of London's nineteenth-century private palaces.

Yet for all the similarities to West End architecture, a walk down
the hill nowadays from Canonbury, with the soaring tower of Canary
Wharf almost straight ahead, is an immediate reminder of how close
Islington is to the City. By the nineteenth century, City businessmen
were prepared to separate office and home. And there were many
more of them than in the past. The urban development which gripped
Islington by the middle of the century was in a sense an extension of
the district's traditional role: from being a resort for City families on
a day out, it turned into their dormitory and retirement home. It was
near, and so much healthier and prettier than the smog-bound town.
David Hughson, writing in the first decade of that century, enthused

that the views from Islington formed a combination of beauty rarely to be met with in any village. However, he goes on,

> this will in all probability soon cease, from the rapid progress of the builders, who are extending their works to every spot of unoccupied land surrounding this place and the city of London.

Nevertheless, it was still possible as late as 1835 for a prospectus for 'superior residences' on the Barnsbury estate to describe the area as being of a rather retired character. It was some time before the penalty of being so near town had fully to be paid.

In Kip's view of Beaufort House, Chelsea, the three Kensington mansions, captioned with their names, glimmer on the horizon. Sutton Nicholls adopts the same device in his *London Described* of 1731. In his drawings of the northern London squares, in the distance beyond untouched fields, stand the 'northern heights' inscribed with the names of the hill villages of Islington, Hampstead and Highgate, symbols of Arcadia, the antithesis of urban filth and commotion. It is no surprise, one thinks, that, short-sighted or not, the Duke of Bedford fought so hard against the New Road, or that Lady Home, originally on the south side of Portman Square, moved over to the north. And if the views upwards to the hills were so alluring, what of those the other way about, downwards on London? Hughson lauded the prospect from Islington, while Malcolm, in his *Londinium Redivivum* of virtually the same date, declared that the most perfect and delightful landscape was that from Hampstead Heath when the wind blew from the east.

Like Islington, Hampstead was at one time celebrated for its spas, and in 1700 you could buy Hampstead water by the flask in Fleet Street. There was horse racing on Hampstead Heath. Ned Ward, the journalist who depicted the Strand in its decline, satirized the visitors to Sadler's Wells in a soft-porn pamphlet entitled *A Walk to Islington*, while the playwright Thomas Baker went one better with his comedy *Hampstead Heath*, performed at Drury Lane in 1705, in which he contrasts country and London pleasures, and describes the people to be found. What fine ladies does the place afford, he asks rhetorically:

We have court ladies that are all air and no dress; city ladies that are over-dressed and no air; and country dames with broad brown faces like a Stepney bun; besides an endless number of Fleet-Street sempstresses, that dance minuets in their furbeloe scarfs, and their cloathes hang as loose about them as their reputations.

But the differences between Islington and Hampstead are marked. Hampstead and Highgate were not on the main road nor easily reached; they lacked posting houses or much in the way of inns, nor were they approached through ribbon development. Their topography, the hills on which they stood, protected them. In the case of Highgate the protection was particularly robust, for access up the hill was often impossible in winter. (That may well have been a blessing, since according to one guidebook writer, 'the air of Highgate is so very keen in winter, that many constitutions cannot endure it.') In fact, Francis Bacon, who at one time incidentally rented the great

View from Hampstead in 1760. Reproduced from
Walford, *Old and New London*, 1897, vol. v.

house at Canonbury, died of a chill in 1626 while staying at Highgate. As well as Arundel House, where Bacon died, there was Ashurst House, built about 1710 by a Lord Mayor of London, and two earlier mansions. One was Dorchester House, which was demolished, with its site given over to building, in the 1680s. The other was Lauderdale House, a portion of which still remains in Waterlow Park, built by the seventeenth-century politician the Duke of Lauderdale (builder too of Ham House on the Thames near Hampton Court) and which passed, for a short period before his bankruptcy, to the Mayfair developer John Hinde.

Hampstead's prosperity faded as the spas went out of fashion, to recover in the mid-eighteenth century as it evolved into a popular summer resort. The cycle of decline and revival is vividly illustrated by the experience of the Belsize estate on Haverstock Hill. Belsize House, originally White Lodge, was built as a gentleman's house in the early years of Charles II's reign. It quickly lost its original character, and from the 1680s was occupied by under-tenants. By the early eighteenth century, it was a smart amusement and pleasure garden

A view down Highgate Hill. Engraving by T. M. Baynes, 1822. Access up the hill was often impossible in winter.

with Charles Povey, the sub-tenant who managed it, supplementing its amenities with a chapel where he offered cheap weddings, free if the couple then dined in the gardens. In 1720, a new sub-lessee took over, closed the chapel, but opened a luxurious ballroom and held concerts. He even organized deer hunts. But fashion moved on and prostitutes moved in: renamed The Wilderness, Belsize was called 'a rendezvous of sharpes and strumpets'. Later the house was abandoned, to be rebuilt and, in 1798, leased by Spencer Perceval, who as Prime Minister was assassinated at the House of Commons in 1812. Like Bacon, Perceval, the son-in-law of Hampstead's lord of the manor, was a lawyer as well as a politician. He was, in fact, just one of a number of rich lawyers – and law in the eighteenth century was a profession which made its leading practitioners very rich indeed – who acquired houses on the northern hills. One reason they selected the area was that they were usually self-made men, unencumbered by agricultural estates located miles away from the capital. Among them was Lord Mansfield, the most eminent lawyer of the century, who bought Kenwood, the palace which stands on the edge of Hampstead Heath and now belongs to the National Trust. Robert Adam, who with his brother enlarged and remodelled Kenwood for Mansfield in the 1760s, declared that it displayed 'a noble view . . . of the city of London, Greenwich Hospital, the River Thames, the ships passing up and down . . . To the north-east, and west of the house and terrace, the mountainous villages of Highgate and Hampstead form delightful objects.' At various times, two Lord Chancellors, Erskine and Rosslyn, and a Master of the Rolls, Sir Thomas Clarke, also lived in the district.

John Gwynn in his study of 1766 warned that if the builders were not restrained '. . . we may expect to find that the neighbouring hills of Hampstead and Highgate will soon become considerable parts of the suburbs of London.' His concern was not unfounded, for by the 1820s many small houses had made their appearance in south Hampstead. Yet where Hampstead and Highgate differed not only from Islington but from most other London suburbs was in largely escaping cheap building, a success which was vital to the particular character they possess today. Above all, it was their topography which preserved them, with the Heath and the hills, which did not make

Church Row, Hampstead – fashionable, and with many
of its houses occupied only in summer. From Walford,
Old and New London, 1897, vol. v.

for an easy disposition of squares and terraces. In 1833 the writer Lucy
Aikin, in a letter to a friend, described why she found Hampstead
so congenial:

> . . . in many respects the place unites the advantages and escapes
> the evils both of London and the provincial towns. It is near
> enough to allow its inhabitants to partake in the society, the
> amusements and the accommodations of the capital as freely as
> even the dissipated could desire; whilst it affords pure air, lovely
> scenery, and retired and beautiful walks; and because everyone is
> supposed to have a London set of friends, neighbours do not
> think it necessary, as in the provinces, to force their acquaintance
> upon you.

According to the 1826 edition of *The Original Picture of London*,
a possible disadvantage was that while Hampstead 'abounds in

delightful villas and elegant mansions', many of the houses and parts of houses were let furnished as temporary lodgings. It was a summer resort, and in Church Row, for example, the most fashionable street in the village, while some houses were occupied all the year round, others were used only in summer. Lucy Aikin, however, was of the opinion that the summer residents were often agreeable people and provided a pleasant variety to life.

The lawyers gave place to other professionals and to merchants. Lord Rosslyn's house went to Robert Milligan, a West Indian merchant and then to the Secretary of the General Post Office. Fenton House, close to the centre of the town, and which, like Kenwood, now belongs to the National Trust, is named after a Riga merchant who owned it in the late eighteenth century. The attraction for moneyed newcomers in the nineteenth century was the simulated country houses, set in several acres and embellished with paddocks, parkland and meadows. A writer on the topography of Hampstead in 1814 noted that for successful business and professional men 'the possession of a country villa is incomplete without the addition of something which may be called a *farm*.' It was a pleasant illusion of real country. For never far away were the streets which attached Hampstead to the metropolis, and behind the screen of trees was another house, another villa, another unit of a residential housing estate. Socially, it was not like 'real' country either. There was no indigenous nobility. The lords of the manor were once the earls of Gainsborough but they sold out at the beginning of the eighteenth century. At that time, the original Kenwood, a medium-sized house rated at twenty-four hearths, belonged to the fourth Lord Berkeley of Stratton, who sold out to move to Twickenham. He was succeeded by the Duke of Argyll who, after a gap, sold to George III's Lord Bute, who in turn sold to Mansfield. The earls of Chesterfield were the leaseholders of Belsize, but interested in it only as an investment. The nobility were transitory and absentee. Much the same could be said of the gentry. Landownership was highly concentrated, and excluding the Heath, five estates shared nearly three-quarters of the area. The lords of the manor were the Wilson (later Maryon-Wilson) family, who owned two blocks of land, which together totalled 416 acres, but they lived on their Charlton estate at Greenwich. The

Belsize landowners were the Dean and Chapter of Westminster, while another significant proprietor, the Howard family, also lived elsewhere. Not even the landowners' stewards were on the spot, for they were usually London attorneys.

In such circumstances it would not have been surprising had the landowners proved ready sellers or mass developers themselves. Fortunately they were not – for one thing they were constrained by family settlements, and for another they were rich enough to choose their own pace. The estate at Belsize, for example, reverted to multiple tenancies after Perceval, but it was not given over for building until 1853. A complication was the prevalence of copyhold tenure which gave tenants the right to renew their leases almost automatically on payment of a fine, and so was not easy to reconcile with building leases. The experience of the Tufnell family in Barnsbury, Islington, shows how the problem could be overcome; that of the Maryon-Wilsons in Hampstead how difficult it could prove.

The Tufnells again were absentee landowners, builders of the twin buildings on the north side of Cavendish Square which, distinguished by an Epstein *Mother and Child*, are now the property of a convent. In 1822, amplifying previous private legislation, they applied to parliament for an estate act with two objectives. First, there was the familiar one, the enablement of a trustee to issue building leases during the minority of the heir; the second was to make it possible for him to provide financial incentives to copyholders so that they would agree to development. The Tufnell bill was successful. The elder Sir Thomas Maryon-Wilson, along with his mother, had encouraged his copyholders to build, but he seems to have been hostile to wholesale development. In the 1820s, his son, the younger Sir Thomas, wanted to go further and to grant building leases on Hampstead Heath. His position was compromised by the effect of his father's will, which, by allowing him no more than a life-tenancy, prevented his granting anything more extensive than conventional twenty-one-year agricultural leases. Sir Thomas was a bachelor and possessed no son with whom a resettlement could have been agreed. Still, it was not impossible to come to an understanding with the 'remaindermen', the contingent heirs under his father's will. The real problem was the common land of the Heath. Back in the seventeenth century, Lord Leicester had been permitted to enclose Leicester Fields on the condition that he allowed people with customary rights to continue to use them. Times, however, had changed. It was not just that copyholders and those with equivalent rights were less co-operative and more influential, it was that Hampstead Heath was not considered by Londoners – and their MPs – as just another village common. It was a cherished amenity. Maryon-Wilson's bill of 1829 was rejected, and so were five subsequent bills that he put forward. When, in 1856, parliament passed the Leases and Sales of Settled Estates Act which made it easier to change family settlements, Maryon-Wilson was debarred from its benefits.

Hampstead Heath provides the best-known example of successful resistance to enclosure. But, in fact, all over the suburbs of London in the later nineteenth century a struggle broke out between landowners wishing to exercise what they often considered a traditional right and local communities, more confident than in the past and supported by articulate public opinion. In the eighteenth century, to encroach on common land or land with a poorly defined ownership was, if not a traditional right, a traditional practice, in Britain and on the Continent. (In the dense forests of Aquitaine, enterprising owners until very recently allegedly increased their property and wealth by surreptitiously pushing forward their boundaries year by year.) The Duke of Argyll created his estate of Whitton Park out of Hounslow Heath. Even if, in the end, Hampstead Heath became closely protected, it was not before pieces along the edge had been absorbed into private holdings. There was even a nibbling of the royal parks, at the eastern edge of Green Park and at Hyde Park Corner, legitimized later by the old system of licensing. It was a near thing that Hyde Park and Kensington Gardens survived in their present form. Included in John Gwynn's proposals was one that revived the 'John James' scheme of half a century earlier to build a new royal palace in the park. He suggested too that the New Road be linked to the Thames by a thoroughfare following down Park Lane and beyond: a more perfect situation, he thought, could hardly be conceived of for 'persons of distinction'. Shortly before his death in 1809, John Fordyce, the Surveyor-General of Land Revenues with responsibility for the royal lands, drew up a more modest plan whereby nine large mansions with stables, offices and gardens were to be established within the park walls, facing Park Lane at its northern end. In the 1820s the full-blown proposal was revived again, apparently much to the excitement of the always excitable George IV.

As it happened, the most sweeping development of the time, indeed of any time in London's history since the Great Fire, took place on Crown land and its approaches. Its origin was in relation to the ancient hunting grounds of Marylebone Fields, our Regent's Park, which were leased to the Duke of Portland until 1811 and sublet by him to farmers. The Duke's request for a renewal of his lease was opposed by Fordyce, and after Fordyce's death, by his successor – who held a different title – John Nash. Two alternative proposals for the development of the fields were put forward. One of them, while allowing for some villas, advocated that the familiar grid of adjoining Marylebone be extended. Nash, whose scheme was accepted, urged something revolutionary, a country park with grand houses for the rich. It was to be more planned and more extravagant than 'an assemblage of villas and shrubberies like Hampstead, Highgate, Clapham-Common and other purlieus of the Town.' But on its own scale it was based on the same premise, that the rich would prefer open spaces with all their country dirt to London squares however quiet and protected. It was after all the Romantic Age, when poets and painters were opening fresh eyes on Nature and its charms.

John Nash, aged fifty-seven when he succeeded Fordyce, was a highly experienced architect and developer in both London and the country. He regarded with dismay the policy of the landowners whose properties bordered Marylebone Fields. There was Mr Portman, who had so far discarded the high standards he had imposed on contractors for his main estate as to let his land north of the New Road to David Porter, a local chimney sweep turned developer, with scarcely a restriction on the standard or type of building to be erected. There was Lord Southampton – a different family from the original Bloomsbury developer – who in 1809 granted forty-year building leases for 500 houses of mediocre quality, 'miserable modern erections' in the words of the Duke of Portland's agent. On Lord Somers's Somers Town, started in 1786, and Lord Camden's Camden Town, of 1791, land was let off by the acre, encouraging builders to pack in as many houses as possible. In Nash's opinion, there was space enough on the lower ground of north London to meet the housing demands of the poorer classes. None of these landowners, he considered, nor the Duke of Portland, nor Colonel Eyre of St John's Wood for that matter, was serving his own best interest.

How much money was waiting, ready to invest in expensive new property, could only be a matter of opinion. While Nash took an optimistic view, he was clear that the people he wanted would not relish exile in a remote suburb. To attract them to Marylebone Fields, it would be necessary to transform its communications with Westminster and St James's. He wrote:

> It is highly essential and is the leading principle of the plan . . .
> that the connection between the present Town and Mary-le-bone
> Park should be made as to lose even the impression of crossing
> the New Road without which it will be vain to expect houses of
> consequence to be built in Mary-le-bone Park.

And . . . 'To effect this the security of continued and unbroken metropolis of streets & houses must be preserved.' Thus, though Nash was concentrating on the rich, the implications of his ambitious scheme would profoundly affect the poor. Integral to the plans was the resuscitation of impoverished parts of central London. However, the poor must be kept out of the exclusive residential streets, so

> . . . that the whole communication from Charing Cross to Oxford
> Street will be a boundary and complete separation between the
> streets and squares occupied by the nobility and gentry, and the
> narrow streets and meaner houses occupied by mechanics and
> the trading part of the community.

His purpose, he wrote later, was 'as a sailor would express himself, to hug all the avenues that went to good streets'.

To sell this unprecedented project to the Commissioners of His Majesty's Woods, Forests and Land Revenue, and to the Treasury, depended above all on the support of the man with whose name it was to be so closely attached – the Prince Regent. Nash was well placed on this count, for he was a flamboyant character, a congenial figure at Court. There was also a rumour that his wife was the Regent's mistress. Others who were closely involved were the senior commissioner, Lord Glenbervie, son-in-law of the Lord North of the American War, and his successor – and much more formidable – the politician William Huskisson. The Prime Minister was Spencer Perceval, who was well acquainted with Marylebone Fields since he had ridden over them daily on his way from Belsize House to Westminster. He interviewed Nash and decided on a reduction in the number of villas planned.

Once, with the Regent's backing, the scheme was approved, negotiations started with the current occupiers of the Fields. One of them was Mr Willan, whose family, so he claimed, had been in possession of a farm on the Fields for many years; he was allowed to carry on at a month's notice and with a restriction on grazing rights to minimize the risk of damage to fences. Willan pleaded for time, that he be allowed to keep some barns and cows in place over the winter of 1812/13 since the local poor depended on them for their milk. Then valuations had to be agreed with Willan for farm property which he could not move elsewhere. All this, however, was simplicity itself compared to the negotiations with the local landowners. Crucial was the attitude of the Duke of Portland in respect of Portland Place, which Nash considered the most magnificent street in London, and which could be made to lead directly – or what amounted to directly – into the eastern end of the Park. The splendour of Portland Place, for which the Adam brothers had provided their skills and John Elwes much of the finance, was magnificently attuned to Nash's conception of the new West End. However, it was a private road, with barriers which must be removed. It became a question of what the Duke would demand in return: he wanted a roadway through the Park to his sixty-five-acre Primrose Hill estate beyond; or, alternatively, he might sell this Primrose Hill land to the Crown, or exchange it for a slice of Marylebone Fields. In any event, he objected to the large army barracks planned at the edge of the Park next to Primrose Hill.

Then there was another neighbour, Colonel Eyre, with his estate in St John's Wood, represented in negotiations (since he himself was

Marylebone, including Regent's Park, from C. and J.
Greenwood, *Map of London* ... of 1827.

serving in India) by his brother Walpole Eyre, a barrister. The Crown wanted to purchase a strip of his land to guarantee communications on the western side of the Fields. The Eyres would sell only if buildings on this land were prohibited. Naturally too they were eager to benefit from the glittering prospects next door, so they also insisted that in return for what the Crown wanted, they be given an undertaking that high quality houses be built along the banks of the Regent's Canal.

The Regent's Canal was an extension of the Grand Junction Canal that ran from Braunston in Northamptonshire to Brentford and then on to Paddington. It caused a lot of trouble. Nash originally planned its course as passing through the Park, but the Commissioners were worried about bargees and others getting loose among the villas. So it was positioned instead along the boundary separating Regent's Park from Primrose Hill to the north. Later on, in the late 1820s, a similar concern for propriety led to the rejection of a proposal that the new King's College be allowed a site. Residents were in uproar. As Sir John Summerson puts it, 'With students in the Park, they

The Regent's Canal passing through Park Village East on the eastern boundary of Regent's Park, *c.* 1825. Reproduced from James Elmes, *Metropolitan Improvements or London in the Nineteenth Century*, 1827.

declared, their more timorous women-folk would never feel safe, their maid-servants would be insulted. It would be worse than the Zoological Society's gardens, which had been opened in the previous April. There, at any rate, the animals were behind bars.' Other alterations to the original scheme involved the transfer of the barracks to the eastern side of the Park, where provision was also made for a hay market and the accommodation of service staff.

Regent's Park, original as it was in conception, was at least to be established in open countryside. Its counterpart, the restructuring and rebuilding of the centre of London all the way down to Charing Cross, required immense expenditure and a wholesale disturbance of existing interests. Its core was a street – called the New Street – which traversed the New Road from the Park by means of a superior version of a roundabout of which today's Park Crescent is the southern arc, and proceeded along Portland Place to cross Oxford Street and sweep down the great colonnaded curve of a newly built Regent Street over Piccadilly Circus. It culminated in the Prince Regent's Carlton House, which stood on the slight rise which now marks Carlton House Terrace. 'It will quite eclipse Napoleon,' declared the Regent in triumph. And, if it comes to that, the project was, in fact, a precursor of Baron Haussmann's reconstruction of central Paris under Napoleon III half a century later.

By an act of parliament of 1813 the plan was authorized and borrowings of public money sanctioned. It was anticipated that 741 houses would need to be demolished, of which 386 were property of the Crown. Appeals and protests flooded in from those affected. There were compromises to be made. It was necessary that the views from the windows of such as the Duke of Hamilton and Sir Thomas Baring, who lived in upper Marylebone, should not be entirely ruined. The residents of St James's Square effected a slight shift westward in the course of the New Street, and those of Cavendish Square a modest switch to the east. The extra expense of buying up property in such districts added to the force of their arguments. It was next door to Cavendish Square that, in physical terms, Nash was confronted by his most intractable single obstacle in the form of Foley House.

In 1764, a routine meeting of the tradesmen and farmers who composed the Marylebone vestry was startled by the irruption of

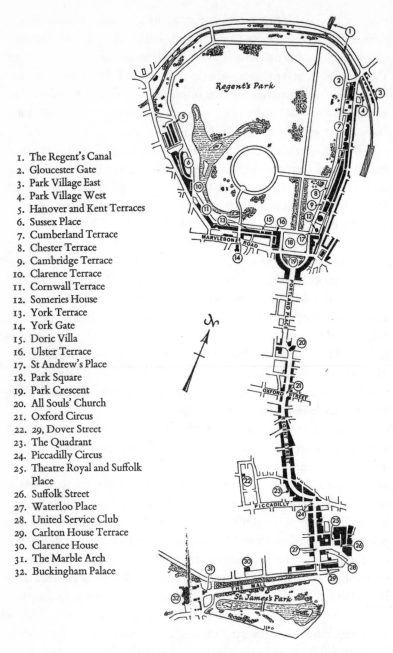

John Nash's plan for the 'New Street' leading from Carlton House to Regent's Park, 1814. Reproduced from Sir John Summerson, *The Life and Work of John Nash, Architect.*

seven noblemen. They were led by Lord Foley, who moved that a petition be submitted to parliament for the reconstitution of the vestry as a 'select vestry', that is, one more subject to oligarchic control. Two generations later, by the time of Nash and Regent's Park, the Foleys were best known for their chronic financial troubles, but in the 1760s they were very shrewd businessmen who, though Lord Foley failed in his attempt to win control of the vestry, managed to persuade their cousin the Duchess of Portland to allow them a quite amazing real-estate bargain – later fiercely contested by her son – a lease on possible building land to the north of Cavendish Square. Standing on this land was the large and free-standing Foley House which, now recast as the Langham Hotel, destroyed Nash's hope for a straight, uninterrupted thoroughfare down Portland Place to Regent Street.

Southwards, particularly south of Piccadilly, planning was less difficult since most of the land belonged to the Crown, and leases were falling in. Even so, the Crown Estate's papers show how busy the commissioners were kept. A Colonel Stanley had been uprooted from his house in Pall Mall and was to be reinstated in an equivalent new house in Foley Gardens, now Langham Place. That was not too difficult; more common was the type of negotiation necessary with Lord Galloway who, turned out of his house in Charles Street (now Charles II Street), was demanding compensation for loss of interest resulting from late payment of what was owed to him. (To rub it in, it was not now intended to pull down Lord Galloway's house after all.) Lord Longford, also of Charles Street, was exigent over the reimbursement he expected on special fitted furniture which it was impractical to move. The elderly George Martin saw no possibility of finding suitable alternative premises in the neighbourhood for the school on which he depended for his living. It is something of a change to read a letter from James Hunt, evicted from Pall Mall:

I feel particular gratification even at the sacrifice of my own personal interest in promoting a plan which it is reported to be the wish of His Royal Highness the Prince Regent to accomplish.

He had to lay it on with a trowel, since he was the Prince's wine merchant, an account which must indeed have been worth keeping. But Hunt did go on to wonder how he was going to replace the vaults which he had installed at such an expense.

In exchange for the turmoil and the inconvenience, residents of the West End were to live in more splendid surroundings, with a magnificent new square, Waterloo Place, set out in front of Carlton House. The flow of traffic would be improved, and there would be a superb shopping centre in Regent Street. The tenements and slums which lurked around the corner of even such districts as Grosvenor Square and St James's Square were to be uprooted. Access into smart London from Soho – now far descended from its past glory – would be cramped and uninviting. In Regent's Park itself, the canal would protect the northern end from the less couth world and its high-built banks would deter the bargees. Elsewhere, the buildings round the edge would face determinedly inwards, and lodges and gates would assert the right of private property to keep out strangers

The insulation of Regent's Park reduced its potential advantages to adjacent landowners. Primrose Hill, across the canal, never attracted the wealthy residents which its owners, Eton College, might have anticipated. Partly it was Eton's own fault for so long postponing development that they were overtaken by the disastrous slump of 1825. The Eyres in St John's Wood encountered other difficulties. Mainly there was the hostility of the Portmans, who interrupted access from the New Road and in order to affirm the superior social standing of their own tenants, erected a brick wall between the two estates. St John's Wood, however, did benefit when Lord Portman proved unhelpful to the Marylebone vestry about providing a new burial ground. The vestry looked to the Eyres, who supplied the land for the St John's burial ground opposite Lords, and in return acquired their link with the New Road. The chapel that went with the ground – now the church – was also helpful in that it drew house-hunters of a respectable and prosperous type. St John's Wood was not rich London, but it is important architecturally with its series of villas, detached and, above all, semi-detached. The word 'villa' starts its devaluation. The classic London villa, with its full Italianate associations, was Lord Burlington's supremely elegant Chiswick House.

View from Regent Circus (Piccadilly Circus) south to
Carlton House in 1822. Engraving by T. H. Shepherd.

By the end of the eighteenth century, the word, in Mark Girouard's
definition, had come to signify a small to medium-sized gentleman's
house in a rural setting which might or might not be near a town.
While intended for the rich, the Regent's Park villas were medium-
sized houses and even the largest, Holford House (though in illustration it looks vast), cost only something in the region of £6,000
(£350,000 today). That might be compared – with the value of money
rather higher in the 1770s – with Mrs Montagu's £20,000 spent on
her 'country house' in Portman Square. However, the term was elastic:
John Dawes's Highbury House, costing £10,000, was referred to as
a villa, and long after, in the 1850s, a cultivated American used the
word to describe the Grosvenors' enormous Eaton Hall in Cheshire.
The St John's Wood semi-detached villas were not remotely in the
Regent's Park class; for all their comfort and attractiveness, they are
the forerunners of the mass-produced houses which were to become
the hallmark of suburbia. To the rich, the expression 'suburban villa'
was to come to mean banality and philistinism.

While the great enterprise of Regent's Park and New Street was revolutionary in scale and consequences for the existing town, its management in many ways resembled that adopted on private estates. Nash's role had much in common with that of the contemporary estate surveyor. However, a passage in the diary of his immediate chief Lord Glenbervie, now dropped by the government as senior commissioner and consequently resentful, reveals the hazardous political and financial background. The entry is for the 15 August 1816:

> I walked down Whitehall Place. The line of houses, from the office, has been continued for four or five new houses since I went abroad. The project of the new street seems to be in a deplorable way and Nash I hear is held in universal abhorrence, except by his royal master and dupe. The lessee of the Circus at the end of Portland Place has broke.

Parliament had authorized borrowings of £600,000 but, when it came to it, Nash had badly underestimated the compensation which would need to be paid. In the end, financing was obtained, not only from the Bank of England but from the Royal Exchange Assurance, which put up a £300,000 loan. Nevertheless, as Glenbervie noted, the Portland Place contractor had failed and, faced with what was generally a hostile financial climate and wariness on the part of possible buyers, Nash had no alternative but to risk his own money and to accept daunting responsibilities. Matters were the more difficult since the Crown, unlike some of the large private landowners, did not provide mortgages to site lessees. When progress on the Regent's Canal faltered in face of opposition from landowners in its path, Nash stepped in. He took on all the leaseholds in the Quadrant, the critical area of Regent Street by Piccadilly Circus. He bought out the Foley family for a huge sum, although even that did not enable him to redevelop the site as he wished.

As time went on and the depression lifted, the sites began to sell. In the Park, with its lake and vistas and carefully planted shrubs and trees, the villas appeared, and if in the end only six were actually built (out of twenty-six originally planned for), beyond them, spaced along the perimeter, there emerged huge and splendid terraces. 'Dream palaces' in Summerson's description; and there was in fact an element of 'dream', or at least of fantasy, about the whole place. More than a decade later, when the Park was largely completed, the German actress Caroline Bauer was smuggled in one evening in the early summer of 1829. She was the mistress of Prince Leopold, the widower of George IV's daughter Princess Charlotte and shortly to be appointed King of the Belgians. At the time, there was some talk of a morganatic marriage, but it never materialized. Caroline Bauer was installed in one of the new villas, almost certainly The Holme, shut up, as she put it, in 'a charming golden cage'. She had ample time to consider her surroundings, while she awaited the occasional visits of her prince. Of her arrival she noted,

> I looked with curiosity at the cottages, villas, and the great houses in magnificent terraces, that were already partly lit up, half-hidden by wonderful old trees, and shrubberies in flower. In the pond on the huge grass lawn the first stars were glittering. Nightingales were singing from the bushes.

And later:

> But how quiet it was all round this remote part of Regent's Park! One saw indeed a few similar gardens and villas, but only rarely a solitary person walking or a silent park-gardener.

She was struck by the number of children: 'They played about on the fresh green lawn with their pretty little ponies and goat carriages, while the fashionable world, in the most elegant *toilettes*, drove or rode on horseback in the "ring" or the surrounding park.'

Nash had intended something Romantic, but he had in mind as residents the *beau monde* not the *demi-monde*. At St Dunstan's Villa (now, in rebuilt form, Winfield House, the residence of the American ambassador), he got both. The lease was taken by the Marquess of Hertford, who put together the Wallace Collection at Hertford House. He was also the original for Thackeray's Marquess of Steyne and known as 'the Caliph of Regent's Park'. Like Prince Leopold, it was the seclusion which drew him: at St Dunstan's Villa he could assemble not just a single mistress, but, it seems, the pick of the *corps-de-ballet* for private orgies. Another leaseholder, less colourful but there again for the privacy, was Lord Dundonald – disgraced for fraud although later exonerated – at Hanover Lodge.

In his book *Metropolitan Improvements or London in the Nineteenth Century*, published in 1827, James Elmes comments on Regent's Park and its magnificent buildings:

> They surely must all be the abodes of nobles and princes! No, the majority are the retreats of the happy free-born sons of commerce, of the wealthy commonalty of Britain.

John Nash had envisaged a superb new district for the patricians. Lord Hertford was certainly that, and so was Marquess Wellesley, elder brother of the Duke of Wellington, and in his day Foreign Secretary and Lord Lieutenant of Ireland, who leased another villa, St John's Lodge in 1829. At Albany Cottage (now transformed into the Islamic Cultural Centre) lived the fashionable Thomas Raikes, dandy and diarist; and the first occupant of Sussex Lodge was Lord Bective, heir to a marquisate. Nevertheless, occupants tended to be transitory tenants rather than lessees. Whoever the elegants were that Caroline Bauer noticed in 'the ring', the smart address was Portland Place, where it was recorded in 1833 that residents included the Earls of Mansfield, Sheffield and Stirling, Viscount Boyne, Lord Walsingham and the dowager Duchess of Richmond.

The representatives of Elmes's 'wealthy commonalty' who took the villas were interesting people. The first house to be built, The Holme, completed in 1818, was occupied by James Burton, the contractor who built Waterloo Place and whose contribution to the creation of the Park and New Street was second only to that of John Nash himself. With him was his son Decimus Burton, the architect of most of the villas as well as many other London buildings. St John's Lodge went first to an MP, and then, after Wellesley, was tenanted by Isaac Lyon Goldsmid, financier and banker, the first Jewish baronet and notable as a philanthropist and President of the Royal Society. South Villa was sold in the 1830s to a vintner, George Bishop, President of the Royal Astronomical Society and Fellow of the

Royal Society, who constructed next door a famous astronomical observatory. Grove House was built in 1822–24 for George Bellas Greenough, MP, a distinguished natural scientist and President of the Geological Society. Lord Bective at Sussex Lodge was followed by the painter Francis Grant, President of the Royal Academy. The largest of the villas, Holford House, was built by Decimus Burton for wine importer and financier James Holford. It was the last of them, completed in the 1830s, and was destroyed by a bomb during the Second World War.

As Regent, George IV had intended for himself a pavilion in the Park, a complement to Carlton House at the other end of New Street. The project came to nothing, a fact which had much to do with the eventual lack of interest on the part of the patricians. In 1826, declaring that he wanted a palace which was not, as he put it, 'standing in a street', he pulled down Carlton House and, taking John Nash along to deal with the rebuilding, moved down the Mall to Buckingham House. It was a transposition which would influence the future of

Grove House, Regent's Park, built by Decimus Burton, 1822–4, renovated 1986.

the area to the west, what would be Belgravia, but it removed much of the underpinning of the great project of New Street and Regent's Park. Moreover, in the same year, the Commissioners brought their contribution to the Regent's Park development to an end. Even so, if Regent's Park has remained at a remove from the West End, if Regent Street has lost its original grace and Portland Place, imposing as it may be, is nevertheless no street of palaces, central London was permanently transformed and, to this day, the context changed, Regent Street's eastern side provides a firm social wall. James Elmes dedicated his book to the King, whose contribution to London he compares to that of Augustus to Rome. To paraphrase Dr Johnson on 'lapidary inscriptions', nobody was on oath when writing a dedication to the great. Yet there was widespread agreement that what had been done was a remarkable achievement. Prince Pückler-Muskau, in England in the late 1820s, visited John Nash ('No artist is more handsomely lodged in town') and complimented the King on the extraordinary 'embellishment' of London since his last visit. He was just one foreigner to be impressed. And innumerable Londoners were impressed too. The diarist Charles Greville, writing in October 1830, thought London a thousand times more beautiful than it had been nineteen years before. In 1835, the magazine *John Bull* reminded its readers of what some of central London had been like before Nash and the Regent got to work, reflecting on 'the huddled mass of wretched streets and houses which twenty years ago covered the site of Regent Street, the Quadrant and Waterloo Place; . . . [and] the still more wretched courts and alleys, dens of infamy and haunts of thieves, which maze-like spread themselves from St Martin's Church to the neighbourhood of Covent Garden.'

7

The Villages to the West

*

Sir Richard Phillips, author of a *A Morning's Walk from London to Kew*, published in 1817, was not a fan of the Prince Regent. As he started his walk to Kew along the Mall, he glanced disdainfully at the garden wall of Carlton House, the Prince's 'puny, though costly, palace', with its 'inside adorned like the palace of Aladin'. A good example, in fact, of the man's extravagant schemes. Phillips is no better humoured when he passes a bit further on 'what are called the Gardens of Buckingham House'. He is an acerbic, rather idiosyncratic person who gives off a distant echo of Jonathan Swift, whose route to Chelsea he is in the act of following.

The St James's that Phillips sees in 1817 is not splendid. The palace is run-down and the park is not as it used to be. Blind and crippled beggars are everywhere. Phillips reflects sardonically on what a wonder it is that statesmen 'who have superfluous means for covering the country with barracks, should find themselves unable to establish comfortable asylums for all the poor who are incurably diseased.' His spirits lift somewhat at the sight of the mothers, nurses and children attracted by the prospect of milk warm from the cows in the park. But he is a sentimental man and he cannot but regret the disappearance of 'those crowds of beauty, rank, and fashion' in the park on Sunday evenings during spring and summer. Partly it is the result of a later time for dinner, partly because of the modern custom of abandoning the metropolis for the coast or the country as soon as the fine weather sets in. Another facet of modern life strikes him as he makes his way against the flow of pedestrians going the other way. These are commuters. First, before 9 a.m., come the clerks from civil-service offices, and from banking and merchanting firms; then, after that, the senior people. Phillips calculates that if, along with those on foot, one takes account of the crowded stagecoaches, the private coaches and chariots, the gigs and chaises, the many people on horseback, and then assumes twenty routes into London, the total must come to something like 16,000 people. It was a phenomenon, he thought, unique to London, one which occurred nowhere else in the world.

Phillips leaves the park along our Buckingham Palace Road (to him the main street of Pimlico). Opposite Buckingham House and its dubious gardens was Stafford Row, its name evoking for him the thought of a long-vanished mansion called Tart Hall which had once stood there, 'the rival in size and splendour of its more fortunate neighbour, Buckingham-House'. On one side, for him as for Swift, lies the swamp of Tothill and Millbank. There is also (postdating Swift) the disagreeably noisy Chelsea Waterworks, and opposite, 'the manufactory of the ingenious Bramah, whose locks baffle knavery.' In Chelsea, Phillips has a clear objective, the site of Ranelagh Gardens on the Royal Hospital grounds. Ranelagh had been closed down fourteen years before. In its day it was the grandest of the London pleasure gardens, more fashionable than the longer-lasting Vauxhall on the other side of the river. Said Horace Walpole, in 1744, soon after the gardens opened, 'Every night constantly I go to Ranelagh, which has totally beat Vauxhall.' To Phillips this is a pilgrimage:

> I passed up the avenue of trees, which I remember often to have seen blocked up with carriages. At its extremity, I looked for the Rotunda and its surrounding buildings; but, as I could not see them, I concluded, that I had acquired but an imperfect idea of the place, in my nocturnal visits! . . . At length on a spot covered with nettles, thistles, and other rank weeds, I met a working man, who in answer to my enquiries, told me, that he saw I was a stranger, or I should have known that Ranelagh had been pulled down, and that I was standing on the site of the Rotunda!
>
> . . . This vile place, I exclaimed, the site of the once-enchanting Ranelagh! – It cannot be – the same eyes were never destined to see such a metamorphosis! All was desolation! . . .

No glittering lights! – No brilliant happy company! – No peals of laughter from thronged boxes! – No chorus of a hundred instruments and voices!

The 1811 census had given Chelsea a population of 18,262, nearly half as much again as Fulham and Hammersmith combined. In his necessarily rough estimates, Sir Richard Phillips reckoned that of the commuters he met on his walk, 200 might come from Pimlico; 300 from Chelsea; 200 from the King's Road and Sloane Street; 50 from Fulham and Putney; and 50 from Battersea and Wandsworth. From the point of view of the rich, the growth of Chelsea was not an advantage, the rural atmosphere had gone. To find that now, it was necessary to go further out. The development of Sloane Street and the creation of Hans Town had above all made the difference. On the death of Sir Hans Sloane in 1753, the manor of Chelsea had been divided between his two daughters, Sarah, who married George

The interior of the Rotunda at Ranelagh. Painting by Canaletto, 1754.

Stanley, and Elizabeth, who married Charles Cadogan. In 1771, the architect Henry Holland (responsible for the remodelling of Carlton House and later of the Brighton Pavilion), himself a Chelsea man, had put forward a proposal to Lord Cadogan for the development of the eastern part of his estate. Agreement was reached, with Holland reserving for himself twenty-one acres on which he planted picturesque gardens and built a house called the Pavilion, a Gothic country seat complete with artificial ruins intended to represent the remains of a priory. The name lingers in Pavilion Road, a long mews running parallel to Sloane Street. If here, though, there was an addition to the great houses of the district, elsewhere there was a falling away. Beaufort House had followed Danvers House into oblivion; the Bishop of Winchester's palace at the river end of the present Oakley Street, in its day employing forty servants, was demolished in 1828. The nearby Shrewsbury House was a wallpaper factory, and Sir Robert Walpole's mansion, designed by Vanbrugh, was incorporated into the Royal Hospital. Gough House, in our Tite Street, was a school. Hans Sloane's 'new' manor house was demolished soon after his death, and even the Botanic Gardens had been superseded in importance by Kew. There was, and is, however, a survivor in Lindsey House on Cheyne Walk, which stands so close to the street and to the river that a passer-by is apt to miss it. Originally it was the site of Sir Thomas More's farmhouse, the later mansion being built in 1674 by the Earl of Lindsey and passing to the dukes of Ancaster. In 1750 a long lease was acquired by Count Zinzendorf on behalf of the Moravian Brotherhood, a Protestant sect of which he was the leader and which traced its descent from the followers of John Hus. The Moravians are still there in Chelsea, their property located behind a gate at World's End, at the top end of Milmans Street. Inside the gate are their burial ground, chapel and exhibition centre, which occupy part of what were the gardens of Beaufort House. Zinzendorf, a charismatic and controversial man with a taste for lavish spending, drew up plans for an extensive community, but in the end financial difficulties forced their cancellation and the sale of Lindsey House. The house was then divided into five apartments, one of which was lived in by the Brunels, father and son.

The 1826 *Original Picture of London* gives a description of the

Thames and its banks which might – with the excision of the word 'villas' – have been lifted from Defoe a hundred years before.

> It is impossible to conceive the beauty and variety of the numerous objects, which, on every side, delight the eye of the passenger. The whole voyage exhibits a continued series of villages, magnificent seats, splendid villas, beautiful pleasure-grounds, and highly cultivated gardens.

The wealthy could appreciate the river and its social life in comfort. The Duke of Wellington's friend Mrs Arbuthnot wrote of the summer 'water parties', of the so-called breakfast parties held by the Duke of Devonshire at Chiswick House which started at 3 in the afternoon and ended at midnight, and of dining at Ham House and being rowed back in style to London afterwards. More humdrum but very popular were the river buses. In 1824, T. Hughes published what is thought to be the first guide for steam boats, as a means of promoting tours with Captain Reynolds in his 'fast-sailing packet' *Diana*. The main attractions were the fine houses along the banks of the river.

By the time the guide was published, the most exciting of these had just been pulled down, leaving on its grounds only two cottages. This was Brandenburgh House, between Fulham and Hammersmith, in origin 'the most magnificent mansion' which had belonged to Sir Nicholas Crispe and which had attracted such scorn from the seventeenth-century Duchess of Beaufort. At that time it had been taken by Prince Rupert for his mistress Mrs Hughes. It was remodelled in the eighteenth century for a famous placeman, the politician Bubb Dodington, owner also of a house in Pall Mall and of the huge Eastbury in Dorset. In 1792, it was acquired by the Margrave and Margravine of Anspach (she being better known to scandal as Lady Craven) who installed a theatre and provided the setting for spectacular parties. It held a staff of thirty servants and a stud for sixty horses. The last resident of Brandenburgh House was the woman whose misadventures divided the nation – Queen Caroline, wife of George IV, who died there in 1821. Also on the north bank of the Thames were to be seen three buildings of outstanding importance. One was Fulham Palace, the summer residence of the bishops of London and

Chiswick Mall, 1820. Engraving from Walford,
Old and New London, 1897, vol. vi.

the last moated house within the London area. There was also the
Duke of Northumberland's Syon House, rebuilt by Robert Adam.
And thirdly Chiswick House, built by the Earl of Burlington and
inherited by the dukes of Devonshire, of which, in its original form,
Lord Hervey declared that it was '. . . too small to inhabit, and too
large to hang one's watch'. Chiswick House, the classic London 'villa',
was not designed for family living but rather as a 'kind of multiplied
drawing room' for the exhibition of paintings and sculpture. At
Chiswick there remains Inigo Jones's baroque gateway of 1621 transferred from Beaufort House by Hans Sloane. Other important buildings along the north bank were Horace Walpole's Strawberry Hill,
and Marble Hill built by George II for his mistress.

These are the survivors. There were plenty of other mansions
and villas for the guide books to praise but which have since disappeared. The first one selected in Hughes's guide for the stretch of
water between Chelsea and Fulham was the elegant Broom House.
This was nabob territory. The guide attributed it to Lady Nepean,

The Sulivan family at Broom House, Fulham,
in the 1860s.

widow of the nabob Sir Evan Nepean, although it had in fact been
sold in 1823 to Laurence Sulivan, grandson of a famous Laurence
Sulivan, eight times chairman of the East India Company. Another
'nabob house' was Bradmore House, formerly Butterwick House, at
Hammersmith, the family home of Sir Elijah Impey, Chief Justice
of Bengal in the late eighteenth century. A further rather exotic
resident of these parts was Anthony Sampayo, a Portuguese merchant,
one of the foreign businessmen whose importance was to grow as
the century progressed. Sampayo had lived at Munster House away
from the river on the northern side of the Fulham Road, which he
sold to J. W. Croker, Secretary to the Admiralty and memoirist. He
himself had moved to a new house at Parsons Green built on the site
of Peterborough House, in its day one of the best-known mansions
in the western suburbs of London and celebrated for its associations
with Locke, Addison, Swift and Pope.

While the topography of the northern and western approaches

to London was very different, the economic structure was not. The economy of Fulham, for instance, could be compared with that of Hampstead and Islington, for in its neighbourhood, so it was said, were produced half the vegetables sold at Covent Garden, and, like the two northern villages, Fulham prospered as a popular summer resort. An essential distinction, however, was the presence of Windsor and the Court, which gave to the west a social focus lacking elsewhere. What north and west both lacked was political focus. Brentford was a thriving commercial and industrial town, but it was not the county town where the justices of the peace met to govern the county. They convened at Westminster in a building on Parliament Square. The low reputation of these magistrates reflects the confused nature of Middlesex as a county, a certain absence of authenticity. The county gentry who composed the magistrates' bench in the rest of rural England were often rough and ready, but they felt a deep attachment to their roots and a sense of duty to their employees and tenants and poorer neighbours. In the transient society of Middlesex, however, such people were hard to find, with the rich for the most part disengaged. Genealogists have done their best to track down the old county families: yet E. P. Shirley, researching his *Noble and Gentle Men of England* of 1859, could identify no gentry family in Middlesex who had held land there before 1485; and W. J. Loftie, in his 1883 history of London and Middlesex, found only three families who had been settled in the county for more than 200 years. Loftie's families were the Woods of Littleton, near Shepperton (also with property at Hampton), but by the time he wrote, they had gone, withdrawn to an estate in Wales; there were also the Taylors at Staines, and the Clitherows of Boston Manor next door to Osterley. The Clitherows were descended from Sir Christopher Clitherow, Lord Mayor of London before the Civil War and one of the most prominent merchants in the City, whose son purchased the manor of Boston in 1670. By the nineteenth century, they at least were certainly regarded as true county magnates.

There were of course a number of noble families, some of enormous wealth, like the Jerseys at Osterley and the Northumberlands at Syon. They were influential, for after all they provided considerable employment. They were, though, too busy and too occupied elsewhere to lead the county. The same would have been true of the great Whig potentates of Scotland, the dukes of Argyll, with their much more modest Whitton Park, famous for its gardens. Another great family was the Berkeleys of Berkeley Castle, Gloucestershire and 16 Berkeley Square, Mayfair, who since 1618 had owned Cranford Park, in Hounslow and close to what is now Heathrow Airport. The earls of Berkeley had not only accumulated their own wealth but had inherited that of their distant kinsmen, the barons Berkeley of Stratton, the first of whom had been the friend of John Evelyn. A photograph in the *Country Life* issue of 9 March 1935 shows Cranford Park in its last days as an abandoned, overgrown, ruined hulk due for demolition and replacement by mass housing. In the 1820s, however, it was still far away from the sprawl of London. The Berkeleys at the time were famous on the one hand for a sensational society scandal, and on the other for their passion for hunting. The scandal was caused by the union of the fifth Earl of Berkeley and Mary Cole, the daughter of a Gloucester butcher, and the fact that no marriage took place until four sons had already been born. A lost peerage case in the House of Lords magnified the drama. The passion for hunting was longstanding, and many years back a Lord Berkeley had kept hounds in the village of Charing, until forced out by the spread of London. The fifth earl had himself hunted the country all the way from Kensington Gardens to Berkeley Castle and Bristol, although by his time, in the later part of the eighteenth century, Kensington should really have been out of bounds, as Lady Mary Coke, who lived on Campden Hill, next door to Holland House, made clear one day in 1774:

I have had another vexation that never happen'd to me before, the having a pack of hounds in my garden, & several men on Horseback broke into my grounds, leap'd into my North Walk, & from thence into Lord Holland's lane. These things are disagreeable, and so near London was not to be expected.

In 1810, after the death of her husband, Lady Berkeley settled at Cranford with her two legitimate sons, Moreton and Grantley. The latter wrote a memoir later in life about hunting in the country west of London in the 1820s.

Grantley was an energetic and enterprising man who resolved early on that he was not going to end up 'an old beau, with a bald head bobbing about like an apple on the sea, or a dreadful wig, dancing, anxious to leave the ball before day-light and the growth of the white stubble on his chin contrasts with the deadly hue of his stained and blue-tinted whiskers.' He served briefly in the Coldstream Guards and commanded a piquet on duty at Carlton House. However, the army got in the way of sport and so he resigned. The shooting at Cranford was excellent, but it was hunting on which his heart was set. In fact, while there was already a Mr Coombe at Gerrards Cross who hunted a pack of fox hounds called the 'Old Berkeley', Grantley and his elder brother went ahead to form their own pack of stag hounds, importing deer from Berkeley Castle and from Hampstead. The hunt quickly became fashionable, for it was well situated socially, close to Hampton Court and Twickenham where, according to Grantley Berkeley, there were balls and dinner parties without end.

But the real question was whether it was well situated from another point of view; whether the outer western suburbs were really still hunting country, whether in fact they could be called country at all. The terrain proved very difficult, with the market gardens, and with the ground pervaded by drains and spread over with brick kilns and rubbish dumps. One day a stag took hounds away from their 'legitimate' line of country towards the built-up area of Hounslow, Isleworth and Brentford. Lord Alvanley, wit and man about town, decided enough was enough and retired rapidly from the hunting field to White's. The asparagus beds were awfully heavy, he told his fellow club-members, and you trampled through glass. On another day, matters almost came to a head, as Grantley Berkeley relates:

> . . . a fine stag, covered with foam and stained with blood, entered London by the Regent's Park, and ran the streets to No. 1, I think, Montague Street, Russell Square. My brother Moreton and Mr Henry Wombwell, who whipped in with me, had stopped the hounds outside the Regent's Park, all but two couple, who went at the flanks of the deer pell-mell into the town. I followed them, of course, to see the termination. Women screamed, children cried, men shouted, and horses shied, as the unwonted

animal came down the pavement or swerved from the passengers across the streets . . . [Finally] the stag was obliged to stop and turn to bay, backing his haunches against the street door of No. 1, and looking wildly over into the area, into which I could see he had a mind to jump. I stopped opposite him, when, at the same instant, the dining-room window was raised, and two very pretty young ladies looked out, full of sweet pity for the deer and bland commiseration! They had scarcely uttered, 'Poor dear thing!' when cap in hand, I instantly joined issue, and implored them 'to have the street door opened, or the innocent and graceful animal would be killed.'

The story then turns into farce, for just as the girls were about to help, they were interrupted by 'a prim but choleric and elderly gentleman' who mistook Berkeley for a showman 'with an animal that would, perhaps, dance on its hind legs to please the company for halfpence' and threatened to send for the beadle. (It is noteworthy that Berkeley does not seem usually to have killed his stags, and at the end of the season the survivors were sent back to Berkeley Castle.)

It could not go on, with the metropolis so near and spreading, and with the attitude of the farmers and nurserymen who were 'no sportsmen'. Grantley Berkeley persisted, nevertheless, for twelve years, and, as he said, had a great deal of fun. But enclosures of heath and common followed one after another, and land which was once the habitat of fish and snipe was covered by villas. 'The spot,' wrote Berkeley, 'where my father shot the highwayman on Hounslow Heath, as he went in the evening from Cranford to dine with Justice Bulstrode . . . became the centre almost of a town.' The end was precipitated by a riot: a stag, which Grantley Berkeley intended to save, got trapped in a barn near Harrow and a fight broke out between farm labourers and the hunt field. The quarrel ended in a court case in which the verdict – and damages – went against the hunt. It became 'very evident to me that, if I kept hounds, it must no longer be in my father's country.' Berkeley moved to Bedfordshire, where he formed a pack of fox hounds. But 'it went to my heart to quit Cranford'.

By now, and even by the later eighteenth century, roads between the villages and towns were much improved, and the choice of where to live, particularly for those rich who combined a London life with one in the suburbs, was accordingly wider. Lady Mary Coke often travelled backwards and forwards in the day, even in winter, between Campden Hill and the house she rented near Green Park. Though highwaymen still infested the roads and caused her some alarm, she moved about freely to see her friends, to the Duchess of Norfolk at Seagreens in Hammersmith; to Richmond; to visit King George III's aunt Princess Amelia at Gunnersbury Park, north of the present-day M4 motorway. This last was in summer, for the Princess spent her winters in Cavendish Square, in what had been one of the Duke of Chandos's houses. Mary Coke also went frequently to Kew, when the Court was in residence. When Sir Richard Phillips took his *Morning Walk* in 1817, Kew was past its best days, but in Lady Mary's time it was, at the appropriate time of year, filled with the highest society. It was the favourite resort of Frederick, Prince of Wales, later of his widow, and then of their son George III. Most of Lady Mary's visits involved the playing of the card game Loo, sometimes for very high stakes. One day she lost 50 guineas (say £5,750), on another she won 76. She could more or less afford it, for she was a daughter of the second Duke of Argyll, a distinguished soldier, and her portion on marriage had been £20,000 (£2.25 million today).

In her journal, Mary Coke leaves an occasionally vivid picture of north Kensington in the late eighteenth century. Her marriage in 1747 to Viscount Coke had been a total disaster. They separated, and he died in 1753, when she was still only twenty-six. A sad and paranoid woman, in 1767 she took a lease on Notting Hill House at the top of Campden Hill. It was her 'Country House', her refuge from the cruel world. Since in reality she needed the world, or at least the 'great world', Kensington, like everything else in her life, was a muddle. She asserted that the workmen employed on the house spent their time eating and drinking, that her gardener was always drunk, that a local butcher had made off with twenty-five of her sheep, that her neighbour Lady Holland snubbed her. She gives, however, a sympathetic vignette of Robert Phillimore, the owner of 64 acres immediately to her south, which originally made up a large part of the old Campden House estate. Phillimore cut down some of his trees to improve her view and confided to her that his land had doubled in value. What could be done with it became clear some years later when his eldest surviving son, William, inherited, and started to build. Mary Coke's house, now known as Aubrey House, is a survivor, which, apart from some Victorian additions, was at any rate until very recently essentially the same structure as it was in her day. With the exception of Thorpe Lodge, at one time occupied by the long-serving Governor of the Bank of England Montague Norman, and preserved as part of the Holland Park Comprehensive School, the ten detached houses built by the Phillimores have been demolished, along with their own eighteenth-century mansion. Some of them were large by almost any standards. Bedford Lodge, first occupied in 1815, was, during the residence of the sixth Duke of Bedford – who bought the lease in 1823 as a retreat from St James's Square – actually at one point more highly assessed for rates than Holland House itself. When the Duke's widow died in 1853, the lease passed to the seventh Duke of Argyll, who the 1871 census shows as employing twenty-seven servants and a governess to look after a family of eight. Another mansion, Bute House, was occupied between 1830 and 1842 by the second Marquess of Bute, like Bedford a man of enormous wealth, and later in the century was to pass to a Lascelles and then to the sixth Duke of Rutland. Holly Lodge was taken by Lord Macaulay, who died there in 1859. Campden Hill was for many years a remarkable enclave of the London rich, with most of its houses surviving in one form or another until after the Second World War.

Kensington has been described as 'the very citadel of Victorian London'. During the nineteenth century its population soared: the census of 1821 gives a figure for Kensington parish of 13,428, while fifty years later it is 120,299, a rate of increase far above that of London as a whole. Holland House, a few hundred yards away from Bedford Lodge and Bute House, was its very centre. During the first half of the nineteenth century, the third Lord Holland, with over 200 acres of land, was the largest landowner. In social terms, Holland House was pre-eminent not only in Kensington but in all London. It was regarded in those times, wrote G. W. E. Russell – than whom no one was better informed – as the very temple of luxury. Late on in the century, in 1872, Gustave Doré chose a Holland House garden party to depict London high society at play. On top of that, from

A drawing by Sir Edwin Landseer of the third Lord
Holland, taken from a sketch sheet.

the death of Charles James Fox in 1806 until that of Lord Holland
himself in 1840, this Kensington mansion was the headquarters of
the Whig party.

Henry, the third Lord Holland, grandson of Henry Fox, the first
Lord Holland, a baby when he succeeded his father Stephen in 1774,
was the political and spiritual heir of his uncle Charles James Fox.
By all accounts, Holland was an absolutely charming man. To take
one of many testimonials, that of Macaulay, who said of Holland, 'I
admire him, I think, more than any man whom I know . . . [and]
. . . The sight of him spreads good humour over the face of everyone
who comes near him.' His wife, on the other hand, no one could
describe in such terms. A very shy young man was sitting next to her
once at dinner, when, plunging her hand into his pocket, she drew
out his handkerchief which, with a sniff of disgust, she gave to a

servant with the words 'Take that to the wash.' Yet that Lady Holland
was a brilliant hostess, an inspirer and orchestrator of conversation,
is not in doubt. Putting it in characteristically measured terms, Lord
Melbourne told Queen Victoria that at Holland House you encountered people whom you wished to know, and had no chance of
meeting elsewhere. The range and distinction of the guest list could
hardly be more impressive. Regulars at various times included Byron,
Macaulay and the Whig leaders, Dickens, and the wits Sydney Smith
and Samuel Rogers. William IV (one of whose daughters by Mrs
Jordan married the Hollands' eldest but illegitimate son) dined frequently at Holland House before and after his accession to the throne.
The guest list was also very cosmopolitan. The memoirist Charles
Greville, a constant visitor, wrote of the salon at Holland House that
when it should end, 'a vacuum will be made in society which nothing
will supply. It is the house of all Europe.' Lafayette was a close
friend, and Greville reported that Talleyrand, while in his last post
as ambassador to Britain in the 1830s, would arrive at Holland House
at 10 or 11 in the morning and stay 'as long as they will let him'. The
Americans, the future president Martin Van Buren and the brilliant
Daniel Webster were guests. Another American, the scholar George
Ticknor, left an account of a dinner in 1835 which among other aspects
of grand life illustrates the authority still exercised by the patrician
rich. He was rather dazzled by the company, which included Lord
Melbourne, the Prime Minister, and Lord Grey, his immediate
predecessor, both, noted Ticknor, highly cultivated men. The conversation turned to public business and to a parliamentary motion on
whether dissenters should be admitted to the universities, which was
scheduled for debate on the following Tuesday night. It was thought
likely, however, that since Lady Jersey was giving a grand dinner that
night she might well succeed in having the debate postponed. (It is
reminiscent of Horace Walpole's report to Horace Mann of sixty-five
years before, that the House of Commons adjourned to allow attendance at a masquerade at Mrs Cornelys's house in Soho Square.)

The distinguished diplomat Henry Lytton Bulwer – two names
to conjure with in Victorian Britain – afterwards Lord Dalling, once
said to a friend on leaving Holland House that 'I have seen most of
the palaces and palatial residences of Europe, and if I was asked to

'Holland House – A Garden Party'; engraving by
Gustave Doré in *London – A Pilgrimage*, 1872.

choose one to live in for the remainder of my life, I would choose
this.' Yet whatever the congeniality, the glamour and the political
importance, Holland House embodies in its history during the nineteenth century (as it did with Henry Rich, Earl of Holland, in the
seventeenth) the fragility of wealth. By 1840, when Lord Holland
died, the patricians of Britain, challenged politically as they were,
disposed of riches which were the envy of the world. Forty, fifty years

later, many of their great fortunes would be melting into thin air. The great wealth made by Henry Fox, the first Lord Holland, as paymaster general had been largely exhausted by his payment of the colossal gambling debts incurred by his eldest son Stephen and by Charles, that 'very prototype of all gamesters'. Kingsgate, the Kentish villa, had been sold to pay further debts as soon as Charles inherited it on his father's death. Many of the contents of Holland House were sold at Christie's. What probably saved Holland House in the years before 1800 from demolition, or from the fate of its neighbour Campden House – conversion into a school or other institution – was the long minority of the third Lord Holland, which allowed it to be let over a period of twenty years. Holland's marriage to Elizabeth Webster after the annulment of her previous marriage, helped less than it might have done. She was born Vassall, of a New England family. They did not actually go over in the *Mayflower*, they just owned it. Later they became one of the richest of the West Indian families, but, as we have seen, by the early nineteenth century the sugar fortunes were in rapid decline. (In the circumstances, it was to Holland's credit, disciple of Fox as he was, that he opposed slavery.)

The third Lord and Lady Holland moved into Holland House in 1797. Its state was alarming. The painted ceiling in the Jacobean dining room had fallen in, there was subsidence in both wings, and at least two of their friends urged that the house be abandoned. Repairs were undertaken, but the problems continued. Rain came through the roof, the whole front wall needed rebuilding. The place was atrociously cold in winter: the Hollands' son Henry Edward wrote in his journal during the winter of 1821 that the house was 'colder than ice, and we all caught violent coughs, colds and catarrhs'. In the 1830s, Charles Barry, the architect, installed central heating, which helped, although Henry, after he had inherited the house, still found it 'piteous cold'. Apart from the costs of maintaining a large house more than 200 years old, there was further expense in resisting a legal attack on Lord Holland's title to the house and estate brought by Lord Kensington, from whose family they had been acquired. It cost £4,000 in an out of court settlement. 'I have paid more than I can well afford . . . for this speedy, quiet and undisputed possession of what was already my own,' wrote Lord Holland wryly.

Back at the turn of the seventeenth and eighteenth centuries, the journalist Ned Ward had lamented that lapsing of 'the old hospitality' at Northumberland House. A century later, and more, lavish entertainment was still regarded as an essential function – a *raison d'être* – of a great house. Whatever their financial anxieties, it seemed to the Hollands more natural to shut down Holland House altogether than to cut out the dinner parties. In 1823, the lawsuit finished with, they thought seriously about closure. The alternative – which they adopted – was to sell building leases on the estate, and take out mortgages to help pay for the initial costs, and Lord Holland commissioned the designation of sites on what was to become Addison Road. Another solution, or partial solution, to money worries might come about through government office and an official salary. Holland never led the Whig party; it would not have been a role for which he was suited. However, when after years in the political wilderness, the party returned to power in 1830 under Lord Grey on a programme of reform, he was appointed to a seat in the cabinet and the post of Chancellor of the Duchy of Lancaster with a generous salary. When suddenly the Whigs fell from office – for what in the end was a matter of only ten days – the Hollands were desperately worried. Lady Holland wrote to her son Henry to say: 'To us, who could hardly keep afloat, the loss of *upwards* of £3,000 a year is calamitous indeed.' In the event, Holland, by now a sick man, kept the appointment for the remaining few years of his life.

In the five years of her widowhood, Lady Holland was obsessed with the need for economy, although she continued to entertain at her house in Mayfair. Ampthill, a house in Bedfordshire inherited by her husband, was sold and to the horror of her son, the new Lord Holland, she also started selling some of the contents of Holland House at auction. Henry, the fourth Lord Holland, a diplomat, was an uneasy figure with poor health. He had loved his father, but found his mother very difficult. He had admired many of the celebrities and grandees who formed his parents' circle, though in his early journals he draws the line at the malicious, gossipy Samuel Rogers. Byron was a friend, and in Italy Henry had succeeded to his mistress Teresa Guiccioli. He found her temperament, and her 'carnality', difficult to cope with. 'Poor Lord Byron! I do not wonder at his going to

Greece,' he wrote in his journal after a particularly stormy passage. Like his father and his great-grandfather, the new Lord Holland was no countryman. In his youth, he wrote in his journal after a period of 'endurance vile' at Holland House that 'I shall be delighted to return to *old smoky*, ruralities and frost don't agree'. Aged twenty-seven, he noted his impressions of a coach journey from London to Brighton.

> My journey was rapid and had no other merit. The country (indeed like almost all the country in this island) is tame and uninteresting; perpetual small country-houses with their mean trimness and Lilliput ostentation. There are few of those worst of all sights on this road – a vast green field, dotted with trees, surrounded by a wall, and damped by a variety of swampy ponds, which call themselves *country seats*.

When, however, on his mother's death, he became outright owner of Holland House, his views had mellowed. Anyway, with London sprawling over Kensington, the question was hardly one of how to settle into country life. 'Dear old H.H. must be sacrificed or at least sadly beset by buildings,' he thought, but yet with elbow room Holland House could become a fine town house, and still be enjoyable. Again substantial renovation and repair were needed. Holland provided them, taking out the first of a series of mortgages on the house and grounds, and erected the buildings in the gardens which are now so important a feature of the park. On a return visit in 1857, George Ticknor noted 'The house now much altered and made very luxurious.'

The house might be improved but the financial situation of the family was only the more dire. But the magnificent parties resumed and to the outside world there was really not much change. And it was certain that the new Lady Holland was much nicer than the old one. The fourth Lord Holland died without an heir in 1859, leaving the property to his wife. The large garden parties carried on and capital was consumed at an alarming rate as Lady Holland sold off freeholds to the railway and for building. A friend and financial advisor put it succinctly in a letter: 'When you live at Hd. He. you need not entertain all London.' To no avail. During the 1860s she was reduced to planning the disposal of all that remained of the estate, a recourse which would indeed have left Holland House itself 'sadly beset by buildings'. Nothing immediate happened, but virtually at the moment that Doré celebrated the superb garden parties in *London – A Pilgrimage*, Lady Holland was considering an offer of £400,000 (£23 million today). There was, however, a happy ending. She turned to her late husband's cousin the fifth Earl of Ilchester, the great-grandson of the first Lord Holland's elder brother, who took on the estate and Holland House, allowing her to live there for the rest of her life. He also provided her with an annuity.

The development of the Holland estate was very protracted. Addison Road, for example, was started in the 1820s but not finished until the end of the 1850s. Nevertheless, the estate produced three of the grandest streets in Kensington – Addison Road, a mix of detached villas and terraces; Holland Villas Road; and between 1860 and 1880, the eighty villas, almost all of which have survived, in what is simply called Holland Park, a grouping of streets, which includes a long mews down the middle for stables and coach houses.

But even the majestic houses of Holland Park fade when set beside the Crown Estate development of Kensington Palace Gardens, which runs down the western side of Kensington Gardens, and was constructed on grounds belonging to Kensington Palace. Certainly this is the most splendid of Kensington's residential streets and squares, and with half a mile of great detached houses ('palaces' in the old description), their carriageways fronting a broad avenue, it stands the equal of any in London. It is very impressive, but odd. To start with, it is the last of the private roads, with gates still manned by lodge-keepers to exclude undesirables on lines that had once been common practice in Regent's Park and elsewhere in the richer areas. These sentries turn away traffic which has no business in the road, and are apt to look sceptically even at pedestrians. And they are supported by police, for this is a precinct of foreign embassies and ambassadors' residences, as well as a means of access to Kensington Palace. But Kensington Palace Gardens is odd too in that, as Mark Girouard has pointed out, it has an air of never having been digested into London. 'The street,' he has written, 'retains a curious atmosphere of not quite having made it, of not being altogether the genuine article.' That seems to have been true from the start. The first tender

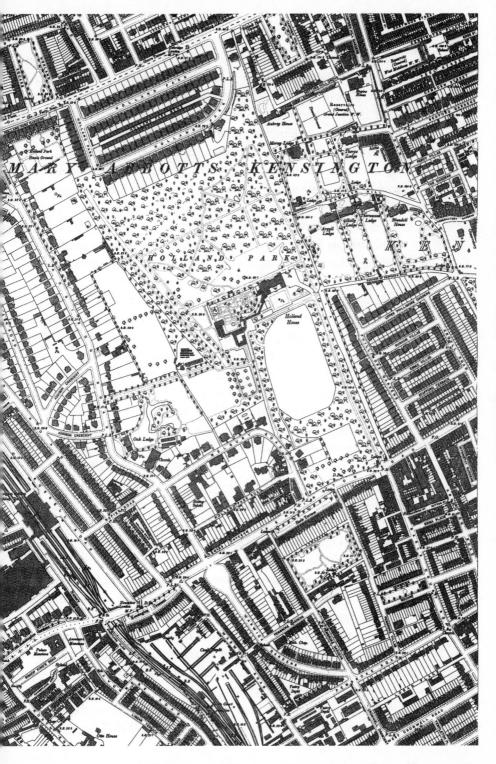

Holland Park and its surrounds in 1894, showing Aubrey House and the 'Dukeries' of Campden Hill and also the artists' quarter of Melbury Road. From *Ordnance Survey*, Middlesex.

was presented to the Commissioners of Woods and Forests in 1842 but progress was slow – not least because of the bankruptcy of the principal contractor – and much of the building did not take place until the 1850s or later. There were few buyers, and by 1851 only eight of the fifteen houses completed were occupied. Then Lord Harrington, a South Kensington landowner, contracted to build himself what is now No. 13, and after that demand was lively. Yet, despite Harrington, the road was not aristocratic; as Campden Hill was nicknamed 'the Dukeries', so Kensington Palace Gardens became 'Millionaires' Row', the home of very rich businessmen, many of them foreign. It was the precursor, and later the counterpart, of Park Lane nearly two miles away on the other side of the parks.

When Professor Benjamin Silliman, Professor of Chemistry, Mineralogy and Geology at Yale, arrived at Liverpool in 1851, he had behind him the memory of his one previous visit made forty-five years before, when as a young man he had been commissioned to buy books and scientific apparatus for the university. Then he had approached London from Oxford by the Henley road, perched on top of a stagecoach. 'From Slough onward,' he had recalled in his memoir of the trip published soon afterwards, 'the crowd of post chaises, coaches and six, and splendid equipages, of every description, indicated our approach to the capital.' He was told that this was more than an ordinary crowd since the Queen that night was to give a splendid ball at Windsor. That was 1805; in 1851, after disembarking from his steamship and with some sightseeing on the way, Silliman and his party joined the Great Western Railway at Gloucester bound for a meeting in London of the Geological Society, of which Silliman was an honorary member. Rooms had been reserved at Morley's Hotel in the recently completed Trafalgar Square. Silliman was, as he said, in 'the very heart of London', and as he looked upwards at the figure of Nelson on its towering column, he remembered that in August 1805, two months before Trafalgar, he had seen the living Nelson walking in the Strand.

It was a new London, as Silliman described it:

The extensive station-house at the terminus [the first Paddington station, immediately north-west of the present one], on the West of London, is in a region which was quite in the country in my early days here; and we drove from it through streets that are principally new since that period. Then the Edgeware road was the extreme limit of London, at the end of Oxford-street, and beyond Hyde Park. Now the Edgeware road is far within the city; and as we approached the region with which I had been best acquainted, we passed through Regent-street and the Crescent, which are entirely new.

He visited a friend who lived in Chester Square. That was Belgravia, which was new too. Only when he called on Barings in the City and travelled by the Strand and Fleet Street did he find himself in familar territory. For the rest . . .

Indeed, while opening my eyes again upon England, I seem to myself to have been awakened like Rip Van Winkle, from a long oblivion, from a sleep of more than twice twenty years; or to have returned like the genii of Arabian tales, after a still longer lapse of time, and to find such changes, that in many places I should not suspect that I had ever been there before.

The district of Paddington grouped round the station at which Professor Silliman had arrived was indeed new. The little village to the north-west of the city had been undistinguished, not the sort of place in which the wealthy chose to spend their summers or their retirement. Its very modesty gave the point to the jingle, ascribed to Canning, which mocked the replacement in 1801 of the great Pitt as Prime Minister by the inconsiderable Addington. It ran,

> Pitt is to Addington
> As London is to Paddington.

Paddington and its surrounds, otherwise known as Tyburnia, were Church of England land, within the diocese of the Bishop of London. The Church was one of the biggest of London landowners, with widely scattered estates. Whereas the other landowners had opened their land for development by granting leases of a length sufficient to give enough security of tenure to appeal to contractors, the Church had been content to abide by the limitations set by parliament. Often its leases were for only forty years; often, as in the case of Paddington, they were on the basis of 'three lives' which was even less helpful from the point of view of development. Under a lease for lives, the leaseholder nominated three people, possibly but not necessarily himself, his son, and his grandson. When all were dead the lease terminated; and in the meantime, as each new 'life' succeeded, a fine was paid to the freeholder. So long as they were prepared to ignore the long-term implications, landlords of course found attractions in short-term leases which, after all, guaranteed income from fines as well as rent, whereas with a long lease the landlord might earn nothing except rent, perhaps just ground rent, for generations. While Church leases were usually in practice automatically renewed, the risk that they might not be was sufficiently real to discourage lessees from making the substantial investment involved in building. What is more, leases for lives, falling in as they must at different times, effectively ruled out comprehensive development.

Another problem was conflict of interest. The additional income derived from these leases came to count as part of a bishop's or other functionary's income. In the 1860s, the Clarendon Commission on the public schools questioned the provost and fellows of Eton – in form an ecclesiastical foundation – on what was a direct contravention of the school's charter. While rents paid by tenants on Eton's lands were entered in the accounts and credited to the school, renewal fines, which constituted a large proportion of the total revenue, were not subjected to audit, and were simply pocketed by the provost and fellows as their own perquisites. The college registrar could only plead that such had always been the practice, and that 'the same is applicable to every religious body . . . [and] . . . of every dean and chapter unless brought under the control of the Ecclesiastical Commissioners.' Ninety-nine-year building leases would indeed upset the apple cart. With Eton's Chalcots estate, which included a Primrose Hill estate, fines were traditionally levied on tenants every seven years, but there was in the end no alternative to a change of policy if the school were to exploit the opportunity provided by the development of Regent's Park. But change was left too late, and Primrose Hill failed to become a fashionable district.

Eton made the change at Primrose Hill in the same way as did individuals burdened by restrictive family settlements – through a private estate act. And in 1795 the Bishop of London, or rather his representatives, made an agreement with his Paddington lessees, now at second generation on their leases, for a joint development with shared profits, to be implemented by an estate act. In practice, very little happened for years and the first building agreement, that for Connaught Place – now a cramped cul-de-sac just north-west of Marble Arch – was not signed until 1807. The delay resulted from a number of causes. There was difficulty over drainage and, to assure a high standard of construction, only small areas were developed at a time. There was, moreover, the distraction of the Grand Junction Canal with its branch to Paddington, and later its extension to Regent's Park. The result was that in the earlier years of the nineteenth century the district was an agglomeration of miscellaneous building. Only too apparent was a shanty town inhabited by Irish labourers working on the canal: they paid low rents and planted potato patches around their huts, and when the ground they occupied was needed for something else, they simply moved their huts on. Craven Hill, slightly further off, preserved a rustic charm. The Novello family, prominent musically – having left London for Bayswater, as one of them remembered it – took consecutively two cottages in Craven Hill in the 1830s, 'when that place retained its primitive simplicity, and consisted of small detached dwellings with gardens, instead of the grand houses which now rise there in lofty rows'. William Hazlitt, grandson of the essayist, was told by his mother, born in 1804, that when as a child she lived on Craven Hill, there were no buildings between her family's house and Harrow. Hazlitt himself could remember the tea gardens at a time when Lancaster Gate was a field with a hedge between it and the highway that later became the Bayswater Road.

From the 1830s the area changed dramatically. Paddington, Tyburnia (the name applied to the section nearest Marble Arch) and, a little further west, Bayswater, rapidly turned into one of the smartest parts of the capital. Partly this was as a result of the property interests of Paddington winning oligarchic control of the vestry, converting it from 'open' to 'select', and so being able more effectively to counter any move which would detract from the district's social standing. *Building News* declared Lancaster Gate to be the most handsome terrace in London. Paddington was a 'city of palaces' claimed a book written in 1853. The *Builder* in 1869 stated that

> Commencing at Lord Grosvenor's mansions, near the Marble Arch, and continuous along the whole park border nearly as far as Notting-hill Gate, the ranges of noble mansions, in terraces, have been completed along the Bayswater-road, which, facing the park and Kensington Gardens, and fronting the south, make them the most favoured residential abodes.

Again the rich were forming a suburb on the edge of town with the open fields immediately behind, while, generally speaking, the middle income groups and the poor stayed on the inside. Architecturally, with its mainly brick houses and the usual squares, much of Bayswater resembled Marylebone across the Edgware Road. Along the Bayswater Road, however, the design changed. For one thing the buildings were faced with stucco. For another, Hyde Park provided the trees and grass, itself taking the place of a square garden. It sounds natural that it should, but it had not been true, and still was only partially true of the eastern side of the park fronting Park Lane where, as may be remembered, the houses at the northern end had been designed to face inwards towards the town. At the same time, in some places along the Bayswater Road, most notably in the eastern section of Hyde Park Gardens, there were planted what amounted to supplementary communal gardens that communicated directly with the houses which formed the terraces. It was a development of this idea which was to be so characteristic of Notting Hill and the general district of Holland Park.

The view over the Bayswater Road into Hyde Park and Kensington Gardens was a particular attraction to house buyers. Equally desirable was the view the other way, from the south, from Kensington Gore. But here the long terraces had yet to appear and there was little to buy. Instead, overlooking the parks, was a line of fine detached mansions. At the western end, looking over to Kensington Palace, was Kensington House, which had been built long before by one of the Colby brothers and which was by the nineteenth century a lunatic asylum. Then came Noel House, on the site of Palace Gate, once, like Campden House, the property of the Noels, earls of Gainsborough, and rebuilt in 1804; next, where the Albert Hall now stands were Grove House and Gore House, the largest of a number of houses on a 21½-acre estate. Further on, in Knightsbridge, were two mid-eighteenth-century mansions, Kingston House and Rutland House. This last was pulled down in the 1830s, while most of the others were demolished soon after the Great Exhibition of 1851 in Hyde Park, when the whole area was redeveloped.

Of these mansions Gore House stands out. It was built in 1750 and among its residents were Admiral Lord Rodney in the 1780s and William Wilberforce from 1808 to 1821. Its most colourful tenant, however, was Lady Blessington who, with the stunning dandy Comte d'Orsay, created there in the late 1830s a salon which for over a decade came close to rivalling Holland House itself. Lady Blessington and (the third) Lady Holland had from the point of view of personality little or nothing in common, for Lady Blessington was charm personified. What they shared was difficulty in paying the bills for their lavish entertainments. In 1849 Lady Blessington and d'Orsay fled to the Continent to escape their creditors, and Gore House ended its life in style, transformed by the great chef Alexis Soyer into a splendid restaurant next door to the Great Exhibition in Hyde Park.

Behind this row of mansions lay the parish of Brompton, much of it rural and under cultivation. Later, as South Kensington, it was to become fashionable, but at this period, residentially, it was a district mainly of villas and country houses. To the south lay Chelsea, and to the west Knightsbridge, Sloane Street and the part of the Cadogan estate developed by Henry Holland. Near Hyde Park Corner were three hospitals, including St George's on the site of the private mansion of Lanesborough House and now of the Lanesborough Hotel. Plots of land near the hospitals were later to fetch low ground rents, only £4 a year as opposed to the more usual £18 further away down Grosvenor Place. There were also two blocks of tenements, and in Grosvenor Crescent, near what was to become Belgrave Square, the old Tattersalls, the market for horse sales much frequented by the rich. Beyond, towards the Thames, were the marshes, mostly desolate wasteland interspersed with ponds and occasional ruinous farm buildings. It was a region that offered good duck shooting and fishing and, on firmer ground, a place for duels and all sorts of less dangerous sports, including horse racing. The largest building was the enormous Millbank Penitentiary down on the river on the site of our Tate Gallery, in theory a model prison planned as it was on lines advocated by Jeremy Bentham. Not only was its presence oppressive, but it was also considered a likely source of disease. This extensive and neglected area was part of the Mary Davies bequest to the Grosvenors, who had failed to be carried away by the idea of attempting to transform it into another Mayfair. They were at least making a reasonable return from rent paid by market gardeners and the sprawling Chelsea Waterworks. And of course the problems of drainage and flood control were formidable. Moreover, the first Earl Grosvenor (1731–1802) was extremely extravagant and accumulated debts which weighed on the family for a generation after his death. By their own standards anyway, the Grosvenors were short of money, and the first earl's son, the first Marquess of Westminster (1767–1845), was unwilling until after 1819 to provide direct financial assistance to contractors and builders, either in the form of mortgages or by paying for drainage and roads. In any event, the family's inclination for building was amply fulfilled elsewhere, in the new Grosvenor House in Park Lane and the rebuilding of Eaton Hall, their mansion in the country.

The construction of Belgravia is as closely identified with Thomas Cubitt as is that of Regent's Park with John Nash. Cubitt may have escaped the political complications faced by Nash, but the technical challenge to his skills was greater. It was required of him that he create a whole new urban development – for here there was not even a village to build around – that he provide public services on a large scale for a growing population, and that he exercise unremitting control over the environment and tone of the area to ensure the success of its development. Cubitt was the son of a Norfolk carpenter and in his early days in London, builder as he was, he persisted in calling himself a carpenter. By 1825, when the construction of Belgravia began, he was nearly forty years old with an unrivalled experience of work throughout London. He had acted as a contractor in Strand-on-the-Green by Kew Bridge; in Highbury; in the City; in Holborn; in Bayswater; and above all, after 1821, in the enlargement of Bloomsbury, where he was to be engaged for the rest of his life. Cubitt brought to the marshes of Belgravia not only his experience but resources in manpower and expertise which were extraordinary by the standards of his time. While he may not have been the first contractor to employ a direct labour force comprehending all the skills required – as opposed to farming out most of the work to specialist firms – the scale of his enterprise was unprecedented. He had a payroll of up to 2,000 employees, with his own civil-engineering department for the making of roads and pavements, and for the installing of sewers and drains. He developed his own brickfields. On top of that, he was a capable manager of risk: for instance, he limited himself to only three of the houses in Belgrave Square, the centrepiece of the estate. At a time when speculative contractors were going bankrupt all over London, and when the other large-scale developers in Belgravia and Pimlico, Joseph Cundy and Seth Smith, went insolvent and had to come to special terms with the Grosvenors, Cubitt survived to make a great deal of money. He left over a million pounds at death.

The Irish writer Lady Morgan has left a description of life in Belgravia and its neighbourhood at the start of the 1840s, while development was in full swing, and she adds a pleasing snapshot of Cubitt himself. The Morgans were not rich and wanted a house in 'Cubittopolis', as Lady Morgan termed it, which would be cheap and charming. They found one at No. 11 William Street, in one of the two roads that link Knightsbridge with Lowndes Square. Only two or three houses were as yet finished, and, Lady Morgan noted in her diary, 'all looks rather wild and rude (a thing that would be a field if it could)'. Actually she felt it was rather silly to try to keep a diary what with the noise of the workmen and machinery. But she was not the sort of person to give up easily on anything and she turned her attention and energies to bettering her immediate surroundings. She objected to the 'hideous gate of the beautiful Hyde Park' (now Albert Gate), which stood at the bottom of William Street beyond the little bridge over 'the great sewer of this quarter'. There was also the Cannon Brewery with its plume of smoke just by. So she got hold of Mr Cubitt, 'a good, little, complying man', who proved most

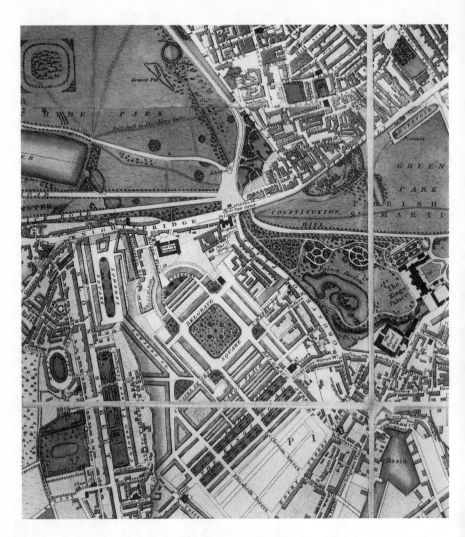

Belgravia in 1827, from C. and J. Greenwood, *Map of London . . .*

co-operative. He was anyway in the market for the brewery in order to pull it down and redevelop the site, and what is more he undertook to pay for an 'ancient gate' into the park. With some others, Lady Morgan initiated a petition to the Queen about the existing gate – this was Crown land – enlisting the support of the Queen's mother, the Duchess of Kent, a neighbour in Belgrave Square. All went well:

we got the new gate, she said, 'just as we got Catholic emancipation, by worrying for it!'

Lady Morgan's house was at the edge of the development, indeed outside the Grosvenor lands. Cubitt was able to demolish the brewery with other buildings on the site by arrangement with the Crown's Commissioners of Woods and Forests and to replace them by the two largest houses which had ever been built on speculation in London. One of them, now the French Embassy, was taken by George Hudson, the 'Napoleon of railways', who shortly afterwards went bankrupt. The other, though intended as a single residence, was split in two, with one part becoming a branch of the London & County Bank. The two sections were reunited in 1875 by the fabulously rich Sassoons.

Within the confines of the estate, Belgrave Square and Eaton Square represented the height of fashion. Eaton Square grew up

Belgrave Chapel and the west side of Belgrave Square, 1828. Drawing by T. H. Shepherd.
Reproduced from James Elmes, *Metropolitan Improvements or London in the Nineteenth Century*, 1827.

around its church, and although started about 1825, progress was delayed by the existence until 1842 of a lease for market gardens on its north side. The square was not in fact completed until the 1850s. Progress in Belgrave Square, however, was rapid, seemingly unimpeded by the financial depression of the late 1820s. Early residents included the Duchess of Kent, the Duke of Bedford, who moved there from St James's Square, Lord Brownlow and Lord Sefton. There were also bankers: the first house completed was occupied in 1828 by Henry Drummond, one of the bankers to Lord Grosvenor. It is easy for Londoners now to forget how very grand the Belgrave Square buildings are. Traditionally the French had dismissed the great London houses when compared to the *hôtels* of Paris. But a French visitor in the 1850s, stating Belgrave Square to be the largest and most splendid of London's residential squares, declared that every house it contained was a palace.

Belgravia is the culmination, the pre-eminent district of London's West End, surpassing even the Grosvenors' other estate in Mayfair, and peopled by what a witness before a Royal Commission in the 1850s described as 'the richest population in the world'. With its building, the series of incisive thrusts into the countryside to the north and west of the City of London came to an end. There were further outward migrations of the rich to come – the Jews to North London, the reoccupation of Chelsea, the infill of South Kensington – but in comparison they are insubstantial. After Belgravia, the rich lost the initiative and thenceforward, until very recent times, they were in retreat, the impulse turned towards concentration and contraction.

8

South of the River

*

Having done with Chelsea, Sir Richard Phillips resumed his walk to Kew, crossing the Thames by Battersea Bridge. The land on the south side of the river was arable and pasture, and like the north side, thick with market gardens. Much of it was marsh. Where it most obviously differed from Chelsea and Fulham and Hammersmith was in the concentration of industry. A hundred yards over Battersea Bridge, Phillips came on a sawmill with a steam engine established by Marc Brunel seven years before, in 1810. In Battersea village, while Old Battersea House remained (and it is still there now), the manor house of the St John family (Bolingbroke) had been replaced by a maltster and distiller, the owner of which, a Mr Hodgson, was happy to show Phillips around. The owner of a pitch and turpentine factory was equally hospitable. The road to Wandsworth was lined with distilleries. Phillips, who was turning increasingly irascible, grumbled about drunkenness. Wandsworth's half-mile-long high street provided more variety with its dyers and calico printers, oil mills and foundries, but Phillips's initial impression of the 'populous, industrious and opulent village of Wandsworth' was overlaid by a more general reflection on villages around London; lively and splendid as they might be in summer, how infinitely dull they were for those who lived in them all the year round. The thought lingered as he passed on, moralizing and sometimes maundering, by Putney Heath, down by Barn Elms – once, as he put it, a 'classical resort' – through Barnes and Mortlake. Roehampton he found a most cheerless place, though he approved the villas, and the dozen or so mansions on the heights above, facing Richmond Park, each set in 20 or 30 acres of garden and park. At Barnes Common 'nature still appeared to be in

← South London in 1827, from C. and J. Greenwood, *Map of London* . . .

a primeval and unfinished state'; while Barnes itself 'consists of a few straggling houses opposite the Common, of a mean street leading to the water-side, and of a row of elegant houses facing the Thames, on a broad terrace nearly half a mile long.'

Richard Phillips might exaggerate, but it was clear to anyone – except perhaps to factory owners – that these south-bank villages, in terms of prosperity, lagged far behind their counterparts on the other side of the Thames. Battersea, after all, was only three miles from Westminster, slightly further than Chelsea which, as we have seen, had grown by the early nineteenth century into a full-blown town. The problem lay in the poor communications. True, there were ferries, but as Boswell found on setting out to dine with the Thrales in Southwark, they could be unreliable, and anyway they were not usually capable of carrying horses or carriages or freight. In 1710, two German visitors, Zacharias von Uffenbach and his brother, crossed the Thames into Southwark. So taken were they with the large and handsome buildings on either side that they were almost half way across the river before realizing that they were on London Bridge itself and not in some ordinary London street. That London Bridge was impressive is not to be doubted, but until the opening of Westminster Bridge in 1750 it made the only 'solid' crossing of the Thames nearer than a timber bridge at Fulham. What delayed the construction of more bridges was less the cost (and, after all, Paris by the seventeenth century possessed numerous bridges across the Seine) than the opposition of vested interests. A proposal for a bridge at Westminster had been put forward soon after the Restoration only to be vigorously and successfully resisted by the City of London and others who worried that it would act as a stimulus to trade and building in the West End. The City was equally effective in 1671 in thwarting the construction of a bridge between Putney and Fulham, where there was a particularly busy ferry crossing. In the House of Commons it was declared to be the Lord Mayor's opinion that 'if carts went over Putney Bridge the City of London would be irretrievably ruined'. The watermen joined in, afraid for their jobs, and their argument weighed the more heavily since they provided a useful reserve of sailors in wartime.

From the point of view of the rich, of course, the very lack of urbanization could be an attraction: after all, they withdrew from Chelsea when it became too built-up. Lambeth and Southwark, with easy access to London Bridge and heavily industrialized, were uncongenial. Richmond and Greenwich, bridgeless and factoryless, one to the west of London, the other downstream to the east, were resorts much favoured by the wealthy. In both cases the initial appeal had been the presence of the monarch. In Richmond, the royal connection was maintained in the eighteenth century by Frederick, Prince of Wales, and by the proximity of Kew and Windsor. At Greenwich, the royal association loosened. Henry VII and Henry VIII had preferred it to nearby Eltham, but Charles II had failed in the end to restore the ruined palace. For a time, fashion moved away, and in the later seventeenth century tax collectors complained their job was complicated by the sub-division of so many old mansions into tenements. Nevertheless, in the early eighteenth century Defoe wrote of 'the people of quality and fashion' who lived at Greenwich, and by his time the district had recovered patrician esteem. There was always the appeal of the surroundings, of Blackheath and Charlton with their superb views. Edward Hasted in *The History and Topographical Survey of the County of Kent* of 1778 described Greenwich both as very populous and to be 'reckoned one of the genteelest and pleasantest towns in England'. Sir Gregory Page's Wricklemarsh at Blackheath, designed by John James and completed in 1721, Hasted considered one of the finest seats in England belonging to a private gentleman. The nobility in the eighteenth century were also well represented with, among others, the Earl of Dartmouth, the Duke of Montague, and the fourth Earl of Chesterfield, the writer of the famous letters, at the Ranger's House, Blackheath. He also built one of the most important of the West End palaces.

But the wealthy who crowded in the early nineteenth century into South London (a conventional but not wholly accurate description since for much of its course the river runs south to north) were not usually weekenders or those in search of a country life, but businessmen who commuted daily north of the river. For them, bridges and a good road system were essential. The prerequisites there were parliamentary approval and investment by private individuals, who in most cases reimbursed themselves for construction

Lambeth Palace from the Thames, 1709. From
Walford, *Old and New London*, 1897, vol. iv.

costs and the buying-out of ferry interests by the levy of tolls. Battersea
Bridge, opened for pedestrians in 1771 and for carriages a year later,
was financed by a syndicate composed of landowners from both sides
of the river, each of whom put up £1,000 capital. The moving spirit
was the first Earl Spencer, whose trustees had bought the manor of
Battersea from the St Johns a few years before and whose family was
to become, through further purchases, one of the principal landowners
of south-west London. At Putney, the bridge dated from 1729 and
one of those requiring compensation, in her case £364 10s. 0d., was
Lord Spencer's grandmother Sarah, Duchess of Marlborough, lady
of the manor of Wimbledon. The Bishop of London from the Fulham
side of the river was paid £23 for his interest in the Putney ferry as
well and also secured exemption from tolls for himself, his successors
and their respective households. For the Richmond bridge, investors
were rewarded by a tontine, a form of life assurance whereby, in early
years, investors or their nominees received little or nothing but the
longer-lived were handsomely rewarded.

Putney Bridge and Village from Fulham. British
School, artist unknown.

The significance of the bridges is obvious enough today. Less
evident, given the mean streets and the congestion of so much of
South London, are the original spacious thoroughfares which were
driven through from the new bridges to the countryside that lay
behind the urban strip along the river. From Vauxhall Bridge, opened
in 1816, the road line, interrupted only by the Oval, runs its mile and
a half straight down the Camberwell New Road to Camberwell and
Denmark Hill. Linking Kennington to the City of London is the
almost equally straight Kennington Road which follows its longer
course to Blackfriars Road and thus to Blackfriars Bridge (1769) –
built soon after Westminster Bridge – and the heart of the City. Free
from smog, beautiful to look at, the newly accessible districts made
an immediate appeal to prosperous Londoners. Even now, you can
sometimes sense how lovely it must have been. Down the Brixton
Road, past Kennington and Camberwell, is Brockwell Park. The
mansion, Brockwell Hall, remains, a rather sad 1816 country villa with
a netball pitch in front and a refreshment room inside. It is uninspiring.
But from the terrace in front with its cedars, those conventional but
evocative ornaments to a gentleman's residence, there opens out a

217

magnificent view of St Paul's and the City, and – nowadays – further off, the British Telecom Tower by Regent's Park. Such a sight makes it easier to comprehend the enthusiasm of pre-railway days, and to respond to Ruskin when he writes of the view southwards from his home in Herne Hill, close by to Brockwell Park:

> The view from the ridge on both sides was, before railways came, entirely lovely: westward at evening, almost sublime, over softly wreathing distances of domestic wood ... On the other side, east and south, the Norwood hills, partly rough with furze, partly wooded with birch and oak, partly in pure green bramble copse, and rather steep pasture, rose with the promise of all the rustic loveliness of Surrey and Kent.

The musicologist Sir Charles Grove, living in Clapham as a child in the 1820s and 1830s, recalled that 'So clear was the air across Battersea Fields that we could see the coloured sails of the barges going up and down the river.'

With perhaps a *Burke's Peerage* in hand, it is not difficult to identify the families who created the West End: their names and associations have been bequeathed to the streets and squares which cover the land they occupied or built over. In Marylebone, for example, are Portman Square and Portman Street, and Bryanston Square, named after the family's country palace in Dorset, and Blandford Street, recalling the local country town. The dukes of Bedford's Bloomsbury teems with such references. From Bloomsbury Square itself, you pass at once into Great Russell Street and Bedford Place, into Southampton Row (named after Rachel Russell's family) and Woburn Place. In another direction are Streatham Street, recalling their Surrey estate, and Bedford Square. Torrington Square looks to the Devonshire estate. Tavistock Square again has a territorial connection, and a personal one as well, since Tavistock is the title assumed by the eldest son. Herbrand Street and Adeline Place carry family associations. In South London, such clues are meagre. Allusions exist, as in Black Prince Road, which commemorates the medieval palace at Kennington, demolished in 1531 to provide building material for Henry VIII's Whitehall, and in Loughborough Park,

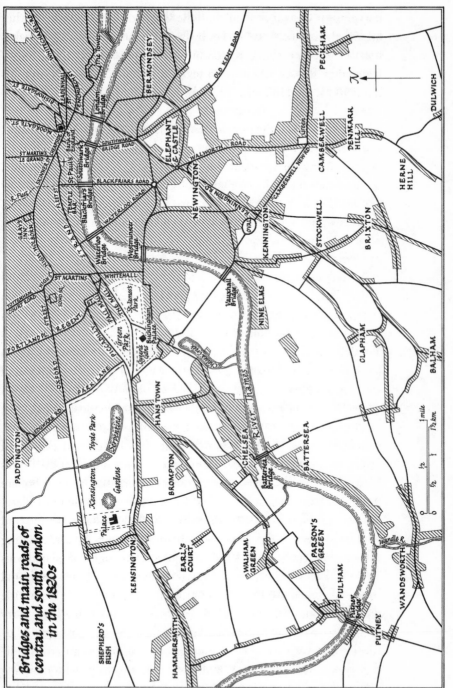

Bridges and main roads of central and south London in the 1820s; based on John Luffman's map of 1820, with additions.

part of the estate acquired by the first (Hastings) Lord Loughborough, a notable Royalist commander in the Civil War, whose house in one form or another survived well into the nineteenth century. While ownership of land was in parts highly concentrated, the proprietors were often corporate bodies. The Archbishop of Canterbury possessed much of Lambeth, and personal names attached to streets usually celebrate past incumbents of his office like Laud and Sancroft. The manor of Vauxhall again was Church land with the Dean and Chapter of Christ Church, Canterbury as landowners. It was on their estate just north of Vauxhall Bridge that there flourished the famous Vauxhall Gardens, long popular with wealthy Londoners. Another important corporate landowner was the Duchy of Cornwall in Kennington.

Apart from Earl Spencer, the most important private landowner in 1800 was the fifth Duke of Bedford at Streatham, whose great-grandfather, the second duke, son of the 'martyred' William, Lord Russell and his wife Rachel, had come into a large South London estate through marriage in 1695 to the heiress Elizabeth Howland, from what was originally a City family. The Thrales, remembered in Thrale Road, bought their estate of Streatham Park from the Duke of Bedford. The Howlands find street names only in Bloomsbury and, more significantly, in the East End of London at Rotherhithe where their wet dock, which survived until the end of the nineteenth century, was for nearly a hundred years the largest in the port of London. To signal the presence of the Bedfords, there is Bedford Hill, a road which runs across Tooting Bec Common, and a (Russell) footpath. The Spencers, with extensive property in Wimbledon (inherited from the Duchess of Marlborough) and Wandsworth and Barnes as well as in Battersea, are better remembered, with Spencer Park by Wandsworth Common ('tastefully planned, but very useless,' commented Sir Richard Phillips as he walked by) and one or two 'Spencer' streets. There are street references to lesser landlords. Baring Road, leading south from the South Circular Road for one and half miles, is a suitable memorial to the Baring family and in particular to Sir Francis Baring, who established himself at Lee, south of Blackheath, with a sizeable country estate. On the other hand, Brodrick Road, just south of Wandsworth Common, is a very modest reminder of the importance of the Brodrick family, minor Yorkshire gentry who made a large fortune in the City of London and settled in Wandsworth during Queen Elizabeth's reign, and who eventually gained an Irish peerage with the title of Viscount Midleton. Sometimes long-dead owners are recalled in the name of a house or other building, as at Barnes, where Milbourne House on the Green seems to have taken its name from the Milbournes or Melbournes, and at Battersea, where the Beaufoy public house on Lavender Hill recalls a rich and philanthropic local family with property there and a factory in Lambeth.

For the family of Clayton, who leased land from the Duchy of Cornwall in Kennington and rank as one of the most important early developers of South London, Clayton Street near the Oval is a quite insufficient memorial, although not far off, at St Thomas's Hospital in Lambeth, the founder of the family fortunes, Sir Robert Clayton, a seventeenth-century scrivener, is honoured as a philanthropist in a statue by Grinling Gibbons. He was a highly influential businessman, one to whom many an old patrician family has cause to be grateful. Clayton transformed the market for mortgages, he initiated loans which avoided the constraints of the usury laws, and devised trusts for his clients – most famously for the second Duke of Buckingham and for William, Lord Russell – which afforded protection against confiscation by the state. Clayton and his partner John Morris were active investors in City real estate after the Great Fire, building residential and commercial property for letting. In Surrey, as well as buying a thirty-one-year lease from the Duchy of Cornwall, they invested in land further afield with purchases of the manors of Marden and Lagham near Godstone, twenty miles away from London, property which remained in the Clayton family – Morris having left his share to his partner – until the twentieth century. The adjacent manor of Bletchingley, which Sir Robert also bought, provided him and subsequent Claytons with a useful parliamentary pocket borough.

Robert Clayton's contemporary and fellow magnate Sir Stephen Fox bought a lease on neighbouring land in South Lambeth from the Archbishop of Canterbury in 1701. There were regular renewals, and between 1820 and 1824 Stephen Fox's great-grandson, the host and politician the third Lord Holland, took out new leases with expiry set for 1923, and let the land to builders and other developers.

Vauxhall Bridge was open and the Hollands were hopeful that Lambeth might revive their shaky fortunes. As with Kensington, however, development was slow, and though some of the buildings initiated by Lord Holland survive, they display little architectural coherence. Take Vassall Road, its name recalling Lady Holland's family. A number of the attractive detached villas are still in place, but their symmetry is wrecked by the ugly timber-board attachments which now connect them one to another. The only 'Holland' name given for the estate in the standard London street directories is Holland Grove, the tiny Lord Holland Lane and Holland Walk being too insignificant to justify a mention. Nevertheless, while Holland Town, the name grandly given originally to the development, failed to live up to expectations, it proved more satisfactory than the Claytons' building projects. Their experience stands as an example of why leaseholders were wary of institutional landowners. In the customary manner, original leases were renewed as they fell due and in the late eighteenth century the Clayton of the day started to issue building leases on terms of up to the usual ninety-nine years. It was a serious misjudgement, for when the head leases expired in 1834, the Duchy of Cornwall, fully aware of the profits now to be made in South London, took back the property (and thus the profits) into its own hands.

The building in Kennington and South Lambeth was instituted by the rich – stretching the word somewhat in the case of the Hollands – but was not for the rich. Even in districts where wealthy businessmen chose to settle, their houses were usually comfortable villas rather than country mansions with extensive lands. Businessmen wanted something imposing but manageable. The fate of Lord Thurlow's great mansion illustrates the change in taste. Thurlow, with one brief interruption, was Lord Chancellor from 1778 to 1792 and acquired an estate of some 1,000 acres mainly in Streatham and Lambeth, employing Henry Holland as architect for a house on Tulse Hill at the junction of what are now Thurlow Park Road and Elmcourt Road. He quarrelled with Holland over costs and never actually took up residence. On Thurlow's death in 1806, his trustees put the estate and house up for sale, but finding no buyer were obliged to obtain a private act of parliament enabling them to sell for building develop-

Kennington Common and church, 1830. From
Walford, *Old and New London*, 1897, vol. vi.

ment. In 1804, J. Hassell published a book of his drawings and
engravings under the title *Views of Noblemen's and Gentlemen's Seats*.
Most of the 'views' are of South London: very few are of noblemen's
seats, and in some cases the houses they depict probably constitute
their owner's claim to gentlemanly status. Again, many of the houses
are villas rather than country houses. Mr Stockwell of the East India
Company, for example, owns an 'elegant villa' at Norwood, while
Mr Lynn at Clapham has retired to a 'homely yet elegant little
cottage'.

Both Hassell and Richard Phillips gave special notice to the
traditional enclosure of the rich at Roehampton, so similar in many
ways to Stanmore on the northern side of London. Roehampton lies
adjacent to and west of Putney with its own western edge touching
the expanse of Richmond Park. Even more than Stanmore, it provides
a natural frontier to London. At the turn of the nineteenth and
twentieth centuries, Charles Booth was to write that Roehampton
'seems to lie a long way from anywhere, except to those such as have

private carriages'. It was two or three miles from the nearest station with a population which consisted of the rich and those 'who in one way or another' served them. Back in the seventeenth century, Christian, the Countess of Devonshire who had held such state in the City, spent much of her time at Roehampton Great House. Later, in the days of Hassell and Phillips, Roehampton residents in summer included the Earl of Bessborough at what is now Manresa House, the Earl of Leven and Melville at Roehampton House (the finest of all, built 1710–12), the marquesses of Downshire and Bristol and the Earl of Ripon. For his *Views*, however, Hassell selected two houses, two villas in fact, with occupants who made no claim to patrician status. At Roehampton Grove, which had replaced Lady Devonshire's mansion, was the banker William Gosling, and at Elm Grove between 1797 and 1808, Benjamin Goldsmid, who with his brother Abraham had established the leading bill brokerage in the City. In the 1830s, Lord Ashburton (a Baring) described the Goldsmids as 'the Rothschilds of their day'.

The presence of Goldsmid, a Jew whose father had immigrated from Holland in the 1760s, represented a sign of the times, but less evidently so in South London than it would have done elsewhere. For this was an area where foreign names abounded. The original developer at Roehampton, the man who built the Great House and Elm Grove, was named Papillon, of an early Huguenot refugee family. Also at Roehampton (and at Putney) were the Vannecks. At Wimbledon the original owners of The Keir, one of the most important of local houses, were the Portuguese Aguilars; at Barnes, the French Castelnaus left their name to the imposing thoroughfare which leads to Hammersmith Bridge. Sir Theodore Janssen of South Sea fame, and later Paul d'Aranda, owned 'Putney Palace', facing the Thames at Putney. Wandsworth in particular owed much to immigrants. It took its name and its original industrial importance from the River Wandle, which runs seventeen miles from its source near Croydon to its junction with the Thames, and the Domesday Book lists at least thirteen corn mills along its banks. Snuff mills flourished there in the eighteenth century along with iron and oil mills, textile workshops and the ubiquitous distilleries. But by that time, Wandsworth's continuing prosperity was as much due to Huguenot refugees who, reviving a local craft, established a great

The Melville family in the grounds of Roehampton
House in 1870.

reputation for the 'Wandsworth Hat' in continental Europe. (Their
least likely market was the Cardinals, who, indirectly of course, bought
their red hats from them.)

The most prominent Huguenot families in South London were
the Minets and the de Crespignys, both of whom had taken refuge
in England at the end of the seventeenth century after the revocation of
the Edict of Nantes. The Minet family of Lambeth and Camberwell,
originally of Calais, made their money as City merchants. In 1770,
Hughes Minet bought from the old Kent family of Knatchbull an
estate variously measured as 109 and 118 acres in the area of Myatts
Field, named after a market gardener tenant who introduced rhubarb
as a vegetable to England. While the building which later covered
their land can claim no particular architectural importance, the Minets
are remembered for their record of communal responsibility. They
provided a site for a church, and in 1889 William Minet gave Myatts
Field of 14½ acres to the London County Council, and at much the

same time donated the Minet Public Library to a trust, or what amounted to a trust, which later transferred it to the Lambeth Library Commission. The importance of the de Crespignys lies in their 80-acre estate on Denmark Hill, Camberwell, a district which became highly sought after by the commercial rich in the first half of the nineteenth century. It was well placed on high ground with magnificent views and, to start with at any rate, was sufficiently distant from the spread of London. Here were built detached and sizeable villas with spacious gardens, whose owners were to mount a firm resistance as the city increasingly threatened their domain.

By origin, the de Crespignys were grander than the Minets. They rebuilt past wealth not as merchants but as lawyers, and added to it through rewarding marriages. The Denmark Hill estate was acquired in 1741 and later extended, and as the family reinstated its wealth it reinstated also its social position. In 1804 Claude de Crespigny and his energetic wife held the first of a series of magnificent garden parties at their house Champion Lodge on the corner of what are now Denmark Hill and Love Walk. A baronetcy followed in recognition of the family's place in society, and thenceforward the de Crespignys depended on Denmark Hill and its rents for their money but not for their home. Champion Lodge remained standing for another generation but in 1841 it was demolished to make way for a more lucrative housing development. While the Minets continued in business, establishing a leading Lloyd's broker, the de Crespignys reverted to country gentry. The fourth baronet, Sir Claude Champion de Crespigny (1847–1939), was a full-time sportsman who published a book of sporting reminiscences. Colourful though he was, nick-named the 'Mad Rider' for his steeplechasing and the 'Fighting Baronet' for his boxing, he would have made a dreadful businessman; in fact early in his career he was faced with bankruptcy proceedings. The Duchess of Westminster remembered him in his old age as 'a fire-eater with a piercing bloodshot eye and a barrack-square manner.'

As at the time of the South Sea Bubble, business was still a very precarious occupation, for which a gentlemanly upbringing was often a poor preparation. One can return to the experience of that other South Londoner, Henry Thrale, for it provides an excellent case in point. The Southwark brewery Thrale inherited was steeped in the

Grove Lane, Camberwell, in the 1870s. From Walford,
Old and New London, 1897, vol. vi., where it is
designated Camberwell Grove.

vigorous and venerable London tradition of the Industrious Apprentice, that of the poor boy who by prudence and hard work makes good. At the start of the eighteenth century, the brewery's proprietor was Edmund Halsey, who in time-honoured fashion had arrived in London from the country with no more than a few shillings in his pocket. There was a family connection with the brewery and so its owner appointed him 'broomstick clerk', the term for the lowly employee who swept the yard and performed other menial jobs. Halsey did so well that he ended up marrying the boss's daughter and inheriting the business. In his turn, being without a son and having married his daughter to Lord Cobham – and peers did not run breweries – Halsey was faced with the problem of succession. He solved it by recruiting another impecunious countryman, his nephew Ralph Thrale from St Albans, who in due course saved enough from the brewery profits to buy out the Cobham interest.

Ralph Thrale had lacked the opportunity to turn himself into a gentleman and his son Henry was born in what his wife described as a miserable Southwark alehouse. Yet, as time went on, the stream of profits from beer and the social ambition of his father washed Henry clean, anointed him a gentleman. In his youth he was sent to stay with his grand relations at Stowe; he was educated at Oxford and went on the Grand Tour. As we have seen, he was a familiar figure at Mrs Cornelys's, owned a pack of hounds, and kept a smart mistress. On their marriage in 1763 – by which time he had inherited the brewery – Hester judged him 'nearly the handsomest man in England'; he probably was, since she was in no way blinded by love. Nevertheless, Henry Thrale was determined to establish himself as a brilliant businessman. With his background he would have needed exceptional gifts to do so, and such gifts he patently failed to possess. His overweening ambition, his passion for gambling and his poor sense of reality, all but drove the brewery into the ground, and it was saved only by the efforts of Hester and the brewery manager John Perkins. When Thrale died in 1781 in the aftermath of a stroke precipitated by the news of another venture gone disastrously wrong, his wife took charge, supported by a Dr Johnson quite carried away by the excitement of signing large cheques. Hester was not lacking in confidence: 'Women', she claimed, have a manifest advantage over men in the doing of business; everything smooths down before them, & to be a female is commonly sufficient to be successful, if she has a little spirit & a little commonsense.

But when it came to it, she had second thoughts, for she was well aware that she lacked the necessary technical knowledge and was in the hands of John Perkins. With a Thrale son, she might have allotted Perkins a larger share of the profits – he anyway had to be made a partner – and kept the business in the family. But, as things were, a sale was inevitable even had the brewery been left in a more flourishing condition. Of the twelve Thrale children, all the boys died, and there were left just four daughters; and, as Dr Johnson said, 'what can misses do with a brewhouse?' Had ages and circumstances fitted, the solution might have been to marry one of the daughters to Perkins. But probably not, for his heavy, no nonsense North Country features and the ungainly body look altogether too proletarian to be acceptable to the fastidious Thrales. Anyway, the ages were all wrong. On top of that, Perkins did even better for himself since, as his second wife, he married Amelia Bevan, the widow of an important City Quaker who was also a grandson of the yet more important David Barclay the elder (1682–1769). Through her, Perkins became part of a group of London rich with very different values to the Thrales. The Quakers, brought up in a separate educational, cultural and social tradition, introduced an especial dedication and dynamism to business. Perkins and two members of his new clan united to buy out the Thrale interest in the brewery. They at once installed a Boulton & Watt steam engine (which was to last for a hundred years) as if to signal the resolve which was to turn the business, henceforward known as the Angel Brewery, into the largest brewery in Europe and one of the sights of London.

The Quakers were also remarkable for their philanthropy and general sense of communal responsibility. David Barclay the younger (1729–1809), the man who directed the purchase of the Thrale brewery, emancipated his slaves in Jamaica at great personal loss and poured money into charity. It was natural that such a family should gravitate to the South London suburb of Clapham. Like Bloomsbury several generations later, the word 'Clapham' at the end of the eighteenth and the beginning of the nineteenth centuries denoted not only the place itself but also a moral and intellectual attitude. Clapham, on its hill less than two miles from the river, had long been a favourite with the rich. It was there that Samuel Pepys retired, a rich man, to live in the magnificent house of his one-time clerk William Hewer. Pepys was followed by others, most notably perhaps the commanding City merchant Sir John Barnard, who settled at Clapham in the middle of the eighteenth century. The Barclays arrived slightly later, initially in the persons of David Barclay's brother, John, and Robert Barclay, the nephew given immediate charge of the Thrale brewery. Clapham was a district for business rather than for patrician money although, as it happened, one of its most eminent (and reclusive) residents was the great chemist Henry Cavendish, grandson of the second Duke of Devonshire. That was Clapham the place; as a figure of speech, Clapham signified an evangelical movement associated with its residents, the members of which became known as the Clapham Sect or alternatively the Saints of Clapham.

The analogy with Bloomsbury can be taken too far although, as it happened, one of the leaders of the Clapham movement, James Stephen, was great-grandfather of Virginia Woolf. However, just as Bloomsbury was the repudiator of Victorianism – with *Eminent Victorians* its most famous work – so Clapham could claim to be its initiator. The revolution that took place in social attitudes and behaviour between the beginning of the nineteenth century and its middle years still seems extraordinary. In a series of articles which appeared in January and February 1851, the *Economist* looked back at the previous half century, declaring that 'not only has that period been rich beyond nearly all others in political events of thrilling interest and mighty moment, but in changes and incidents of moral and social significance it has had no parallel since the Christian era' began. The articles deal with economic and social change, with the invention of the railways, with scientific discovery, and not least with the change in manners and behaviour on the part of the upper class.

Language which was common in our fathers' days would not be tolerated now ... *Debt*, which used to be regarded as an

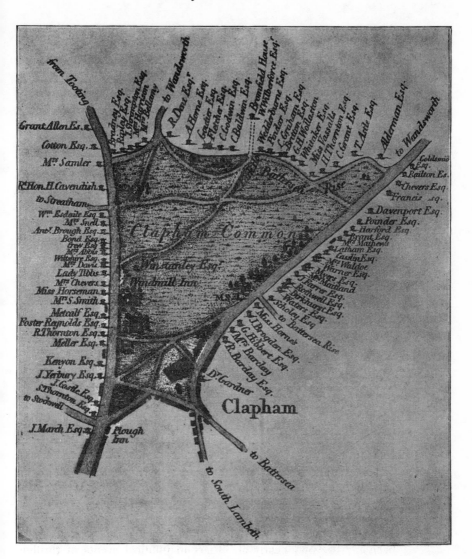

Clapham Common, 1800. From C. Smith, *Actual
Survey of the Road from London to Brighthelmston.*

indispensable characteristic of a man of fashion, is now almost
everywhere scouted as disreputable; and reckless extravagance is
no longer regarded as an indication of cleverness and spirit . . .
Generally speaking, even where there is not purer morality, a
better moral *taste* prevails.

The article goes on:

> *Now*, intemperance is as disreputable as any other kind of low debauchery, and, except in Ireland and at the Universities, a drunken gentleman is one of the rarest sights in society.

Or, as someone else put it, '. . . a toper in St James's became as rare as a bishop in a billiard room'. Between 1780 and 1850, to use the words of Professor Perkin, the English were transformed from one of the most aggressive, brutal, rowdy and bloodthirsty nations in the world into one of the most inhibited, polite, tender-minded and hypocritical.

Obviously, no group of reformers can change society on its own. Not Clapham, nor the late twentieth-century reform movements on gender and race with which it has much in common, could of themselves *create* a sea change in standards of behaviour, in ways of thought and moral consciousness. Rather they exploit the circumstances which permit it. The evangelism of the Clapham reformers, their crusade (for that was what it was), focused on the disenchantment with the cynical world of the *ancien régime* and set out to restore a sense of religious belief and stricter moral values. William Wilberforce, Henry Thornton, James Stephen, the Barclays and their colleagues were so influential because of the shock of the French Revolution and the fast-increasing power of the middle classes with their traditional desire for an ordered world. Clapham was a movement with a purpose extending far beyond London. 'That confederacy which, when pent up within the narrow limits of Clapham, jocose men invidiously called a "Sect", is now spreading through the habitable globe,' wrote Stephen's son, Sir James Stephen, perhaps the most illustrious civil servant of his time. A more famous son yet, Lord Macaulay – son of Zachary Macaulay, a leading Clapham reformer – wrote to one of his sisters in 1841 that 'from that little knot of men emanated all the Bible societies, and almost all the missionary societies in the world.' Nevertheless, Clapham was first of all a mission of Londoners to London. The target was the influential, the opinion formers, the powerful, and that meant London. To the King, George III, Henry Thornton, with Wilberforce the movement's central figure,

was a 'canting Methodist': certainly he was an evangelical, but one
who held firmly to the Church of England. In fact, it was a principle
of the reformers not to allow themselves to be confused with dissenters.
John Wesley's success had been in the provinces and among the
poorer classes; his message of moral renewal had hardly touched the
rich. To Henry Thornton, Wesley and Whitefield gave 'much needless
offence'. His own father, John Thornton (1720–90), usually considered the founder of the Sect, was, in his view, 'naturally rough,
vehement and eager', not at all characteristics which would help in
the conversion of the upper class. Ironically Henry was himself short
on the social graces. In 1782, aged twenty-two, he was returned at a
by-election as one of the two MPs for Henry Thrale's old constituency
of Southwark, and soon afterwards encountered Fanny Burney at a
party given by Hester Thrale. Very uncouth, she thought him. His
close friend and cousin, the highly sophisticated Wilberforce, would
never have made that impression. He was a man who moved naturally
in the highest social circles, he dined with the Prince Regent, his
intimate friend was William Pitt. Yet at the same time Wilberforce
abhorred the 'profane self-sufficiency' of the upper class. 'Pride, pride,'
he said, 'was the universal passion.' Allied with them though they
were in detestation of the slave trade, the Clapham evangelicals could
only regard as disreputable such people as Charles James Fox and
Sheridan: to them, political principle which did not rest on private
morality was a chimera. (But Byron's story of the watchman finding
Sheridan dead drunk in the street deserves to be remembered. The
watchman asks his name and gets the answer 'Wilberforce!')

Clapham talked as rich to rich. The Thorntons were very rich
indeed, even though much of their income went to charity and other
good causes. The older Thornton, Henry's father, was described in
his obituary as 'the greatest merchant in Europe, except Mr Hope of
Amsterdam', while Henry himself was a successful banker. He was
intelligent and severely practical. In the parliament of 1807, he was
naturally a strong supporter of Wilberforce's bill to abolish the slave
trade, but he was also energetic in his attacks on Old Corruption and
in his advocacy of Economical Reform. Earlier he had published his
Enquiry into the Nature and Effects of the Paper Credit of Great Britain,
a book which, while it might overstretch the Bloomsbury analogy to

compare it with Keynes's *General Theory*, was sufficiently distinguished to be reissued in the twentieth century under the editorship
of Professor Hayek.

Better known as a writer and one who played an important part
in the Clapham movement – though not herself a Clapham resident
– was Hannah More. Yet most of the leading members were people
of a practical rather than an intellectual background. 'We are all City
people and connected with merchants, and nothing but merchants
on every side', Henry Thornton remarked of his family on one
occasion, distancing them from aristocratic associations. No less
entrenched in business were the Barclays. The brewery was a sideline,
for primarily they were bankers, whose business was to evolve through
Barclay, Tritton and Bevan into Barclays Bank. Others brought a
different sort of practical experience. There were Lord Teignmouth,
who as Sir John Shore had been Governor-General of India; and his
friend Charles Grant, also from India and later to be chairman of

The wedding of one of Mr Allnutt's daughters at their
home, Clapham Common, 1842. Painting by David
Cox, Junior.

the East India Company. There was Lord Barham, the great naval administrator. Stephen was a barrister, Zachary Macaulay a business-man and colonial governor. Henry Thornton's two brothers were also MPs. As was to be expected with such company, Clapham's evangelism was promoted in the most professional way. What, for instance, could be more businesslike than Henry Thornton's brother John in his buying up of advowsons as a way of increasing Clapham influence in the Church of England? Even its language of devotion, as one writer has pointed out, was sometimes borrowed wholesale from the market-place.

Of Professor Silliman's memories of his trip to London in 1805, perhaps none was stronger than that of the night he had spent as guest of Henry Thornton at Battersea Rise House on the north-western side of the Common. He described the house as spacious and elegant. In terms of spaciousness at least that seems something of an under-statement, for it contained thirty-four bedrooms plus nursery on the upper floors (and incidentally on the ground floor a library designed by William Pitt) and was set in extensive grounds. The company at table Silliman recalled as being 'uncommonly intelligent and agree-able', and at breakfast the next morning he was delighted to meet William Wilberforce the 'distinguished friend of mankind', who lived next door. On his return in 1851 Silliman crossed the river to Clapham to look up old haunts. The large, fine houses he remembered were still there but of course 'all who adorned them' were gone. In fact, the Thornton family still lived at Battersea Rise House, but while the Barclays stayed on for many years, most of the leading spirits of the movement had – in the geographical sense – quite soon drifted away. Wilberforce, for instance, sold his house Broomwood, and moved in 1808 to Kensington Gore. Yet Clapham, particularly the Common, remained a very popular district for wealthy City families and others. It was not surprising that in the 1820s Thomas Cubitt chose it as home for his large family, taking first the house and grounds which had belonged to Henry Cavendish and later a nearby house, which he rebuilt. Nor was it surprising that he saw in Clapham an opportunity for real estate development on a massive and splendid scale. Although Professor Silliman in 1851 thought of Clapham as a 'beautiful suburban village', by then Cubitt's New Park on the eastern

Battersea Rise House on Clapham Common's westside, ~~the home of Henry Thornton. This photograph was~~ taken *c.* 1890.

side of the Common was far advanced. Cubitt, though, would have been gratified by Silliman's description, for he intended a rural environment amply planted with trees and with houses of high quality to be built not on speculation, but to order. He did not intend terraces around the edge as at Regent's Park, but, like Nash, he was determined to keep New Park exclusive, and to shelter it from down-at-heel Brixton next door.

Yet while it might be possible to keep out Brixton, it would be quite another matter to keep out everybody. And by 1851 it was a real danger that New Park might be challenged on all sides. The problem for would-be developers of inadequate communications no longer applied. Bridges had gone up one after the other with Waterloo in 1817 followed by Southwark in 1819 and Hammersmith in 1827. There were omnibuses and now railways. London contained more rich than in 1800 but also many more on middling or small incomes. A population of less than a million in 1800 had multiplied by 1851 to around 2.36 million. For many landowners and developers the situation was a boon; with such potential demand they could cover the countryside and the existing elegant suburbs with dense terrace housing.

Clapham enjoyed a considerable advantage in its geographical situation. The Common lay almost directly south of Hyde Park Corner and – as the crow flies – near enough to the West End shops. In 1844 Cubitt put forward a proposal for a highway north to south carried across the Thames by a new bridge on the edge of the Grosvenor development at Pimlico, where he was himself the chief contractor. In 1809 the Vauxhall Bridge Company had obtained an act of parliament authorizing the construction of a broad thoroughfare leading from Hyde Park via their bridge and thence to the south bank. More than anyone, Cubitt, with his interests in Pimlico and New Park, was in a position to weigh the possibilities. In the 1840s he was also working in Nine Elms, a trading and industrial area on the south bank of the river, on the site now occupied by the old Battersea Power Station. He was well informed about the effect of railways for not only was Nine Elms the location for one of the first of London's stations, but he had also waged a successful battle to prevent the Great Western Railway establishing their terminus on the northern approach to Vauxhall Bridge. The idea of turning a section of South London into an extension of the West End was reminiscent of the scheme attributed to John James in Queen Anne's reign of a road and bridge link between a Hyde Park palace and Wimbledon, and of course of Nash's conception of Regent's Park. And Regent's Park at least had partly worked; if it was not quite incorporated in the West End, it was nevertheless a district from which proletarian London was held at arm's length.

The project remained in the air, to become a much more practical proposition in the 1850s. Clapham could add to its attractions the prospect of the Museum area at South Kensington, for which it was well placed. More than that, the vital bridge – paid for by government money – became a fact with the opening of Chelsea Bridge in 1858. By that time Cubitt was dead, but his place in Clapham had been taken by the energetic developer and architect James Knowles the younger, better known as founder of the journal *Nineteenth Century*, and responsible for some large buildings on the edge of Clapham

Common. Plans were now far advanced for an ambitious development over Battersea Fields, a loose description of an area which included the later Battersea Park and extended up the slopes leading to Clapham Common. Hopes were high and the new town, to be called Park Town, was greeted as being 'ultimately destined to form another Belgravia'. This was nonsense, for what was planned – a huge array of small villas; 3,000 was a figure mentioned – would in no way be comparable to the palatial houses in Belgrave Square and its surrounds. But 'Belgravia' had become a magic word. Denmark Hill was the 'Belgravia of South London' and – with more reason – Pimlico was sometimes known as South Belgravia.

What happened is clear from the standard London road maps. Best (in this instance) is the *A–Z London Street Atlas*. Half a mile south of Chelsea Bridge, where Queenstown Road meets Battersea Park Road, it shows an agglomeration of railway lines heading for Clapham Junction, mixed up with railway workshops. This is what became known as the Battersea Tangle. The influential Clapham committee and its vociferous supporters were too late. In 1860, the London, Chatham and Dover Company announced its intention of buying the land in question, and the London, Brighton and South Coast Railway were also involved. Proposals for tunnels or viaducts crumbled in face of their opposition and Park Town, when it materialized, was grim with its packed terrace houses. Some South London districts, Wimbledon and Dulwich for example, were able to hold this invasion by cheap housing at bay but at Clapham nearly all of Thomas Cubitt's handsome New Park villas were to disappear, to join Battersea Rise House and its fellows in oblivion.

9

Monster City

*

Two visitors to London at the very beginning of the nineteenth century – Louis Simond, a Frenchman who had lived in America for twenty years, and the Dane A. A. Feldborg – vividly described the routine of life in the West End during the Season. Nothing stirred in the elegant streets and squares until about 10 in the morning. Before that, there were 'no carts, waggons, fishwomen, dustmen . . . only a solitary Jew, now and then, crying "old clothes, hare skins, old clothes?"' As the shops started to open, milkmaids appeared, their pails suspended on yokes over their shoulders, delivering their milk from door to door. About midday, footmen were to be seen as they emerged from the houses, and nannies and maids taking children out for the 'morning' air. Finally, at about 3 or 4 in the afternoon, the fashionables surfaced, to visit the shops and to drop cards on each other, returning home to dress for dinner and to prepare for the hectic night life of the city. If you were not dressing for dinner, it was for something else. According to Chateaubriand, French ambassador in London in 1822, one never stopped changing clothes. As ambassador, his routine was necessarily untypical. He was up at 6 a.m. for a breakfast party in the country – 'breakfast' in town was between 4 and 5 p.m. – and back in London for lunch. He then changed his clothes for a walk in Bond Street or Hyde Park. After that, he changed for 7.30 dinner. Then came the opera and another set of clothes, followed – changing again – by the evening assembly known as a 'rout'. What a life, he thought; the galleys would be a hundred times preferable. Chateaubriand's opposite number, Richard Rush, the American minister, spoke of parties ending at 2 or 3 a.m. and wondered how MPs and men of affairs could cope with so punishing a schedule. The Persian envoy, Abul Hassan – the balls he attended went on until 5 a.m. – sighed that 'Night and day it seems, the English think only of pleasure.' He then reflected that with the watchmen calling out the hours, it was anyway impossible to sleep in the early morning.

William Austin, an American in London at much the same time as Simond and Feldborg, was bemused by some of the conventions. For instance, he found it difficult to obtain admittance to a house where he was invited to dine. He had knocked only once, and, in London, gentlemen, ordinary gentlemen, knocked three times (but not too hard) while knights gave six knocks with a few faint raps at the end. Noblemen were entitled to knock long and loud. And in spite of all the changes in behaviour over the next fifty years, such customs lingered. The protocol of knocking still applied even if endangered by the installation of door bells in new buildings. The milkmaids with their yokes were still to be seen, and the cows in St James's Park remarked on by Sir Richard Phillips still produced their milk, even though it was, as somebody observed, of a decidedly 'metropolitan flavour'.

But cows and milkmaids give a picturesque impression. And picturesque was the last word visitors were likely to use about London in the early and middle years of the nineteenth century. There are, of course, exceptions, as with Léon Faucher, a distinguished journalist and reformer, and minister of the interior in the 1848 French republican government, who published his impressions of England in 1856. He marvelled at the London parks; imagine, he wrote, the vegetation of Saint-Cloud and Neuilly transplanted to the middle of Paris. He admired the square gardens, with their trees and lawns: how, he asked rhetorically, should young English girls not dream of streams and meadows and woods when even in the heart of London they have this country scene constantly under their eyes. There was the otherwise derogatory Edmond Texier, taken by what he described as the long avenue of parks and charming cottages which extended the six miles from London to Kew. Yet, to most foreigners, London presented three overwhelming impressions, none of them romantic – its immensity, its materialism, and the extremes of riches and poverty. It was the 'Monster City'; to some also a 'monstrous' city. Nathaniel Hawthorne wrote, 'I have never had the same sense of being surrounded by materialism and hemmed in with the grossness of this earth's existence anywhere else.' The ultra-radical Flora Tristan, a frequent French visitor in the 1830s, wrote that in London one breathed sadness in the air, that it entered through one's pores. The atmosphere nullified even the luxury which constituted the dominant passion of the rich:

> To judge from the elegant comfort enjoyed by the rich Londoner one might believe him to be happy; but if one takes the trouble to study his expression, one recognises in his features with their imprint of boredom and lethargy, and in his eyes where the life of the soul is extinguished and the suffering of the body manifest, that not only is he wholly unhappy but that he is placed in conditions which prevent him from aspiring to happiness.

Many of the criticisms recall those of the Casanovas and Kielman-segges of a century before. There is the boredom of Sunday, and of Sunday in the rain when London is like 'an immense and a well-ordered cemetery', the dislike of the weather generally, a distaste for the obsession with money, and the monotony of much of the architecture. By now, though, the sense of exhilaration is missing; inevitably perhaps since London, so slightly known, so strange, to eighteenth-century visitors, was less likely to prove a revelation. Often what the strangers saw confirmed views already held. Certainly there was less risk than before of being lectured on the perfection of the British constitution, and whatever they might feel about Palmerston, they could not accuse his milieu, or that of Gladstone and John Russell, of the corruption and cynicism attributable to the generation of Henry Fox. The hypocrisy was new. They could not cease to wonder that a nation apparently so strait-laced, so ready with its moral precepts, could tolerate the grinding misery in which so many of its citizens lived, or the hordes of audacious prostitutes which they encountered almost anywhere they went.

The patricians bore a reputation abroad for an excessive arrogance. If they did not flaunt their grandeur in public, for instance in Hyde Park, it was because they were so sure of their position that they had no need to do so. The arrogance was expressed by an absolutely icy

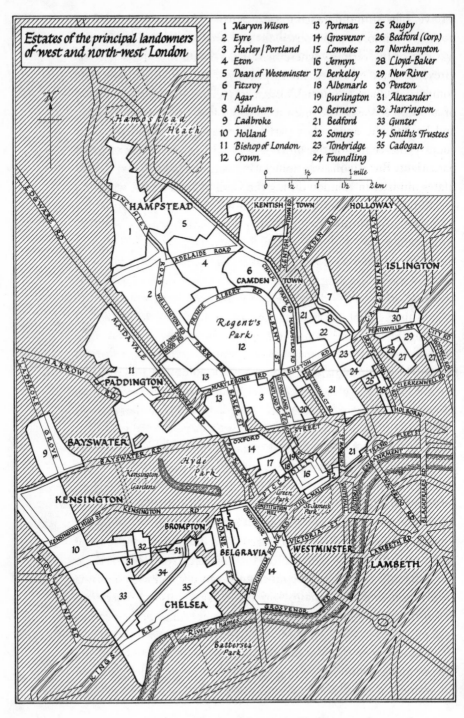

Estates of the principal landowners of west and north-west London.

reserve, plus an indifference to what anyone thought of them. The novelist Fenimore Cooper observed that Lord Grey's house in London was one of the very few where he was not made to feel a foreigner: Grey, he said, expressed no surprise that he spoke English! His compatriot Charles Francis Adams, son of one president, grandson of another, spoke of the intense egotism. The English, he thought, and he had the upper class particularly in mind, considered their country the centre of the universe and all outside its limits to be barbarians. But Adams was unlucky in his timing, for he was United States minister in London during the Civil War, at a time when the great majority of the upper class supported the South. His successor John Lothrop Motley lived at ease in the highest society. Another American, Henry Colman, in Britain during the 1840s, referred to the universal attention to good manners. (He was greatly taken with London and its 'dazzling splendour': even in unfashionable December, he wrote, it was never dull, 'for there is one continual stream of life ... rushing, bubbling, gushing, spreading along the whole time.') Here again is a reminder of the previous century, when visitors, disconcerted at the extreme reserve, suddenly found that they had broken through. Colman after all carried with him excellent introductions and he was also – which would have made him the more congenial – an agricultural expert. He could penetrate further than most into this unwelcoming society.

The German Max Schlesinger in *Saunterings in and about London* of 1853 probed the questions of reserve and social conventions carefully and with sympathy. What we see as a mincing chilliness of address, he wrote, is to the British a decent reserve. And as the English grow older, the more open they become. Hippolyte Taine, the eminent French philosopher and critic, agreed on that and admired the common sense and pragmatism of the English. Nevertheless, there is a difference to the past; the nineteenth-century melting point was clearly more difficult to attain. A friend of Taine's, also a Frenchman, described the patricians as suffering from an 'inertness of the nervous system'.

Thus the men. They fit into the familiar 'stuffed shirt' stereotype. The women are more interesting and more surprising. The stereotype for women of the Regency period, what with Caroline Lamb and

Lady Jersey, is clear enough. A letter from the popular Abul Hassan, here in 1809 and 1810, written in his special English to the *Morning Post*, is in accord. He is enjoying London social life enormously but should there not be limits? 'I always afraid some old Lady in great crowd come dead. . . I think old ladies after 85 years not come to evening party that much better.' He decided not to include another sentence which runs '. . . among the wonders I have seen – 100 year-old men trying to seduce young girls and 100 year-old ladies flirting with young men at parties so crowded that you cannot move and so hot you could roast a chicken.' By Victorian times it seems the dowagers were safely in bed at an unexceptionable hour, but it is not easy to identify the demure Victorian miss of nineteenth-century fiction. In England, wrote Jules de Prémaray in 1851, *'on est tutoyé par les regards des femmes.'* Francis Wey, another Frenchman, was told by an English friend that 'there are no more relentless flirts in the world than English girls.' While Captain Gronow in his memoirs shows signs of suffering from a conviction that everything is going to the dogs, what he says of upper-class girls in 1860 must have some basis. Unmarried girls nowadays, he complains, discuss with young men the merits of 'Skittles' (a well-known courtesan) and her horses. Too many 'seem to have taken for their ideal something between the dashing London horse-breaker and some Parisian *artiste dramatique* of a third-rate theatre; the object of whose ambition is to be mistaken for a *femme du demi-monde*'.

Taine did find some demure young Englishwomen but he did not deny that in the 'fishery for husbands' the restraints sometimes broke down. For him, it was a result of the freedom (which generally he found admirable) that English girls enjoyed. French girls could not act in the same way because they were too closely watched. To others the explanation was more sombre: the 'inertness of the nervous system' bred suppression of sensibility. The Comtesse de Boigne, a sympathetic observer who lived for years in London as a refugee, wrote of the emptiness of life for older women. Once they have married off their daughters, everything goes downhill. The husband takes to his club, marriages break up, the husband dies. It is then that the English system bears so heavily, for as widows they are turned out of the family house, and their income reduced to a fraction of what it was. Relations with their children are rigidly formalized: in

West End ladies. From *Gavarni in London*, 1846.

no other country, asserted Madame de Boigne, are the words of St Matthew that 'a man shall leave his father and mother, and shall cleave to his wife' so strictly interpreted. The close family feeling of the French does not exist. Francis Wey's English friend talked of the 'prodigious mass of marriageable girls, raised, as they are, in utter segregation and eager to escape from their life of dependence to a home of their own.' Faced with this 'prodigious mass' the rich young men, brought up anyway to be cold and independent, are necessarily on the defensive and guarded. His grim conclusion was that 'happiness in England depends on our having no affections'.

Yet, for all the differences of temperament and custom, the wealthy of London and Paris had one deeply important anxiety in common. It is illuminated in a passage from Chateaubriand's *Mémoires d'Outre-Tombe*. One evening in 1822, Chateaubriand, the ambassador, and Lord Liverpool, the Prime Minister, sat talking after dinner by a window overlooking the Thames. As Chateaubriand praised the solidity of Britain with its balance of liberty and order, Liverpool, pointing outside to the buildings looming huge in the smoke and fog, asked, 'What can be stable about these enormous cities? a serious insurrection in London and all is lost.' To both men it was a very pertinent thought. In 1780 Liverpool was only a boy, but nevertheless the Gordon Riots of that year, when for a week the mob controlled London, would have been firmly imprinted on his mind. Even during his own premiership, only a year or two before, he had been faced with the Cato Street Conspiracy and the Queen Caroline riots. And then – a searing memory – neither he, and certainly not Chateaubriand, nor anyone else of their generation, would for an instant have forgotten Paris in 1792, when the working class streamed out of the slums to slaughter their former masters. For the rulers were confronted with something quite new. They were living in cities of unprecedented size. London in particular was growing at an extraordinary rate. Its population by the 1801 census was less than a million, by 1822 it was around 1.4 million, by 1841 close on 2 million, by 1851, 2.36 million.

In fact, for all their self-assurance, the elegant West End streets and squares could give more than a passing hint that they were under siege. There were the celebrated screens, 200 ft. long by 80 ft. high, erected by the fifth Duke of Portland at Harcourt House in Cavendish Square. Max Schlesinger wrote that,

> . . . in the front of palaces, club-houses, and other public build-
> ings, the railings are so high and strong as to engender the
> belief that the thieves of England go about their business of
> house-breaking with scaling-ladders, pick-axes, guns, and other
> formidable implements of destruction.

Charles Francis Adams passed Devonshire House in Piccadilly many times before he actually went inside, always under the impression that it was a warehouse or barracks. Then there were the barriers constructed by ground landlords. They blocked off their streets with gates and porters' lodges, perhaps during the day allowing non-residents' carriages through, perhaps not. At night, the gates were closed altogether, forcing members of the public to make what could

Devonshire House, Piccadilly. A magnificent interior,
but from the outside it could be mistaken for a barracks.

be lengthy detours. An example given was of someone obliged to go
nearly a mile out of his way in order to reach his house, which was
actually situated only 200 yards from his starting point. Fire engines
too were forced to comply.

Even the richest and most self-indulgent Londoner could not
avoid the realities of life. Once outside the cosseted neighbourhoods,
the air was filthy with smuts, the streets with mud which befouled
vehicles and passers-by, anyway buffeted by 'whirlwinds of dust,
straw and paper'. The traffic roar was ceaseless and the traffic jams
inordinate. The Thames stank like a sewer, and everywhere was the
stench of horse manure and overflowing cesspools. In 1848, the first
Board of Health was established; it met at Gwydr House in Whitehall
where, in the basement, there were no less than nine cesspools, full
and overflowing. The rich could not avoid the poor. Inside the
fashionable precincts, Léon Faucher noted, such poor as existed could
be hidden away by the stables situated in the backstreets, in the mews.

It was true that most of the London poor lived far off in the East End, in such districts as Whitechapel and Bethnal Green. And of Bethnal Green, according to its vicar, 'as little was known about . . . as the wilds of Australia or the islands of the South Seas'. Nevertheless, slums, 'rookeries' as they were called, also stood on the doorstep of fashionable London. One area of startling poverty lay east of Portland Place, John Nash's 'most magnificent street in London', and the Americans at their legation there described Great Portland Street as a slum. Whitehall, the heart of Westminster, the hub of the Empire, quartered some of the grandest of London's mansions, but close by on its western side was Devil's Acre, an area between Victoria Street and the Thames. Like the other West End slums it was not merely the scene of appalling human misery but a centre of criminal life, an Alsatia. A City missionary reported of Devil's Acre that he had seen 'upwards of forty policemen beat out of Old Pye Street, by the inhabitants, while attempting to take a thief.'

Worst of all was St Giles, which included the notorious Seven Dials, intended originally as a district for the wealthy. 'In common parlance,' wrote Thomas Beames in his *The Rookeries of London* (first edition, 1850), 'St Giles's and Billingsgate are types – the one, of the lowest conditions under which human life is possible, the other, of the lowest point to which the English language can descend'. The worst of this slum was cleared away by the construction of New Oxford Street, but even after the clearance, George Augustus Sala could write this terrifying description. He supposes the reader to be making a morning call in Bedford Square, walking there from the new Covent Garden opera house a mile away. St Giles is with you, says Sala, all the way – 'always before, behind, and about you . . .'

From a hundred foul lanes and alleys have debouched, on to the spick-and-span-new promenade, unheard-of human horrors. Gibbering forms of men and women in filthy rags, with fiery heads of shock hair, the roots beginning an inch from the eyebrows, with the eyes themselves bleared and gummy, with gashes filled with yellow fangs for teeth, with rough holes punched in the nasal cartilage for nostrils . . . awful deformities, with horrifying malformations of the limbs and running sores ostentatiously displayed.

The slums of Westminster – Devil's Acre as seen by
Gustave Doré in 1872.

If the revolutions which exploded across Europe in 1848 spared
Britain, if the Chartist threat faded away, the problem remained.
Thomas Beames wrote of Westminster that it was 'at once the seat
of a palace and a plague spot; senators declaim, where sewers poison.'
It was an ever-present fear on the part of the rich that the disease
and sickness which inevitably infested the slums, perhaps the cholera
that haunted London in the first half of the century, might spill
over. Charles Dickens warned that '. . . if you once have a vigorous
pestilence raging furiously in St Giles's, no mortal list of Lady Patron-
esses can keep it out of Almack's.' Add a moral dimension as well. After
all, educated Victorians, hypocritical as they often were, possessed a

genuinely disinterested sense of social responsibility. Practical and moral considerations then united. The rich were aware that their own desertion of the declining areas of London was partly responsible for the dire situation. They were no less aware that to allow a particular class to stagnate in poverty while the nation as a whole advanced in prosperity year by year, was to store up grave trouble. The first of these propositions carries an echo from the seventeenth century; in the second there is an intimation of a late twentieth-century anxiety. The difficulty was that goodwill and money could not of themselves do away with the slums.

Two rehousing schemes on sites within a couple of hundred yards of each other provide examples of how the rich tried to tackle the problem. They were built on land which once formed part of the grounds of Weld House (sometimes called 'Wild House'), owned by a Mr Humphrey Weld. This was original West End, close by Lincoln's Inn Fields and with Drury Lane and Great Queen Street next door. By 1665, Weld House, a large mansion assessed at 37 hearths, was already showing conventional signs of decline. It was divided into three, although the principal occupier was the Marquess of Winchester, an undoubted grandee. The grounds were put out for development and houses went up in Wild Court, intended for obviously substantial tenants, probably lawyers. In 1855, when Dickens's *Household Words* reported a rehabilitation scheme for thirteen houses in Wild Court, some of the expensive fittings and decoration survived, quite out of place in what had become classic tenements, divided and subdivided again and again. The condition of the buildings was appalling: open troughs of ordure passed through the upper rooms into a half-stagnant open sewer in a parapet immediately below the upper windows, the cellars were full of refuse, and the backyards 'ankle deep in all abomination'. The foundations of the houses were rotten with filth.

The leases for the houses were acquired by the Society for Improving the Condition of the Labouring Classes, which set about restoration. Where there had been 200 families, say 1,000 people, plus drifting homeless who crowded in at night on to the staircases, the Society intended 100 families totalling 300 to 400 people, with a resident building superintendent. The snag was, what would happen to the 600 to 700 displaced? Their work, often purely casual work, was in London,

probably within two miles of Temple Bar. They could not afford the
rail or omnibus fares which would allow them to commute from the
suburbs, and while cheap housing for the poor had been built in some
areas of north London – usually itself turning rapidly into slums –
distinctive working-class housing was as yet rare. A witness before a
Royal Commission in 1846 stated: 'A poor man is chained to the
spot; he has not the leisure to walk, and he has not the money to
ride.' The evicted could only move to some other London tenement,
or to a squalid lodging house which would be no better. The slum
problem, alleviated in one place, was worsened somewhere else.

The Wild Street (then Great Wild Street) development was
much more successful in providing decent homes for the poor. Like
the Wild Court conversions, it relied on private money. The buildings,
bleak but efficacious, were constructed in the 1870s on a 1½ acre site,
and unlike the Wild Court buildings, they are – apart from some
destruction by bombing during the Second World War – still in
place. The money was provided by a trust set up by the American
businessman George Peabody, a leading figure in the City of London,
the project one version only of a number of purpose-built Peabody
estates distributed around London.

The trouble was that none of these schemes, nor the deliberate
policy of the Marquess of Westminster (the new title for the Grosvenors; the dukedom came in 1874) in providing cheap sites for model
dwellings, nor the large amounts of money produced for the East
End by Baroness Burdett-Coutts, could provide a solution. In 1875,
the dedicated and practical Octavia Hill pointed out that all the
private acts of benevolence in London in the previous thirty years
had housed only 26,000 people, a figure which was not much more
than the increase in the city's population every six months. The task
was beyond private enterprise, a legacy for the London County
Council and a broader conception of the city and its organization.

But at mid-century the demographic pressure on the West End
was as much the result of an enormous growth in the number of
well-to-do middle class and of a change in their mode of living. At
the beginning of the century the Franco-American Louis Simond
commented that a businessman moving into the West End risked
being snubbed should his spending power be less than £3,000 (say

£170,000 today) a year. A figure of £6,000 would be safer. Nathan Mayer Rothschild had very much more than that when in the 1820s, yielding to family pressure, he moved from his combined home and office ('a poor obscure looking place,' said one visitor) to the newly built No. 107 Piccadilly. It was the start of a trend which rapidly gathered momentum and was encouraged by the increasing demand in the City for more office and commercial space. By the 1840s – from a residential point of view – virtually all the richer businessmen had left. In 1845 the journalist David Morier Evans wrote that at seven in the evening, in the centre of the City, you would wonder where everyone had gone:

> Round 'Change, you would not find a soul; in Bartholomew-lane, the only cry heard would be that of the Bus-conductor for Paddington and Holloway; and in Lombard-street the police would watch you, as though you contemplated a burglary at Glyn's or Barclay's.

At the time Evans wrote, the City's resident population was still around 130,000, concentrated in the boundary parishes. In 1861 it was 113,000; in 1871, 76,000; in 1901, 27,000.

Many of the former City dwellers were, of course, living in the suburbs, but Evans added that here too taste had changed, and that 'in a great number of cases' businessmen had turned to the West End. Few followed the Rothschilds to Piccadilly or Mayfair, but by moving to Marylebone or Bayswater they were dragging richer London further west, a gravitational pull already strengthened by the development of Belgravia. Lincoln's Inn Fields had dropped away, and by the 1850s the effect was marked in Bloomsbury. At the start, in the seventeenth century, along with some lesser – but still most respectable – buildings, the Bedfords' Bloomsbury estate contained three large town houses which lay, spaciously, in a row, looking out over country as yet untroubled by the New Road. East to west, they were Bedford House (alternatively Southampton House), Montagu House, which belonged to the Duke of Montagu and his wife, the half-sister of Rachel Russell, and – not quite so grand – Thanet House, which was leased by the earls of Thanet. Montagu House, too expensive for its owners to maintain, went first, sold to the government to be opened as the British Museum in 1759. Bedford House disappeared at the end of the eighteenth century, demolished like its predecessor in the Strand a hundred years before, in order to make room for more intensive building development. Like the Strand house, its location was no longer attractive enough to outweigh commercial opportunity.

Thanet House remained. The Tuftons, earls of Thanet, formerly of Aldersgate, once one of the richest English families and still very wealthy in the eighteenth century, moved on in 1730 to Grosvenor Square, leaving the lease of Thanet House to a daughter and her husband. Shortly after the lease expired in 1755, the house was given by the Duke of Bedford to his son Lord Tavistock. By the 1780s it was let to Lord Mansfield whose own town house had been burned down in the Gordon Riots. But it was clear by then that while patricians might figure as passing tenants, they were no longer interested as buyers. So, in 1787, Thanet House was split in two, with the larger part taken by a brewer and MP, Harvey Christian Combe, Lord Mayor of London in 1800. When he went, the house was again subdivided and a new front added by Thomas Cubitt, the prime developer for the new, expanding Bloomsbury. It was by now an investment for its leaseholder, rather than a home for him to live in.

A section of Thanet House, now 100–102 Great Russell Street, is still there, easily identified by a blue plaque announcing it once to have been the home of Dr Johnson's friend Topham Beauclerk, one of the transient late eighteenth-century tenants. Like a number of large London houses, Thanet House just subsided quietly into obscurity. It was often the same with streets or even whole districts. This passage from *Gavarni in London*, published in 1849, catches the pathos of such a moment of decline. The place is Great Ormond Street, just outside the Bedfords' Bloomsbury estate, once the site of Powis House, among the most important of the London town houses of its time. This is very much Nicholas Barbon territory, and Nos 55 and 57 Great Ormond Street are attributed to him.

The houses, even in their decay of quality, have a respectable look. Their style of architecture is passé, it is true; but they evidently make a great struggle to keep up appearances ... All the furniture is rubbed up to the last degree of friction polish, and the carpets are brushed cleanly threadbare. The window-curtains, blanched in the sun of thirty or forty summers, until their once crimson hue has paled to a doubtful buff ... Even the ancient landladies have given the same conservative care to their flaxen fronts and remarkable caps. They are grave and dignified in their demeanours, for they believe Great Ormond Street still to be the focus of the West-End.

A great deal was done to preserve Bloomsbury's appeal. Gin palaces and pubs were kept out, commercial intrusion generally was restrained, and a multitude of gates protected the residents. The new squares and streets which replaced Bedford House and the fields to the north and west were usually of a high architectural standard, and Bedford Square, still almost unspoilt, is one of the finest of London's squares. However, fashion and convenience were too much for the best-laid plans, and it was true that the new development took a long time to complete and its design came to look old-fashioned. The Duke of Bedford's agent Christopher Haedy put his finger on the central issue: a constant struggle existed in many of the wealthier families between the businessmen and lawyers who found Bloomsbury convenient – if rather far from the West End clubs – and their wives and daughters who hankered after the more fashionable and exciting West End. The wives and daughters won. Haedy doubted whether Bloomsbury could sustain more expensive grand houses. Cubitt's argument was that cheaper houses would tend to drag down prices in general and make it more difficult to sell or let those which were already there. In the end, Cubitt was to admit that Haedy had been right. Bloomsbury and its neighbourhood did not decline into rookeries; as with the landladies of Great Ormond Street, a genteel standard was maintained, the larger houses being divided into apartments and lodgings and private hotels. But in *The Small House at Allington* published in 1862, Anthony Trollope makes Lord De Guest recommend to the impecunious John Eames that he live in Bloomsbury Square because there, he is told, you can get a house for nothing. The pull of the Grosvenor empire to the west was having its effect on other parts of once-fashionable London as well. In 1830, Lord Hatherton's servants warned him that they could not be expected to move from Portman Square in Marylebone to such an unheard-of part of the world as Grosvenor Place, Belgravia. However, in Thackeray's *The Newcomes* of 1854, a hostess living in Bryanston Square says to her nephew by marriage, 'What . . . is it possible that you do me the honour to come all the way from May Fair to Marylebone. I thought you young men of fashion never crossed Oxford Street.' George Augustus Sala takes up the theme of fashion in his *Twice Round the Clock* (1859), satirizing the unpolished residents of one of the 'quietly grim squares in the semi-aristocratic North-west End', a description in which he includes Portman and Manchester Squares. This is the sort of house, he says, 'where they keep a footman, single-handed – a dull knave, who no more resembles the resplendent flunkey of Eaton Square or Westbourne Terrace, than does the cotton-stockinged "greencoat" of the minor theatres.' The coupling of Eaton Square with Westbourne Terrace – now hardly more than a useful link between Hyde Park and the Westway flyover – would later seem unlikely. A second glance, though, at this Bayswater street is illuminating as it brings into focus the imposing, ornamented, stuccoed terraces, standing back from the main road and protected from it by trees and shrubs. Bayswater in fact remained a district for the rich, including the very rich, particularly for businessmen, right through the last part of the nineteenth century. No. 1 Westbourne Terrace was the home of Henry Gardner, who left £600,000 in 1879 (say £34 million now), half of it for the benefit of the blind. The Russia merchant Giles Loder, one of the richest men of his time, who left £2.9 million, lived nearby at No. 1 Clarendon Place, Hyde Park Gardens. It was in Bayswater that Trollope in *The Small House at Allington* places the newly-wed Adolphus Crosbie and his wife Lady Alexandrina. With so much building work going on, there were disadvantages, but nevertheless the area was acknowledged to be 'a quite correct locality'. Near the Crosbies were an ambassador – from South America – a few bankers and senior clerks, and a peer.

For the would-be fashionable but no more than well-to-do Crosbies, the alternatives were limited. There were no resurrections of old *faubourgs*, which in any event were increasingly occupied by

Westbourne Terrace, Bayswater, in its original glory.
Engraving by J. Johnston in the middle of the
nineteenth century.

warehouses and offices. In the last part of the eighteenth century, the
brothers Adam had attempted such a resurrection with the construction of the Adelphi, twenty-four elegant terrace houses between the
Strand and the river, built on the site of the slum which had replaced
the old Durham House and its grounds. The project failed. In the
1820s, Mrs Arbuthnot's husband was offered the treasurership of the
navy at the enticing salary of £3,000 a year. But it would have meant
living in the Strand and neither Mr nor Mrs Arbuthnot could bear
to do that. Back in fictional life, Crosbie and his bride had considered
two alternatives to Bayswater. One was St John's Wood, rejected by
Crosbie because his future sister-in-law lived there rather than because
of its reputation as a 'love nest'. For those villas which set an architectural model for other suburbs were, with their leafy gardens surrounded by high walls, ideal for arrangements which their owners
preferred to keep clandestine. Here rich men kept their mistresses

from the demi-monde. Harriet Howard, the mistress of the future emperor Napoleon III, lived in Circus Road, the location also of a well-known brothel patronized by Swinburne. When in 1863 George Eliot with her lover George Henry Lewes bought a villa on North Bank, just above the canal, Lady Cork commented: 'Of course, poor dear, where else *could* she go.' For the Crosbies, the other alternative was Pimlico. But be careful about Pimlico, a married friend warned Lady Alexandrina: '. . . for heaven's sake, my dear, don't let him take you anywhere beyond Eccleston Square!' Actually, Warwick Square, situated in the prohibited area, could claim a number of titled residents, but nevertheless Pimlico, constructed over the marshlands at great expense by Thomas Cubitt, was socially tricky, in part a respectable suburb for professional people, in part a light industrial estate, and always with the great bulk of Millbank Penitentiary set down next door.

With the Great Exhibition of 1851, a flurry of guidebooks appeared for what were to be more than 6 million visitors. Apart from the Exhibition itself, they proposed an impressive list of places to see – the Tower, the Abbey, St Paul's, the British Museum, Madame Tussaud's, the zoo in Regent's Park, the palaces (if mainly from the outside), the steamers on the Thames and the bridges over it. Then there were the theatres, and the panoramas, dioramas and cycloramas, precursors of cinema, where interacting revolving cylinders gave an illusion of moving images. At least two of the guides recommended a visit to the Barclay Perkins brewery as the largest establishment of its kind in the world. As was to be expected, they are less concerned with the strictly residential districts than with the shopping, entertainment and hotel area around Piccadilly Circus. Although even there smart residential enclaves were to be found, most obviously in St James's Square and – down from the Circus, at the bottom of (Lower) Regent Street – in Carlton House Terrace, a row of magnificent houses built by Nash after Carlton House itself had been pulled down. North-west of Piccadilly Circus were the shops of Regent Street, now without the colonnade which had originally graced the Quadrant. Visitors required shops and obviously they also required hotels. Morley's Hotel in Trafalgar Square, where Benjamin Silliman stayed, was a favourite with Americans. The two best hotels in London, though, were north of Piccadilly, in Mayfair. One was

Mivart's, with entrances in Brook Street and Davies Street, and the other, the larger Clarendon Hotel, stood on the site of the old Clarendon House gardens, with its entrance in New Bond Street. A French guide, the *Guide-Chaix*, warned its readers that while the best London hotels were extremely luxurious, they were also very expensive. For French visitors it recommended Leicester Square, where there were three multilingual French-owned hotels.

Leicester Square was by 1851 a fully fledged commercial centre. After the death of Frederick, Prince of Wales, a hundred years before, Leicester House had gone down in the world, converted into a natural history museum before demolition at the end of the eighteenth century. Savile House, once Ailesbury House, was still more or less in existence: it had been attacked and looted during the Gordon Riots and by now was a sort of commercial tenement, containing an assortment of activities, among them a shooting gallery, a bazaar, a coffee room, and places for wrestling and billiards. One reminder of old times remained, at least for the first half of the Exhibition year, in a statue of George I brought from the Duke of Chandos's Canons, and which stood in the bedraggled square gardens. Mid-year, however, it got buried under a large new exhibition hall. Leicester Square was well placed for restaurants and for shops, one of which thought it expedient to advertise to foreign visitors that they would be charged the same prices as English customers.

The *Guide-Chaix* also highly recommended the Hotel Dubourg in the Haymarket. That would have been a riskier choice. By day, and for most of the evening, the Haymarket, running parallel to Lower Regent Street, was just another of the West End streets in the Piccadilly area, though with rather more than the average number of restaurants, coffee houses and gin palaces. At midnight it changed character: in the words of the *Saturday Review*, it was the street where 'vice reigns without a rival'. Here was prostitution at all prices, for the poor, and, as J. Ewing Ritchie makes clear in his *The Night Side of London*, for the rich. 'There are an immense number of women all splendidly dressed', he wrote.

> Some are borne away in broughams, some in cabs, but the most on foot. Let us now look at the men. You cannot see a finer set

Repainting the Mall front of Carlton House Terrace in 1898.

anywhere. Are not the flower of our youth and manhood there?
... Young fellows from the army and navy, men from all our universities and inns of court, gents from the city and the Stock Exchange, and respectable middle-aged country gentlemen stopping
in town a night, and just dropping in to see what is going on.

Yet if in 1851 there were a new exhibition hall in Leicester Square
and a mainly commercial utilization of the area around Piccadilly
Circus, the architecture was largely traditional. Apart from the
churches, most of the buildings followed the old 'Barbon model',
their exact size of course dependent on circumstances and the influence
of the Building Acts. The standard building proved astonishingly
adaptable, converted as it might be into a lodging house, a restaurant,
a shop, or even an hotel. Mivart's Hotel, for example, had been put
together steadily through the acquisition of neighbouring houses.
Even the less standardized building of Schomberg House – its façade

Burlington Arcade in the 1820s. A fashionable shopping
precinct of which George Augustus Sala wrote, 'I don't
think there is a shop in its enceinte where they sell
anything that we could not do without.' Engraving by
T. H. Shepherd.

still there now in Pall Mall – built at the end of the seventeenth century as a ducal mansion, having passed through various phases, emerged a century later as London's first department store. Equally adaptable were town houses on Crown land around Whitehall, which took on a new life as government offices as their leases fell in.

The really new and sensational buildings were the purpose-built club houses. They were impressive architecturally certainly, but what attracted particular attention was their social significance. One of the 1851 guides, *London, As It Is Today*, devoted a chapter to the gentlemen's clubs, and declared them to have had 'a very decided influence on the state of society'. 'Of late years', it added, they have 'assumed a splendour unknown to the ideas of their originators.'

The clubs were the natural descendants of the chocolate and coffee-houses, even of some of the more reputable taverns, which from the start had flourished around St James's and Pall Mall. Lord Ossulston, the peripatetic peer of Queen Anne's day who figured in Chapter 4, needed coffee-houses, inns and taverns nearby, whatever his changes of habitat, He entertained in them, and in the course of his ten-year diary records no less than 251 visits. White's Club descended from White's Chocolate House founded in 1698, the proprietor of which was a Mr White. Mr Brookes, who gave his name to Brooks's Club, was a wine merchant and money lender. Mr Crockford, who once kept a fish stall, was the creator of the famous gambling club of that name. The assembly rooms at Mrs Cornelys's Carlisle House and the Oxford Street Pantheon were club-like – when they could get away with it – in the strictness of their admissions policy. Above all, there was Almack's, in King Street off St James's Square, the most splendid and fashionable of all the assembly rooms. The journalist James Grant (admitting he can only write at second-hand) rhapsodizes over Almack's in *The Great Metropolis* of 1838 in terms worthy of Sir Richard Phillips on the site of the ruined Ranelagh. Almack's, wrote Grant,

What a sound! With what powerful emotions does many a fair bosom beat at the mere mention of it! It is the subject of the nocturnal visions of thousands of both sexes in the fashionable world: it is the subject also of their day dreams.

By the 1860s, indeed by 1851, the clubs had multiplied in number and largely changed their character. Crockford's wilted in the new era of respectability – skin-deep as it often was – inaugurated by the young Queen and her consort, although Crockford himself managed to die a very rich man. The assembly rooms passed away, and if White's and Brooks's retained their aristocratic individuality, the new clubs such as the Athenaeum, opened in 1830 and described by one of the 1851 guidebooks as 'a sort of palace', the Travellers (1832), and the Reform (1841), which was furnished with an especially famous kitchen, as well as with running hot and cold water in the bedrooms, were more orderly and without a hint of the old raffishness. The gambling had calmed, and the expression 'reeling home from the club' was no longer current.

By now, the clubs usually belonged to their members and not to an entrepreneur. They were splendid, comfortable, well organized and so numerous that anyone, given an appropriate social level, could find a club to suit his taste. The Reform was Liberal, Boodles popular with country gentlemen, the Garrick – excellent for 'a snug party' – was for actors, writers and painters. In contrast to Almack's, which was controlled by a self-elected committee 'of very grand women' – a 'feminine oligarchy' in the words of Grantley Berkeley – they were almost self-consciously male; indeed their maleness was an important reason for their success. And they were cheap. 'For a few pounds a year,' wrote J. Timbs in his *Club Life in London*, 'advantages are to be enjoyed which no fortunes, except the most ample, can procure.' The competition they provided was considered an explanation for the shortage of good London restaurants. Particularly where there were bedrooms, but even where there were not, the clubs provided what was in effect a second home for the upper and upper-middle classes. It is noteworthy that so popular were they that the Adelaide at Euston, the first of the railway hotels, chose to advertise itself as being intended to serve more as a 'respectable club-house' than as an ordinary hotel.

While the guidebooks described the exteriors of the great town houses, their real enthusiasm was for what they contained. Given the bleak impression that Devonshire House and many of the others made on passers-by, we, now, are fortunate in the four surviving

Five o'clock p.m. The fashionable club. Drawn by
William McConnell for G. A. Sala's *Twice round the
Clock*, 1859.

examples with which a present-day Londoner is most likely to be
familiar. They are all approachable in the figurative as well as in the
purely physical sense. One is Apsley House, the so-called No. 1
London, but actually No. 149 Piccadilly, which stands majestically at
Hyde Park Corner. The other three, half a mile to the east, form a
line fronting Green Park. To the north, towards the Ritz Hotel, is
the eighteenth-century Spencer House, recently restored through the
generosity of Lord Rothschild and regularly open to the public. Next
door is the Italianate and far from austere Bridgewater House, now
offices, and, separated from it by two more modest buildings, is
Lancaster House, used for state receptions. As Stafford House, Lancaster House was the grandest and largest of all the private palaces.
It was here that the young Queen Victoria said to her hostess the
Duchess of Sutherland, 'I come from my house to your palace.' Lady

Eastlake, wife of the director of the National Gallery, agreed: 'The house surpasses in splendour anything that can be imagined: Buckingham Palace is nothing to it.' Stafford House and Bridgewater House owed their existence to the same aggregation of great fortunes. One source was money accumulated by the Leveson Gower family over generations; another was the vast holdings in the Scottish Highlands owned by the ancient earls of Sutherland; a third was the inheritance from the 'Canal Duke' of Bridgewater. The first Duke of Sutherland, the Canal Duke's nephew by marriage, who died in 1833, left Stafford House to his elder son and Bridgewater House (in the form of its predecessor, Cleveland House) to his younger, who was also the heir to the canal properties. Charles Greville, brother-in-law to the younger son, believed Sutherland to be 'the richest individual who ever died.'

The most satisfactory measure of the value of individual houses is probably the Inhabited House Duty tax, which was based on rental value, or, in the case of freeholds, imputed rental value. In 1833, a list of the hundred most highly assessed houses in the country was published in the Parliamentary Papers, showing the rental figure applied to each. Top of the list, by far the most costly private house in Britain, let alone London, was Stafford House, assessed at a rental level of £3,900 (£225,000 today). The architect Charles Barry estimated in 1842 that the building alone should be insured for a million pounds (approaching £60 million now), although in fact this is actually much more than it appears to have cost to build. Next came Devonshire House in Piccadilly at £2,500; Chesterfield House, by the present Dorchester Hotel, at £2,000; the Duke of Wellington's Apsley House at £1,850; and Lansdowne House in Berkeley Square at £1,650. The East India Company's building in the City was assessed on a par with Devonshire House and, to use another measure of comparison, £1,500 was attributed to the Lord Mayor's Mansion House. A particularly expensive group of buildings lined up in Arlington Street, which leads off Piccadilly by the Ritz Hotel, and is now rather nondescript. It contained three houses, including Cecil House, each assessed at more than £1,000. The London values were much higher than provincial ones, with, for example, the most expensive house in Manchester listed at £600. Brighton is a partial exception, with Thomas Cooper's mansion there assessed at £1,150. (Mrs Fitz-herbert at Brighton comes in at £308.) There is a marked difference between town and country, with the Duke of Sutherland's Stafford-shire palace of Trentham assessed at only £300. With the Duke of Bedford the difference is less: he was taxed on £800 for 6 Belgrave Square and £600 for Woburn.

While the comparison of London and country values reflects the improvements made to town houses in the early nineteenth century, the grandees by no means neglected the country. For instance, the sixth Duke of Bedford, with all his spending on Bloomsbury and Campden Hill as well as his rebuilding of Covent Garden market, erected a new country house in Devonshire at a cost of £70,000–£80,000, with more yet spent on the laying out of its very extensive grounds. The Grosvenors altered Eaton Hall in the 1820s, the 1840s and 1850s, and reconstructed it entirely in 1870. The second Duke of Sutherland owned not only Trentham (which he rebuilt) but Dun-robin in Scotland and, later, Cliveden on the Thames. Whether a family saw its headquarters as situated in London or the country varied between families and between generations. In the late eight-eenth century, for instance, the Devonshires were immersed in London social and political life, but for twenty years or so, starting in the 1820s, their concentration shifted to Chatsworth, leaving Devonshire House put away to the side. The dukes of Norfolk treated Norfolk House, St James's Square, as home until the coming of the railways made access to their Arundel estate in Sussex much easier. Yet overall, there was from the late eighteenth century a refocusing by the very rich on London in what amounted to a competition in splendour. The number of new houses which they built was quite small; what they did do was to spend a great deal of money on the remodelling and extending of existing mansions, notably in the construction of ballrooms, and of art galleries to house the magnificent collections of pictures accumulated by their families. It was generally agreed that, whatever the disappointments from the outside, the interiors were magnificent.

The location of a family's art collection indicated where priority lay. A 1798 valuation of contents showed an amount of £29,285 as applicable to Devonshire House against £22,321 at the much larger

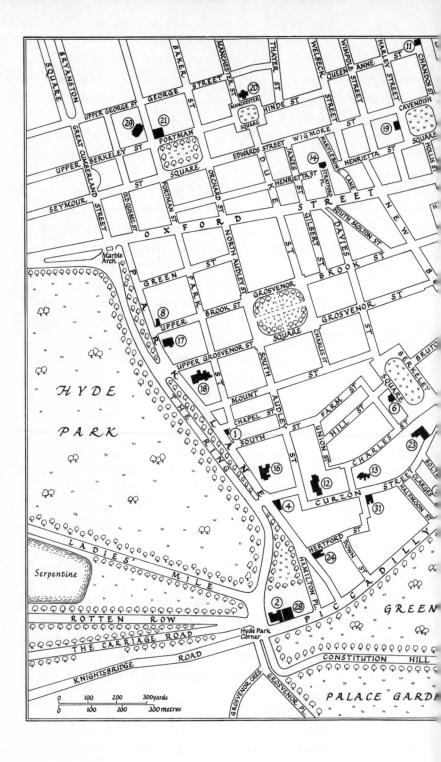

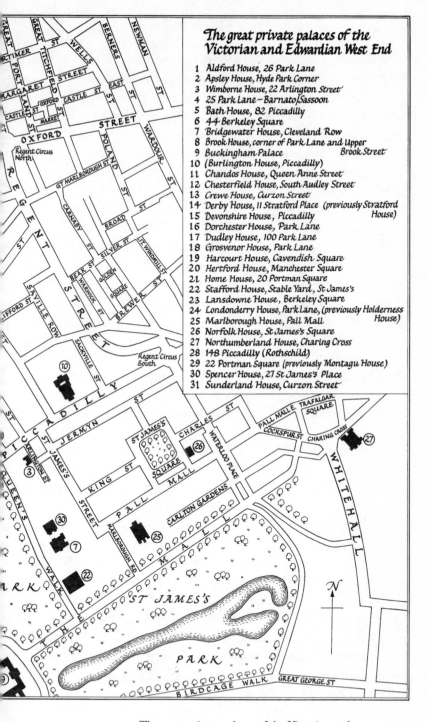

The great private palaces of the Victorian and Edwardian West End.

The great private palaces of the Victorian and Edwardian West End

1 Aldford House, 26 Park Lane
2 Apsley House, Hyde Park Corner
3 Wimborne House, 22 Arlington Street
4 25 Park Lane – Barnato/Sassoon
5 Bath House, 82 Piccadilly
6 44 Berkeley Square
7 Bridgewater House, Cleveland Row
8 Brook House, corner of Park Lane and Upper Brook Street
9 Buckingham Palace
10 (Burlington House, Piccadilly)
11 Chandos House, Queen Anne Street
12 Chesterfield House, South Audley Street
13 Crewe House, Curzon Street
14 Derby House, 11 Stratford Place (previously Stratford House)
15 Devonshire House, Piccadilly
16 Dorchester House, Park Lane
17 Dudley House, 100 Park Lane
18 Grosvenor House, Park Lane
19 Harcourt House, Cavendish Square
20 Hertford House, Manchester Square
21 Home House, 20 Portman Square
22 Stafford House, Stable Yard, St James's
23 Lansdowne House, Berkeley Square
24 Londonderry House, Park Lane, (previously Holderness House)
25 Marlborough House, Pall Mall
26 Norfolk House, St James's Square
27 Northumberland House, Charing Cross
28 148 Piccadilly (Rothschild)
29 22 Portman Square (previously Montagu House)
30 Spencer House, 27 St James's Place
31 Sunderland House, Curzon Street

Chatsworth, this last figure moreover including farming stock and implements. Much of the London valuation consisted of the art collection. In 1798, however, the London houses were not yet the semi-public museums which they were to become: while country houses were often open to a select public, London houses were not. Then, in 1806, the Duke of Sutherland (then Marquis of Stafford) allowed public viewing in London of his incomparable pictures, many of them from the collection of the Duc d'Orléans, sold off in the French Revolution. Increasingly, the great London houses took on the role of public galleries, so that by the time of the Great Exhibition the guidebooks could devote pages to their collections and to the conditions of entry. Apart from Bridgewater House and Stafford House, there were listed, among others, Grosvenor House, Cambridge House and Lord Lansdowne's collection at Lansdowne House in Berkeley Square, which was reputed to hold more 'life-size statues' than the British Museum. Other names mentioned included businessmen. At Bath House, assessed for a rental of £1,320 in 1833, was Lord Ashburton, a Baring, and also in Piccadilly was Mr Hope, a member of the great Amsterdam banking family, both of them fully accepted into the patricians' social world. They were commercial money, but the most respectable commercial money possible. A different matter was Robert Vernon, late of Pall Mall, who had died in 1849, but whose collection of paintings had been left to the nation and was, in 1851, on show free to the public, at Marlborough House, a royal palace temporarily unoccupied. Vernon's money was nothing like so salubrious; it derived from livery stables. Then there were the Rothschilds, still somewhat uncertain socially though certainly not financially. Baron Lionel, with 'a few fine pictures', lived at the twinned Nos. 147 and 148 Piccadilly, topping Apsley House next door. A neighbour was his younger brother Mayer at No. 107, the house acquired by their father, Nathan Mayer Rothschild. Other Rothschilds moved into Piccadilly, giving this part of the road the nickname of Rothschild Row.

By the beginning of the 1860s, another prominent Jewish dynasty, the Goldsmids, were established in one of the older London palaces, Home House in Portman Square. Sir Francis Goldsmid, the second baronet, son of Sir Isaac Lyon Goldsmid and great-nephew of the Goldsmid brothers who have figured earlier in this book, was also

Baron Lionel de Rothschild's 148 Piccadilly topping
next-door Apsley House. It formed part of Piccadilly
Terrace, popularly known as Rothschild Row.

the lessee of St John's Lodge in Regent's Park. He acquired Home
House from the dukes of Newcastle, and his family remained in
occupation until shortly before the lease expired in 1921. Between
them, the Duke of Newcastle and the Goldsmids were the only
leaseholders, and apparently the only occupants, over the whole
ninety-nine-year life of the lease. This comparative stability of occu-
pancy can, however, be compared with the frequent changes that
occurred in the earlier years, during the currency of the original lease.
The Countess of Home died in 1784, leaving Home House to a
schoolboy relative from Jamaica. The house was let, first to a Mrs
Walsh, and then, in 1789, as the French embassy. After the outbreak
of war and the departure of the French, it went to a John Tharp who
appears to have taken it as an investment; over a period of two years,
he carried out alterations and built new stables. He was succeeded

by the Duke of Atholl, who was in residence for eleven years, and then let to sub-tenants. In 1812, the house passed to the future Reform Bill Prime Minister, the second Earl Grey, who built an extension. After him came the Duke of Newcastle, who negotiated a new lease with the Portman estate.

By the later part of the nineteenth century, fashion was drifting away from the old Marylebone houses such as Home House. They did not appeal to servants for one thing, for another they were unlikely to live up to current standards of comfort, not least in terms of plumbing. As an example, there was Stratford House, located in a small aristocratic precinct off Oxford Street, opposite our Bond Street tube station. With ceilings by Angelica Kauffman, and a subdued colouring untouched by new gilding, admired by Augustus Hare, it was a mansion of some distinction. However, even in the 1880s, it possessed only two lavatories, one for men under the stairs and windowless, the other for ladies let into the servants' bedrooms. The kitchens, which incorporated the only hot water tap on the premises, were out of doors, with the disadvantage – in addition presumably to that of cold food – that there was a constant stream of housemaids carrying hot water can after hot water can to the bedrooms upstairs, where incidentally there existed only one, solitary, sink. The cesspit for the house was uncovered.

The Victorian town mansion was not to be like this at all. In the 1860s, the architect Robert Kerr published an influential book entitled *The Gentleman's House* in which he discussed what someone building a house got for his money. Take a house estimated to cost £40,000 (£2.3 million today) in London, or £28,000 to £30,000 in the country. It would be very large, but not the largest; for instance, Bridgewater House, which Kerr examines in some detail, cost around £50,000. No. 12A Kensington Palace Gardens, built for the contractor Sir Samuel Morton Peto in the early 1860s, would have been nearer the mark. Even at this £40,000 level, Kerr's dimensions are breathtaking: the 'family department', which excludes the servants' quarters, is allocated 100 rooms. While that somewhat exaggerates the usable area, since all space, be it for drawing rooms, porches, vestibules or galleries or anything else, is counted, the appointments are still very lavish. The dining room measures 36 × 24 ft., the drawing room 46

× 24 ft., the library 40 × 16 ft., and, in addition, there are 'a saloon or picture gallery', a billiard room, a morning room, a luncheon room, a boudoir, as well as a gentleman's room, described as 'a private room for a gentleman whose mornings are more or less spent in practical affairs'. For sleeping there is a family suite of five rooms and a nursery suite, which is augmented by 20 bedrooms and 10 dressing rooms. Servants and 'offices' are allocated a further 97 rooms.

Kerr was as concerned with comfort as with magnificence, although he emphasized what he termed 'convenience' – 'the arrangement of the various departments, and their various component parts, in such relation to each other as shall enable all the uses and purposes of the establishment to be carried on in perfect harmony'. There should be 'A place for everything, and everything in its place.' Kerr

Bridgewater House: the saloon, which provided one of the grandest spaces of any building in London.

assumes central heating and gas lighting. On plumbing, he is by and large generous: dressing rooms are to be equipped with wash basins, and bedrooms have water closets within easy reach. However, he allows for only two bathrooms in the 'family section', and, in fact, specifies more in plans for terrace houses prepared for the Marquess of Westminster. And there was no bathroom at all in Florence Nightingale's Mayfair house when she died in 1910. But then if you had plenty of servants you might well prefer hip baths in front of a blazing bedroom fire to the best ordered bathroom. More than anything or anyone, it is the servants who make vivid the life of these vanished palaces. Here is Taine on the servants of a great London house:

> They wear white cravats with large faultless bows, scarlet or canary-coloured knee-breeches, are magnificent in shape and amplitude; their calves especially are enormous. In the fashionable neighbourhoods, beneath the vestibule, about five o'clock in the evening, the butler seated, newspaper in hand, sips a glass of port; around him, ushers, corded lackeys, footmen with their sticks, gaze with an indolent and a lordly air upon the middle-class passers-by.

The servants, of course, made these houses possible. They were the measure of comfort; officially even, for the census of 1901 used the number of servants employed as its yardstick.

A substantial, but not large London house, the equivalent of a medium-sized country house with around twenty rooms plus servants' quarters, but excluding any mews attached, would be likely to employ up to twelve living-in servants, a number well in excess of the family itself. The great houses employed around forty permanent servants, with some living out, although the Duke of Sutherland in 1845 employed at Stafford House a staff of forty-eight with another ten in the stables. For special occasions, for balls or 'routs', extra staff would be hired. Such an occasion would have been the party Lady Eastlake attended at Lansdowne House where she estimated the number of guests at over 2,000. Amongst the permanent employees were those who would not have regarded themselves as servants, nor

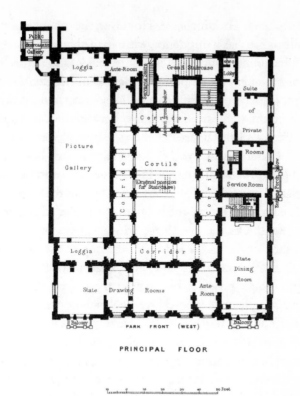

Bridgewater House: plan of the Principal Floor. From
Robert Kerr, *The Gentleman's House*, 1868.

would have been regarded as such by their employers. For instance,
at Bridgewater House, the census of 1861 records a living-in 'physician';
at Londonderry House there was Lord Londonderry's secretary.
Again there were governesses. While the staff might be permanent,
their place of employment changed as their employer moved about.
The Duke of Sutherland was reminded in the 1830s that he was the
only nobleman in the country who kept a regular establishment at
each of his four large houses. (And even he seems later to have
undertaken some modest rationalization.) The 1861 census, which
took place in early April, found many of the owners of the great
houses out of town, although sometimes their children remained in
London. Accordingly, at Devonshire House, only thirteen servants
were present and at Baron Lionel de Rothschild's 147–148 Piccadilly,

only eighteen. At Dorchester House, on the other hand, the Holford family of five was in residence, with, in the house itself, twenty-seven staff, including a nurse and two nursemaids, and in the coach house, seven more and in the porter's lodge, a further two. At the family's country house of Westonbirt in Gloucestershire, there were left, ignoring the stables and the lodge, just three housemaids.

These are the houses of the rich in full glory, at their climax. 'Busy, Clamorous, Crowded, Imperial London,' declaimed *London, As It Is Today* in 1851, 'may be considered not merely as the capital of England, or of the British Empire, but as the metropolis of the civilized world.' For all the bombast it was not an exaggeration. The year 1851 marks the zenith of British power. Britain was still the workshop of the world and by far the richest nation. What is more, for all the technological and social changes of the first half of the nineteenth century, the 'old', patrician rich were still in charge. The insurrection feared by Lord Liverpool had not taken place, the Prime Minister was a brother of the Duke of Bedford and his cabinet predominantly aristocratic. Said the radical Richard Cobden in 1857, '. . . the higher classes never stood so high'. But ten years after that came the second Reform Act, and then, a further ten years on, the onset of a profound agricultural depression. What has been described as the 'age of equipoise' was at an end. The effect on the traditional rich was to be devastating.

IO

The Rich in Turmoil

*

In rapid succession we passed through the fringe of fashionable London, hotel London, theatrical London, literary London, commercial London, and, finally, maritime London, till we came to a riverside city of a hundred thousand souls, where the tenement houses swelter and reek with the outcasts of Europe.

There must be tens of thousands of people who acquired their first impression of the size of late Victorian London from the Sherlock Holmes stories. In *The Adventure of the Six Napoleons*, from which this quotation comes, Holmes and Watson are hot-foot to Lambeth, to the Kennington Road. Often, for Holmes after all was paid for his services, their destination is more glamorous. It could be Fairbank, a good-sized house in Streatham with double carriage-sweep, belonging to the senior partner of the second largest private bank in the City, or The Haven in Lewisham which, Dr Watson reports, resembles 'some penurious patrician who has sunk into the company of his inferiors'. In the middle of monotonous brick streets and weary suburban highways, it stands as 'a little island of ancient culture and comfort'. Holmes interrupts, with 'Cut out the poetry, Watson.' And it is true that by then poetry was seldom appropriate for descriptions of South London; the islands of culture left were too few and far between.

'Interminable' is a word that seems naturally to come to mind. Conan Doyle through Watson speaks of the 'interminable lines of new, staring brick buildings – the monster tentacles which the giant city was throwing out into the country.' Percy Fitzgerald in *London City Suburbs as They Are Today* of 1893 writes of 'Long rows of grim,

275

shabby-looking houses [that] line these dismal avenues, which seem interminable.' Bricks and mortar, everywhere and endless. Of Clapham, the *City Press* in August 1887 declared that 'Wilberforce and Macaulay now would scarcely know the scenes of their boyhood.' William Hazlitt – the grandson – wrote of Battersea Fields:

> I used to think that Battersea Fields, with the Red House and other amenities, were not all that could be desired; yet I would joyfully vote for their restoration instead of the actual scene which they present, with their honeycomb of railway-line and doleful blocks of poverty-stricken houses.

There is John Ruskin, appalled as he revisits the by then important railway junction of Herne Hill to search out the country lane where he used to walk with his mother: '. . . no existing terms of language known to me are enough to describe the forms of filth, and modes of ruin, that varied themselves along the course of Croxted Lane.'

The engulfment of South London, and of North and West London, was a consequence of a prodigious increase in population. Less than a million people lived in London in 1801; the number in 1851 was – as we have seen – 2.36 million; by 1901 it was 4.52 million. Partly the increase was due to a general shift from country to town, but it was magnified by London's pull as the pre-eminent commercial and financial centre, and by its position as the hub of the Empire. For residential purposes, the central zone of the city was shrinking under continued pressure for commercial building and for space to accommodate the railways. Had houses been built higher, had the town grown upwards, no doubt the demands on the suburbs would have lessened. But suburban land was cheap and, until late in the century, high domestic buildings were unpopular, outside the tradition, outside the culture. The demand would have been far less too without the revolution in transport. Above all, of course, that meant the railways. But before them there were the regular omnibus services. Put crudely, the new buses were boxes on wheels, no more than an elaboration of existing coach services. However, they could hold twenty passengers inside, seated on two forms which faced each other down the length of the vehicle. The buses stopped frequently and averaged only about 5 m.p.h., but that was sufficient for the nearer suburbs. In fact, for short distances horse buses remained competitive even against suburban rail services, their use prolonged by the introduction of tram lines in the 1870s, which by reducing the friction on wheels, made for a smoother and more economical ride.

The clamour for houses was especially exigent in the riverside districts of Lambeth, Battersea and Wandsworth, where a population of 130,000 in 1841 multiplied almost three and a half times in the next fifty years. But the crowds pushed on. First came the middle-income groups, then the skilled working class, then the less skilled. As the century progressed so did the national income; people at almost all levels of society were better off and many of the poor could afford something more comfortable than the old-fashioned tenements of inner London. Shorter working hours encouraged commuting. By

The arrival of the Workmen's Penny Train at Victoria Station, from the *Illustrated London News*, 1865.

the 1870s and 1880s, the railway companies, recognizing the value to themselves of commuter traffic, and with government pressure behind them, introduced cheaper fares. In 1883, persuaded by the Cheap Trains Act, they greatly increased the number of 'workmen's trains'. Railway companies joined the City solicitors and the building societies and freehold land societies in advancing money for building finance.

On the wealthy, the effect of trams and suburban railways was twofold: they lost Arcadia but they gained the means of escape to the country beyond. Their withdrawal was gradual. At the start, many of the City merchants of Kennington and its neighbourhood, those recalled by Dr Watson, migrated to the western end of Wandsworth and to Norwood. Some stayed there, clustering on the hilltops, 'little islands' indeed, perched above the flood; the views may have gone, but, for the time being, some privacy remained. But most moved on. In June 1874 *The Times* noted that 'The people who can afford to spend £60 a year in season tickets fly further off and carry Wandsworth and Clapham into the heart of Surrey.' The general manager of the Great Eastern Railway wrote a report in 1884 on what happened in the Stamford Hill, Tottenham and Edmonton area:

> That used to be a very nice district indeed, occupied by good families, with houses from £150 to £250 a year, with coach houses and stables, a garden and a few acres of land. But very soon after this obligation was put upon the Great Eastern to run workmen's trains . . . speculative builders went down into the neighbourhood and, as a consequence, each good house was one after another pulled down, and the district is given up entirely, I must say, now to the working man. I lived down there myself and I waited until most of my neighbours had gone; and then, at last, I was obliged to go.

He was referring to North London, but what he said applied equally to much of South London. More so in fact, for South London, on the wrong side of the river, was literally on the wrong side of the tracks. The commissioners appointed to the Royal Commission on Metropolitan Railway Termini, set up in 1846 in the middle of the great railway boom, make this clear. Intensely concerned about the effect of the railways on central London, they were prepared to let South London and its landowners look after themselves. The all-important Church of England appears to have offered no opposition. Hence the Battersea Tangle and, further east, the New Cross Tangle, which between them covered 300 acres.

The commissioners' priorities were understandable, for the potential disruption to central London was alarming. For one thing, there was the effect on traffic; for another, more fundamental, there was the amount of space required. Each railway company laid claim to its own terminus, with space for tracks, marshalling yards and locomotive sheds. Happily for the rich, the expense to the companies of buying prime residential land plus hostility on the part of the government, kept the railway termini out of the West End. The stations were built in a great arc round central London, in the north placed along the New Road at Paddington, Marylebone, Euston, St Pancras and King's Cross, and in the east, at Liverpool Street and Broad Street near the City's eastern limits. On the southern side, the stations of Cannon Street, Blackfriars and Charing Cross were erected on or by the river. Only Victoria Station pressed in close, with Buckingham Palace and Belgravia nearby. But Victoria replaced slums and the Grosvenor Canal basin, not expensive residential housing. If Lord Westminster proved relaxed over Victoria, however, the same was not true of the Eyres and Portmans when in the 1890s they were confronted with plans for Marylebone station produced by the Great Central Railway. These were a remnant of an old and highly ambitious project to connect Manchester and Paris by means of a direct line across London and a Channel Tunnel. Remnant though the scheme was, it was the most expensive of London rail construction works, and, when put into effect along with some subsidiary work, obliterated twenty-one streets and nearly 900 houses. Among the buildings which disappeared were some attractive medium-sized villas with pretty gardens, but again the district – above the old New Road – was not one much favoured by the rich.

A railway company acquired land through a private act of parliament or through compulsory purchase where no agreement on price or principle could be reached with the landowner. However, parliament made sure that landowners' interests were protected. The Eyre and

Portman estates lost land but they were able to insist on some stringent conditions, including lengthy tunnelling. Eton was able to require tunnelling where the track crossed its Chalcots estate, and Lord Harrington in South Kensington obtained a clause prohibiting the emergence on his estate of ventilator shafts connected with the underground line built by the Metropolitan District Company. Understandably, landowners were often ambivalent about the railways. Lord Jersey from Osterley was initially reluctant to come to terms, but was converted by the prospect of a 'good round sum'. The third Lord Holland was torn two ways: he was in urgent need of a good round sum, but the railway track was scheduled to run down the side of Addison Road, a few hundred yards from Holland House and nearer still to his new building development. A railway line would inevitably be unsightly, dirty and noisy. In the end, all was well, for the company shifted the track to the western end of the estate, and in addition to substantial compensation, provided free a new covered sewer which would help in Holland's plans for future development. To the Edwardes family, the railways were even more important. This family, it may be remembered, descended from Sir Walter Cope and his son-in-law, the sybaritic Earl of Holland, was once the owner of Holland House and most of Kensington. They were still in the early nineteenth century the biggest landowners in the parish, making sporadic but unsuccessful attempts at development. They tried to improve their appeal to developers by buying out their copyholders, but generally the Edwardes were sellers of assets rather than buyers. Mostly they lived off capital. In 1852, William Edwardes, second Lord Kensington (who happily for his family was prevented by settlement from selling off everything), died in near destitution, his household by the 1851 census consisting only of himself, his illegitimate daughter and a single male servant. There were problems afterwards, notably in the loss of the Harrods site and nearby land as a result of foreclosure. However, the railway needed land on their estate and the family was saved. The third Lord Kensington was able to pay off many of the debts and move to Mayfair.

Lord Southampton and Lord Somers with their dilapidated north London estates around Euston and St Pancras were other landowners happy to sell. As John Nash had pointed out, the buildings they had authorized were shoddy, and their reversionary value was low. The Duke of Bedford, however, their neighbour to the south, was not at all pleased by the incursion of the railway, and put up a fight worthy of his grandfather, the opposer of the New Road. Bedford was directly affected in his Fig's Mead estate (sometimes known as Bedford New Town) which lay straight in the path of the railway as it passed through to the new terminus at Euston. But Fig's Mead, unlike the Bloomsbury estate, was not intended for wealthy residents. Bloomsbury was outside the railway's limits but vulnerable to the indirect effect of a station. The extra traffic, the dirt caused by steam trains, the noise in the streets around, the crowds and the shops and hotels which catered for them, could easily ruin the refined atmosphere essential for a fashionable district. Euston accelerated Bloomsbury's decline. Victoria accelerated that of Pimlico, especially at its southern end. However, it was the station at Paddington which had the most dramatic consequences, primarily because it was situated in one of the most sought-after residential districts in London. To begin with, the station was expected to add to its appeal and the Great Western Hotel, opened in 1854, was widely admired. Yet, as the Ordnance Survey map of 1872 makes plain, the railway agglomeration was enormous. It dominates the area. The parish was broken in two by the railway and the existing Grand Junction Canal, with the original nucleus of the community at Paddington Green isolated. Tyburnia continued to flourish as a strip above Hyde Park, but closer to the station, deterioration set in. By the end of the century it was noted by both Percy Fitzgerald in his *London City Suburbs*, and Charles Booth in his mammoth survey of London. Fitzgerald refers to the 'tame yellow houses of Westbourne and other terraces being close by, with a curious general stagnation'. Booth commented on the poverty along the canal banks – lined with industry – though he noted 'a pleasant and successful effort' to utilize the canal as ornamental water at Blomfield Road (Little Venice). As to the humbler streets by the station, they were increasingly given over to seedy hotels and prostitution. It was a standing joke later that the biggest brothel-owners in London were the Ecclesiastical Commissioners, Paddington's main landlords.

As the suburbs grew, the population of the inner boroughs fell.

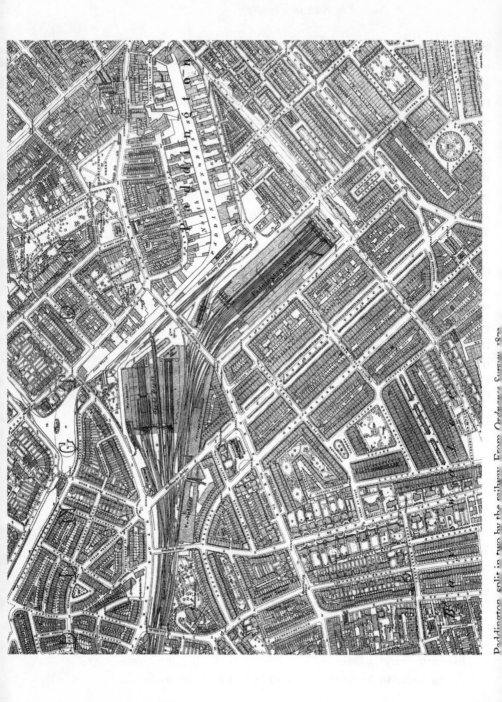

Paddington, split in two by the railway. From Ordnance Survey, 1872.

By the later decades of the nineteenth century, there was an actual net loss of population in central London. The population of Westminster fell from 257,000 in 1861 to just above 200,000 by 1891, and that of Marylebone from 161,000 to 143,000. The inner suburbs to the west became almost as congested as those on the southern side of the Thames. As desirable places to live, Fulham and Hammersmith went steadily downhill. Too close to London and no longer country, they were thrown open by the Great Western Railway, the underground and the trams. James Thorne in his *Handbook to the Environs of London* of 1876 warned that 'Fulham looks its best from the Thames. The shabbiness of too many of the houses is thence little apparent.' The population grew from 12,000 in 1851 to 137,000 by the end of the century. In 1912, William Hazlitt wrote of Hammersmith that few places near London had within the last two generations so thoroughly lost their old aspect and attraction. If the great houses of Syon and Osterley survived, protected by their parks and farmland, they were a rarity. Gunnersbury, to which Lady Mary Coke had travelled from Kensington to visit Princess Amelia, for long stood fast within its protecting fields. The mansion was rebuilt, and Nathan Mayer Rothschild bought the western section of the estate shortly before he died. Later in the century the two parts were reunited. In 1869 a local railway station opened, and after that the Rothschilds gradually sold off much of the land for building. There remain now a public park and a local authority museum. Other notable properties were no more fortunate. Lonsdale House, on the river at Fulham, was famous in the 1860s as high society flocked to the Saturday afternoon garden parties given by its owner, the widowed Lady Shelley. But it was an Indian Summer. The 'nabob' Sulivan family continued at Broom House until 1911, when the last Miss Sulivan died. Of the riverside houses on the London side of Richmond, only Hurlingham survives. Built in 1760 and later enlarged, it escaped the common fate of conversion into an insane asylum to be leased in 1867 as a sporting club – outdoor sports rather than gambling – and remains a fashionable London club.

By the end of the century there was little poetry about the western suburbs either. Still, a certain lyricism embroiders the reminiscences of William Hazlitt. He recalls the cattle grazing on the site of Belgrave

Square, the roadside inns and ancient London markets, and the dreadful road which ran west from Knightsbridge. Married early in the 1860s, he and his wife moved to Addison Road, leaving in disgust in 1881 for the more tranquil Barnes as the city lurched in on all sides. Like others, he remembered the sprawling parish of Brompton with special affection. He wrote of it:

> The scenes amid which I spent much of my youth now survive only in the mind's eye. The ancient mansions which abounded there, the historical sites or records, the fine residences in grounds, the market gardens, and, best of all, the old Vale, have vanished like a dream.

The very name of Brompton has become shadowy, overlaid by the modern South Kensington. Yet Brompton, menaced by town on all sides, stayed predominantly rural for many years. South Kensington was a long time in gestation. A lawyer named Elisha Biscoe, who was connected with a family owning land on the site of Brompton Square, in company with an ironmonger, undertook some speculative building in the 1760s. It continued along what is now the Brompton Road in a desultory way until the 1820s, when serious development resumed. A number of landowners were involved, of whom three merit special mention. One was Smith's Charity, a trust (originally several trusts) holding land also in Chelsea, which was founded in the seventeenth century by a philanthropic City merchant and alderman who stipulated that rents should be applied partly to the relief and ransom of captives enslaved by Turkish pirates, and partly for the benefit of impoverished members of his family. (By 1772 the pirates were no longer in evidence and the trust was consolidated.) Another was the Alexander estate, otherwise known as the Thurloe estate, which owned the land on which South Kensington station was built. The third of these landowners was the Gunter family. Gunter, 'the pastry cook' as Hazlitt called him, ran a highly successful confectionery and catering business in Berkeley Square supplied by produce cultivated on 30 acres of kitchen garden and orchard which formed part of the family's land in West Kensington. By the early nineteenth century the Gunters had become sufficiently accepted socially to hunt with Grantley Berkeley's hounds and were ready to start on the development of their estate, which was to include The Boltons. The family business continued to trade in Mayfair until after the Second World War.

We know something of what it was like to live in South Kensington in the early 1870s from a diary kept by Margaret Leicester Warren. Aged just on twenty-four, she and her older sister and brother were obliged to quit the family house in Mayfair on the remarriage of their widowed father, Lord de Tabley. With the need for economy in mind they started house-hunting in Kensington. The villas on Campden Hill, they found, looked glum and 'unhomelike', and the long rows of half-built houses and dreary heaps of gravel and scaffolding that disfigured Exhibition Road and its surrounds were depressing. They settled on a lease for 67 Onslow Square, and were cheered their first morning by the April blossom in the garden and the pretty church spire. In the afternoon, as the diary puts it, they 'drove into London'. That was the problem: to Margaret Warren, they were living in the sticks. She could never get used to that. She could not forget the sort of remark made by their friend Lord Bathurst while they were still house-hunting: 'How are you going to manage next Season if you live at Phillimore Gardens?' The unsatisfactory state of her love life made things worse – she had just turned down an assiduous but feeble suitor – and when Mrs Gladstone offered to take her to a 'drawing room', she refused, thinking it 'absurd for an old maid from Brompton to go to Court'. One afternoon she found herself returning in a cab from a tea party with Mr Freake, the developer of Onslow Square. Even his unremitting praise of the square's situation and his information that it was once called 'the vale of health' failed to lift her spirits. Happily, marriage to another, this time more lively, suitor carried her away.

In her emotional state Margaret Warren took an odd view of the other residents of Onslow Square. She noted that they were very neighbourly and exchanged food and old newspapers. 'They are all very poor,' she wrote. Whether she included her next-door neighbour Lady Aberdeen in this assessment one does not know, but it hardly accords with a diary entry for August 1871 where she writes that except for themselves everyone in the square has left town. In fact, the census of that year shows an average number per house of 7.85 inhabitants, of whom 4.25 were servants. Such a ratio would have been sufficient to grade Onslow Square among London's wealthier streets in the survey carried out by Charles Booth thirty years later for his *Life and Labour of the People in London.* Nonetheless, Onslow Square is not of an opulence to compare with a self-contained development, the artists' precinct coming into full glory during the 1870s at the southern end of the grounds of Holland Park, and bounded now by Melbury Road, Addison Road and Holland Park Road. The most successful late Victorian artists were decidedly wealthy. If one counted post-humous sales, the richest artist by far living in London during the mid-1870s would be Vincent van Gogh, then working as a master at a small boys' school in unfashionable Isleworth. Leaving him aside, the star is probably Sir John Everett Millais. The journalist Sir Henry Lucy remembered a dinner where the conversation turned to the top level of earnings in the various professions. One of the guests, a royal prince, put the question to a prominent lawyer and to a doctor, and then to Millais. His answer was £35,000 a year, and when the other guests looked incredulous, he mentioned that in the previous year he had earned £40,000 (£2.3 million today) and could have made more had he not prolonged his holiday in Scotland. Even an ordinarily successful member of the Royal Academy could expect an income of £5,000 or £6,000.

The artists' colony of Melbury Road and its immediate neighbour-hood owed its existence to a friendship between G. F. Watts and the fourth Lord Holland, and even more so to one between Watts and the Prinsep family, with whom he moved in at Little Holland House. Another local connection for Watts was with the Greek collector Constantine Ionides at No. 1 Holland Park. Little Holland House was demolished in 1875 to make way for the building projects put in hand by the widowed Lady Holland, but Watts built himself a new house next door to which he gave the same name. (Actually, neither of these two houses was at all 'little'.) Others to arrive and usually to build were Holman Hunt, Luke Fildes, the sculptor Hamo Thornycroft, the caricaturist Phil May and Frederic Leighton, later Lord Leighton. They produced what Ruskin – contrasting them with the artists of Chelsea – described as 'senatorial and authoritative

Sir Luke Fildes's house at 31 Melbury Road (originally
No. 11), designed by Norman Shaw.

art'. While the second Little Holland House has in its turn been
demolished, there still remain, adorned with commemorative plaques,
most of the lavish studios and mansions, above all Leighton's No. 12
Holland Park Road, now a museum, with its profusion of decorative
tiles and a highly ornamented Arab Hall. There is another aspect of
this community which is worth mentioning. It was great fun. Sir
Edward Burne-Jones, a visitor, spoke of Little Holland House (apparently in its first incarnation) as very strange, foreign in its ease and
'brilliancy', with dinner often laid for thirty or forty people. At the
same time there is no doubting the professionalism, particularly on
'Show Sunday', the Sunday before the Royal Academy's Summer
Exhibition, when the artists opened their studios to show the work
they would be exhibiting. In fact, the Melbury Road precinct in its

combination of home and workplace inhabited by people of the same profession was in principle the same as the old homogeneous enclaves in the City of London.

Millais himself lived from 1878 in the newly built neo-renaissance No. 2 Palace Gate, which formed part of the new town emerging on land abutting Hyde Park and Kensington Gardens. As mentioned in Chapter 7, the whole area was redeveloped after 1851. The commissioners responsible for the Great Exhibition and the ambitious projects which followed, purchased great tracts of land to house the scientific and artistic institutions which were established in the area. Some of this land they themselves sold for development in order to raise funds. The main landowners were the Earl of Harrington and the Swiss family of Villars, the joint beneficiaries of marriages in the eighteenth century with daughters of Sir John Fleming of Brompton Park, a mansion which was sited roughly where the Victoria and

Lord Leighton's studio at 12 Holland Park Road
(then 2 Addison Road) in 1895.

Albert Museum stands now. Development had begun well before the Great Exhibition at the western end of Kensington Gardens towards Kensington Palace and Millionaires' Row. Large mansions for the wealthy made their appearance in Palace Gate, Kensington Gate and Hyde Park Gate. In the view of the *Survey of London* the buyers were *too* wealthy: 'The wealth of many of its occupants had an adverse effect on the architecture of [Hyde Park Gate], much of whatever distinction it originally possessed having been mutilated by inappropriate additions.' The eighth Duke of Bedford bought two plots in Palace Gate for Thorney House – probably because his mistress lived nearby – while at the same time keeping his palace in Belgrave Square.

Between 1855 and the early 1880s, terraces composed of very large houses were constructed around Queen's Gate and Exhibition Road (then known as Prince's Gate). A visit now to Queen's Gate Terrace is illuminating, even breathtaking. Numbers 11 to 43 extend in a long Italianate block, each house with basement, and some with five, some with six upper storeys. Each house contained a dining room, breakfast room and billiard room on the ground floor, and a thirty-seven-foot drawing room with conservatory on the first floor. There were nine principal bedrooms, and plenty of space on the attic floor to provide for servants' bedrooms. The households, as shown by the 1871 census, match the space: that of John Fiennes, later seventeenth Lord Saye and Sele, at 16 Queen's Gate Terrace comprised, in addition to his wife and himself, eight children and nine living-in servants. At 56 Queen's Gate, Richard Courage the brewer accounted for a family of nine plus nine servants, while at 25 Queen's Gate (now demolished) Richard Duncombe, by profession 'fundholder', registered a household of twenty, half of whom were servants. (In Grosvenor Square at this time the average household consisted of thirteen or fourteen, of whom ten or eleven were servants.) Many of the original residents of this part of London moved here from other parts of the city, from Belgravia, Bayswater, Mayfair, St James's, Regent's Park.

What might be called Middle Kensington, along with South Kensington, constituted a new town, another colonization of countryside by the London rich. Its residents included a duke (Rutland) and a number of other peers, as well as the Archbishop of York. Yet such

Northumberland House just before demolition. The
shadow of Nelson's Column is falling across the main
entrance.

challenge as it might have posed to Belgravia and Mayfair was
short-lived. Demand was insufficient. The mid-century return to
London from the suburbs went into reverse. The countryside was
syphoning off many of the wealthier businessmen, and, as will be
seen, the landed rich were in no mood for investment in substantial
London properties. Many of the great mansions were soon divided
into flats. The demographic pattern had changed in a fundamental
way. Traditionally the rich occupied the suburbs, now they were
becoming concentrated in an inner zone, encircled by a ring, miles
deep, composed of non-rich. They were losing control of London
too. Symbolic of that was the destruction of Northumberland House.
Among the great private mansions, Northumberland House was
unique, a Jacobean Strand palace that had long outlived its contemporaries. Its appearance and its position on the crucial and historic
crossroads at the base of Trafalgar Square proclaimed a kinship closer
to the Tower of London than to the town houses with which it now
kept company. It had, to quote Knight's *London* of 1844, 'an exclusive,
almost fortified air . . . as if meant to lodge troops of retainers and

keep the "profanum vulgus" at bay'. In 1862, the Metropolitan Board of Works proposed to run a new street (Northumberland Avenue) through the site of Northumberland House and its grounds as a link with the Embankment, which was at that moment under construction. The Duke of Northumberland resisted, but the political pressure was too strong, and in 1873 his successor gave in, accepting a sale at a price only just short of £500,000 (£29 million today). The seclusion of many West End squares and streets was put in jeopardy as the right to keep street barriers came under increasing attack. In 1868 the St Marylebone vestry removed some gates on the Portman estate and were successfully sued for damage to property, with the court ruling that landowners were entitled to retain such gates even when the roadway they blocked – and the cost of its maintenance – had been transferred to the local authority. Public indignation mounted and matters worsened when in 1874 a cab driver died after a fracas with gate-keepers in Bloomsbury. (The Bloomsbury gate-keepers were often ex-prison warders.) In the end, in 1890, despite prolonged resistance by landowners and residents, the newly formed London County Council obtained an enabling act from parliament which led to the abolition of gates and barriers with very modest compensation.

While in the West End the interests of landlord and tenant (likely of course to be a long leaseholder) diverged on the amount of rent to be charged, in many circumstances they were the same. For instance, both favoured well-kept square gardens, both wanted street barriers. The wealthy London tenant was happy with expensive housing packed in terraces and the Grosvenors, for instance, had no possible incentive to cover Belgrave Square with cheap villas. In the suburbs, the arguments were different, because the tenants were there to savour a rural, or at least a semi-rural, life, and few would have relished a Belgrave Square-on-the-Wandle. Occasionally, the land-owner/landlord was in accord. An example is Dulwich, owned by the governors of Dulwich College, who were determined to preserve the existing character of their estate. The college permitted some closely controlled development, but by 1900 Dulwich was still country with wide expanses of green fields, as well as a pretty village and attractive houses. While the population density of Dulwich was seven people per acre, in the rest of the parish of Camberwell the average was

Keeping the public out: the Taviton Street gate and
gate-keeper, Bloomsbury, 1893.

ninety-seven. In some parts of Wimbledon, local regulations prohibited the sale of buildings (and so in effect their construction) where
the price would fall below a certain figure. However, the landlord
had virtually always a judgement to make – was a tract of land going
to make him more money as an estate of expensive but occasional
houses or through mass building?

The issue came to a head over the enclosure of common land
and its use for building. We have seen the frustration of Sir Thomas
Maryon-Wilson at Hampstead Heath, an important case but untypical in that there the landowner's efforts were gravely compromised
by the existence of a restrictive family settlement. The case of Lord
Spencer and Wimbledon Common – an even larger space – was more
straightforward. Spencer was lord of the manor and thus contingent

proprietor of the Common. He did not need to balance the usual pros and cons, to assess whether despoliation of the Common might affect his rents on surrounding land, since his family, loaded with debts, had by the 1860s already sold their South London freeholds. He could thus be indifferent to neighbouring tenants and freeholders. Except politically, for as a prominent politician he was fully aware of the delicacy now necessary with enclosures. The public had seen the railways push ruthlessly through common land, they had seen the disappearance of open spaces everywhere, not least in such districts as Notting Hill, Chelsea, Kensington, Islington and Brompton. Lord Spencer came to a financial agreement with the copyholders who held rights of use and put forward a proposal to parliament whereby he would allocate most of Wimbledon Common as a public park and reimburse himself by selling off 300 acres of the adjoining Putney Heath for building. However, by this time, public concern was thoroughly aroused, wealthy residents of Wimbledon rose in protest, the copyholders had second thoughts, and Lord Spencer found himself obliged to withdraw his private bill. A Commons Preservation Society was formed, to be followed by the Metropolitan Commons Act of 1866 which forbade enclosure of common land within a fourteen-mile radius of Charing Cross. As to Lord Spencer, a few years later he sold out his rights for a substantial annuity.

One group of rich had suffered a striking defeat. The wealthy as a whole had secured their sanctuaries. Open spaces explain the prosperous suburban enclaves which survived around Richmond Park, and at Hampstead, Wimbledon, Barnes, Dulwich and Blackheath. They provided a visual and physical amenity and a natural separation from lower income groups. (And of course they gave the poor some relief from the oppression of the 'monster city'.)

More alarming for the landowners than the actual legislation which restrained their powers was the pronounced shift against them in public opinion and the threat that held for the future. In the later years of the century, critics were attacking the system of urban leasehold on grounds of principle, accusing the landowner in his role as landlord of exercising an intolerable monopoly. An example was the position of a small business established for generations in Mayfair: how could it leave Mayfair when the lease expired without a probably fatal loss of trade? It would be entirely in the hands of the (since 1874) Duke of Westminster and his agents. Its bargaining power would be negligible. Frank Banfield published an influential and critical series of articles in the *Sunday Times*, issued in book-form in 1888 under the title *The Great Landlords of London*. Another book was Henry Lazarus's *Landlordism: An Illustration of the Rise and Spread of Slumland* . . . of 1892 which blamed the slum landlords for the scandalous state of much urban housing. According to Lazarus, in comparison with the 'noble dukes and marquises, the worshipful companies, the churchly commissioners, and the other honourable gentry . . . the mere money-lending Shylocks are but halting parasites.' The greed of the great landlords in 'abolishing altogether breathing space from their estates, compel the better-to-do tenants to move into healthier neighbourhoods, and leave only the very poor behind.' In 1894, Lord Salisbury, the Prime Minister, declared that 'The landlord is assuming the position of the Jew of the Middle Ages or the pariah of India. He is an outcast . . . who has no rights.'

Lady Troubridge, writing in the 1920s, recalled a scene from 1891, a time when there were problems at Covent Garden market over costs and lack of investment. The Duke of Bedford was giving her sister away at a wedding at Holy Trinity, Sloane Square. A crowd had gathered outside the church and gave the Duke a rough reception, a cry going up, 'Stingy old Bedford, give us Covent Garden!' The great London landlords were ill-prepared for such treatment, for the public criticism, and for the falling off of that deference which had always been their due. One commentator suggested that had the Duke of Northumberland possessed a better sense of public relations and allowed wider access to his gardens he might have found stronger public support in his campaign for the defence of Northumberland House. The landlords were, of course, investors intent on making a profit from their estates, but at the same time these properties also held for them – as they had for their ancestors – other values. Like his friend, the fourth Earl Spencer, back in the 1830s, the seventh Duke of Bedford had inherited considerable debts, and he too considered selling off his South London property. He decided against, one reason certainly being the argument advanced by his agent Christopher Haedy, that to do so would put at risk his family's pre-eminent standing in public esteem. But now the arguments were changing, and the old certainties no longer held.

The upper class was confronted by a new political culture; at last the egalitarian pressures dreaded by Lord Liverpool and the Duke of Wellington were gathering force. Their troubles did not come singly, for in the late 1870s the world succumbed to what became known as the Great Depression. Between 1880 and 1895 prices in Britain fell by 28 per cent. For most people the effect was benign: employment levels improved and, overall, real income per head rose by more than 50 per cent in the twenty years to 1900. For those involved in agriculture, however – which meant most of the upper class – the effect could be calamitous. Prices, rents and land values plummeted, driven on their way by the import of cheap American corn. Costs, on the other hand, did not fall proportionately. Country landowners traditionally carried high levels of debt and also obligations under family settlements to pay fixed annuities and capital sums to members of their families. However desirable such arrangements might be in times of inflation, they were dire in a deflation. Thus there occurred an uncoupling of financial fortunes between those dependent on agriculture and those who were not, and equally, between London and the country.

Even before the Depression country landowners had sometimes found London dauntingly expensive. They had to put up with it, for, as in the seventeenth century, they were duty-bound to spend time there as members of parliament in the Lords or Commons, to arrange fitting marriages for themselves or their children, to see doctors or lawyers, to shop, and by engaging in London social life to assert their place in society. They might also just want some fun. The financial strain, though, could be acute, as the Earl of Romney discovered in the 1840s. The first Earl of Romney (1744–1811) had lived expensively: he gambled, he entertained on a grand scale, he leased a London house in fashionable Arlington Street and he rebuilt the family seat, The Mote near Maidstone in Kent. A West Indian income that had helped to sustain his standard of living dwindled, and his son the second earl came into a much reduced inheritance. Family property in London, located on the edge of Devil's Acre in Westminster, was of little help. A survey of one of the houses near the river in Medway

Street reported that water and filth were rising up, front and back, and rapidly destroying the ground floors.

By the 1840s, Lord Romney was elderly and infirm and he and his wife no longer took a house for the London season. There was, however, the problem of Miss Cholmondeley, Lady Romney's daughter by a previous marriage, who was now aged seventeen and due to be 'brought out'. A London house for the Season was unavoidable. At least Miss Cholmondeley possessed money of her own in trust, some of which could be advanced. 'She is rich & I am poor', as Lord Romney put it in a letter. But there remained many expenses for which he would have to take responsibility. It was unnecessary to rent a house in the most fashionable district but there were clear limits; if they went east of Portland Place, ill-natured people would accuse Lord Romney of failing to do his stepdaughter justice. Portman Square seemed a sensible address and perhaps they could limit their stay to three months or even come down to eight or ten weeks. The trouble was that it was more than just a matter of rent and entertaining. At The Mote there were only 'an old coachman & a pair of old horses, fit for very little London work. We keep two footmen. I am too infirm to go out except in a carriage. A London coachman & pair of horses are therefore indispensable, or Miss Cholmondeley would not go out, as she ought to do. There is the same necessity for a third footman. The expense of moving a rather large family, with baggage . . .' Lord Romney could only lament that 'things are very different from what they were.'

It was standard practice for a wealthy family falling on hard times to let or sell their London house and retire to a more frugal life in the country. Yet it could work the other way round for someone prepared to undertake stringent economies. Hippolyte Taine noted that, while for luxurious living London was prodigiously expensive, life on a simple scale cost less than it did in Paris. So during the depression years at the end of the century, many patrician families adopted the solution sought by Edmund Bohun and his wife in the seventeenth century (see Chapter 2). They let their country mansions where they could, or shut them down and sacked the servants if they could not, and settled into lodgings in London. They might or might not follow the Bohun example of looking for a job.

Many of the largest country landowners had diversified their investments, although even then they might not be able to escape the damage caused by the world Depression. The Duke of Devonshire, for example, suffered not only through the fall in agricultural rents but also as a result of the drop in world commodity prices generally, which shattered his considerable investments in Barrow-in-Furness. Some, however, did better than merely survive. The Duke of Northumberland was involved with provincial urban property and docks, and drew a revenue from minerals, which by 1914 constituted nearly 60 per cent of his net income. Lord Bute drew money from Cardiff and its docks and from enormous wealth invested in Welsh coal mines. No one, though, was better placed than the London landlords, for while the countryside floundered, London had never been so prosperous. Rents were soaring. The City was entering its 'Golden Age'. The boom which drove the development of Queen's Gate in Kensington was roaring ahead; it was a time when, in Percy Fitzgerald's words, 'everybody was, or fancied he was, growing rich'. Landlords might be worried by the state of public opinion but on economic grounds it was not the time to sell. In South London, the Bedfords hung on and profited, the Spencers had sold out and lost. In the country, the Duke of Bedford's rents collapsed, but he could say, perhaps too flippantly, 'I, too, should be in a very tight place, only that I luckily own a few lodging-houses in Bloomsbury.' In 1881 the sporting Sir Claude Champion de Crespigny was in a bad way, heavily in debt and up in front of the bankruptcy court. It was pointed out that his income would shortly be transformed as his Camberwell leases came up for renewal. Frank Banfield in his *Great Landlords. . .* was particularly irritated by Lord Portman's intention to increase his Marylebone rents eightfold as the old leases expired. He would charge premiums as well. In 1872 the Duke of Portland received nearly £105,000 from his London property and £88,350 from his country estates; in real terms the differential was greater since the London figure was net of expenses and that for the country gross. With Mayfair and Belgravia, the dukes of Westminster were even better placed. In 1869, the year the future first duke succeeded, the gross London income was about £115,000 a year; by the end of the century it was calculated at £250,000. In one year, 1893, because of high renewal fines, it all but touched £500,000 (£29 million in our money).

In 1874 the first monthly parts of Trollope's *The Way We Live Now* were published, their theme the career of the megalomanic and crooked financier Melmotte set against a background of patrician society in decay. At that moment, rising on slum land once occupied by the Colbys, situated across the road from Kensington Palace and the Millionaires' Row of Kensington Palace Gardens and Palace Green, was a new Kensington House, its architect James Knowles of Clapham, its owner Baron Albert Grant. The barony was Italian and its holder usually believed to be the model for Melmotte. The location of the house was a choice one, advertised in 1868 as 'Almost the only remaining Site in this centre of fashion and haut ton Available for the Erection of Patrician Mansions'. Alternatively, went the publicity, the land could be used for a cathedral or public building. It is doubtful whether any estate agent imagined what London would actually get – a French neo-baroque extravaganza, in its garden an ornamental lake, a skating rink and an 'American bowling alley'. 'Pretentious and frightful', was Augustus Hare's reaction, and most people agreed with him. By the time the house was completed in 1875, Grant was in deep trouble, ejected from the House of Commons for gross election irregularities and with his firm about to go into liquidation. He never lived at Kensington House, in fact, nobody did. After six years lying empty – though let out for parties – it was demolished, the most unsuccessful of London's large town houses.

Whether or not Grant was the prototype of Melmotte, he was certainly a forerunner of a breed of rich financiers due shortly to make a dramatic appearance on the London scene. He resembles too some of the nabobs of the previous century, particularly perhaps General Richard Smith. Yet the nabobs were British, and some of the most prominent of the late nineteenth-century financiers and mine owners were not. Grant himself was born Gottheimer, of a German father and British mother. London, as the world's financial centre, naturally attracted an international business population. Some of the overseas businessmen who came were transients, but many made their home in Britain and became British. In terms of commercial morality they were seldom Baron Grants; many could better be compared with the Huguenots who had made so great a contribution to London's prosperity.

Baron Grant's Kensington House, built on slum land opposite Kensington Palace. This 'pretentious and frightful building' lasted just six years.

One group were the Germans, some of whom arrived like the Huguenots as refugees, escaping the occupation of their home cities by Napoleon's armies. The area around Denmark Hill became known as 'Little Germany'. Here a German Evangelical church was built – its services in German – financed by forty-six contributors headed by Prince Albert and including partners in the merchant banks of Schroders, Kleinworts and Huths. Even as late as the 1890s, Denmark Hill could be described by Percy Fitzgerald as a place where the speculative builder had as yet done little mischief and where there were still 'comfortable-looking mansions, of old-fashioned and formal cut, that seem to doze on in tranquil fashion'. The handsome eighteenth-century terrace houses of Grove Lane, on the slope of the hill, still exist and so do the remnants of the mansions on the hill itself. But mass housing was making inroads. In 1909 the Kleinworts, who in the 1850s had moved into a substantial house, The Glebe, where they employed a staff of twelve indoors and six outside, sold up and headed for Curzon Street. (At much the same time, the Thorntons at last abandoned Battersea Rise; Percy Thornton, the local MP, was to the end highly conscious of his duty 'towards the surging population which ever more thickly encircled the secluded garden and grounds.')

The immigrants have left few traces in the form of great town houses. There exists, however, a particularly striking memorial to one important group which is to be found at the West Norwood Cemetery in South London, the burial place incidentally of Thomas Cubitt and Baron de Reuter. Familiar grandiose nineteenth-century monuments greet the visitor passing through the gates, but as he or she walks on, they give way to the simple gravestones of the twentieth century. Then, at the eastern end of the grounds, on a slight mound, there arises in total contrast a railed precinct of miniature temples, mausoleums and statuary packed densely together. Even from a distance, before it is possible to decipher the lettering, it is clear that this is a Greek burial-place. It was created by a small number of Greek families, Rallis, Argentis, Rodocanachis, Schillizzis and a few others, refugees from Turkish massacre during the Greek War of Independence in the 1820s, and all of them natives of a single island, Chios, which lies just off the Turkish coast. These were patrician families with commerce in the blood, who held none of the reservations about trade so common to their counterparts in Britain and continental Europe. They intermarried, and for decades retained a certain separateness, building up considerable fortunes in the City. John S. Schillizzi, who died in 1908, left over £2 million at death, a sum sufficient to put him among the thirty-five richest businessmen who died during the hundred years to 1914. Sir Lucas Ralli died in the middle of the Depression in 1931 and left much the same amount.

Then there were the American rich. Earlier in the century, one of them, Joshua Bates, rejuvenated Barings and lived in a splendid house in Arlington Street. The most intriguing was Judah P. Benjamin, in turn attorney-general, war minister and secretary of state in the Confederate government, who fled the collapse of the South to rebuild his career in London as a very distinguished QC. Most famous is probably J. P. Morgan, who inherited Dover House, Roehampton, as well as a house in Prince's Gate from his father Junius Morgan, who was at one time the partner of George Peabody. In the last decades of the century, alongside the men were the women, the more enthusiastic for London after the extinction of the Second Empire took the glamour off Parisian social life. In his *Social Transformations of the Victorian Age* of 1897, the prominent commentator T. H. S. Escott declared that 'New York and London have become socially one and the same capital, having their pleasures, their lions and lionesses, their favourite composers, authors, dramatists and players, in common.' William Waldorf Astor, whose family had dominated New York society and who, with ownership of much of Fifth Avenue (as well as tracts of slums), was perhaps the nearest equivalent to the Grosvenors, arrived to settle down permanently in London. In 1899 he became a British subject. It was the American daughters, though, who really struck the public imagination. They were quick and lively – everyone agreed they were lively – prepared to be entranced by the romance of the Old World, its civilization, or alleged civilization, its ancient castles and glittering titles. They may have had doubts: Consuelo Yznaga, later Duchess of Manchester, for instance, announced, 'England is all right for splendor, but dead slow for fun'; but if so, their mothers helped to remove them. 'Buccaneers' was Edith Wharton's word for these girls, and Mrs Wharton was born Jones, a member of one of the best New York families. Certainly many of them fancied the idea of a British husband, and equally certainly many patrician bachelors, buffeted as they were by the agricultural depression, were just as eager for an American marriage. They could not remain unmoved either by the American habit of bequeathing a fair share of family money to daughters. One hundred and four marriages by peers and their sons – one tenth of all such marriages – took place to Americans in the period 1870 to 1914.

The most significant of these marriages was the love match of Jennie Jerome, whose father owned perhaps the most magnificent of New York's private palaces, to Lord Randolph Churchill. The grandest was that of Consuelo Vanderbilt to the Duke of Marlborough. Dollars repaired many acres of crumbling country roofs, but in London their effect visibly was less evident. Nevertheless,

Goelet money enabled the Duke of Roxburghe to elevate himself from Chesterfield Gardens to a tenancy of Chesterfield House. Captain Naylor-Leyland of the Life Guards and his bride Jeannie Chamberlain from Cleveland, Ohio, took one of Cubitt's giant houses at Albert Gate. Moreover, the Marlborough marriage brought London one of the last of its town palaces. This was Sunderland House in Curzon Street, on the corner of Shepherd Market, for which the Duchess's father paid a colossal £500,000 (£29 million today). Sunderland House was needed, for the Marlboroughs had lacked what they regarded as a proper town house since 1817 when Marlborough House, in St James's, built for the first duke, reverted to its freeholder, the Crown, to become, in the later years of the nineteenth century, the home of the Prince of Wales. Since by then Queen Victoria was hardly in evidence, Marlborough House constituted the effective Court, casting in time-honoured fashion a rosy glow on its surrounds, in particular on Carlton House Terrace, which speedily turned into a preferred place of residence for American wives. If the Americans were drawn to the Prince, or anyway to what he stood for, he, like his grandson Kind Edward VIII, delighted in them. London Society as a whole, however, took a more ambivalent view. As early as the 1870s, a group of aristocratic ladies asked the help of the Archbishop of Canterbury in organizing a mission to check the decline in moral standards in high society which they attributed to Americans in the Marlborough House set. The Americans came to exercise a huge influence on the style of living. They (naturally) made it more cosmopolitan, and they prompted the Edwardian fashion for rushing to and fro between Mayfair and Paris and Monte Carlo and Homburg.

There was little ambivalence about the attitude of Society towards another group of the Prince of Wales's friends, the new super-rich who became known as 'the Plutocrats'. Money may be what rules us now, wrote the dowager Countess Cowper to her son, but what right have such people as Baron Grant to force themselves into our society? Edith Wharton's term 'invaders' for the New York equivalents conveys more of the nature of the new men. Both their values – gross materialism – and their background – obscure if not downright proletarian – were in sharp contrast to the taste of London society. For upper-class London was very snobbish indeed. The great American historian of the Spanish conquests of Mexico and Peru, William Hickling Prescott, after his visit in 1850, commented on the deference paid to caste. Nowhere was it greater than in London, he pronounced, not even in Spain in the days of the Philips. The success of the Plutocrats in London society was indeed ironic.

No one in the world was better equipped than Disraeli to understand what was happening, and a passage from his *Endymion*, published in 1880 and touched on earlier, is worth quoting in full.

The great world then, [in the 1820s] compared with the huge society of the present period, was limited in its proportions, and composed of elements more refined though far less various. It consisted mainly of the great landed aristocracy, who had quite absorbed the nabobs of India, and had nearly appropriated the huge West India fortunes. Occasionally an eminent banker or merchant invested a large portion of his accumulations in land, and in the purchase of parliamentary influence, and was in time duly admitted into the sanctuary. But those vast and successful invasions of society by new classes which have since occurred, though impending, had not yet commenced. The manufacturer, the railway kings, the colossal contractors, the discoverers of nuggets, had not yet found their place in society and the senate.

According to Disraeli's one-time lover, the charming Lady Dorothy Nevill, society, albeit unconsciously, hoped again to absorb the newcomers. But it did not work out that way; the opposite was true. The new men 'have imported the bustle of the Stock Exchange into the drawing-rooms of Mayfair'. This time it was the City which conquered the West End. G. W. E. Russell, grandson of the sixth Duke of Bedford and a member of Liberal governments in the 1890s, wrote,

So profoundly has all society been vulgarised by the worship of the Golden Calf that, unless people can vie with alien millionaires in the sumptuousness . . . they prefer not to entertain at all. An emulous ostentation has killed hospitality.

Vulgar, alien and Jewish. That was the generalization, but often true. And not Jewish like the Rothschilds, or the admired Sir Moses Montefiore or, a generation back, the immensely rich but dignified and cultivated Sir Isaac Lyon Goldsmid. Lord Romney, a subsequent one, trying to restore the family fortunes in the 1870s, decided to rent out The Mote. But he disliked the idea of the Jewish Reuben Sassoon, and preferred to make do with a lower rent from a 'more desirable tenant'. Rather later, Beatrice Webb, the daughter of a successful Victorian entrepreneur, regretted that the South African millionaires were without manners or morals and far inferior to the Barings, Glyns, Lubbocks, Hoares and Buxtons, their predecessors as representatives of money power in London Society.

The confusion that followed the arrival of the new rich in a society weakened by depression later supplied good material for British films. In *Rolling in Money* (1934), for instance, a straitened duchess schemes to marry her daughter to a newly rich cockney barber, and in the 1937 musical *Take My Tip* a lord and lady are servants in their rich butler's hotel. Then there is *Spring in Park Lane* of 1948, in which Michael Wilding plays an impoverished lord posing as a footman in love with Anna Neagle, the daughter of a diamond magnate. That the plot – and the location given to it – were by then decades out of date merely emphasizes the power of association. For Park Lane was to plutocracy what Clapham had been to philanthropy. In an attack on the government at the very end of his spectacular career, Joseph Chamberlain accused ministers of collusion with "magnates" who are not creditable acquaintances and who live in palaces, usually in Park Lane.' In *Tono Bungay* (1912), H. G. Wells exhibits Park Lane as the home of 'moneylenders and Jews [and] bold financial adventurers'.

The road, which runs from Piccadilly up the east side of Hyde Park, contained a number of large town houses, of which four, perhaps five, could be described as palaces. Near the Piccadilly end stood Holderness House, renamed Londonderry House, rebuilt by the third Marquess of Londonderry and his wife (the greatest heiress of her generation) for £243,000 (£14 million today) in the 1820s. Chesterfield House, further up the street, from which it stood well back, was built in 1748 for the famous Lord Chesterfield at a time when Tyburn

Park Lane – the southern end in 1885.

Lane, as Park Lane was then called, was considered remote and dangerous by night. Chesterfield, a francophile, provided his mansion with an extensive garden and placed a large courtyard in front, a feature as rare in London as it was common in Paris. Chesterfield was by nature urban through and through. To him,

> Congenial Society is, in the end, the greatest joy in life, and it can only be found in capitals. It is on this principal [*sic*] that I am at the present in the process of ruining myself by building a fine house here.

The most important individual contribution to ruin, had it come about, would have been the magnificent arcaded staircase of marble and bronze which Chesterfield purchased at the sale of the contents of Chandos's Canons.

Further on were two other palaces. Grosvenor House has already entered these pages, but Dorchester House has rated only the barest

The drawing room at Chesterfield House in 1894.

mention. Built in the 1850s and modelled by its architect Lewis
Vuillamy on the Villa Farnesina at Rome, Dorchester House was
acknowledged as the rival of Stafford House itself. To G. W. E.
Russell, it was architecturally the finest thing in London; to the
eminent historian of London and its houses, E. Beresford Chancellor,
it was the finest private dwelling in the city. Dorchester House was
singular in itself, and also by reason of the origin of the money which
built it, the fortune which lay behind its owner, Mr Robert Stayner
Holford. Augustus Hare recalled a dinner party in 1874 when 'the
most airified man in London said to his dinner neighbour, apropos
of a dinner at Dorchester House, "Pray who *are* these Holfords?" –
"Oh," said Lady Katherine, "I believe they are the people who have
got a little shake-down somewhere in Park Lane."' The 'airified' man
was not alone in his ignorance of this venerable London family that
so suddenly and so dramatically broke in on the London social scene.

Murray's *Handbook for Modern London* of 1851 refers to Holford as 'a retired Russia merchant'. *The Times* in its obituary in 1892 designates a Gloucester bank as the source of his wealth. Actually, Gloucester did make some sense, since the Holfords had owned the Gloucestershire estate of Westonbirt since the mid-seventeenth century. There was inevitably too some confusion with the originally Manchester Holfords of Regent's Park. But despite Gloucestershire, the Park Lane Holfords were rooted in London and owed everything to London. In the 1560s, Richard Holford bought Aldwych Close, a field he was already occupying that formed part of the Lincoln's Inn property of Purse Field. As the area took urban shape, his descendants lived first in Bedford Row on the northern side of High Holborn, and from 1765 until well into the nineteenth century at No. 1 Lincoln's Inn Fields. Their wealth had three sources. One was the law, and from the seventeenth century the Holfords provided three successive masters in Chancery. (One of them Hester Thrale described as a 'most eminent bore'.) The other sources, through the medium of the New River Company, were water supply and London real estate; three generations of Holfords were governors of the company which, if the Grosvenor estate is left out of account, must rank as arguably the most successful purely London business ever. By the later part of the nineteenth century the New River held exclusive right of water supply for nearly all the northern suburbs, for the whole of the City, and for a large part of Westminster.

Robert Stayner Holford left £422,000 in personal property at death as well as 14,500 acres of country land and the freehold of Dorchester House. He was rich, but not as rich as his one-time neighbour Samuel Lloyd, first Baron Overstone, who left £2.12 million in 1883 in addition to land for which he had paid over £1.5 million. Such riches classed him as one of the wealthiest men of the century. Between 1818 and 1858, Overstone occupied a family house – for some of the time two houses – at the northern end of Park Lane with its entrance in Dunraven Street, at that time called Norfolk Street. (It was one of the peculiarities of the road that the front doors of most of the houses opened on to side streets.) To some of the more old-fashioned residents of Mayfair the disagreeable odour of commerce must have hung over both Holford and Overstone, but neither

The west front of the Sutherlands' Stafford House.
Watercolour by T. H. Shepherd, *c.* 1845.

could be classed as a 'plutocrat'. The Holfords were indisputably old
gentry and R. S. Holford's passion in life was the forming of an
outstanding art collection. Indeed the lodgement of that collection was
a principal reason for the building of Dorchester House. Overstone's
father had been a Welsh Unitarian preacher – worthy rather than
grand as a profession – but had seen the light, gone into private
banking, and sent his son to Eton and Trinity, Cambridge. Private
banking, where Overstone himself made his money, was definitely a
gentlemanly pursuit. By 1870 or so, anyway, new money was commonplace in Mayfair. In a few years' time, Samuel Lewis, extremely rich
but a moneylender in Cork Street (quite different to a private banker
in the City), was living in Grosvenor Square itself. And at Chesterfield
House was the North Country brewer Michael Bass, who as Lord
Burton was a founder member of what came to be called the Beerage.

Barney Barnato – a semi-literate cockney born in Petticoat Lane,
his father Isaac Isaacs, original profession bar-room bouncer and

Above: The Anchor Brewery, belonging to Barclay Perkins & Co. in Southwark, 1835.
By the time of the Great Exhibition it was recommended to tourists as one of the sights
of London. British School, artist unknown.

Below: 'I implored them to have the street door opened.' The Berkeley stag hounds
pursue their quarry into deepest Bloomsbury. One of John Leech's illustrations to
Grantley Berkeley's *Reminiscences of a Huntsman*, 1854.

Above: The suburban frontier: West London in 1840 by B. R. Davis.

Below: Rotten Row in the 1840s. Engraving after William Henry Barraud.

Right: Hampstead in 1835. A detail from George Cruchley, *New Plan of London and Its Environs.*

Above: The grand staircase of Stafford House, painted *c.*1850 by J. Nash. Said Queen Victoria to the Duchess of Sutherland, 'I come from my house to your palace.'

Left: *Going to Business*, oil painting by James Tissot, *c.*1879.

Dorchester House, Park Lane, in the 1890s.

tapster, maker of one of the great Kimberley diamond fortunes – was altogether a different matter. The inscription on his visiting card announced it even before you met him: 'I'll stand any man a drink, but I won't lend him a fiver.' Barnato hired Spencer House from the precarious Spencers, and one day in 1896 attended court to stand bail for a friend. 'Where do you live?' demanded the magistrate. 'Spencer House.' 'But that's Lord Spencer's house. Are you his major-domo?' 'I'm my own bloody domo,' shouted back Barnato, then quickly apologized. More questions followed and finally the magistrate enquired, 'What are you exactly, Mr Barnato?' 'A diamond merchant and a director of a couple of companies', was the reply, accompanied by a broad wink at members of the public in court. 'And I've got a bit of freehold in Park Lane.' But Barney Barnato did not live long enough to inhabit the great mansion he was building at 25 Park Lane; he suffered a breakdown, probably delirium tremens, and fell off the ship, assumed a suicide, on his way back from South Africa.

The enormous house, Renaissance style, fully centrally heated, with two billiard rooms and a vast ballroom, was taken by Edward

Sassoon, married to Aline Rothschild of the French Rothschilds. The Sassoons of Baghdad, then of Bombay, possessed huge wealth based mainly on cotton and opium and were socially the opposite of Barnato. Whatever Lord Romney's reservations, they were friends of the Prince of Wales and positively exotic, their Jewishness the more acceptable since it was of so unfamiliar a type. Other members of the family lived in Belgrave Square and at Albert Gate. To Brook House in Park Lane, near to where both Disraeli and Moses Montefiore had once lived, came Sir Ernest Cassel (1851–1921) closer still than the Sassoons to Edward, as Prince of Wales and as King. Cassel was a dominating international financier, originally from Germany. His financial achievements included the Aswan Dam, an important contribution to American railways, and what became the Central Line on the London Underground. He bought Brook House from Lord Tweedmouth and converted it at vast expense into a town house of extraordinary lavishness. A lady asked Cassel for his opinion on her necklace of lapis lazuli. 'Very pretty stuff,' he apparently replied. 'I've got a room made of it.' Three other of the Park Lane mansions went to 'Randlords', Disraeli's 'discoverers of nuggets' whether of diamonds or gold: No. 15 to Frederick Eckstein; and Dudley House, a fine building famous for its balls lately the property of Lord Dudley, to the universally unpopular Joseph Robinson. The third was Aldford House at 26 Park Lane, rebuilt on two storeys only by the reserved and attractive Alfred Beit, who with his partner Julius Wernher (who acquired Bath House in Piccadilly) owned what by the 1890s was the largest of the Rand mining houses.

In the old days, that is before the 1880s, nobody in society, stated Lady Dorothy Nevill in her reminiscences, talked about money or their health. Now they hardly stop, conversation is without wit or learning. The evidence, in fact, is conflicting. Lady Dorothy, 'cosmopolitan to her finger tips', no doubt participated in the best that was going, but the American Richard H. Dana was told by Earl Russell (formerly Lord John Russell) in the 1870s that the general society of the Court was about on the level with a 'dancing-hall barroom'. T. H. S. Escott, certainly no radical, declared in 1904 that 'such humanising influences as leaven fashionable London to-day largely come from the Jewish element'. Alfred Beit, for example, was

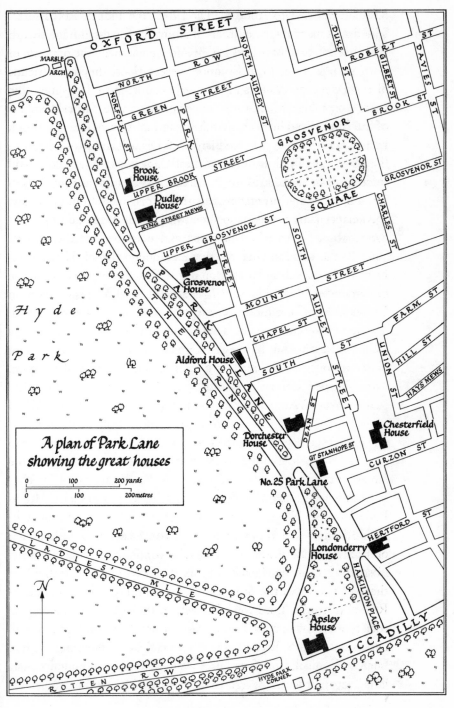

A plan of Park Lane, showing the great houses. Based
on the *Ordnance Survey* of 1894.

a munificent donor to the arts. The Duke of Westminster refused to lease any of his property to Barney Barnato; the Duchess of Buccleuch, from her palace of Montagu House, Whitehall, the prototype, somebody said, of a nineteenth-century Grand Hotel, stood out for the old social standards; Mrs Lowther – a great hostess – of Lowther Lodge, on Kensington Gore, now the premises of the Royal Geographical Society, was less than enthusiastic about welcoming the new rich to her parties. Yet by and large Society fell into line.

'Everyone wants to come to London' was a constant and rueful refrain which sounded throughout the years leading up to the war. The plutocrats were unmistakably urban in their tastes, with Brighton the nearest thing to a country town which they were likely to enjoy. They owned or rented country houses but, according to G. W. E. Russell, they seldom inhabited them. And, said Russell, if the plutocrat builds a country house for himself, it reproduces 'the worst monstrosities of Park Lane'. Sir Henry Lucy paid a visit in 1896 to Colonel North, a flamboyant and crafty company promoter known as 'the nitrate king', at his newly built fifty-room mansion, Avery Hill, near Eltham in south-east London. Suburb as it was, a farm with livestock was included, and the colonel, 'as well known on the turf as in the City' was in country mood.

'He was dressed,' reported Lucy,

> in what I fancy he regarded as the best style of a country gentleman – light trousers and coat, with white waistcoat and a flowered silk necktie. In further keeping with the character he carried an umbrella, though a cloudless sunlit sky hung over Avery Hill.

Inside the house, the Colonel glanced with satisfaction at the immense collection of empty champagne bottles. Lucy clearly rather enjoyed his visit, although he was taken aback by the two blackened mummies dug up from the nitrate grounds which his host had recently brought with him from Chile. Avery Hill was only slightly more successful than Grant's Kensington House. North died shortly after Lucy's visit. A few years later, in 1902, the estate was bought by the London County Council for a fraction of its cost, for use as a public park. The mansion was damaged by a flying bomb during the Second

Barney Barnato – once a bouncer in a bar, by the 1890s he had become the most powerful financier in South Africa.

World War and what is left of it is now a teachers training college.

On the face of it, the patrician attitude to town and country was less clearly defined. The moribund countryside was depressing, London, for those who could afford its pleasures, was exciting. Yet, as Sir Edward Cadogan remembered, convention held – even when your address was Chelsea House, Knightsbridge – that the country was always preferable. A book published in 1907 with the misleading title of *London Leaders – Historic Families . . . Ancestral Estates* provides an insight. As an analytical study it is worthless. Reasonably so, since it was printed for subscribers and clearly intended for businessmen and local dignitaries living in Middlesex. Thrown in are some grand names like Leopold de Rothschild, the Duke of Bedford and the Duke of Norfolk. The Duke of Westminster, a 'London leader' if there ever was one, does not figure at all. The 'ancestral estates' of the title turn out to be almost entirely country estates, and there is, for instance, a long description of the Cecils' Hatfield. The numerous photographs are almost always of country houses. Evidently what pleased the subscribers were non-London associations: the old businessman-turning-gentleman syndrome was still alive and well.

As it happened, a moment of choice between town and country was imminent. Over the next fifteen years there were to be massive land sales both in London and the country. While the grandees would fight hard to keep their country seats, London palaces were a different matter. Were they worth the cost of maintaining? Could they any longer fulfil their function as centres of social and political life? The Settled Land Act made it easier for trustees of a life tenant to reinvest. The heavier taxes falling on the wealthy, particularly the alarming Death Duties, the threat of confiscation even as some saw it, much increased the attraction of alternative investments. For anyone who wished to stick to land, it was there, in boundless quantities, in the dominions and the colonies. The town houses were rented out, like Spencer House and now Dorchester House. Lord Lansdowne declared that he would not let Lansdowne House outside his family, but he did – to the Astors, who would later acquire their own town house in St James's Square. Most significant though was the decision made by the Duke of Sutherland just before the war to sell Stafford House. The property empires started to go. While the leasehold system for residential property would largely hold until 1993, the auspices were poor. Moreover, prices were falling anyway, even in Mayfair, enhanced in attraction as it had been by recent rebuilding. Sales began with the Edwardes Kensington estate at the beginning of the new reign. The *Building News* announced it as 'the largest and most important transaction yet effected in a London estate.' Then in 1913 the Duke of Bedford started negotiations (only fully completed five years later) for the sale of half his London estate, including Covent Garden.

But this is not the note which catches the spirit of London in the ten or twelve years before 1914. For despite worries over taxation and what in 1911 the Duchess of Sutherland spoke of as the 'suicidal despair of the ruined aristocracy', despite Ireland and industrial turbulence on an unprecedented scale, these years celebrate London at its zenith. They celebrate too the London rich in an apparent heyday. The newspapers assiduously report the most mundane activities of Society; the children of the poor cluster outside the big houses to see the guests arrive. 'Night by night, during the summers of 1913 and '14,' remembered Osbert Sitwell, 'the entertainments grew in number and magnificence. One band in a house was no longer enough, there must be two, three even.' With our knowledge of what was about to happen, the carnival seems an hallucination. After the slaughter, the world was quite different, garishness was vulgar and flamboyance provocative, and the rich lay low, slipping from the limelight. The Park Lane plutocrats melted away and the London palaces came tumbling down.

II

Resurgence

*

Sometimes it appears that not much has changed. In November 1939, two months after the outbreak of war, Chips Channon was lunching at the Ritz with his friend the Duchess of Sutherland, whom he had not seen since the previous summer. He reflected on what a summer it had been. In his diary he described it as 'that feverish season when night after night we went to balls and fêtes, each one more splendid and sumptuous than the others.' None of the parties was more memorable than that given at Holland House in the last days of the Season. The antiquity of the buildings and the splendid setting amid gardens and woods invested Holland House, as always, with a particular attraction, but the dance of 6 July 1939, held for the débutante Rosalind Cubitt, was especially magnificent. There were over a thousand guests, among them the King and Queen (who dined at the house first) and the Queen of Spain, and they danced to Ambrose's fourteen-piece band. It was the climax, and the end, of two hundred years of incomparable entertaining. A little over a year afterwards, the house was bombed: first, three high-explosive bombs fell in the grounds, slightly damaging the house; then, a few nights later, on 27–28 September, there was a direct hit. Holland House stood derelict for seventeen years, much of it to be demolished in 1957, by which time what was left of it, along with the park and gardens, had passed into the ownership of the London County Council.

'The ancien régime dies hard in England,' Channon had written in his diary in the spring before the war, his eyes dazzled by the jewels and tiaras which graced a gala performance at Covent Garden. The owners of the great town houses still played their part socially with

Holland House. The library, before and after bombing.

lavish parties, but also politically. Lady Londonderry accomplished the social seduction of Ramsay MacDonald. Wimborne House in Arlington Street served as a background for negotiations during the General Strike of 1926. Sir Philip Sassoon's 25 Park Lane was a centre of political entertaining. The teetotal Lady Astor might have made a political salon of her St James's Square mansion, wrote one commentator, had it not been that the politicians dreaded lemonade. The very rich could still afford to live in great style. At Londonderry House there was a staff of twenty-eight in the kitchen and sixteen in the steward's room, no less than one would have expected a hundred years before. Chips Channon at No. 5 Belgrave Square employed fifteen servants to serve his wife and himself and their small child, as well as, admittedly, a steady flow of guests. Also in Belgrave Square were two fully staffed houses belonging to the Duke of Bedford, even though he himself very rarely visited London, preferring to remain in traditional state at Woburn, served by fifty or sixty indoor servants and more yet out of doors.

But the base was fragile. In his memoirs published in 1937, the Duke of Portland wrote that of the great palaces only Londonderry House, Apsley House, Bridgewater House and Holland House remained in private hands. Devonshire House was pulled down in 1925, Grosvenor House in 1927, Dorchester House in 1929. Lansdowne House, in recognizable form, and Chesterfield House both went in 1937. In fact, by the end of the First World War, during which many of their houses had been used as hospitals or convalescent homes, most of the grandees had come to accept that the time had arrived to settle for less extensive accommodation, both in terms of housing and of gardens. Not all, for Lord Lascelles, later Earl of Harewood, married to the future Princess Royal, with a flourish worthy of his West Indian forebears, bought and occupied Chesterfield House. However, it was the Depression, not a return of the good old days, which lay ahead, and after ten years he and his wife gave up and moved to 32 Green Street off Park Lane, bought for them by Queen Mary. Here they were neighbours to the Duke of Sutherland and his wife who, having sold the Crown lease on Stafford House to Sir William Lever, later Lord Leverhulme, moved after a short interval to Hampden House at Nos. 60 and 61 Green Street. Visually Hampden

House was (and is) austere, not to be compared with Stafford House in either looks or size. In 1914, the latter was assessed at a rateable value of £4,167, which compared to a figure of £1,250 for Hampden House. Still, the Sutherlands were not cramped. The Duke added a ballroom and there was a tennis court in the garden and enough space for 700 people at a party. Their friend 'Bendor', the capricious second Duke of Westminster, renowned for his generosity, his yachts and his wives, also sold out to Leverhulme and occupied Bourdon House, a charming detached building on his own Mayfair land in Davies Street. Here the discrepancy in terms of 1914 rateable value was yet more marked – £3,750 against £550. The Duke of Norfolk abandoned Norfolk House in St James's Square, which, counting its predecessor on the site, had belonged to his family for 214 years. He went to Belgrave Square. The Duke of Devonshire, in the process of selling the remainder of the Chiswick estate inherited by his family from the Earl of Burlington, chose Carlton Gardens, the western extension of Carlton House Terrace. To most people the house seemed palatial enough, but the Duchess was heard to remark that 'It's interesting to see what the pictures look like in a small house.'

With Lord Leverhulme the purchaser of two such outstanding patrician town houses, it would look as though new money had now overwhelmed old. However, Leverhulme (who lived in Hampstead) intended neither of them for himself personally; his motives were largely public spirited. Stafford House, renamed Lancaster House, he gave to the government for use as the London Museum and as a conference and entertainment centre. Grosvenor House he visualized as a public art gallery. But he died too soon, and his executors felt compelled to sell. To convert redundant private palaces into galleries or museums was one way of preserving them. Montagu House in Bloomsbury, though replaced by the British Museum of today, was in its time an example, and so to an extent is Burlington House. More recent was Hertford House in Manchester Square – the old Manchester House – presented to the nation by the widow of Sir Richard Wallace, the natural son of the fourth Marquess of Hertford, which was followed in the 1920s by Kenwood House on Hampstead Heath, the gift of the Earl of Iveagh. Both these mansions passed with superb collections of pictures, furniture and artefacts. Yet that

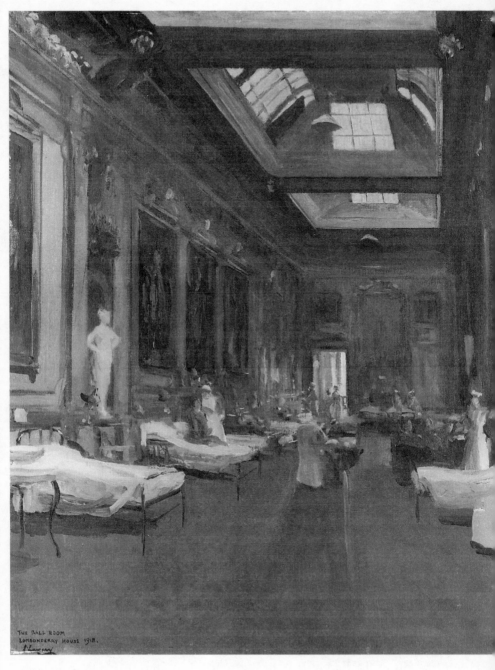

THE BALL ROOM
LONDONDERRY HOUSE 1918.

Londonderry House: the ballroom in use as a
hospital during the First World War. Painted by
Sir John Lavery.

does not answer the question about the strength of new money. It is true that by the time of the First World War the new fortunes were coming to surpass the old, but by the twenties and thirties there was no longer a battle to be won. The contrast between the old and new rich was less stark. For one thing, many of the new rich held peerages, for another their families conformed to type; if, for instance, the first Lord Cowdray was a bit on the rough side, his successors were impeccable. The Randlords had drifted from the scene, leaving only heiresses. Sir Ernest Cassel's granddaughter and heir, Edwina Ashley, married into the highest aristocracy. So did the Sassoons. The present Duchess of Westminster is the great-granddaughter of Sir Julius Wernher. Moreover, the old patrician families, seldom able to live entirely on their investments, were more directly engaged in business. Even before the First World War, G. W. E. Russell was complaining that 'scions' of the aristocracy would produce tea samples or floor cloths from their pockets and attempt, 'winningly', to make a sale. In 1920 a quarter of the nobility were directors of significant firms, and before that, the tenth, eleventh and twelfth earls of Leven and

The demolition of Devonshire House, Piccadilly, 1925.

Melville had established their own banking dynasty. Above all, petty quarrels were out of place when the rich as a class were subjected to heavy taxation which they believed, correctly, would become heavier yet. They were on the defensive, seeking to maintain their wealth in unpromising circumstances. However flamboyant the nightclubs and parties, the jewels at Covent Garden, and individuals such as the Duke of Westminster, generally speaking it was considered indiscreet to flaunt money. Clothes and demeanour became more subdued. Sociologists and market researchers complained that it was all but impossible to persuade the rich to provide a straight answer to questions about their wealth. Though no doubt the rich bared their hearts and files to the Inland Revenue, official statistics were often unhelpful, since, increasingly, wealthy parents passed on much of their fortune to their children during their own lifetime.

While entrepreneurs with a colour and flair reminiscent of the old-time plutocrats have continued to thrive, it is argued that the mammoth business corporations which had emerged by the 1920s and 1930s were likely to prefer less individualistic talents in their leaders. There were famous and vivid newspaper magnates such as Lord Beaverbrook (living at Stornaway House ensconced between Lancaster House and Bridgewater House) but it is significant that the most successful British businessman of the first half of the twentieth century was a hybrid, an entrepreneur certainly, but one who behaved like a stereotype of the dried-out accountant. This was Sir John Ellerman (1862–1933), second generation British of a German, non-Jewish father, who, to quote Professor W. D. Rubinstein, was the only Englishman whose riches could be compared with those of Americans like Rockefeller and Mellon. At his death in the depths of the slump he was worth nearly £37 million (£1.35 billion today). Ellerman was dominant in shipping, powerful in newspapers, breweries and collieries, and – having started with virtually nothing – before he finished, owned London property on the scale of Lord Portman. Ellerman's wealth far surpassed not only that of the grandees, even the Duke of Westminster, but also that of such men as Iveagh, Leverhulme, Northcliffe and Wills. Lord Nuffield alone is probably comparable. On a personal level, 'genial' is about the most exciting adjective that can be applied. He hated parties, he belonged to no clubs. The boisterous late-Victorian and Edwardian plutocrat was an enthusiast for Brighton; Ellerman preferred Eastbourne, where he owned a house on the sea front. But wherever he was, he was not a man to spend money on grand houses. In London he lived at No. 1 South Audley Street. It may have been a 'stuffy old museum', in the description of his American son-in-law, but it was not a particularly big one. The 1914 rateable value was £667, less than the figure attributed to other houses in the street and much less than that of its immediate neighbour, Chesterfield House.

In 1920 Ellerman bought part of Covent Garden; in 1925 he bought 21 acres of Marylebone from Lord Howard de Walden. In 1929 he acquired nearly 14 acres of the Cadogan and Hans Place estates and, in the same year, 82 acres of South Kensington freehold which originally formed part of the old Edwardes estate. (This last he soon resold.) Such sales, together with others made in London at the time, were highly important. However, they should be seen also in the context of the immense disposals of land being made in the country as a whole by traditional landowners during the 1920s. With high taxes, especially the taxes on death, the sales are not surprising. But it was not only taxes. People were demoralized, by the loss of so many young men in the trenches and by the evident running down of the British economy. London itself had yielded financial and social leadership to New York, and to many now it was a drab place. Yet at the same time it continued to grow, it was still disjoined from the industrial north. Right through the twenties and through the depression of the thirties, London expanded, its population of 7.5 million in 1921 rising to 8.2 million in 1931 and 8.7 million in 1939. Between the wars, something like a third of the total increase in the population of England and Wales applied to London, and (between 1923 and 1939) two-thirds of new jobs. Factories and warehouses proliferated on the approach roads to the city, many along the Great West Road and the North Circular. In the twenty years between the wars, London more than doubled its built-up area.

The whole of this massive growth took place outside the County of London itself, in the development of yet another dense ring of suburbs. Inevitably, retreats for the rich on the outskirts which had survived the mass migrations of before 1914 now disappeared.

Sir Philip Sassoon and the Hon. Mrs Dudley Ward at
the Wimbledon tennis championships, 1922. Sassoon
lived in great style in Park Lane until his death in 1939.
According to Chips Channon 'royalties haunted his
house'.

Roehampton with its large houses made a natural centre for hospitals,
nursing homes and training colleges. By the 1980s it was otherwise
mainly council housing. The village of Charlton in the south-east
was swallowed up. It was much the same story at Stanmore and at
Edgware, where at the turn of the century you could still encounter
besmocked yokels. *Where to Live Round London*, a book published in

1906, rated Stanmore as 'a picturesque and beautiful district enjoying high favour among City men as a place of residence'. It possessed its own plutocrat in the banker Sir Henry Bischoffsheim, who was visited there by Edward VII. At Canons, a substantial house even if not to be classed with its eighteenth-century predecessor, was Sir Arthur du Cros of Dunlop Rubber. Canons survived the post-war onrush, and with a reduced but still attractive park, the house was acquired and adapted by a leading girls' school, the North London Collegiate School. But the district in general succumbed to the motor bus and the tube and to the spread of industry.

Industry flourished in the suburbs because of the space and manpower available. It was also discouraged from more central areas by the strict environmental controls imposed by the London County Council. Nevertheless, the West End in its familiar character was under intense pressure from other forms of business. There was an irresistible demand for office and other commercial space. Tracts of Marylebone were absorbed: Harley Street, Wimpole Street and Queen Anne Street and their surrounds were now almost monopolized by doctors and medical suppliers; and the new stores along Oxford Street put pressure on the streets and squares immediately behind. For obviously, the department stores, like the railway stations of the previous century, brought the crowds. Cavendish Square and Portman Square were less agreeable places to live in, as were Hanover Square and its neighbourhood on the other side of Oxford Street. Regent Street was rebuilt with massive steel-framed buildings, and Park Lane started to resemble New York's Fifth Avenue. Car showrooms, smart shops, hotels and offices took over. The West End lost its privacy, its exclusive atmosphere. Now no one from outside needed to feel diffident about strolling anywhere they wished; Hyde Park, with its carriage parades and social rituals a matter of history, was open to all. Moreover, not only was Mayfair less pleasant, with the commercial competition for space it was also more expensive.

In other times the rich would have reacted by colonizing new territory. But now there were fewer rich. As we have seen, the very wealthy, while adapting perhaps to less extended living space, continued to enjoy much the same standard of comfort, but for those one economic grade down, it was a different matter. They possessed improved means of transport and other conveniences previously unavailable, but the higher taxes and the much increased expense of servants and maintenance entailed a sharp reconsideration of their housing. Keeping two homes, one in the country, one in London, was now often beyond them. Some chose one, some the other. The Duke of Portland, in the late thirties, stated that the great country houses were usually left unoccupied except for a very few days a year, with the shooting either let or abandoned. On the other hand, there were many who stuck to the country, with the effect, it has been calculated, that by 1940, 60 per cent of the landed aristocracy (defined as descendants or survivors of the aristocrats of 1880) were without homes in London.

Financial pressure and also a profound change in taste and fashion altered what was expected of the home. It was said that it 'has ceased to be a background and a setting, and has sunk to being once more a shelter'. The well-off, the young especially, looked outside for enjoyment, and one of the growth industries of Mayfair was restaurants and nightclubs. There is where we entertain ourselves now, said the Duke of Portland. The Prince of Wales, following in his grandfather's footsteps, set the pace. The Embassy Club in Old Bond Street, the Café de Paris off Leicester Square, Quaglino's in St James's, the old Berkeley Hotel off Piccadilly, the Ritz and the Dorchester. This was the great era of cabaret, of the sophisticated lyrics of Cole Porter, the smoky voice of Hutch, the bands of the sort that played at Holland House.

And so if the home is no more than a shelter, why not live in a flat? When he wrote his memoirs, the Duke of Portland had just lost the house in Grosvenor Square where he had lived for forty-five years. It had been demolished to make way for a block of flats. The face of what remained of residential Mayfair was in course of change. In 1930 the mansions on the east side of Berkeley Square were pulled down to be replaced by an enormous apartment block, and on the opposite side of the square Lansdowne House suffered something of the same fate. Lord Lansdowne let the house to Gordon Selfridge during the twenties, subsequently selling it to another American, Benson Greenall. Permission for wholesale demolition to allow space for an hotel was refused. However, by 1935, Lansdowne House,

Party scene at a night club in the 1920s.

largely reconstructed for flats, was virtually unrecognizable. Most of
Portman Square was converted, and in Arlington Street, three of
the four substantial town houses which stood as neighbours to
Wimborne House had disappeared by the thirties. Dolphin
Square on the Embankment provided the largest block of flats in
Europe.

The first flats in London appeared in Victoria Street in 1853, and
were followed by many others particularly in the last years of the
nineteenth century. They were not unchallenged: suited as they might
be to Paris, an out-of-doors city, the habitat of the single man and
the café, they were, so the argument ran, inappropriate to London,
a city designed for family and home. In both Britain and the United
States, this new type of accommodation was actually called 'French
flats'. There is no mistaking the sniffiness. To the *Architect*, the
splendid Haussmann boulevards were morally objectionable: 'An
immense amount of dawdling and frittering away of life must be put

down to the broad ways of Continental cities,' it judged. Robert Kerr, in a speech to the RIBA in 1894, advanced the more sophisticated argument that the English idea of domestic comfort depended on privacy, especially in the complete separation of family and servants. Certainly it was expensive to achieve such segregation, and few could hope to emulate Mrs E. H. Hutton with her fifty-four-room apartment (replicating her original house) at 1107 Fifth Avenue. But it was not unobtainable. In March 1930, *Country Life* carried an article on a new block of flats at what had been Stratton House on Piccadilly, the home in the nineteenth century of the immensely rich and immensely philanthropic Baroness Burdett-Coutts. The larger flats were of three reception rooms, four principal bedrooms and two or three bathrooms, plus maids' rooms. The specimen floor plan shows the servants' quarters as almost separate. Since, unlike a house, there is no back door – in London usually the basement door – family and servants meet in a common entrance lobby. But on either side of the lobby are two self-contained apartments connected only through the dining room. Anyway, many of the people interested in flats were concerned above all with finding something small and manageable.

However, flats failed to tempt many of the very rich until after the Second World War. The Duchess of Westminster stated that practically no one that she and her husband knew lived in a flat. How odd it was, she thought afterwards, that in the twenties and thirties the tall houses of Mayfair and Belgravia had been inhabited – apart from servants – by a single family, sometimes only husband and wife, sometimes just one person, with nobody feeling in the least overhoused. It was not that these houses were convenient, for they had been planned for dinner parties and Victorian 'At Homes' and not for what she termed 'cosy daily life or dances'. Hardly any of them, the Duchess added, were equipped with lifts. Her husband's houses in Eaton Square provide an excellent example of the contrast between this style of living and what the rich required after the Second World War. In 1939, 95 per cent of the Eaton Square houses were in single family occupation; in 1945, the proportions were reversed. Maintenance costs and difficulties had become serious factors, and above all there was the question of staffing. Very few people indeed were in a position to afford, or even find, anything like the dozen or so servants these houses had been intended for.

To decide on the future of Eaton Square and for that matter on that of the rest of their property, the Grosvenor estate, working in conjunction with architects and a firm of developers, undertook an analysis of probable demographic trends. It was necessary to form a view on the future shape of the West End. They were sceptical of the London County Council's declared intention to retain Mayfair as a primarily residential district; the pressure for office space, they correctly judged, would prove overwhelming. It appeared virtually certain that more and more, following a trend noticeable before the war, the rich would favour Belgravia; it would be 'the new Mayfair'. The newcomers, though, were clearly not going to be interested in palaces. Belgrave Square then, with its huge buildings, several of them free-standing, would not fit the bill. No one, for instance, was likely to take on Seaford House, built in 1842 for the third Earl of Sefton and later redesigned for Lord Howard de Walden, or Forbes House, just round the corner in Halkin Street, at one time leased to the Fitzwilliams and which had later passed to Forbes, eighth Lord Granard and his rich American wife. Since the Belgrave Square houses did not lend themselves to conversion into flats, it was decided to lease them for embassies and for institutional use, while converting the Eaton Square houses into luxury flats – sometimes constructed to extend across two houses – offering preferential treatment to existing leaseholders to persuade them to co-operate.

With the data gathered mainly about 1930, there was published in 1934 *The New Survey of London Life and Labour*, a sequel to Charles Booth's great survey carried out at the turn of the century. It shows a marked improvement in the situation of the poor. As a result of emigration from the County of London and slum clearance, and of the national shift in income distribution from rich to poor, thirty years had brought about a large drop in the proportion of Londoners living in poverty. The reduction was especially large in Hampstead, Kensington and Westminster. On the wealthy, *The New Survey* is much less informative than its predecessor, but it is clear that Fulham and Hammersmith had continued in decline, while Chelsea was on a rather tentative upward path. By then the migration westward of the wealthy was well established. If it was in Belgravia that most of them settled, there was still an overspill into Chelsea. By 1927, Harold Clunn in his *London Rebuilt* could go so far as to say that Chelsea could now be 'considered a fairly handsome quarter of London', adding, however, that the King's Road has never enjoyed anything like the same degree of popularity as a shopping centre as most of the other principal London streets. He also regrets the failure of an attempt to convert the poor neighbourhood around Sloane Avenue between the King's Road and Fulham Road into one suitable for the wealthy. Chelsea was rising but not yet fully rehabilitated, not yet fashionable. Even Pont Street, leading directly into Belgravia, was not smart. The Duchess of Westminster, then Loelia Ponsonby, recalled that in the early twenties, when 'dancing was more than a craze, it had become a sort of mystical religion', she and her friends might sometimes attend 'what we scornfully called a "gramapont" – that is, a gramophone dance in Pont Street, a district we despised'. One trouble, wrote Patrick Balfour in his sparkling *Society Racket* of 1934, was that to the older generation, Chelsea 'connotes ... the epitome of all that is abandoned in London life.' A reputation for sluminess and Bohemianism took some getting over.

Chelsea's main landlord, Lord Cadogan, started the full-scale development of the Hans Town area – which included Pont Street – in the late 1870s after the expiry of the lease granted to Henry Holland. Further improvements in the district followed, culminating in extensive building around Trafalgar Square in the 1930s and its rechristening as Chelsea Square. Here were constructed substantial houses, some with outbuildings, wholly suitable for wealthy occupiers. But one of the most obvious attractions of the borough was in its old heartland, on the riverside at Cheyne Walk and Chelsea Embankment, on the old Beaufort House grounds and their vicinity. This was an area largely preserved from the deterioration elsewhere, with a number of considerable houses looking out over the Thames, among them anyway the core of the Moravians' Lindsey House. After a visit to a friend in Cheyne Walk, Margaret Warren noted in her diary (in the early 1870s) that 'One feels there, as if one had got into one of Henry Kingsley's Chelsea stories, or into the reign of Queen Anne.' Swan House – destroyed in the Blitz – was much admired, and at

Long-suffering Husband: 'I say, Monica, do let's leave
Chelsea and sit on chairs again.' A cartoon in *Punch* of
1924 by Frank Reynolds.

the end of the 1870s the judge Sir Robert Collier, later Lord Monkswell, built Monkswell House, also known as Chelsea Lodge, immediately to the front of Dilke Street, where he employed some eighteen
indoor servants. His daughter-in-law claimed it to be 'one of the
nicest houses in London'.

To the young, the Bohemian reputation, otherwise known as the
Artistic Tradition, fostered by Wilde, Rossetti, Whistler and, further
back, Turner, was a draw. It became smart to occupy the artists'
studios still to be found in Chelsea, with an effect on rents that forced
more dedicated artists to decamp, according to Patrick Balfour, to
Montmartre and later to Cassis and Cagnes in the South of France.
After the Second World War, the rich and those with expectations
of becoming rich moved in *en masse*. In 1935, twelve peers lived in
Chelsea; in 1965 there were forty-three, and this at a time when the
overall number of peers with homes in London had declined. The
artistic tradition was by then much attenuated and more palpable to

outside visitors to the King's Road on Saturday afternoons than to the increasingly sedate residents. The young – the expectant rich – appreciated the cheerful atmosphere but what above all attracted them were the terraces of houses built in Victorian times, and sometimes before, for the working class and lower middle class. They provided exactly the right amount of accommodation for young families, with probably an au pair and someone to do the cleaning, but without traditional servants.

The appropriation of Chelsea by the affluent was to be the forerunner of a type of demographic movement which was to emerge as so dramatic a feature of London's development in the last thirty years of the twentieth century. But before coming to that, there is the migration of the Jewish community to consider. It was a migration which partly broke new ground and partly occupied old. As we have seen in relation to Park Lane, by the beginning of the twentieth century the Jews formed a very important section of the London rich. For instance, they make up more than 15 per cent of all non-landed millionaires dying between 1900 and 1914, when their share of the total population was only 0.5 per cent. They had been strongly represented in the City long before that. Many of the richer members of the community were settled in the district around Finsbury Circus and Finsbury Square which had been built on Moorfields just north of the City proper about 1790. Around 1830 they started to move out, with one group setting off westwards, the other to the north. The western route can be followed in the course taken by the family of Sir George Jessel (1824–83), master of the rolls and a Liberal attorney-general. The Jessels started in Finsbury Square, moved to Montagu Square in Marylebone, then to Cleveland Square in Paddington, and after that to Hyde Park Gardens overlooking Hyde Park. Alternatively one can note the location of the West End synagogues – the Central Synagogue in Great Portland Street (behind the modern BBC building), the West London Synagogue in Upper Berkeley Street, virtually on Edgware Road, and finally the New West End Synagogue in St Petersburgh Place, Bayswater, placed a few hundred yards from another demographically significant landmark, the Greek Orthodox Church in Moscow Road. A section of numerous but less wealthy Jews also settled in Maida Vale.

The other stream ran northwards to Hampstead and Highgate, and to Islington and Stoke Newington and the eastern part of Hackney. It was familiar territory in the sense that Jews, like other City businessmen, had favoured the northern villages and landscape for their country houses. Daniel Defoe wrote that in his day Highgate was a favourite retreat for wealthy Jews. Later in the eighteenth century, Benjamin Goldsmid, married to the heiress Jesse Solomon of Clapton, part of the parish of Hackney, took a country house at neighbouring Stamford Hill before promoting himself to Roehampton. Nathan Mayer Rothschild rented a house at Stamford Hill before his purchase of Gunnersbury. A synagogue was opened in Barnsbury in 1868, but by then much of the congregation had swept on to Highbury and to Mildmay Park in Stoke Newington. Later many Jews settled in Finchley or pushed further to Golders Green. In the thirty or so years before the First World War, North London developed into the major residential area for the London Jewish community.

If there is no Goldsmid Street or Rothschild Road to commemorate the importance of this part of London to wealthy businessmen, there does exist a Cazenove Road leading off Stoke Newington High Street to mark the estate of the Huguenot Philip Cazenove, founder of the most eminent of London stockbrokers. With its late eighteenth-century manor house close to the parish church of St Mary's – a fine example of Victorian ecclesiastical architecture with excellent stained glass – Stoke Newington gives an impression of impeccable Anglican conformity. In practice, the district held a special appeal for religious minorities, in particular the Quakers. It was described as 'a very Elysian field of nonconformity'. While Stoke Newington could not rival Clapham – with which it was compared – in the number of its distinguished residents, it did produce two men who made their mark in the wider world. One was Defoe, who wrote *Robinson Crusoe* at his home in Stoke Newington, the other, the banker-poet-wit Samuel Rogers, whose original choice of vocation was that of a Presbyterian minister. A startling idea, though of course one in accord with local taste. Henry Luttrell, another Holland House habitué, told Charles Greville that much of the popularity of Rogers's poetry was 'owing to its being so carefully weeded of everything approaching to indelicacy', but that Rogers himself was the greatest sensualist of all the men he had ever known. It is no surprise that this caustic, socially ambitious man early abandoned Stoke Newington for a house which he built for himself in St James's Place overlooking Green Park.

By the time Rogers died at the age of ninety-two in 1855, Stoke Newington and the rest of North London were in the second stage of occupation by Londoners. First, there had been the rich to establish country houses, to be followed by businessmen a rung or two lower in the economic scale. In the third phase came the lower middle class and the poor. As it happened, of the northern villages, Hampstead and Highgate, like Wimbledon and Dulwich in the south, were able to check the mass migration of stage three. Islington, Stoke Newington and Hackney were not. They were overwhelmed, above all because geographically they were so accessible to the poor. The 1934 *New Survey of London* showed that the proportion of the better-off in Islington's population had fallen by more than half in one generation, a decline greater than that in Camberwell or South Lambeth. Barnsbury, once so elegant, was now one of the most overcrowded districts of London.

Then, in barely more than another generation, this inner-city borough, badly bombed, much of it a slum, much of it derelict, became the terrain for a new phenomenon, the recovery by the middle class of a district abandoned by their grandparents. The very closeness to London which had made it so vulnerable was now a factor in its regeneration. That, and the existence of a multitude of fine and capacious houses – split of course into tenements and lodging houses – set around some of what were architecturally the most handsome and unspoilt squares in London. Another factor was the availability of freeholds. The newcomers were wary of leases, not least because they did not appeal to Building Societies and Life Assurance Companies on whom they depended for mortgages. As it happened, the Northampton family, the main Islington landlords, had sold out soon after the war, and freeholds were usually in the hands of petty landlords who could make only miserable returns from renting. For the right price – and their aspirations were modest – they were ready to sell, although, of course, protected tenants had to be persuaded to move. (In some cases the means of persuasion were rough.) In the early stages of what came to be called 'gentrification', there were some

334

extraordinary contrasts, the most spectacular probably that of four houses in Islington's Lonsdale Square which between them provided for fifty households. Two of the houses were occupied by newcomers, one family per house, while in the other two there lived forty-eight single working-class tenants in furnished accommodation.

The result of what was happening is shown in the statistics. Between 1961 and 1971, Islington registered an increase of 23.37 per cent in the proportion of males in the professional and managerial classes, with the rise particularly marked in the previously impoverished Barnsbury ward. In neighbouring Hackney, where the fine houses and squares did not exist, the proportion had actually fallen.

Gentrification was by no means unique to London: it was occurring in other British cities, in America, on the Continent, and elsewhere in the developed world. In the United States it was known as the 'back to the city movement', the gentrifiers being migrants from the suburbs, while in London they came from the inner city. In each case, however, it amounted to a reaction against the once irresistible outer suburbs. Convenience and the reduced cost of travel to work played their part. Yet in any event the romance of the suburbs had faded, the association now was with twitching net curtains – a powerful image – and a narrow view of life. If there was anyone with whom the gentrifiers did not identify themselves, it was Mr Pooter. A lively article in *New Society* in 1968 brings out luminously the character of the Islington gentrifiers. Typically they were people who worked in the media, advertising or the professions; often they were teachers. In the spirit of the time they were resolutely progressive. They were not intending a clearance of their poorer neighbours – quite the opposite. 'We'd be sorry if the whole street became homogeneous,' said one newcomer to the *New Society* interviewer. They painted up their houses, knocked down the internal partitions, and held some lively parties, but they were not extravagant or ostentatious. They exemplified a style of what has happily been called 'conspicuous thrift'. Their virtues, though, were less appreciated by their working-class neighbours, both because of the sense of insecurity provoked by their presence and because of some of their customs. Sunbathing on their doorsteps was unpopular, and so was the practice of their children wandering about without shoes.

·

One old inhabitant is quoted in *New Society* as saying that Chelsea had begun to move to Islington. Certainly there were perceptive and reasonably wealthy buyers of Islington property who moved into, for instance, the fine houses of Canonbury Square, who may well have come from Chelsea and who could have afforded to live there had they wished. Certainly many gentrifiers had been privately educated: a limited survey in Battersea in 1985 found that out of thirty-five gentrifiers plus spouses, 80 per cent had received fee-paying education and none had attended a state-run school. But most, in Islington, Hammersmith, Fulham, Wandsworth or in the rehabilitated docklands of the East End, were not rich and their thrift, conspicuous or not, was a reflection of that fact. However, they were young, and the sort of people likely to make good money later on. If they sold their houses, it was often to someone richer. No longer was it a matter of do-it-yourself. Speculators appeared to renovate dilapidated houses for prospective buyers less likely than their predecessors to relish the prospect of carrying out their own conversions. In the context of the rich, the importance of gentrification was that it prepared their way by transforming battered and shabby housing and in revivifying neighbourhoods. It opened out new ground.

Nowhere can the process and effect of upgrading be seen more clearly than on the Ladbroke estate in Notting Hill. At its southern end, the estate looks over Holland Park Avenue up into Campden Hill Square and at the back of the solid Holland Park buildings developed under the auspices of the fourth Lord Holland and his widow. On the western side it follows roughly the line of Portland Road to reach its northern boundary not far short of the Westway motorway. On the east it descends down Portobello Road. In 1965, the ordinarily informed Londoner, asked what he or she knew of Notting Hill, would probably have found it difficult to come up with more than the Portobello Market; race riots; Christie, the necrophile from Rillington Place; and Rachman, the demonized slum landlord who broke on the public consciousness in the wake of the Profumo Scandal. This mid-Victorian suburb, of which the Ladbroke estate forms the centre, had been slumbering on almost undisturbed for years. In 1907, E. Beresford Chancellor, seeming rather put out, condescended in his *The History of the Squares of London* to notice

Ladbroke Square and one or two other neighbouring squares with the words 'they sadly lack historical or antiquarian interest'. It is unlikely that anyone on the Ladbroke estate would have minded much. Even in the 1970s an old inhabitant, apprehensive about the improvements all around, explained that 'this isn't Hampstead or Chelsea, it isn't anywhere'. Ladbroke was in its Victorian day a particularly elegant and cohesive suburb of London on which a lot of money had been spent (and lost) and which never quite made the grade. Mr Ladbroke himself, the original landowner, had disappeared from the scene a long time back. It was largely freehold.

There are a number of explanations for the decline and neglect. The vicinity – and Christie and Rachman were actually at work just outside the estate – was, to put it mildly, unsalubrious. The Potteries and Piggeries on the western boundary were evil-smelling and disease-prone. At the beginning of the twentieth century, they were replaced by London's Laundry Land. The houses, planned for large families, were inconvenient. Moreover, the district was too far out. Far out, and 'North of the Park'. The expression was one of disparagement, for the contraction of fashionable London had bestowed a questionable status on the whole range of tall, self-assured buildings and their hinterland which stretched from Notting Hill east to Marble Arch. Writing in the 1970s, the novelist Monica Dickens recalled her youth at 52 Chepstow Villas, Notting Hill. In her childhood, she said, if one had to live north of the Park, the address was quite a decent one. The real change only occurred in the late 1930s when the area began to go downhill. Family houses were broken up into flats and bedsitting rooms, front gardens were concreted over or filled with rubbish. It was a dingy neighbourhood to which she was ashamed to invite new friends home.

The war rendered it dingier yet. Unattended stucco is most depressing. Bombs took their toll, with the houses replaced by flats or utilitarian substitutes. Nevertheless, Ladbroke remained very much as built. A history of No. 39 Lansdowne Road compiled by its owner, gives a sense of continuity, of the type of people who lived in the house, and, most significant for the future, the measure of space available. The house was built in 1845 and the first occupants (going by the census of 1851) were a civil engineer and his wife from Lancashire, with four young children and three living-in servants, one of whom was the children's nurse. By 1861 they had been succeeded by a widow with her two daughters and her son, a soldier who was secretary to the Council for Army Education. With them in the house were three granddaughters and again three servants. By the time of the 1871 census this family had been replaced by a 'gold laceman', his wife and two others, plus two servants. In the 1890s the house was enlarged, with ten people in residence. The laceman died, but his widow, a second wife, remained until her death in 1915. The house, apparently unoccupied for three years, passed to an occupant about whom little is known – census records are not yet available – who sold in the early 1930s to a distinguished civil servant, with a wife and four children. He in turn sold the house to the present owner and her husband in 1947. Lansdowne Road, like most of the centre of the estate, qualified for the wealthiest category in Charles Booth's 1901 survey, although probably by a narrow margin. One would judge its inhabitants to have been prosperous but not rich.

Roughly speaking, 1965 is the turning point. More well-to-do people started buying, attracted by the price of the houses, the space they provided, the environment, and also the luxuriant Victorian decoration and fittings which were returning to fashion. Subsiding houses were underpinned and dry rot purged. A philistine impulse on the part of the council was countered and more consistently philistine developers thwarted. The Ladbroke estate is now very expensive with prices for the largest semi-detached houses in the most favoured streets running at over £3 million at the time of writing. Since many of the buyers undertake extensive alterations, the overall cost is sometimes considerably more. 'You have to be a banker to buy a house here now', is a common observation. The elegant street pattern and the presence of fifteen communal gardens (which, apart from other advantages, provide security for children) help. Above all, though, it is the size of the houses which is the draw.

The regeneration of Notting Hill and of North Kensington more generally, is part of a London-wide phenomenon, one that could hardly be foreseen by the planners of 1945 faced with the prospect of reviving a shattered city. They could have no foreknowledge of the economic growth which would so much influence what happened, for their experience, after all, was rooted in the Depression of the inter-war years. They believed that planning and the prudent allocation of resources were fundamental to London's recovery, and they had no time for aesthetic frills. Sir Isaac Hayward, leader of the London County Council, was approached about the restoration of Holland House. His reaction was unequivocal: 'Holland House should go, it is a relic of an outdated aristocracy and anyway, it would cost £25,000 to restore.' (The figure of £25,000 in 1945 is the equivalent of rather over £500,000 now.) If the politicians and planners were narrowly focussed and pessimistic, they were in good company. That Theory of Progress embraced by the nineteenth century hardly included London. Arthur Sherwell in his *Life in West London* of 1901 declared that 'It requires no great stretch of imagination to forecast a time when the wealthy mansions of Kensington shall give place to warehouses and shops, or be let out in one and two-room tenements.' Isaac Hayward's predecessor, Lord Rosebery, the first chairman of the London County Council, stated, 'there is no thought of pride associated in my mind with the idea of London. I am haunted by the awfulness of London.' In 1945 it was anticipated that segregation would increase and that inner London would come to be divided into two clearly differentiated zones – one zone with council-owned blocks for the poor, the other with owner-occupied houses and flats for the rich. Conflict would presumably be inevitable. Indeed, Notting Hill at one stage seemed a battleground between the newcomers, between the well-to-do and the very poor, the West Indian immigrants.

By 1945 the Duke of Portland's list of great private palaces had shrunk from four to two. Bridgewater House, unlike Holland House, was repaired after bombing but destined for use as offices and to figure as Marchmain House in the television series *Brideshead Revisited*. Londonderry House and Apsley House were left. The first continued as a private house into the 1960s when, like its erstwhile neighbours, Dorchester House and Grosvenor House, it was replaced by an hotel. Apsley House, with an apartment allocated to its then owner, the Duke of Wellington, was converted into a museum. Of the great houses more generally only fragments were left – the odd stretch of wall, the seventeenth-century watergate to the Duke of Buckingham's

York House, the façade of Schomberg House in Pall Mall, the music room of Norfolk House, St James's Square, now, like the section of Sir Paul Pindar's Bishopsgate mansion, to be found at the Victoria and Albert Museum. And also – especially poignant – a gateway from Northumberland House set into the wall of an East End playground.

Of the second-line houses, No. 57 South Audley Street, formerly Bute House, in reversion to a traditional pattern, became the Egyptian embassy, and Stratford House, the one with Angelica Kauffman ceilings and plumbing deficiencies, was occupied by the Oriental Club. The dukes of Sutherland moved on from Green Street to a smaller house just off Belgrave Square and the Duke of Westminster's Bourdon House is now the showroom of a prominent antique dealer. Such houses, in one form or another, have been more likely than the giants to survive, and, at a level down, housing grants have stimulated

The ballroom of Wimborne House in use as an office in the 1950s.

the repair and restoration of buildings which would otherwise have perished, just as planning controls and the institution of conservation areas have preserved buildings and neighbourhoods. Nevertheless, by 1971, when Hermione Hobhouse published her *Lost London*, there seemed little to be optimistic about. Not only had much of old London gone, but what was replacing it was at best mediocre.

Yet there was one considerable improvement which has greatly added to London's appeal. For many of the overseas and European visitors who have appeared in this book, London was too big, too monotonous architecturally, and above all too dirty, too polluted. It is no longer the 'monster city', for by world standards it is now only of medium size. More important is the lifting of the smog, that affliction which to foreigners often seemed the very essence of London, what they thought of first (and their descendants sometimes still do) when London came to mind. To a few, usually artists, the tricks of light and smell were exciting and evocative. It was true of Claude Monet with his 'I adore London, it's a mass, a whole . . . But what I love more than anything in London is the fog.' And there is the almost lyrical, tragic but not brutal, Jack the Ripper sequence in G. W. Pabst's 1929 film *Pandora's Box*. But that was a specialized reaction. The smog left you choking for air, it dirtied your clothes and your furniture, it disfigured the buildings with its grime. Henry James writes of the 'miles of smoke-darkened stucco'. Londoners could not cure the smog, the eminent geographer Elisée Reclus accepted, but why have not 'rich Englishmen, so scrupulously careful of the cleanliness of their persons and homes, adopted more extensively the Portuguese and Brazilian fashion of covering their houses with glazed bricks, which can be washed'? But now, the buildings are cleansed, the impenetrable fogs, exorcized by the Clean Air Act, are a memory no more recent than the early 1960s. The monotony of the architecture, notwithstanding the mediocrity of much new building, offends less, partly because taste has shifted and partly because white and gleaming stucco is more impressive than stucco drenched with soot. Another alleged drawback mentioned by Reclus appears now as an advantage. London, he wrote, unlike Paris, lacks a collective personality, it is an agglomeration of distinct towns. To us, the diversity adds interest, and seems to act as a stimulus. For the rich (who after all do not have to endure the broken-down underground system), and even for the merely well-to-do, London is a more agreeable place to live than it used to be.

By 1971, when Hermione Hobhouse published her book, the process of gentrification had yet to advance sufficiently to be much more than a curiosity. By 1981, however, it was clear that sections of previously deteriorating London were reviving. By then, a book such as this would have treated what was happening as interesting, but as no more than a coda to the history of the rich in London. But now, at the turn of the century, such a view is impossible, for London finds itself at the centre of an explosion of wealth and building as dynamic and exuberant as that brought about by the patricians of the seventeenth century, the West Indians of the eighteenth, the aristocracy and gentry again (gingerly mixed with the businessmen) of the

London Fog. Relief from the dense and choking fogs of the past has made London a more attractive place to live for rich and for poor.

early nineteenth century, and the plutocrats of a hundred years ago.

The boom started in the mid-1980s, to coincide with the deregulation of the securities market – the 'Big Bang' – and a deluge of overseas investment in the City. Salaries rose to international levels, and property values reacted to the huge profits being made in the City and to the urgent demand for centrally placed accommodation. Buildings with familiar names, dozing in the background for years and with a seemingly most uncertain future, have suddenly emerged. Lady Mary Coke's Aubrey House on Campden Hill, has been sold for a reported £20 million to a buyer who plans private occupation once major alterations are completed. It will have twenty-one bedrooms, and reception rooms on a comparable scale. There is another 'country house', the early eighteenth-century Old Rectory, off Old Church Street, Chelsea, sold by the Church Commissioners in the 1980s and now bought by a private buyer for her personal use. In Park Lane, Sir Ernest Cassel's Brook House was replaced in the 1930s by a block of comfortable flats; in turn they have gone, supplanted by a new block with flats of an altogether more palatial type. At Regent's Park, all the remaining villas, St John's Lodge, Hanover Lodge, The Holme and Grove House, have reverted from institutional to private occupation. (Also in Regent's Park several reproduction Regency villas have been built and sold as private residences.) At the southern end of Park Lane, the Barnato/Sassoon mansion, now numbered No. 45, used during the Second World War as an American officers' club and afterwards as the Playboy Club, was bought in 1992 for conversion into a private palace by Prince Jefri Bolkiah, a brother of the Sultan of Brunei and owner of the Dorchester Hotel and Asprey's.

Two other mansions in southern Mayfair have been converted back from commercial use. One is 38 South Street, built for Lord Aberconway and now called Aberconway House, a rarity in being a large house built in Mayfair after the First World War. The other is the Marlboroughs' Sunderland House in Curzon Street. As a private palace Sunderland House enjoyed a short life, but it was nevertheless on a scale to rank among the very grandest; its rateable value in 1914 was more than twice that of Crewe House across the road (now the Saudi Arabian embassy) and more than that of either Chesterfield

The Old Rectory, Chelsea earlier in the century.

House or Londonderry House. Such one-time private mansions come on the market mainly because advances in technology with their requirement for broad expanses of lateral space render them unsuitable as offices. One more great house should be added to this list. At 43,000 sq. ft., Home House (now No. 20 Portman Square), much the same size as Sunderland House, was in its later years the home of Samuel Courtauld and then of the Courtauld Institute. Unlike its neighbour, the one-time Montagu House, it survived the Blitz. Now, incorporating two next-door houses – in all 60,000 sq. ft. – it has opened as a members club.

'People are going back to the way of life of 150 years ago,' observed Richard Crosthwaite of the estate agents Knight Frank. Like the neglected houses, neglected sections of what was once the West End – a term which now tends to mean Theatre Land – have come back into fashion residentially. Mayfair certainly, Regent's Park spectacularly, Marylebone tentatively. Others, such as Belgravia, still the home of 'old money', and Knightsbridge, Kensington and Chelsea are as desirable as and more expensive than ever. Further away from the centre are St John's Wood, Hampstead and Wimbledon, offering

One of the 1980s villas built in Regent's Park: the
dining room of Quinlan Terry's Gothick Villa.

space which is in shorter supply elsewhere, and which benefit apparently from a Russian weakness for suburban *dachas*. Who then are
these new high-flying London rich? Like the old Plutocrats, they are
of diverse nationality. In their way of life they are truly international,
since modern business and modern means of transport dictate and
allow that they be so. Some are British, 'new money' and members, so
to speak, of the same club as the numerous foreigners, the Americans,
Arabs, Swedes, Greeks, Russians and other East Europeans, Hong
Kong Chinese, Nigerians, Japanese, Indians, and more nationalities

345

yet. The new rich travel by private plane and helicopter. They possess other houses, perhaps in New York, Paris, the Caribbean. They are accompanied by bodyguards and a large staff. They demand not only comfort but luxury, and their London houses – which they may rent rather than buy – will be equipped with swimming pools, air conditioning and the most sophisticated communications equipment. What they spend initially when they buy a house is only a start, for the interior is likely to undergo wholesale reconstruction. The exterior, probably governed anyway by planning controls, remains essentially the same although additions may well be made. (In the case of the Old Rectory, it appears that the purchase price was something like £25 million and that a further £10 million has been spent on remodelling and redecoration.) Since most of the new rich are highly competitive and entertain lavishly – often of course for business purposes – the size of reception rooms is particularly important and considerably influences the price. (One of the reasons for the popularity of The Boltons in South Kensington is the spaciousness of these rooms.) Reception rooms must possess 'wall power', that is they must be hung with expensive paintings.

The rich have seldom bothered much about the level of local taxes or the whereabouts of local schools, but they have been concerned about communications. Notwithstanding the broad area of London they occupy, the newcomers are likely to be concerned about ease of access to Heathrow airport. (It will be interesting to see whether the fifteen-minute rail shuttle from Paddington stimulates demand for housing in Bayswater.) Choice of location is also influenced by the inclination, always particularly marked in the case of foreigners, to live among friends or at least among people of similar background. This tendency is at its most visible in North London, along The Bishop's Avenue, a road running northward from Kenwood which was for long the preserve of the Jewish and show-business communities. Gracie Fields and Billy Butlin had houses there. Standing on either side of the road are houses which are in every way, except in the generosity of the space they fill, the opposite of the decorous country mansions of Aubrey House and (before remodelling) the Chelsea Old Rectory. Ostentatious, mock-Tudor, mock-everything, Beverly Hills-in-London, this is a multi-national precinct indeed. And very rich. Also in Hampstead, an enormous Lutyens-style mansion is in course of building, while at Highgate nearby is Wittanhurst, owned by a Syrian businessman, which is reputedly one of the largest houses in the London area.

It is a new and final context in which to look at the London rich. Like the Plutocrats, the super-rich restore and rebuild grand houses. Around them, cascading money from the City or elsewhere reinstates and smartens old upper and middle-class neighbourhoods and transforms areas such as the Docklands. The discontinuance of the penal rates of income tax on high income which so influenced the contraction of wealthy London earlier in the century has increased spending and borrowing power.

Of the super-rich, however, the old question is highly pertinent. How far do they count as Londoners? The patricians of the past often spent no more than two or three months a year in London; in old age, like the nineteenth-century Lord Romney, they might keep almost entirely away. Their loose attachment to the capital was clear in reliance on lodgings or on the shortest of tenancies, and also in the ease with which great town houses passed from one family to another. Between 1838 and the end of the nineteenth century, for instance, No. 22 Arlington Street was at different times known as Beaufort House, Hamilton House, Walsingham House and Wimborne House. Even business families, albeit with notable exceptions, have departed quickly to the countryside once their fortunes were made. Of the very rich newcomers of our day, some – American bankers are an example – are temporary residents likely to be called elsewhere professionally within a few years of arrival. For another category, the London house is merely an investment, a safe lodgement for capital in a country perceived as politically stable. In The Bishop's Avenue, for example, while the houses are fully staffed all the time, the owners are sometimes in residence for no more than three weeks a year. Elsewhere, it may be that only the womenfolk come, perhaps for a couple of months in summer. Such people are most unlikely to look for assimilation into any indigenous London community; they will indeed have only the most tenuous connection with whole-time Londoners.

While the nature both of the rich and of their creation the

'West End' has changed, the overall conception of London remains remarkably constant. Economically, London, carrying with it the south-east corner of the British Isles, is sometimes now compared to a City State, to Hong Kong of a year or two back, seen to be 'unhooked' from the rest of the country. For good or ill, it may be true, but then in varying degrees it has been so since the days of the Great Fire and before. Sir John Reresby's speech of 1685 comes to mind: 'this one county [London] drained all England of its people ... our tenants all coming hither'. London has always drawn off talent and capital. In the earlier days the businessmen were making fortunes from overseas trade, and the patricians supplemented their rents with sinecures and jobs earned at Court. Even in the nineteenth century, notwithstanding the Industrial Revolution, industrial fortunes were overshadowed by those generated in the City. One is aware nevertheless of an extreme volatility. In 1992, a book, *The Crisis of London*, compared the lethargy of London to the vitality of Paris. But by 1997, Parisian tourists were streaming over here to imbibe the energy of London. As for the businessmen – how depressing to be the French ambassador, wrote the City correspondent of *Le Monde* in an article in April 1998. Every time he dines out he is compelled to listen to other guests discussing the exodus from Paris. After the Huguenots, the article went on, after the royalists [during the Revolution], the exiled Communards, the Gaullists, today it is the turn of the very rich, of the high earners and the entrepreneurs '*dans la force de l'âge*' to find refuge on the other side of the Channel. As well as facing more volatility, London's economy must be more generally vulnerable than in the past, partly because its financial markets and support services, the engines of its prosperity, are no longer fortified by a strong manufacturing base or by the once famous, now defunct, Port of London. Partly too because so many City firms are owned by overseas institutions. Yet, for all the uncertainties of the future, it is difficult in the historical context not to be struck by the steadiness of London's economy, by its resilience, and by its success over so many generations as a creator of wealth.

Sources

Abbreviations

HMC   Historical Manuscripts Commission
VHCE   *Victoria History of the Counties of England*
DNB   *Dictionary of National Biography*
PRO   Public Record Office

1 Before the Fire

In this chapter, as in all those that follow, the *Survey of London* is a basic source. In Chapter 1 the volumes concerned are 13 (Palace of Westminster) and 18 (the Strand). For general background Lewis Mumford *The City in History* (1961) is useful. For medieval and Renaissance London see Gwyn A. Williams *Medieval London* (1970 edn) and Sylvia Thrupp *The Merchant Class of Medieval London* (1948), and as mentioned in the text, John Stow *A Survey of London* (1598). For Crosby Hall see P. J. Norman 'Crosby Place' in *London Topographical Record*, 6 (1909), and for Sir Paul Pindar, C. Goss *Sir Paul Pindar and His Bishopsgate Mansion* (1930). The history of Devonshire House is set out in M. Sefton-Jones *Old Devonshire House by Bishopsgate* (1923). For population figures see R. Finlay *Population and Metropolis: The Demography of London, 1580–1650* (1981).

E. J. Davis in her 'The Transformation of London', in *Tudor Studies* (ed. R. Seton-Watson, 1924), gives an excellent account of the requisitioning of ecclesiastical lands. For Martin Lister on the difference demographically between London and Paris, see his *An Account of Paris at the Close of the Seventeenth Century* (revised G. Henning, 1823) while Valerie Pearl's *London and the Outbreak of the Puritan Revolution* (1961) provides a vivid description of restrictions on new building.

349

The French ambassador's view of overcrowding is taken from 'A French Ambassador's Impressions' in *The Nineteenth Century and After*, 446 (April 1914). For the Great Fire see W. G. Bell *The Great Fire of London* (1920), which also refers to Pudding Lane as a 'pitiful lane'. The census figures for Pudding Lane in 1638 are to be found in T. C. Dale *Inhabitants of London in 1638* (1931) and the Hearth Tax returns in the PRO.

Samuel Pepys's reference to Mrs Backwell occurs in *The Diary of Samuel Pepys*, vol. 3 (ed. R. Latham and W. Matthews, 1970). The manuscript of Humphrey Mildmay's diary is in the British Library, reference Harley Ms. 454; Diary of Sir Humphrey Mildmay. For Mildmay's furniture at Danbury, see Essex Record Office, Chelmsford, file D/DU 261/3. The diary is also published in R. L. Ralph *Sir Humphrey Mildmay: Royalist Gentleman* (New Brunswick, NJ, 1947), which as a biography is incomplete, relying as it does almost exclusively on the diary. For the earls of Bedford and Bedford House in the Strand, see G. S. Thomson *Life in a Noble Household* (1937) and for references to travelling 'like a prince', *The Memoirs of Sir John Reresby* (ed. J. J. Cartwright, 1875).

For Buckingham and his jewels, the source is H. Chapman *Great Villiers* (1949). For Evelyn see *The Diary of John Evelyn* (ed. E. S. de Beer, 1959). The reference to the Turkish curse is taken from Francis, Viscount Shannon *Discourses and Essays* (1696). For Lady Anne Clifford, there are several editions published of her diary: recently there is *The Diary of Anne Clifford*, ed. Katherine O. Acheson (New York, 1995). For the Strand palaces, see David Pearce *London's Mansions* (1986); N. Brett-James *The Growth of Stuart London* (1935); and H. B. Wheatley *London Past and Present*, vol. 3 (1891), based on P. Cunningham's *Handbook of London*. Sorbière's account of his visit to London was published in his *Relation d'un voyage en Angleterre* (Paris, 1664). The quotation relating to Buckingham comes from Roger North *Lives of the Norths*, vol. 1 (ed. A. Jessopp, 1890), and Rochester's City excursion from V. de Sola Pinto *Rochester: Enthusiast in Wit* (1962). Many of the facts relating to the early West End in this chapter and the next are based on books and articles by Lawrence Stone: in the case of the directory of 1677 from his 'The Residential Development of the West End of London in the Seventeenth Century' in B. B. Malament (ed.) *After the Reformation* (1980). For Backwell see J. Martin *The Grasshopper in Lombard Street* (1892). Roy Porter in his *London: A Social History* (1994) brings out the ignorance at Whitehall over the Fire. The eighteenth-century foreign visitor was J. W. von Archenholz, quoted from his *Picture of England* (English trans. 1789). The Lord Mayor's letter of protest is printed in Lawrence Stone *Family and Fortune* (1973).

For the Verney family see *Memoirs of the Verney Family*, vol. 1 (ed. F. Verney, 1892), for William Petty *The Petty Papers*, vol. 1 (ed. Marquess of Lansdowne, 1927), and for Reresby, the *Memoirs* as referred to above. In addition to Pearl *Outbreak of the Puritan Revolution*, as above, information on building regulations is to be found in F. Fisher 'The Development of London as a Centre of Conspicuous Consumption in the Sixteenth and Seventeenth Centuries' in *Transactions of the Royal Historical Society*, 4:xxx (1948). Lord Bedford's licence for Covent Garden is described in Christopher Hibbert *London: The Biography of a City* (1977 edn); Lord Clare's development in Holborn and the building in Lincoln's Inn Fields are described in Lawrence Stone *Crisis of the Aristocracy* (1965). For Lincoln's Inn see also *Survey of London*, vol. 3. Pepys's visits to Lincoln's Inn Fields are recorded in several of the volumes of his *Diary*.

The quotation about the Chancery Lane address can be found in Verney *Memoirs*, as above, vol. 4. Aristocratic landholdings are listed in Stone *Crisis*, as above. For Mary Davies see C. Gatty *Mary Davies and the Manor of Ebury* (1921).

2 London Breaks Its Bounds

For the demolition of the Strand palaces, see *Survey of London*, vol. 18. For Evelyn's advice see *The Diary of John Evelyn* (ed. E. S. de Beer, 1959). For 'ruinous heap' see Samuel Rolls *Londons Resurrection* [*sic*] (1668). Sir Dudley North's experience of pollution in the City is taken from Roger North *Lives of the Norths*, vol. 1 (ed. A. Jessopp, 1890), and the Simond quotation from his *An American in Regency England* (ed. C. Hibbert, 1968). For Clarendon on class-consciousness during the Civil War, see L. Stone 'The Residential Development of the West End of London in the Seventeenth Century' in B. B. Malament (ed.) *After the Reformation* (1980), and for Reresby's experience of it *The Memoirs of Sir John Reresby* (ed. J. J. Cartwright, 1875). Evelyn's *Character of England* was published in *Harleian Miscellany X* (1813). For Russell see *Letters of Rachel, Lady Russell* (ed. Lord John Russell, 1853).

For letting to the 'very door of the their mansion house', the reference is J. Thirsk and J. Cooper *Seventeenth-Century Economic Documents* (1972), and Pepys's reference to country gentlemen making their wills is to be found in *The Diary of Samuel Pepys*, vol. 9 (ed. R. Latham and W. Matthews, 1976). For travel see *The Diary of Anne Clifford* (ed. Katherine O. Acheson, New York, 1995), M. Coate *Social Life in Stuart England* (1924) and L. Stone 'Residential Development', in Malament (ed.) *After the Reformation*, as above. Bohun's diary is published in *The Diary and Autobiography of Edmund Bohun* (ed. S. Rix, 1853). For St Albans and the development of St James's see *Survey of London*, vol. 29 and N. Brett-James *The Growth of Stuart London* (1935). The Fiennes quotation is from *The Journeys of Celia Fiennes* (ed. C. Morris, 1948).

Samuel Butler's satire on courtiers is published in 'Characters' from H. Morley (ed.) *Character Writings of the Seventeenth Century* (1891). The Folio Society edition (1968) has been used for *The Letters of Dorothy Osborne to Sir William Temple*, while Temple's own view is given in his *Of Popular Discontents* (1814 edn). For Chesterfield see Earl of Chesterfield *Letters to His Son*, vol. 2 (ed. O. Leigh, New York, nd); for Reresby *Memoirs*, as above, and Bramston *The Autobiography of Sir J. Bramston* in Camden Soc. 32, 1845. The Post Office pensions are published in the *Calendar of Treasury Books*, vol. XIX, 1704/5 held by the PRO. Very valuable on anything to do with emoluments, Court or otherwise, are the studies by W. D. Rubinstein, in particular here his *Elites and the Wealthy in Modern British History* published in the UK in 1981. For Ailesbury see *The Memoirs of Thomas, Earl of Ailesbury* (1890).

Francis Sheppard discusses Baker and Panton in *Robert Baker of Piccadilly Hall and His Heirs*, London Topographical Soc., publication 127 (1982). For Lord Leicester see HMC, *De Lisle and Dudley*, vol. 6; and also for Leicester Fields, *Survey of London*, vol. 34, and Roy Porter *London: A Social History* (1994).

Christopher Wren's anxiety over Soho is noted in C. A. Edie's

'New Buildings, New Taxes' in *Journal of British Studies*, 6:2 (1967). Reactions in the House of Commons are given in Edie, and also in Anchitell Grey *Debates in the House of Commons*, vol. 2 (1763). For the reluctance to permit new taxes, see *The Diary of Sir E. Dering* at the Centre for Kentish Studies, Maidstone, file U275. Lord Ailesbury's experience is related in his *Memoirs*, as above.

For developers in general see the excellent 'Speculative Housing and the Land Market in London, 1600–1730' by P. Booth in *Town Planning Review*, 51:4 (1980). For Nicholas Barbon, a most lively, as well as contemporary, source is Roger North in his *Lives*, as above. Norman Brett-James wrote on Barbon in *Transactions of the London & Middlesex Archaeological Society* ns, VII (1933), and the episode of Essex House is discussed in *Archaeologia*, 73 (1922–3). For Barbon and insurance, see J. Carswell *The South Sea Bubble* (1960).

For Pulteney see *Survey of London*, vols. 31 and 32, and for Soho, vol. 33. For Macclesfield see Dering *Diary*, as above. The Civil War forts are depicted in F. Barker and P. Jackson *The History of London in Maps* (1991 edn). Lord Southampton and his development of Bloomsbury are treated by Lawrence Stone in his *Family and Fortune* (1973) and in G. S. Thomson *The Russells in Bloomsbury* (1940). For Rachel Russell see Lois G. Schwoerer *Lady Rachel Russell* (Baltimore, 1988). For family trusts see also F. T. Melton 'A Rake Refinanced' in *Huntington Library Quarterly*, 51 (1988) (San Marino, Calif.). Also for Bloomsbury see D. J. Olsen *Town Planning in London* (1964).

The Berkeleys are the subject of B. Falk *The Berkeleys of Berkeley Square* (1944), and Evelyn's involvement is recorded in his *Diary*, as above. For Hinde and Mayfair see B. H. Johnson *Berkeley Square to Bond Street* (1952). The attitude of Lord Leicester and his son Lord Lisle to development can be seen in HMC, as above. There is further discussion of Barbon's importance in Sir John Summerson *Georgian London* (1948 edn). Summerson also writes in this book on building leases, as does Andrew Byrne in *London's Georgian Houses* (1986).

3 Suburban Splendour

For Henry VIII's laborious journey to London, see R. Milward *Historic Wimbledon* (1989) and for Evelyn, his way of life and his opinion of Eltham, see *The Diary of John Evelyn* (ed. E. S. de Beer,

1959). Valence House and its history are described in *VHCE*, *Essex*, vol. 5; Forty Hall in D. Pam *A History of Enfield*, vol. 1 (1990). Charlton Park is referred to in Evelyn, as above, and is the subject of A. R. Martin *Charlton House, Kent* (1929); for Bruce Castle see *Haringey History Bulletin*, 28, published by the Hornsey Historical Society. For Eastbury see *VHCE*, *Essex*, vol. 5, Daniel Defoe *A Tour thro' the Whole Island of Great Britain*, vol. 1 (1724) and T. H. Clarke *Eastbury Illustrated* (1834). W. Addison, in his *Wanstead Park* (1977), provides a full account of this important house.

Cassandra Willoughby, later Duchess of Chandos, left ample records of her life. Her journeys through England before her marriage are described in the (unpublished) 'Journal of Cassandra, Duchess of Chandos', which forms part of the Stoneleigh Papers at the Shakespeare Birthplace Trust Records Office, ref. D 18/20/21. Her (unpublished) 'Letterbook' reveals her life at Canons and belongs to the North London Collegiate School, Canons Park, Edgware. Life at Wollaton Hall figures in Cassandra, Duchess of Chandos *The Continuation of the History of the Willoughby Family*, vol. 2 (ed. A. C. Wood, 1958). Joan Johnson has written a biography, *Excellent Cassandra* (1981). For the Duke of Chandos see C. H. C. Baker and M. I. Baker *The Life and Circumstances of James Brydges, First Duke of Chandos* (1949) and Joan Johnson *Princely Chandos . . . 1674–1744* (1984). Onslow's description of Chandos was published in *Huntington Library Quarterly*, 15 (1951–2) (San Marino, Calif.). Defoe's eulogy is to be found in *Tour*, as above, vol. 2. For the house in St James's Square see C. S. Sykes *Private Palaces* (1985) and *Survey of London*, vol. 29; for Bedford House see G. S. Thomson *Life in a Noble Household* (1937).

The Abbé Le Blanc recorded his visit in his *Letters on the English and French Nations* (English trans. 1747). Defoe's enthusiasm for the Thames west of London is again taken from his *Tour*, as above, vol. 1. For Uffenbach, see *London in 1710 from the Travels of Zacharias Conrad von Uffenbach* (trans. and ed. W. H. Quarrell and M. Mare, 1934). The comparison with Venice is made by J. de Rochefort, writing in 1672, and translated in *The Antiquarian Repertory*, vol. 4 (compiled F. Grose, 1809). For Bedford see Thomson, *Life*, as above. For Thoresby see D. H. Atkinson *Ralph Thoresby the Topographer*, vol. 2 (1885). *A Voyage up the Thames* (1738) was ascribed to 'Weddell'.

Particulars and Inventories of the Estates of the Late Sub-Governor, Deputy Governor and Directors of the South-Sea Company, published in 2 volumes in 1721, gives a unique view of the assets held by rich men at the time of the South Sea Bubble. J. Carswell's *The South Sea Bubble* (1960) provides a lucid account of the great financial boom and collapse. For Clayton see *Sir Robert Clayton and the Origins of English Deposit Banking* (1986) by F. T. Melton. Janssen's investment in Queen Square is recorded by Isobel Watson in her *Westminster and Pimlico Past* (1993), while his purchase in Wimbledon is reported in Milward *Historic Wimbledon*, as above. For Worcester House see John Stow *A Survey of the Cities of London and Westminster, Brought down from the Year 1633 to the Present Time by J. Strype*, vol. 2 (1720) and for Lord Worcester (Beaufort) see HMC 12th Report, appendix pt. 9, *Ms. of the Duke of Beaufort and others*. Beaufort House and its history are recorded in R. Davies *The Greatest House at Chelsea* (1914). For where peers lived, see C. Jones 'A London Directory' in *London Journal*, 18:1 (1993).

Swift's experiences in Chelsea are drawn from the 'Journal to Stella' in *The Works of the Rev. Jonathan Swift*, vol. 5 (ed. T. Sheridan, 1784). For the Duke of Buckingham see Sykes *Private Palaces*, as above, quoting from Buckingham's *Works*. C. de Saussure in his *A Foreign View of England in the Reigns of George I and George II* (trans. and ed. Mme. Van Muyden, 1902) talks of the crowding around Buckingham House. Hugh Phillips in his excellent *The Thames about 1750* (1951) describes the terrain.

The proposals for a new palace are printed in the *Oxford Papers* contained in HMC *Portland Papers* 10, under reference Hyde Park. For the history of this area of Kensington see *Survey of London*, vol. 37, and Sir G. Evans *Kensington* (1975). Lady Cowper's comment on the temporary safety of roads comes from the *Diary of Mary, Countess Cowper 1714–1720* (ed. Hon. S. Cowper, 1865).

There are a number of histories of Holland House and its inhabitants. For the earlier days which are treated in this chapter, most useful are the Earl of Ilchester's *The Home of the Hollands, 1605–1820* (1937) and his *Henry Fox, First Lord Holland*, 2 vols. (1920); and also Derek Hudson's *Holland House in Kensington* (1967). Sala's quip comes from his *Twice round the Clock* (1859) and Clarendon's sketch of Henry Rich, first Earl of Holland, from his *The History of the Rebellion*, vol. 4 (1849 edn). For the criticisms of Henry Fox, first Lord (Baron) Holland, see G. O. Trevelyan *The Early History of Charles James Fox* (1880) and L. B. Namier *England in the Age of the American Revolution* (1930). Lady Susan O'Brien described Fox's eccentric view of the young in an entry under March 1818 in her *Journal*, which is catalogued under Additional Manuscripts no. 51359 in the British Library. For Motley, see *The Correspondence of John Lothrop Motley*, vol. 2 (ed. G. W. Curtis, 1889).

4 Casualties

For interest rates see T. S. Ashton *Economic Fluctuations in England 1700–1800* (1959). For Mary Davies, the ultimate poor little rich girl, see again C. Gatty *Mary Davies and the Manor of Ebury* (1921), and also Simon Jenkins *The Selling of Mary Davies and Other Writings* (1993). Barkstead's career is recounted in M. Ashley *Cromwell's Generals* (1954), and in terms of the act of parliament in C. H. Firth and R. S. Rait *Acts and Ordinances of the Interregnum*, vol. 2 (1911). Chandos and his financial difficulties are traced in the relevant books listed under Chapter 3, particularly in Baker and the Duchess of Chandos's 'Letterbook' at Canons Park.

The property boom of 1716–18 is described in Ashton as above and the construction of Hanover Square in Simon Jenkins *Landlords to London* (1975). For Cavendish Square see Hugh Phillips *Mid-Georgian London* (1964), Sir John Summerson *Georgian London* (1948 edn), and G. Mackenzie *Marylebone* (1972). Horace Walpole's letter to Mann is published in *The Yale Edition of Horace Walpole's Correspondence*, vol. 18 (ed. W. S. Lewis, 1955). For the surveys see C. Jones 'A London Directory' in *London Journal*, 18:1 (1993). Lord Ossulston's peregrinations are tracked, also by C. Jones, in 'The London Life of a Peer in the Reign of Anne' in *London Journal*, 16:2 (1991). For St James's Square see *Survey of London*, vol. 29, and for the Lord Mayor's misgivings *The Diary of Samuel Pepys*, vol. 4 (ed. R. Latham and W. Matthews, 1971). The appellation 'terror of many a mother' is quoted from J. T. Smith *A Book for a Rainy Day* (ed. W. Whitten, 1905). For Clarendon House and its owner see Earl of Clarendon *Life of Edward, Earl of Clarendon*, vol. 3 (1827 edn) and I. Halstead *Bond Street* (1952).

The later history of Beaufort House is set out in R. Davies *The Greatest House at Chelsea* (1914) and St J. Brooks *Sir Hans Sloane* (1954). For Edmund Howard see his *Narration of Some of the Occurrances in the life of Edmund Howard*, dated 1785, in the Chelsea Reference Library catalogued SP 210 (B). For Nicholas Barbon, see his *An Apology for the Builder* (1685). For the Duke of Norfolk see Hugh Phillips *The Thames about 1750* (1951), and for Lord Dorset, C. J. Phillips *History of the Sackville Family* (1930). The fate of the theatre in Dorset Gardens is described in P. Hartnoll (ed.) *Oxford Companion to the Theatre* (1983, 4th edn), while that of the Strand is recounted in the *Survey of London*, vol. 18. For the Cecils see Lawrence Stone *Family and Fortune* (1973) and for Lord Holland, Lawrence Stone *Crisis of the Aristocracy* (1965). For the 'Wild-Fire Engine' refer to Chapter 3, the reference under Weddell. The degeneration of Covent Garden and Clare Market is described by M. D. George in her *London Life in the XVIIIth Century* (1925) and by E. J. Burford *Wits, Wenches and Wantons* (1986). For Boswell and Wapping see Roy Porter *London: A Social History* (1994).

The early history of Southwark is recorded in M. Concanen and A. Morgan, *History and Antiquities of the Parish of St Saviour's, Southwark* (1795), and in M. Carlin *Medieval Southwark* (1996). Mrs Thrale's life in Streatham and Southwark is comprehensively documented in her own *Thraliana*, 2 vols. (ed. K. C. Balderstone, 1942); H. L. Piozzi *Anecdotes of the late Samuel Johnson* (1925 edn); *Autobiography, Letters and Literary Remains of Mrs Piozzi* (ed. A. Hayward, 1861). M. Hyde's *The Thrales of Streatham Park* (1977) fills in background as does J. L. Clifford *Hester Lynch Piozzi* (1941). For Samuel Crisp see *Diary and Letters of Madame d'Arblay*, vol. 1 (ed. C. Barrett, 1904). For social status in the graveyard see W. Rendle *Old Southwark and Its People* (1878), for Boswell see W. K. Wimsatt, jun. and F. A. Pottle (eds.) *Boswell for the Defence* (1960). Samuel Johnson's admonitions to Hester Thrale are published in *The Letters of Samuel Johnson*, vol. 3 (ed. B. Redford, 1992). The name given to the brewery garden no doubt reflects the influence of R. Wood's *The Ruins of Palmyra* published in 1753.

5 'Devouring Luxury'

For estate acts in general see G. Bramwell *Table of Private Statutes* (1813) and Maurice Bond 'Estate Acts of Parliament' in *History*, 49 (1964). For the Grosvenors' early difficulties see C. Gatty *Mary Davies and the Manor of Ebury* (1921) and for Grosvenor Square the *Survey of London*, vols. 39 and 40. For Defoe see *Survey of London*, vol. 39. This advantage of the leasehold system is noted in H. J. Dyos *Victorian Suburb* (1961). The information on the Conduit Mead estate is given in I. Doolittle 'The City's West End' published in *London Journal*, 7 (Summer 1981), and on the Berners estate in J. Slater *A Short History of the Berners Estate* (1918). Soho in the 1760s is discussed in Hugh Phillips *Mid-Georgian London* (1964). Heidegger's career is described in the *DNB*, and for Mrs Cornelys see E. F. Rimbault *Soho and Its Associations* (1895). Casanova's record of his London visit is taken from *Mémoires de Jacques Casanova de Seingalt*, vol. 6 (Paris, nd).

Walpole's letter to Mann is published in *The Yale Edition of Horace Walpole's Correspondence*, vol. 23 (ed. W. S. Lewis, 1967). Lady Dalkeith's letter on the deserted West End is among those in the Duke of Argyll *Intimate Letters of the 18th Century* (1910). For Mme. du Bocage see her *Letters Concerning England, Holland and Italy* (English trans. 1770). For Kielmansegge see his *Diary of a Journey to England* (English trans. 1902). J.W. von Archenholz in his *A Picture of England* (English edn of 1797) used the term 'devouring luxury'. For the bagnio see H. Meister *Letters Written During a Residence in England* (English trans. 1799). Saussure's comment on women's interest in money comes from his *A Foreign View of England in the Reigns of George I and George II* (trans. and ed. Mme. van Muyden, 1902) and the reference to Voltaire is from D. Flower *Voltaire's England* (1950). For Gontaut see the *Memoirs of the Duchesse de Gontaut* (English trans. in 2 vols., 1894); for Grosley, M. Grosley *A Tour to London* (English trans. 1772). The Marquise de La Tour du Pin wrote a fascinating memoir of her experiences in the period of the French Revolution in *Journal d'une femme de cinquante ans* (Paris, 1913). Joshua Johnson's horror at the cost of living in London is expressed in his *Letterbook* (ed. J. Price, 1979, for the London Record Society). For Levis, see the Duc de Levis *England at the Beginning of the 19th Century*, vol. 1 (English trans. 1815). For Simond see Louis

Simond *An American in Regency England* (ed. C. Hibbert, 1968). The Abbé Le Blanc's impressions were recorded in his *Letters on the English and French Nations* (English trans. 1747). See C. P. Moritz *Journeys of a German in England* (trans. and ed. R. Nettel, 1965). Lichtenberg's experience with the traffic is taken from *Lichtenberg's Visits to England* (trans. M. Mare and W. Quarrell, 1938). Walpole's reference to the size of late eighteenth-century London is contained in his *Correspondence*, as above, vol. II (1944). For Sophie von la Roche see *Sophie in London 1786* (trans. C. Williams, 1933), for Governor Hutchinson's daughter, *Diary and Letters of Thomas Hutchinson*, 2 vols. (comp. P. O. Hutchinson, 1883).

The great wealth of London and the consumer boom are discussed in N. McKendrick et al., *The Birth of a Consumer Society* (1982), in F. Braudel, *Civilisation and Capitalism*, vol. 3 (English edn 1984), and in G. Rudé *Hanoverian London* (1971). Dr Trusler's assertion is made in his *The Way to be Rich and Respectable* (1796 edn). Dr Johnson on the breakdown of 'subordination' is quoted by Roy Porter in his *English Society in the Eighteenth Century* (1982). For Gouverneur Morris see his *A Diary of the French Revolution*, vol. I (ed. B. C. Davenport, Cambridge, Mass., 1939). For Van Schaack see *The Life of Peter Van Schaack* (New York, 1842).

For nabobs and West Indians in general see J. M. Holzman *The Nabobs in England* (New York, 1926), T. G. P. Spear *The Nabobs* (1932), D. Knight *Gentlemen of Fortune* (1978) and L. J. Ragatz *Absentee Landlordism in the British Caribbean 1750–1833* (1931). Lord Chesterfield's problem with the House of Commons seat is to be found in Earl of Chesterfield *Letters to His Son* (ed. O. Leigh, New York, nd). Correlli Barnett is referring to the later British rulers of India in his *The Lost Victory* (1995). For where the nabobs lived in Soho see Phillips *Mid-Georgian*, as above. For Samuel Johnson see *The Letters of Samuel Johnson*, vol. 3 (ed. B. Redford, 1992). Beckford's attack on the oligarchy is taken from Lucy Sutherland, 'The City of London in Eighteenth Century Politics' in R. Pares and A. J. P. Taylor *Essays Presented to Sir Lewis Namier* (1956). Namier himself quotes the anonymous West Indian in *Crossroads of Power* (1962). The West Indian lobby is discussed by R. A. Smith *Eighteenth-Century English Politics. Patrons and Place-hunters* (1972).

For Fielding see A. S. Turberville *Johnson's England*, vol. 1 (1933). Boswell's visit to a neglected Chatsworth comes from *Boswell in Extremes* (ed. C. Weis and F. A. Pottle, 1971). For Walpole, see his *Correspondence*, as above, vol. 9 (1941). For the background and the development of Marylebone see G. Mackenzie *Marylebone* (1972), and also F. H. W. Sheppard's impressive *Local Government in St Marylebone* (1958). Sir John Summerson in his *Georgian London* (1948 edn) gives an overview. For Marylebone Gardens see W. Wroth *The London Pleasure Gardens of the Eighteenth Century* (1896). For the Berners estate see Slater *Berners Estate*, as above. J. T. Smith in his *A Book for a Rainy Day* (ed. W. Whitten, 1905) remembers Marylebone when it was still thought of as country. Boswell's astonishment at the growth of London is expressed in *Boswell for the Defence* (ed. W. K. Wimsatt, jun. and F. A. Pottle, 1960). Land contracts for Marylebone in the eighteenth century are recorded in the Middlesex Land Register at the London Metropolitan Archives.

Captain Topham in his *The Life of Mr Elwes, the Celebrated Miser* (1795 edn) gives an entertaining account of this extraordinary man. For the Pantheon see B. Weinreb and C. Hibbert *The London Encyclopedia* (1983), a most useful book for London buildings generally. Rateable values for Marylebone are registered at the Westminster City Archives. For the Barrett family see J. Marks *The Family of the Barrett* (1938).

6 Migration to the North

For the New Road see F. H. W. Sheppard *Local Government in St Marylebone* (1958), G. S. Thomson *The Russells in Bloomsbury* (1940) and *Survey of London*, vol. 21. The background to the growth and development of Islington is described by the earlier writers D. Lysons *The Environs of London*, 2 vols. (1811) and S. Lewis, jun. *The History and Topography of the Parish of St Mary, Islington* (1842) and more recently in *VHCE, Middlesex*, vol. 8, and P. Zwart *Islington* (1973). The 'romantic tale' of elopement is discredited by Lawrence Stone's 'The Peer and the Alderman's Daughter' in *History Today*, 11 (1961). For the Northamptons see W. B. Compton (sixth Marquess of Northampton) *History of the Comptons of Compton Wynyates* (1930). David Hughson warns of what is likely to happen in *London; being an accurate history* . . . vol. 6 (1809). The prospectus for the Barnsbury estate is taken from *The Family of Tufnell*, with a foreword by E. B. Tufnell (1924).

J. Richardson in *Highgate Past* (1989), and *Survey of London*, vol. 17, provide background for Highgate, while F. M. L. Thompson's *Hampstead: Building a Borough, 1650–1964* (1974) is an accomplished example of local history, which gives a clear analysis of land tenure. Baker's 'Hampstead Heath' is quoted in J. J. Park *Topography and Natural History of Hampstead* (1814). The dangers of Highgate air are remarked upon in J. Hassell *Picturesque Rides and Walks* (1817). For Lucy Aikin see *Memoirs, Miscellanies and Letters of the late Lucy Aikin* (ed. P. Le Breton, 1864). The 1826 *The Original Picture of London* was edited (or rather re-edited) by J. Britton. The necessity for 'a farm' in Hampstead is taken from Park *Topography*, as above. The Tufnell estate act is registered under 3 Geo.IV Cap 18, 1822; for Maryon Wilson see Thompson, *Hampstead*, as above.

For encroachment on Crown land see R. B. Pugh *The Crown Estate* (1960). For the 1820s plan for Hyde Park see *The Journal of Mrs Arbuthnot, 1820–1832* (ed. F. Bamford and the Duke of Wellington, 1950).

The description of the development of Regent's Park and Regent Street (the New Street) relies primarily on Sir John Summerson's *The Life and Work of John Nash, Architect* (1980) and more generally on his *Georgian London* (1948 edn) as well as on Ann Saunders *Regent's Park* (1969). Also fundamental as a source is Hermione Hobhouse *A History of Regent Street* (1975). For further background and for tenants and residents of central London displaced by the ambitious project, see the Crown Estate Records in the PRO, references CRES 2/741; 2/742; 2/746; 2/1736; 26/17. For the intervention of Lord Foley and his family, see G. Mackenzie *Marylebone* (1972) and F. H. W. Sheppard *Local Government in St Marylebone* (1958). For the Eyre estate see *London Topographical Record*, 27 (1995). The cost of Mrs Montagu's house in Portman Square is recorded in J. V. Beckett *The Aristocracy in England 1660–1914* (1986), and Eaton Hall as a 'villa' in B. Silliman the Elder, *A Visit to Europe in 1851*, vol. 1 (New York, 1854). For villas, see also Mark Girouard *Life in the English Country-House* (1980 edn). Lord Glenbervie expresses his disillusion in *The Diaries of Sylvester Douglas, Lord Glenbervie*, vol. 2 (ed. F. Bickley, 1928). For the villas built in Regent's Park see particularly Ann Saunders *The Regent's Park Villas* (1981) and Enid Samuel *The Villas in Regent's Park and Their Residents* (1959). Caroline Bauer is the subject of D. A. Ponsonby *A Prisoner in Regent's Park* (1961).

For Prince Pückler-Muskau see his *A Tour in England, Ireland and France* (revised English trans. Zurich, 1940). For Greville see *The Greville Memoirs*, vol. 2 (ed. L. Strachey and R. Fulford, 1938 edn).

7 The Villages to the West

Horace Walpole is quoted in A. Beaver *Memorials of Old Chelsea* (1892). The disappearance of Chelsea's rural atmosphere is commented on in J. N. Brewer *Middlesex*, vol. 4 (1816). For the houses of Chelsea see Beaver *Memorials*, as above, and W. Gaunt *Kensington and Chelsea* (1958). For Mrs Arbuthnot see *The Journal of Mrs Arbuthnot, 1820–1832*, vol. 1 (ed. F. Bamford and the Duke of Wellington, 1950), and for riverside houses, T. Hughes *The Steam-Boat Companion* (1824) and Brewer *Middlesex*, as above. Lord Hervey's criticism of Chiswick House is quoted in T. Faulkner *History and Antiquities of Brentford, Ealing and Chiswick* (1845), and the description 'multiplied drawing room' comes from W. Draper *Chiswick* (1973 edn).

For the investment in west London see D. A. Reeder 'Capital Investment in the Western Suburbs of Victorian London' (Ph.D. thesis, University of Leicester, 1965). The classic book on Fulham is C. J. Fèret *Fulham Old and New* (1900). For the Woods of Littleton see London Metropolitan Archives, accession 1302. For the Berkeleys see B. Falk *The Berkeleys of Berkeley Square* (1944) and for Coke *The Letters and Journals of Lady Mary Coke*, 4 vols. (ed. Lady L. Stuart, 1970 reprinted from 1889–96 edn). Grantley Berkeley described hunting in west London in G. C. G. F. Berkeley *Reminiscences of a Huntsman* (1854), while for the difficulties of the terrain around London see M. D. George *London Life in the XVIIIth Century* (1925). The *Survey of London*, vol. 6, gives the Duchess of Norfolk's address as 'Seagreens'. For Campden Hill and the spectacular growth in Kensington's population see *Survey of London*, vol. 37.

For Holland House in this chapter see Earl of Ilchester *The Home of the Hollands 1605–1820* (1937) and *Chronicles of Holland House* (1937), Derek Hudson *Holland House in Kensington* (1967) and Leslie Mitchell *Holland House* (1980). Russell's description comes in G. W. E. Russell *Collections and Recollections* (1898) and the handkerchief anecdote from R. Nevill *Yesterday and Today* (1922). For Greville see *The Greville Memoirs*, vol. 2 (ed. L. Strachey and R. Fulford, 1938 edn). Ticknor describes his dinner at Holland House in the *Life, Letters, and Journals of George Ticknor*, vol. 1 (ed. G. Hillard, 1876). For Walpole see *The Yale Edition of Horace Walpole's Correspondence*, vol. 23 (ed. W. S. Lewis, 1967). Charles James Fox is described as a prototype of gamblers in W. B. Boulton *In the Days of the Georges* (1909). Sonia Keppel in her biography of Lady Holland *The Sovereign Lady* (1974) supplies the *Mayflower* connection. For the fourth Lord Holland when young see *The Journal of Henry Edward Fox* (ed. Earl of Ilchester, 1923). For the 1857 visit to Holland House see Ticknor *Life*, as above, vol. 2.

For northern Kensington in the nineteenth century see *Survey of London*, vol. 37, and for Kensington Palace Gardens, Mark Girouard in *Country Life*, 11 November 1971 and 18 November 1971.

For Benjamin Silliman (the Elder) in England see his *A Journal of Travels in England, Holland, and Scotland . . . in . . . 1805 and 1806*, vol. 1 (2nd edn, Boston, 1812) and his *A Visit to Europe in 1851*, vol. 1 (New York, 1854). G. P. Fisher in his *Life of B. Silliman*, 2 vols (New York, 1866) supplies some background. For the Church and leases see G.F.A. Best *Temporal Pillars* (1964) and also W. Robins *Paddington: Past and Present* (1853). The effect on Eton College finances is related in *Archives*, 5:27 (1962). The development of Paddington is set out in *VHCE*, *Middlesex*, vol. 9; see also George, as above, and C. Knight *Passages of a Working Life*, vol. 1 (1864). For the Novello family see M. C. Clarke *Life and Labours of Vincent Novello* (1864). The Hazlitt description is contained in W. C. Hazlitt *The Hazlitts*, Pt. 2 (1912). D. J. Olsen gives considerable attention to the growth of Bayswater in his *The Growth of Victorian London* (1976). For Kensington Gore see *Survey of London*, vols. 37 and 41.

For Belgravia, Hermione Hobhouse *Thomas Cubitt, Master Builder* (1995 edn) and M. J. Hazleton-Swales 'Urban Aristocrats – The Grosvenors and the Development of Belgravia and Pimlico in the Nineteenth Century' (Ph.D. thesis, Bedford College, 1981) are especially useful. Lady (Sydney) Morgan wrote of her experiences in her *Memoirs* (1862). For the French visitor see Francis Wey *A Frenchman Sees the English in the Fifties* (adapted V. Pirie, 1935).

8 South of the River

For the south bank of the Thames and Vauxhall see *Survey of London*, vol. 23; for Lambeth see *Survey of London*, vol. 26. D. J. Olsen's *The Growth of Victorian London* (1976) gives valuable background to the growth of South London.

Uffenbach's description of London Bridge is to be found in *London in 1710 from the Travels of Zacharias Conrad von Uffenbach* (trans. and ed. W.H. Quarrell and M. Mare, 1934), and John Pudney *Crossing London's River* (1972) discusses the building of the new bridges over the Thames. The Lord Mayor's protest is recorded in E. Hammond *Bygone Putney* (1898). D. Lysons *Environs of London*, 4 vols. (1792 edn) provides a contemporary view. *VHCE*, Surrey, vol. 4 refers to the watermen's fear for their jobs. For Greenwich see Beryl Platts *A History of Greenwich* (1973). For Battersea Bridge, see E. Hammond *Bygone Battersea* (1897), and for Richmond Bridge, Bamber Gascoigne *Images of Richmond* (1978).

John Ruskin's admiration of the view is expressed in his *Praeterita*, vol. 1 (1886) and Grove's in C. L. Graves *The Life and Letters of Sir George Grove* (1903). The Barings at Lee are mentioned in Philip Ziegler *The Sixth Great Power . . .* (1988). For the Brodricks see Rita Ensing 'Dunsford Manor and the Brodrick Family' in *Wandsworth Historian*, 42 (September 1984). The Clayton family in South London are discussed in *VHCE*, Surrey, vol. 4 and the importance of Sir Robert Clayton as a businessman in F. T. Melton *Sir Robert Clayton and the Origins of English Deposit Banking* (1986). The Duchy of Cornwall's role as landlord is taken from Crispin Gill (ed.) *The Duchy of Cornwall* (1987). The development of Kennington and South Lambeth is largely based on *Survey of London*, vol. 26, as above. For Roehampton see *VHCE*, Surrey, vol. 4 and Donald Gerhold *Putney and Roehampton Past* (1994).

For Lord Ashburton's description of the Goldsmids see Stanley Chapman *The Rise of Merchant Banking* (1984). The importance of the Huguenots in Wandsworth is described in E. Hammond *Bygone Wandsworth* (1898). For the Minet family see the Minet Papers at the Minet Library, Lambeth. The development of Camberwell is closely traced by H. J. Dyos in his *Victorian Suburb* (1961). For the de Crespigny family, along with the more general books on South London already mentioned, see the *Camberwell Society Newsletter*, 38 (July 1977). For the fourth baronet see Loelia, Duchess of Westminster *Grace and Favour* (1961).

For general references to the Thrales see the bibliography under Chapter 4. For the 'misses . . . brewhouse' quotation see *The Letters of Samuel Johnson*, vol. 2 (ed. B. Redford, 1992). The history of the brewery is set out in *Three Centuries – The Story of Our Ancient Brewery* published by Barclay Perkins (1951) and in the *Courage Papers* (Accession 2305/1–8) deposited at the London Metropolitan Archives. For the Barclays see *A History of the Barclay Family*, pt. 3, comp. Lt.-Col. H. F. Barclay and Alice Wilson (1934).

The description of the Clapham Movement is based primarily on Ford K. Brown *Fathers of the Victorians* (1961) and David Spring 'The Clapham Sect' in *Victorian Studies*, 5 (1961–2). M. J. Quinlan *Victorian Prelude: A History of English Manners 1700–1830* (New York, 1941) discusses moral attitudes of the time. For Henry Thornton more particularly see Standish Meacham *Henry Thornton of Clapham* (Cambridge, Mass., 1964). For Fanny Burney's encounter with Thornton see *The Diary and Letters of Madame d'Arblay*, vol. 2 (ed. C. Barrett, 1904). The quotation from Macaulay comes from J. W. Grove *Old Clapham* (1887), and that from George III from *The Diaries of Sylvester Douglas, Lord Glenbervie*, vol. 1 (ed. F. Bickley, 1928). The Sheridan anecdote is taken from Linda Kelly *Richard Brinsley Sheridan: A life* (1997). The reference to topers in St James's is provided by T. H. S. Escott *Social Transformations of the Victorian Age* (1897). For Perkin see Harold Perkin *Origins of Modern English Society, 1780–1880* (1969). The history of Battersea Rise is given in E. M. Forster *Marianne Thornton* (1956) and Benjamin Silliman the Elder's visits to Clapham recounted in his *A Journal of Travels in England, Holland, and Scotland . . . in . . . 1805 and 1806*, vol. 2 (2nd edn, Boston, 1812) and *A Visit to Europe in 1851*, vol. 2 (New York, 1854).

For Cubitt see Hermione Hobhouse *Thomas Cubitt, Master Builder* (1995 edn), for the Vauxhall Bridge Company, Pudney *Crossing London's River*, as above, and for the Battersea Tangle, Priscilla Metcalf *The Park Town Estate and the Battersea Tangle* (1978).

9 Monster City

As general background to this chapter, H. J. Dyos and M. Wolff *The Victorian City*, 2 vols. (1973) and Francis Sheppard *London 1808–1870: The Infernal Wen* (1971) are particularly useful.

For Louis Simond see *An American in Regency England* (ed. C. Hibbert, 1968). A. A. Feldborg wrote under the pseudonym J. Andersen in his *A Dane's Excursions in Britain*, 2 vols. (1809). For François-René, Vicomte de Chateaubriand see his *Mémoires d'Outre-Tombe*, vol. 2 (Paris, Pléiade edn, 1957). Richard Rush reminisced of his time in London in *Memoranda of a Residence at the Court of London* (Philadelphia, 1833). For the irrepressible Abdul Hassan see *A Persian at the Court of King George* (trans. M. Cloake, 1988). For Austin see W. Austin *Letters from London* (Boston, 1804). G. A. Sala referred to the 'metropolitan flavour' of the milk in *Twice round the Clock* (1859). Léon Faucher published his impressions in his *Études sur l'Angleterre* (Paris, 1856), and Edmond Texier in his *Lettres sur l'Angleterre* (Paris, 1851). For Hawthorne see H. Jennings *Pandaemonium 1660–1886* (1985). Flora Tristan's views of London are made plain in her *Promenades dans Londres* (Paris, 1840); she uses (in translation) the term 'monster city'. For other visitors' impressions see J. Fenimore Cooper *Gleanings in Europe: England. With Sketches of Society in the Metropolis*, 3 vols. (1837); for C. F. Adams see N. B. Ferris 'An American Diplomatist Confronts Victorian Society', *History Today*, XV (1965); Henry Colman *European Life and Manners*, 2 vols. (Boston, 1850); H. T. Taine *Notes on England* (3rd edn, trans. W. F. Rae, 1872); Jules de Prémaray *Promenades sentimentales dans Londres* (Paris, 1851). For Wey see *A Frenchman sees the English in the Fifties* (adapted V. Pirie 1935). Gronow's recollections of girls' behaviour were published in *The Reminiscences and Recollections of Captain Gronow*, vol. 1 (1900 edn).

For Mme. de Boigne see *Mémoires de la Comtesse de Boigne*, vol. 2 (Paris, 1907), for Chateaubriand, his *Mémoires*, as above. Max Schlesinger's observations on the besieged look of London buildings are contained in his *Saunterings in and about London* (English trans. 1853). The street barriers of the time are discussed in J. Hogg *London as It Is* (1837), and sanitation at Gwydr House in A. S. Wohl *Endangered Lives* (1983). The Bethnal Green reference is taken from N. Thrift and P. Williams *Class and Space: The Making of Urban Society* (1987). For Great Portland Street see Ferris in *History Today*, as above. The Devil's Acre reference and that for Westminster as a plague spot come from T. Beames *Rookeries of London* (1852 edn), and the quotation about St Giles from Sala *Twice round the Clock*, as above. Charles Dickens is quoted in *Endangered Lives*, as above. For Victorian slums more generally see G. Stedman Jones *Outcast London* (1971) and H. J. Dyos 'Slums of Victorian London' in *Victorian Studies*, 11:1 (September 1967).

For the poor as being 'chained to the spot' see J. R. Kellett *The Impact of Railways on Victorian Cities* (1969). Octavia Hill's terrible and salutary reminder is taken from Jack Rose *The Dynamics of Urban Property Development* (1985). D. M. Evans described the after-hours abandonment of the City in *The City; Or, the Physiology of Business* (1845). For the earls of Thanet and Thanet House, Bloomsbury, see Hermione Hobhouse *Thomas Cubitt, Master Builder* (1995 edn) and *Survey of London*, vol. 5. Bloomsbury is the main subject of D. J. Olsen *Town Planning in London* (2nd edn, 1982). For Hatherton see E. Walford *Old and New London*, vol. 5 (1897); in fact Hatherton in 1830 was still plain Edward Littleton, since his peerage was not granted until 1835.

For Gardner and Loder (and indeed for a classic analysis of the London rich and their wealth in general) see W. D. Rubinstein *Men of Property* (1981). The Arbuthnots' rejection of the Strand is noted in *The Journal of Mrs Arbuthnot, 1820–1832*, vol. 2 (ed. F. Bamford and the Duke of Wellington, 1950). For Lady Cork and George Eliot see Stella Margetson *St John's Wood* (1988). Leicester Square and its neighbourhood are discussed in *Survey of London*, vol. 34, and their more disreputable side in Ronald Pearsall *The Worm in the Bud* (1971). The advertisement reassuring foreign tourists on prices was printed in *The English and Continental Guide . . .* (1851). The quotation from Ritchie's *The Night Side of London* comes from the 1861 edition. The effect of Building Acts on standardization is reviewed in Sir John

Summerson *Georgian London* (1948 edn) and in D. J. Olsen 'Victorian London' in *Victorian Studies*, 17 (1973–4). Other particularly informative books on types of housing and their evolution are Stefan Muthesius *The English Terraced House* (1982 edn) and C. C. Knowles and P. H. Pitt *The History of Building Regulation in London 1189–1972* (1972). For Schomberg House as a department store see Alison Adburgham *Shopping in Style* (1979). For the conversion of private mansions into government offices see M. H. Port 'Pride and Parsimony' in *London Journal*, 2:2 (November 1976). Timbs's *Club Life in London* was published in 1866. The reference to the Adelaide Hotel comes from Jack Simmons *The Victorian Hotel* (1984).

For London town houses, in the nineteenth century and before and after, Christopher Simon Sykes *Private Palaces* (1985) and David Pearce *London's Mansions* (1986) provide essential information, which is supplemented by papers presented at a conference held by the Institute of Historical Research at Spencer House and the Royal Academy in July 1993 and printed in *London Journal*, 20:1 (1995).

For Queen Victoria's compliment to Stafford House see Lord Ronald Gower *My Reminiscences* (1884), and also see Lady Eastlake *Journals and Correspondence*, vol. 1 (1895). The 'Return of Assessment for Inhabited House Duty in London and Country' is published in *Parliamentary Papers for 1833*, vol. xxxii. Barry's estimate is taken from J. Cornforth in *Country Life*, 14 November 1968. Building projects by the aristocracy come from F. M. L. Thompson *English Landed Society in the Nineteenth Century* (1963) and J. V. Beckett *The Aristocracy in England 1660–1914* (1986). The information on Home House is based on the booklet *History of Home House* printed privately for the Home House Club. For Stratford House see Sir Shane Leslie *The Film of Memory* (1938), for Peto in Kensington Palace Gardens see *Survey of London*, vol. 37, and for Florence Nightingale, Carol Kennedy *Mayfair* (1986). Census returns are lodged at the Family Record Centre, Clerkenwell. The quotation from Richard Cobden is taken from G. Best *Mid-Victorian Britain* (1975).

10 The Rich in Turmoil

For Sherlock Holmes see also *The Adventure of the Beryl Coronet* and *The Adventure of the Retired Colourman*. William Hazlitt looks back at Battersea Fields in *The Hazlitts*, pt. 2 (1912) and Ruskin at Herne Hill in 'Fiction – Fair and Foul' in *Nineteenth Century* (June 1880). David Reeder in *Suburbanity and the Victorian City* (1980) discusses attitudes to the suburbs. For buses see T. C. Barker and M. Roberts *A History of London Transport*, vol. 1 (*c.* 1976); and H. Pollins et al. (eds.) *London, Aspects of Change* (1964). For railways in general and their demographic effect, see J. R. Kellett *The Impact of Railways on Victorian Cities* (1969). The fate of Lambeth and the other riverside boroughs of South London is described in J. Roebuck *Urban Development in 19th Century London* (1979). The general manager is quoted from Barker and Roberts *History of London Transport*, as above. For the attitude of the railway commissioners and the positioning of London's railway stations see S. R. Hoyle in the *London Journal*, 8:2 (Winter 1982) and Kellett *Impact of Railways*, as above. The effect on estates in northern Marylebone is described in *London Topographical Record*, III (1906).

Lord Jersey's negotiations with the railway companies in September 1834 are recorded in the *Jersey Archive* deposited at the London Metropolitan Archives. For Lord Holland and the Edwardes family see *Survey of London*, vols 37 and 42. The decline of Paddington and other inner boroughs is recorded in *VHCE*, *Middlesex*, vol. 9. See also F. M. L. Thompson *The Rise of Surburbia* (1982). The fall in population is registered in J. T. Coppock and H. C. Prince (eds.) *Greater London* (1964). For Hazlitt see *Hazlitts*, as above. For Brompton see *Survey of London*, vol. 41. Margaret Warren's diary was published privately as Margaret Leicester Warren *Diaries* in 1924 with the Onslow Square description in volume 2.

Late Victorian artists are considered in a demographic context in (Lady) Frances Horner *Time Remembered* (1933); Giles Walkley *Artists' Houses in London, 1764–1914* (1994); and Mark Girouard 'The Victorian Artist at Home' in *Country Life*, 16 November 1972. See also *Survey of London*, vol. 37. For Millais see Sir Henry Lucy *The Diary of a Journalist*, vol. 2 (1920); the Ruskin quotation is taken from W. Gaunt *Kensington and Chelsea* (1958). The development of the Queen's Gate area is described in *Survey of London*, vol. 38. The ratio of servants in Grosvenor Square is given in Carol Kennedy *Mayfair* (1986).

For Northumberland House and its demolition see G. L. Gomme

London in the Reign of Victoria (1898). For street barriers and the battle to abolish them see P. Atkins 'Freeing the Streets of Victorian London' in *History Today*, March 1993. The success of Dulwich in preserving its original atmosphere is set out in H. J. Dyos *Victorian Suburb* (1961). For the struggle to preserve common land see N. Plastow (ed.) *A History of Wimbledon and Putney Commons* (1986) and A. Forshaw and T. Bergstrom *The Open Spaces of London* (1986). Lord Salisbury is quoted in Harold Perkin *The Rise of Professional Society: England Since 1880* (1989). For the Duke of Bedford see Laura, Lady Troubridge *Memories and Reflections* (1925), and on the importance of public relations R. Nevill *Yesterday and Today* (1922). For incomes in the late nineteenth century see Perkin *Rise of Professional Society*, as above. For the earls of Romney see Romney of The Mote papers at the Centre for Kentish Studies, Maidstone.

For aristocratic wealth during the period of the Agricultural Depression and up to 1914 see J. V. Beckett *The Aristocracy in England 1660–1914* (1986), F. M. L. Thompson *English Landed Society in the Nineteenth Century* (1963), Mark Girouard *The Victorian Country House* (1979 edn), and David Cannadine *The Decline and Fall of the British Aristocracy* (1990). For the Duke of Westminster the main source is G. Huxley *Victorian Duke* (1967), and G. W. E. Russell's *Land and Lodging Houses* (1897) quotes the Duke of Bedford on his lodging houses. For the special factors influencing London's economy see J. Parry Lewis *Building Cycles and Britain's Growth* (1965). Baron Grant's Kensington House is described in *Survey of London*, vol. 42. See Duke of Portland *Men, Women and Things* (1937) for reference to the house being hired out for parties.

Youssef Cassis in *City Bankers, 1890–1914* (English trans. 1994) discusses residential preferences; for bankers on Denmark Hill refer to R. Roberts *Schroders* (1992), and J. Wake *Kleinwort Benson* (1997). *Wandsworth Historian*, 30 (1981), contains an article on the last days of Battersea Rise. W. D. Rubinstein in his *Men of Property* (1981) and his *Elites and the Wealthy in Modern British History* (1987) lists probate valuations of many wealthy Londoners including that of J. S. Schillizzi; for Ralli see valuation at Probate Office, 42–49 High Holborn WC1. Timotheos Catsiyannis, Bishop of Militoupolis has written several books on the Chios families, including *The Schillizzi*

Family (1990). For the influx of American heiresses see G. MacColl and C. Wallace *To Marry an English Lord* (New York, 1989); F. M. L. Thompson *The Rise of Respectable Society* (1988); and M. E. Montgomery *Gilded Prostitution* (1989). For Lady Cowper see Mark Girouard *The Victorian Country House*, as above. Prescott's comment on snobbery comes from *The Literary Memoranda of William Hickling Prescott*, vol. 2 (ed. C. H. Gardiner, Norman, Okla., 1961). For Nevill see *The Reminiscences of Lady Dorothy Nevill* (1906); for Russell, *An Onlooker's Notebook* (1902); for Romney, as above; for Webb *My Apprenticeship* (1926).

The Joseph Chamberlain quotation is taken from Geoffrey Wheatcroft *The Randlords* (1986 edn) and that for Lord Chesterfield from C. S. Sykes *Private Palaces* (1985). For Hare on the Holfords see A. Hare *In My Solitary Life* (ed. M. Barnes, 1953) and for the background to the Holfords in London see *Survey of London*, vols 3 and 5, and also B. Rudden *The New River* (1985) and the *New River Papers* at the London Metropolitan Archives. For probate refer to Probate Office. The careers of Overstone and Barnato are set out in David Kynaston *The City of London*, vol. 1 (1994) and vol. 2 (1995) respectively. For Barnato see also J. B. Jackson *The Great Barnato* (1970). The new rich in general are the subject of Jamie Camplin *The Rise of the Plutocrats* (1978). For the Cassel anecdote see A. R. Allfrey *Edward VII and His Jewish Court* (1991). The history of the Grosvenor property in Park Lane and Mayfair generally is given in *Survey of London*, vols. 39 and 40. For Lady Dorothy Nevill see above and her memoirs *Under Five Reigns* (ed. R. Nevill, 1910). For R. H. Dana see his *Hospitable England in the Seventies* (1921). Escott on the humanizing influence of the Jews is published in A Foreign Resident (his pseudonym) *Society in the New Reign* (1904). For the Duchess of Buccleuch see Pamela Horn *High Society* (1992) and for Mrs Lowther, G. W. E. Russell in *Social Silhouettes* (1906). For Colonel North see Lucy *Diary of a Journalist*, as above, vol. 1 (1920). Sir Edward Cadogan's memoirs were published as *Before the Deluge* in 1961. For the Duchess of Sutherland see Denis Stuart *Dear Duchess* (1982). For Sir Osbert Sitwell see *Great Morning* (1948).

11 Resurgence

For Channon see *Chips: The Diaries of Sir Henry Channon*, ed. R. Rhodes James (1967) and for Holland House, Pamela Horn *High Society* (1992), Angela Lambert *1939: The Last Season of Peace* (1989) and *The Times*, 7 July 1939. For Astor, see Patrick Balfour *Society Racket* (1934). For Bedford, see John, Duke of Bedford *A Silver Plated Spoon* (1959), for Londonderry, James Lees-Milne, *Prophesying Peace* (1977) and Portland, the Duke of Portland *Men, Women and Things* (1937). Lord Lascelles at Chesterfield House is taken from *Survey of London*, vol. 40. For Mayfair see also *Survey of London*, vol. 39. Rateable values are recorded at the Westminster City Archives. The Duchess of Devonshire's reaction to more modest accommodation is supplied by Loelia, Duchess of Westminster in her *Grace and Favour* (1961). G. W. E. Russell's complaint is made in his *One Look Back* (1912). For Ellerman see W. D. Rubinstein *Elites and the Wealthy in Modern British History* (1987); David Jeremy (ed.) *The Dictionary of Business Biography since 1860* (1984); R. McAlmon *Being Geniuses Together* (1938); and James Taylor *Ellermans: A Wealth of Shipping* (1976).

For the growth of twentieth-century London see J. T. Coppock and H. C. Prince (eds.) *Greater London* (1964), Gavin Weightman *The Making of Modern London 1914–1939* (1984) and Anthony D. King *Global Cities* (1990). Rural Edgware is described in Michael Robbins *Middlesex* (1953) and its urbanization in K. Hoggart and D. Green (eds.) *London: A New Metropolitan Geography* (1991). The effect of encroaching commerce is recounted in F. M. L. Thompson 'Moving Frontiers' in *London Journal*, 20:1 (1995).

For the Duke of Portland, as above. The quotation on the home as a shelter is taken from Hermione Hobhouse *Lost London* (1971). For nightclubs see Stella Margetson *The Long Party* (1974). For flats, see Chris Hamnett and Bill Randolph *Cities, Housing and Profits* (1988); Antonia Tatham *Lansdowne House* (1988); D. J. Olsen *The Growth of Victorian London* (1976); Anthony D. King *Buildings and Society* (1980) and his *Global Cities*, as above. For the conversion of Eaton Square see the *Architect and Building News*, 18 June 1953. For 'dancing as a craze' see Loelia, Duchess of Westminster *Grace and Favour*, as above. The improvements to the Cadogan estate are recorded in Olsen *Growth*, as above; for Warren see Margaret Leicester Warren *Diaries*, vol. 2 (1924), for Monkswell House, E. C. F. Collier (ed.) *A Victorian Diarist – Extracts from the Journals of Mary, Lady Monkswell 1873–1895*, vol. 1 (1944). The numbers of peers in Chelsea are noted in Jack Rose *The Dynamics of Urban Property Development* (1985).

W. D. Rubinstein discusses Jewish wealth in his *Elites and the Wealthy in Modern British History* (1987). For Jewish migration to the west and north see V. D. Lipman 'The Rise of Jewish Suburbia' in *Jewish Historical Society of England, Transactions 1962–1967*, 21 (1968) and *VHCE, Middlesex*, vol. 9. For Jessel see Israel Finestein *Jewish Society in Victorian England* (1993). For Cazenove see David Kynaston *Cazenove & Co.* (1991), and for Stoke Newington as an 'Elysian field', A. J. Shirren *Daniel Defoe in Stoke Newington* (1960). For Samuel Rogers see *DNB* and *The Greville Memoirs*, 8 vols. (ed. L. Strachey and R. Fulford, 1938 edn).

The progress of gentrification is plotted in S. Humphries and J. Taylor *The Making of Modern London* (1986); Ruth Glass, in the introduction, and J. Westergaard 'The Structure of Greater London' in H. Pollins et al. *London, Aspects of Change* (1964); Hamnett and Randolph *Cities*, as above; J. Bugler 'The Invaders of Islington' in *New Society* (15 August 1968); and Chris Hamnett and P. Williams 'A Study of Gentrification' in *London Journal*, 6:1 (1980). For demographic change in Battersea see I. Munt 'Economic Restructuring . . . a Case Study in Battersea' in *Environment and Planning A*, 19 (1987).

In his *The Selling of Mary Davies and other Writings* (1993) Simon Jenkins outlines the early problems of development in Notting Hill. For the history of the district see also *Survey of London*, vol. 37, and Ashley Barker in F. Gladstone and A. Barker *Notting Hill in Bygone Days* (1969). Monica Dickens remembers her youth in Notting Hill in *An Open Book* (1978). Eleanor Boyle has produced privately a study of 39 Lansdowne Road which she has kindly allowed to be used.

For the planners' view of post-war development see A. W. Evans *The Economics of Residential Location* (1973). The *Annual Report of the Kensington Society 1988/1989* contains a recollection of Sir Isaac Hayward's dismissal of Holland House. For Rosebery see Martin J.

Wiener *English Culture and the Decline of the Industrial Spirit, 1850–1980* (1981). Monet's appreciation of the London fog is taken from René Gimpel *Diary of an Art Dealer* (English edn, 1966). Reclus's question as to why the existence of the fog did not affect the architecture appears in his *The Universal Geography vol. IV, The British Isles* (ed. E. G. Ravenstein, 1887). For Aubrey House and the boom in expensive London residential property see *Financial Times*, 28–29 June 1997 and 27–28 December 1997. Also *The Times*, 7 January 1998. For Reresby see Chapter 1. *The Crisis of London* was edited by Andrew Thornley and the article in *Le Monde* appeared on 14 April 1998.

Index